LITTLE DORRIT.

IN TWO BOOKS.

BOOK THE SECOND.—RICHES.

32

CHARLES DICKENS, ESQ.

CHARLES DICKENS.

Philadelphia:

T. B. PETERSON, No. 102 CHESTNUT STREET.

LITTLE DORRIT.

BY

CHARLES DICKENS.
(BOZ.)

WITH FORTY ILLUSTRATIONS.

FROM DESIGNS BY PHIZ AND CRUIKSHANK.

IN TWO VOLUMES.

VOL. II.

Philadelphia:
T. B. PETERSON, NO. 306 CHESTNUT STREET,
GIRARD BUILDINGS, ABOVE THIRD.

CONTENTS.

BOOK THE SECOND—RICHES.

CONTENTS.

LIST OF ILLUSTRATIONS.

LITTLE DORRIT.

CHAPTER XXXVII.

FELLOW TRAVELERS.

In the autumn of the year, Darkness and Night were creeping up to the highest ridges of the Alps.

It was vintage time in the valleys on the Swiss side of the Pass of the Great Saint Bernard, and along the banks of the Lake of Geneva. The air there was charged with the scent of gathered grapes. Baskets, troughs, and tubs of grapes, stood in the dim village doorways, stopped the steep and narrow village streets, and had been carrying all day along the roads and lanes. Grapes, spilt and crushed under foot, lay about everywhere. The child carried in a sling by the laden peasant-woman toiling home, was quieted with picked-up grapes; the idiot sunning his big goître under the eaves of the wooden chalet by the way to the waterfall, sat munching grapes; the breath of the cows and goats was redolent of leaves and stalks of grapes; the company in every little cabaret were eating, drinking, talking grapes. A pity that no ripe touch of this generous abundance could be given to the thin, hard, stony wine, which after all was made from the grapes!

The air had been warm and transparent through the whole of the bright day. Shining metal spires and church-roofs, distant and rarely seen, had sparkled in the view; and the snowy mountain-tops had been so clear that unaccustomed eyes, cancelling the intervening country, and slighting their rugged height for something fabulous, would have measured them as within a few hours' easy reach. Mountain-peaks of great celebrity in the valleys, whence no trace of their existence was visible sometimes for months together, had been since morning plain and near in the blue sky. And now, when it was dark below, though they seemed solemnly to recede, like spectres who were going to vanish, as the red dye of the sunset faded out of them and left them coldly white, they were yet distinctly defined in their loneliness, above the mists and shadows.

Seen from those solitudes, and from the Pass of the Great Saint Bernard, which was one of them, the ascending Night came up the mountain like a rising water. When it at last rose to the walls of the convent of the Great Saint Bernard, it was as if that weather-beaten structure were another Ark, and floated away upon the shadowy waves.

Darkness, outstriping some visitors on mules, had risen thus to the rough convent walls, when those travelers were yet climbing the mountain. As the heat of the glowing day, when they had stopped to drink at the streams of melted ice and snow, was changed to the searching cold of the frosty rarefied night air at a great height, so the fresh beauty of the lower journey had yielded to barrenness and desolation. A craggy track, up which the mules, in single file, scrambled and turned from block to block, as though they were ascending the broken staircase of a gigantic ruin, was their way now. No trees were to be seen, nor any vegetable growth, save a poor brown scrubby moss, freezing in the chinks of rock. Blackened skeleton arms of wood by the wayside pointed upward to the convent, as if the ghosts of former travelers, overwhelmed by the snow, haunted the scene of their distress. Icicle-hung caves and cellars built for refuges from sudden storms, were like so many whispers of the perils of the place; never-resting wreaths and mazes of mist wandered about, hunted by a moaning wind; and snow, the besetting danger of the mountain, against which all its defenses were taken, drifted sharply down.

The file of mules, jaded by their day's work, turned and wound slowly up the steep ascent; the foremost led by a guide on foot, in his broad-brimed hat and round jacket, carrying a mountain staff or two upon his shoulder, with whom another guide conversed. There was no speaking among the string of riders. The sharp cold, the fatigue of the journey, and a new sensation of a catching in the breath, partly as if they had just emerged from very clear crisp water, and partly as if they had been sobbing, kept them silent.

At length, a light on the summit of the rocky staircase gleamed through the snow and mist. The guides called to the mules, the mules pricked up their drooping heads, the travelers' tongues were loosened, and in a sudden burst of slipping, climbing, jingling, clinking, and talking, they arrived at the convent door.

Other mules had arrived not long before, some with peasant-riders and some with goods, and had trodden the snow about the door into a pool of mud. Riding saddles and bridles, pack-saddles and strings of bells, mules and men, lanterns, torches, sacks, provender, barrels, cheeses, kegs of honey and butter, straw bundles and packages of many shapes, were crowded confusedly together in this thawed quagmire, and about the steps. Up here in the clouds, every thing was seen through cloud, and seemed dissolving into cloud. The breath of the men was cloud, the breath of the mules was cloud, the lights were encircled by cloud, speakers close at hand were not seen for cloud, though their voices and all other sounds were surprisingly clear. Of the cloudy line of mules hastily tied to rings in the wall, one would bite another, or kick another, and then the whole mist would be disturbed: with men diving into it, and cries of men and beasts coming out of it, and no bystander discerning what was wrong. In the midst of this, the great stable of the convent, occupying the basement story, and entered by the basement door, outside which all the disorder was, poured forth its contribution of cloud, as if the whole rugged edifice were filled with nothing else, and would collapse as soon as it had emptied itself, leaving the snow to fall upon the bare mountain summit.

While all this noise and hurry were rife among the living travelers, there, too, silently assembled in a grated house, half a dozen paces removed, with the same cloud enfolding them, and the same snow flakes drifting in upon them, were the dead travelers found upon the mountain. The mother, storm-belated many winters ago, still standing in the corner with her baby at her breast; the man who had frozen with his arm raised to his mouth in fear of hunger, still pressing it with his dry lips after years and years. An awful company, mysteriously come together! A wild destiny for that mother to have foreseen. "Surrounded by so many, and such companions, upon whom I never looked, and never shall look, I and my child will dwell together inseparable, on the Great Saint Bernard, outlasting generations who will come to see us, and will never know our name, or one word of our story but the end."

The living travelers thought little or nothing of the dead just then. They thought much more of alighting at the convent door, and warming themselves at the convent fire. Disengaged from the turmoil, which was already calming down as the crowd of mules began to be bestowed in the stable, they hurried shivering up the steps and into the building. There was a smell within, coming up from the floor of tethered beasts, like the smell of a menagerie of wild animals. There were strong arched galleries within, huge stone piers, great staircases, and thick walls pierced with small sunken windows—fortifications against the mountain storms, as if they had been human enemies. There were gloomy vaulted sleeping rooms within, intensely cold, but clean and hospitably prepared for guests. Finally, there was a parlor for guests to sit in and to sup in, where a table was already laid, and where a blazing fire shone red and high.

In this room, after having had their quarters for the night allotted to them by two young Fathers, the travelers presently drew round the hearth. They were in three parties; of whom the first, as the most numerous and important, was the slowest, and had been overtaken by one of the others on the way up. It consisted of an elderly lady, two gray-haired gentlemen, two young ladies, and their brother. These were attended (not to mention four guides) by a courier, two footmen, and two waiting-maids: which strong body of inconvenience was accommodated elsewhere under the same roof. The party that had overtaken them, and followed in their train, consisted of only three members: one lady and two gentlemen. The third party, which had ascended from the valley on the Italian side of the Pass, and had arrived first, were four in number: a plethoric,

THE TRAVELLERS.

hungry, and silent German tutor in spectacles, on a tour with three young men, his pupils, all plethoric, hungry, and silent, and all in spectacles.

These three groupes sat round the fire eyeing each other dryly, and waiting for supper. Only one among them, one of the gentlemen belonging to the party of three, made advances toward conversation. Throwing out his lines for the Chief of the important tribe, while addressing himself to his own companions, he remarked, in a tone of voice which included all the company, if they chose to be included, that it had been a long day, and that he felt for the ladies. That he feared one of the young ladies was not a strong or accustomed traveler, and had been over fatigued two or three hours ago. That he had observed, from his station in the rear, that she sat her mule as if she were exhausted. That he had, twice or thrice afterward, done himself the honor of inquiring of one of the guides, when he fell behind, how the young lady did. That he had been enchanted to learn that she had recovered her spirits, and that it had been but a passing discomfort. That he trusted (by this time he had secured the eyes of the Chief, and addressed him) he might be permitted to express his hope that she was now none the worse, and that she would not regret having made the journey.

"My daughter, I am obliged to you, sir," returned the Chief, "is quite restored, and has been greatly interested."

"New to mountains, perhaps?" said the insinuating traveler.

"New to—ha—to mountains," said the Chief.

"But you are familiar with them, sir?" the insinuating traveler assumed.

"I am—hum—tolerably familiar. Not of late years. Not of late years," replied the Chief, with a flourish of his hand.

The insinuating traveler, acknowledging the flourish with an inclination of his head, passed from the Chief to the second young lady, who had not yet been referred to, otherwise than as one of the ladies in whose behalf he felt so sensitive an interest.

He hoped she was not incommoded by the fatigues of the day.

"Incommoded certainly," returned the young lady, "but not tired."

The insinuating traveler complimented her on the justice of the distinction. It was what he had meant to say. Every lady must doubtless be incommoded, by having to do with that proverbially unaccommodating animal, the mule.

"We have had, of course," said the young lady, who was rather reserved and haughty, "to leave the carriages and fourgon at Martigny. And the impossibility of bringing any thing that one wants to this inaccessible place, and the necessity of leaving every comfort behind, is not convenient."

"A savage place, indeed," said the insinuating traveler.

The elderly lady, who was a model of accurate dressing, and whose manner was perfect, considered as a piece of machinery, here interposed a remark in a low soft voice.

"But, like other inconvenient places," she observed, "it must be seen. As a place much spoken of, it is necessary to see it."

"Oh! I have not the least objection to seeing it, I assure you, Mrs. General," returned the other, carelessly.

"You, madam," said the insinuating traveler, "have visited this spot before?"

"Yes," returned Mrs. General. "I have been here before. Let me recommend you, my dear," to the former young lady, "to shade your face from the hot wood, after exposure to the mountain air and snow. You too, my dear," to the other and younger lady, who immediately did so; while the former merely said, "Thank you, Mrs. General, I am perfectly comfortable, and prefer remaining as I am."

The brother, who had left his chair to open a piano that stood in the room, and who had whistled into it and shut it up again, now came strolling back to the fire with his glass in his eye. He was dressed in the very fullest and completest traveling trim. The world seemed hardly large enough to yield him an amount of travel proportionate to his equipment.

"These fellows are an immense time with supper," he drawled. "I wonder what they'll give us! Has anybody any idea?"

"Not roast man I believe," replied the voice of the second gentleman of the party of three.

"I suppose not. What d'ye mean?" he inquired.

"That, as you are not to be served for the general supper, perhaps you will do us the favor of not cooking yourself at the general fire," returned the other.

The young gentleman, who was standing in an easy attitude on the hearth, cocking his glass at the company, with his back to the blaze and his coat tucked under his arms, something as if he were of the poultry species and were trussed for roasting, lost countenance at this reply; he seemed about to demand further explanation, when it was discovered—through all eyes turning on the speaker—that the lady with him, who was young and beautiful, had not heard what had passed, through having fainted with her head upon his shoulder.

"I think," said the gentleman in a subdued tone, "I had best carry her straight to her room. Will you call to some one to bring a light?" addressing his companion, "and to show the way? In this strange rambling place I don't know that I could find it."

"Pray let me call my maid," cried the taller of the young ladies.

"Pray let me put this water to her lips," said the shorter, who had not spoken yet.

Each doing what she suggested, there was no want of assistance. Indeed, when the two maids came in (escorted by the courier, lest any one should strike them dumb by addressing a foreign language to them on the road,) there was a prospect of too much assistance. Seeing this, and saying as much in a few words to the slighter and younger of the two ladies, the gentleman put his wife's arm over his shoulder, lifted her up, and carried her away.

His friend, being left alone with the other visitors, walked slowly up and down the room, without coming to the fire again, pulling his black moustache in a contemplative manner, as if he felt himself committed to the late retort. While the subject of it was breathing injury in a corner, the Chief loftily addressed this gentleman.

"Your friend, sir," said he, "is—ha—is a little impatient;

and, in his impatience, is not perhaps fully sensible of what he owes to—hum—to—but we will waive that, we will waive that. Your friend is a little impatient, sir."

"It may be so, sir," returned the other. "But having had the honor of making that gentleman's acquaintance at the hotel at Geneva, where we and much good company met some time ago, and having had the honor of exchanging company and conversation with that gentleman on several subsequent excursions, I can hear nothing—no, not even from one of your appearance and station, sir—detrimental to that gentleman."

"You are in no danger, sir, of hearing any such thing from me. In remarking that your friend has shown impatience, I say no such thing. I make that remark, because it is not to be doubted that my son, being by birth and by—ha—by education a—hum—a gentleman, would have readily adapted himself to any obligingly-expressed wish on the subject of the fire being equally accessible to the whole of the present circle. Which, in principle, I—ha—for all are—hum—equal on these occasions—I consider right."

"Good!" was the reply. "And there it ends! I am your son's obedient servant. I beg your son to receive the assurance of my profound consideration. And now, sir, I may admit, freely admit, that my friend is sometimes of a sarcastic temper."

"The lady is your friend's wife, sir?"

"The lady is my friend's wife, sir."

"She is very handsome."

"Sir, she is peerless. They are still in the first year of their marriage. They are still partly on a marriage, and partly on an artistic tour."

"Your friend is an artist, sir?"

The gentleman replied by kissing the fingers of his right hand, and wafting the kiss the length of his arm toward Heaven. As who should say, I devote him to the celestial Powers as an immortal artist!

"But he is a man of family," he added. "His connections are of the best. He is more than an artist: he is highly connected. He may, in effect, have repudiated his connections, proudly, impatiently, sarcastically (I make the concession of both words); but he has them. Sparks that have been struck out during our intercourse have shown me this."

"Well! I hope," said the lofty gentleman, with the air of finally disposing of the subject, "that the lady's indisposition may be only temporary."

"Sir, I hope so."

"Mere fatigue, I dare say."

"Not altogether mere fatigue, sir, for her mule stumbled today, and she fell from the saddle. She fell lightly, and was up again without assistance, and rode from us laughing; but she complained toward evening of a slight bruise on her side. She spoke of it more than once, as we followed your party up the mountain."

The head of the large retinue, who was gracious but not familiar, appeared by this time to think that he had condescended more than enough. He said no more, and there was silence for some quarter of an hour until supper appeared.

With the supper came one of the young Fathers (there seemed to be no old Fathers) to take the head of the table. It was like the supper of an ordinary Swiss hotel, and good red wine grown by the convent in more genial air was not wanting. The artist traveler calmly came and took his place at the table when the rest sat down, with no apparent sense upon him of his late skirmish with the completely-dressed traveler.

"Pray," he inquired of the host, over his soup, "has your convent many of its famous dogs now?"

"Monsieur, it has three."

"I saw three in the gallery below. Doubtless the three in question."

The host, a slender, bright-eyed, dark young man of polite manners, whose garment was a black gown with strips of white crossed over it like braces, and who no more resembled the conventional breed of Saint Bernard monks than he resembled the conventional breed of Saint Bernard dogs, replied, doubtless those were the three in question.

"And I think," said the artist traveler, "I have seen one of them before."

It was possible. He was a dog sufficiently well known. Monsieur might have easily seen him in the valley or somewhere on the lake, when he (the dog) had gone down with one of the Order to solicit aid for the convent.

"Which is done in its regular season of the year, I think?"

Monsieur was right.

"And never without the dog. The dog is very important."

Again Monsieur was right. The dog was very important. People were justly interested in the dog. As one of the dogs celebrated everywhere, Ma'amselle would observe.

Ma'amselle was a little slow to observe it, as though she were not yet well accustomed to the French tongue. Mrs. General, however, observed it for her.

"Ask him if he has saved many lives," said, in his native English, the young man who had been put out of countenance.

The host needed no translation of the question. He promptly replied in French, "No; not this one."

"Why not?" the same gentleman asked.

"Pardon," returned the host, composedly, "give him the opportunity and he will do it without doubt. For example, I am well convinced," smiling sedately, as he cut up the dish of veal to be handed round, on the young man who had been put out of countenance, "that if you, Monsieur, would give him the opportunity, he would hasten with great ardor to fulfill his duty."

The artist traveler laughed. The insinuating traveler (who evinced a provident anxiety to get his full share of the supper), wiping some drops of wine from his moustache with a piece of bread, joined the conversation.

"It is becoming late in the year, my Father," said he, "for tourist-travelers, is it not?"

"Yes, it is late. Yet two or three weeks, at most, and we shall be left to the winter snows."

"And then," said the insinuating traveler, "for the scratching dogs and the buried children, according to the pictures!"

"Pardon," said the host, not quite understanding the allusion. "How, then the scratching dogs and the buried children according to the pictures?"

The artist traveler struck in again, before an answer could be given.

"Don't you know," he coldly inquired across the table of his companion, "that none but smugglers come this way in the winter, or can have any possible business this way?"

"Holy blue! No; never heard of it."

"So it is, I believe. And as they know the signs of the weather tolerably well, they don't give much employment to the dogs—who have consequently died out rather—though this house of entertainment is conveniently situated for themselves. Their young families, I am told, they usually leave at home. But it's a grand idea!" cried the artist traveler, unexpectedly rising into a tone of enthusiasm. "It's a sublime idea. It's the finest idea in the world, and brings tears into a man's eyes, by Jupiter!" He then went on eating his veal with great composure.

There was enough of mocking inconsistency at the bottom of this speech to make it rather discordant, though the manner was refined and the person well-favored, and though the depreciatory part of it was so skillfully thrown off, as to be very difficult for one not perfectly acquainted with the English language to understand, or, even understanding, to take offense at: so simple and dispassionate was its tone. After finishing his veal in the midst of silence, the speaker again addressed his friend.

"Look," said he, in his former tone, "at this gentleman our host, not yet in the prime of life, who in so graceful a way and with such courtly urbanity and modesty presides over us! Manners fit for a crown! Dine with the Lord Mayor of London (if you can get an invitation) and observe the contrast. This dear fellow, with the finest cut face I ever saw, a face in perfect drawing, leaves some laborious life and comes up here I don't know how many feet above the level of the sea, for no other purpose on earth (except enjoying himself, I hope, in a capital refectory) than to keep an hotel for idle poor devils like you and me, and leave the bill to our consciences! Why, isn't it a beautiful sacrifice? What do we want more to touch us? Because rescued people of interesting appearance are not, for eight or nine months out of every twelve, holding on here round the necks of the most sagacious of dogs carrying wooden bottles, shall we disparage the place? No! Bless the place. It's a great place, a glorious place!"

The chest of the gray-haired gentleman who was the Chief of the important party, had swelled as if with a protest against his being numbered among poor devils. No sooner had the artist traveler ceased speaking than he himself spoke with great dignity, as having it incumbent on him to take the lead in most places, and having deserted that duty for a little while.

He weightily communicated his opinion to their host, that his life must be a very dreary life here in the winter.

The host allowed to Monsieur that it was a little monotonous. The air was difficult to breathe for a length of time consecutively. The cold was very severe. One needed youth and strength to bear it. However, having them and the blessing of Heaven—

Yes, that was very good. "But the confinement," said the gray-haired gentleman.

There were many days, even in bad weather, when it was possible to walk about outside. It was the custom to beat a little track, and take exercise there.

"But the space," urged the gray-haired gentleman. "So small. So—ha—very limited."

Monsieur would recall to himself that there were the refuges to visit, and that tracks had to be made to them also.

Monsieur still urged, on the other hand, that the space was so—ha—hum—so very contracted. More than that. It was always the same, always the same.

With a deprecating smile, the host gently raised and gently lowered his shoulders. That was true, he remarked, but permit him to say that almost all objects had their various points of view. Monsieur and he did not see this poor life of his from the same point of view. Monsieur was not used to confinement.

"I—ha—yes, very true," said the gray-haired gentleman. He seemed to receive quite a shock from the force of the argument.

Monsieur, as an English traveler surrounded by all means of traveling pleasantly; doubtless possessing fortune, carriages, servants—

"Perfectly, perfectly. Without doubt," said the gentleman.

Monsieur could not easily place himself in the position of a person who had not the power to choose, I will go here to-morrow, or there next day; I will pass these barriers, I will enlarge those bounds. Monsieur could not realize, perhaps, how the mind accommodated itself in such things to the force of necessity.

"It is true," said Monsieur. "We will—na—not pursue the subject. You are—hum—quite accurate, I have no doubt. We will say no more."

The supper having come to a close, he drew his chair away as he spoke, and moved back to his former place by the fire. As it was very cold at the greater part of the table, the other guests also resumed their former seats by the fire, designing to toast themselves well before going to bed. The host, when they rose from table, bowed to all present, wished them good night, and withdrew. But first the insinuating traveler had asked him if they could have some wine made hot; and as he had answered Yes, and had presently afterward sent it in, that traveler, seated in the centre of the group, and in the full heat of the fire, was soon engaged in serving it out to the rest.

At this time, the younger of the two young ladies, who had been silently attentive in her dark corner (the firelight was the chief light in the sombre room, the lamp being smoky and dull) to what had been said of the absent lady, glided out. She was at a loss which way to turn, when she had softly closed the door; but, after a little hesitation, among the sounding passages and the many ways, came to a room in the corner of the main gallery, where the servants were at their supper. From these she obtained a lamp, and a direction to the ladies' room.

It was up the great staircase on the story above. Here and there the bare white walls were broken by an iron grate, and she thought as she went along that the place was something like a prison. The arched door of the lady's room, or cell, was not quite shut. After knocking at it two or three times without receiving an answer, she pushed it gently open, and looked in.

The lady lay with closed eyes on the outside of the bed, protected from the cold by the blankets and wrappers with which she had been covered when she revived from her fainting fit. A dull light placed in the deep recess of the window, made little impression on the arched room. The visitor timidly stepped to the bed, and said, in a soft whisper, "Are you better?"

The lady had fallen into a slumber, and the whisper was too low to awake her. Her visitor, standing quite still, looked at her attentively.

"She is very pretty," she said to herself. "I never saw so beautiful a face. O how unlike me."

It was a curious thing to say, but it had some hidden meaning, for it filled her eyes with tears.

"I know I must be right. I know he spoke of her that evening. I could very easily be wrong on any other subject. But not on this, not on this!"

With a quiet and tender hand she put aside a straying fold of the sleeper's hair, and then touched the hand that lay outside the covering.

"I like to look at her," she breathed to herself. "I like to see what has affected him so much."

She had not withdrawn her hand, when the sleeper opened her eyes, and started.

"Pray don't be alarmed. I am only one of the travelers from down-stairs. I came to ask if you were better, and if I could do any thing for you."

"I think you have already been so kind as to send your servants to my assistance?"

"No, not I; that was my sister. Are you better?"

"Much better. It is only a slight bruise, and has been well looked to, and is almost easy now. It made me giddy and faint in a moment. It had hurt me before; but at last it overpowered me all at once."

"May I stay with you until some one comes? Would you like it?"

"I should like it, for it is lonely here; but I am afraid you will feel the cold too much."

"I don't mind cold. I am not delicate, if I look so." She quickly moved one of the two rough chairs to the bedside, and sat down. The other as quickly moved a part of some traveling wrapper from herself, and drew it over her, so that her arm, in keeping it about her, rested on her shoulder.

"You have so much the air of a kind nurse," said the lady,

smiling on her, "that you seem as if you had come to me from home."

"I am very glad of it."

"I was dreaming of home when I awoke just now. Of my old home, I mean, before I was married."

"And before you were so far away from it."

"I have been much further away from it than this; but then I took the best part of it with me, and missed nothing. I felt solitary as I dropped asleep here, and, missing it a little, wandered back to it."

There was a sorrowfully affectionate and regretful sound in her voice, which made her visitor refrain from looking at her for the moment.

"It is a curious chance which at last brings us together, under this covering in which you have wrapped me," said the visitor, after a pause; "for do you know, I think I have been looking for you some time."

"Looking for me?"

"I believe I have a little note here, which I was to give to you whenever I found you. This is it. Unless I greatly mistake, it is addressed to you. Is it not?"

The lady took it, and said Yes, and read it. Her visitor watched her as she did so. It was very short. She flushed a little as she put her lips to her visitor's cheek, and pressed her hand.

"The dear young friend to whom he presents me, may be a comfort to me at some time, he says. She is truly a comfort to me, the first time I see her."

"Perhaps, you don't," said the visitor, hesitating—"perhaps you don't know my story? Perhaps he never told you my story?"

"No."

"O, no, why should he! I have scarcely the right to tell it myself at present, because I have been entreated not to do so. There is not much in it, but it might account to you for my asking you not to say any thing about the letter here. You saw my family with me, perhaps? Some of them—I only say this to you—are a little proud, a little prejudiced."

"You shall take it back again," said the other, "and then

my husband is sure not to see it. He might see it and speak of it, otherwise, by some accident. Will you put it in your bosom again, to be certain?"

She did so with great care. Her small, slight hand was still upon the letter, when they heard some one in the gallery outside.

"I promised," said the visitor, rising, "that I would write to him after seeing you (I could hardly fail to see you, sooner or later), and tell him if you were well and happy. I had better say you were well and happy?"

"Yes, yes, yes! Say I was very well and very happy. And that I thanked him affectionately, and would never forget him."

"I shall see you in the morning. After that we are sure to meet again before very long. Good-night."

"Good-night. Thank you, thank you. Good-night, my dear!"

Both of them were hurried and fluttered as they exchanged this parting, and as the visitor came out of the door. She had expected to meet the lady's husband approaching it; but the person in the gallery was not he: it was the traveler who had wiped the wine-drops from his moustache with the piece of bread. When he heard the step behind him, he turned round —for he was walking away in the dark.

His politeness, which was extreme, would not allow of the young lady's lighting herself down-stairs, or going down alone. He took her lamp, held it so as to throw the best light on the stone steps, and followed her all the way to the supper-room. She went down, not easily hiding how much she was inclined to shrink and tremble; for the appearance of this traveler was particularly disagreeable to her. She had sat in her quiet corner before supper, imagining what he would have been in the scenes and places within her experience, until he inspired her with an aversion, that made him little less than terrific.

He following her down with his smiling politeness, followed her in, and resumed his seat in the best place on the hearth. There, with the wood-fire, which was beginning to burn low, rising and falling upon him in the dark room, he sat with his legs thrust out to warm, drinking the hot wine down to the lees, with a monstrous shadow imitating him on the wall and ceiling.

The tired company had broken up, and all the rest were gone to bed except the young lady's father, who dozed in his chair by the fire. The traveler had been at the pains of going a long way up-stairs to his sleeping-room, to fetch his pocket-flask of brandy. He told them so, as he poured its contents into what was left of the wine, and drank with a new relish.

"May I ask, sir, if you are on your way to Italy?"

The gray-haired gentleman had roused himself, and was preparing to withdraw. He answered in the affirmative.

"I also!" said the traveler. "I shall hope to have the honor of offering my compliments in fairer scenes, and under softer circumstances, than on this dismal mountain."

The gentleman bowed, distantly enough, and said he was obliged to him.

"We poor gentlemen, sir," said the traveler, pulling his moustache dry with his hand, for he had dipped it in the wine and brandy; "we poor gentlemen do not travel like princes, but the courtesies and graces of life are precious to us. To your health, sir!"

"Sir, I thank you."

"To the health of your distinguished family—of the fair ladies, your daughters!"

"Sir, I thank you again. I wish you good-night. My dear, are our—ha—our people in attendance?"

"They are close by, father."

"Permit me!" said the traveler, rising and holding the door open, as the gentleman crossed the room toward it with his arm drawn through his daughter's. "Good repose! To the pleasure of seeing you once more! To to-morrow!"

As he kissed his hand, with his best manner and his daintiest smile, the young lady drew a little nearer to her father, and passed him with a dread of touching him.

"Humph!" said the insinuating traveler, whose manner shrunk and whose voice dropped when he was left alone. "If they all go to bed, why I must go. They are in a devil of a hurry. One would think the night would be long enough, in this freezing silence and solitude, if one went to bed two hours hence!"

Throwing back his head in emptying his glass, he cast his eyes upon the travelers' book, which lay on the piano, open, with pens and ink beside it, as if the night's names had been registered when he was absent. Taking it in his hand, he read these entries.

William Dorrit, Esquire Frederick Dorrit, Esquire Edward Dorrit, Esquire Miss Dorrit Miss Amy Dorrit Mrs. General	And suite. From France to Italy.

Mr. and Mrs. Henry Gowan. From France to Italy.

To which he added, in a small, complicated hand, ending with a long, lean flourish, not unlike a lasso thrown at all the rest of the names:

Blandois. Paris. From France to Italy.

And then, with his nose coming down over his moustache, and his moustache going up under his nose, repaired to his allotted cell.

CHAPTER XXXVIII.

MRS. GENERAL.

It is indispensable to present the accomplished lady, who was of sufficient importance in the suite of the Dorrit Family to have a line to herself in the Travelers' Book.

Mrs. General was the daughter of a clerical dignitary in a cathedral town, where she had led the fashion until she was as near forty-five as a single lady can be. A stiff commissariat officer of sixty, famous as a martinet, had then become enamored of the gravity with which she drove the proprieties four-in-hand through the cathedral town society, and had solicited to be taken beside her on the box of the cool coach of ceremony to which that team was harnessed. His proposal of marriage being accepted by the lady, the commissary took his seat behind the proprieties with great decorum, and Mrs. General drove until the commissary died. In the course of their united journey, they ran over several people who came in the way of the proprieties—but always in a high style and with composure.

The commissary having been buried with all the decorations suitable to the service (the whole team of proprieties were harnessed to his hearse, and they all had feathers and black velvet housings, with his coat-of-arms in the corner), Mrs. General began to inquire what quantity of dust and ashes was deposited at the banker's. It then transpired that the commissary had so far stolen a march on Mrs. General as to have bought himself an annuity some years before his marriage, and to have reserved that circumstance, in mentioning, at the period of his proposal, that his income was derived from the interest of his money. Mrs. General consequently found her means so much diminished, that, but for the perfect regulation of her mind, she might have felt disposed to question the accuracy of that portion of the late service which had declared that the commissary could take nothing away with him.

In this state of affairs it occurred to Mrs. General, that she might "form the mind," and eke the manners, of some young lady of distinction. Or, that she might harness the proprieties to the carriage of some rich young heiress or widow, and become at once the driver and guard of such vehicle through the social mazes. Mrs. General's communication of this idea to her clerical and commissariat connection was so warmly applauded that, but for the lady's undoubted merit, it might have appeared as though they wanted to get rid of her. Testimonials representing Mrs. General as a prodigy of piety, learning, virtue, and gentility, were lavishly contributed from influential quarters; and one venerable archdeacon even shed tears in recording his testimony to her perfections (described to him by persons on whom he could rely), though he had never had the honor and moral gratification of setting eyes on Mrs. General in all his life.

Thus delegated on her mission, as it were by Church and State, Mrs. General, who had always occupied high ground, felt in a condition to keep it, and began by putting herself up at a very high figure. An interval of some duration elapsed, in which there was no bid for Mrs. General. At length a county-widower, with a daughter of fourteen, opened negotiations with the lady; and as it was a part either of the native dignity or of the artificial policy of Mrs. General (but certainly one or the other), to comport herself as if she were much more sought than seeking, the widower pursued Mrs. General until he prevailed upon her to form his daughter's mind and manners.

The execution of this trust occupied Mrs. General about seven years, in the course of which time she made the tour of Europe, and saw most of that extensive miscellany of objects which it is essential that all persons of polite cultivation should see with other people's eyes, and never with their own. When her charge was at length formed, the marriage, not only of the young lady, but likewise of her father the widower, was resolved on. The widower then finding Mrs. General both inconvenient and expensive, became of a sudden almost as much affected by her merits as the archdeacon had been, and circulated such praises of her surpassing worth, in all quarters where he thought an opportunity might arise of transferring the blessing to somebody else, that Mrs. General was a name more honorable than ever.

The phœnix was to let, on this elevated perch, when Mr. Dorrit, who had lately succeeded to his property, mentioned to his bankers that he wished to discover a lady, well-bred, accomplished, well connected, well accustomed to good society, who was qualified at once to complete the education of his daughters, and to be their matron or chaperon. Mr. Dorrit's bankers, as the bankers of the county-widower, instantly said, "Mrs. General."

Pursuing the light so fortunately hit upon, and finding the concurrent testimony of the whole of Mrs. General's acquaintance to be of the pathetic nature already recorded, Mr. Dorrit took the trouble of going down to the county of the county-widower, to see Mrs. General. In whom he found a lady of a quality superior to his highest expectations.

"Might I be excused," said Mr. Dorrit, "if I inquired—ha —what remune—"

"Why, indeed," returned Mrs. General, stopping the word, "it is a subject on which I prefer to avoid entering. I have never entered on it with my friends here; and I cannot overcome the delicacy, Mr. Dorrit, with which I have always regarded it. I am not, as I hope you are aware, a governess—"

"O dear no!" said Mr. Dorrit. "Pray, Madam, do not imagine for a moment that I think so." He really blushed to be suspected of it.

Mrs. General gravely inclined her head. "I cannot, therefore, put a price upon services which it is a pleasure to me to render if I can render them spontaneously, but which I could not render in mere return for any consideration. Neither do I know how, or where, to find a case parallel to my own. It is peculiar."

No doubt. But how then (Mr. Dorrit not unnaturally hinted) could the subject be approached?

"I cannot object," said Mrs. General—"though even that is disagreeable to me—to Mr. Dorrit's inquiring in confidence, of my friends here, what amount they may have been accustomed, at quarterly intervals, to pay to my credit at my banker's"

Mr. Dorrit bowed his acknowledgments.

"Permit me to add," said Mrs. General, "that beyond this, I can never resume the topic. Also that I can accept no second or inferior position. If the honor were proposed to me of becoming known to Mr. Dorrit's family—I think two daughtere were mentioned ?——"

"Two daughters."

"I could only accept it on terms of perfect equality, as a companion, protector, Mentor, and friend."

Mr. Dorrit, in spite of his sense of his importance, felt as if it would be quite a kindness in her to accept it on any conditions. He almost said as much.

"I think," repeated Mrs. General, "two daughters were mentioned ?"

"Two daughters," said Mr. Dorrit again.

"It would therefore," said Mrs. General, "be necessary to add a third more to the payment (whatever its amount may prove to be), which my friends here have been accustomed to make to my banker's."

Mr. Dorrit lost no time in referring the delicate question to the county-widower, and, finding that he had been accustomed to pay three hundred pounds a-year to the credit of Mrs. General, arrived, without any very severe strain on his arithmetic, at the conclusion that he himself must pay four. Mrs. General being an article of that lustrous surface which suggests that it is worth any money, he made a formal proposal to be allowed to have the honor and pleasure of regarding her as a member of his family. Mrs. General conceded that high privilege, and here she was.

In person, Mrs. General, including her skirts, which had much to do with it, was of a dignified and imposing appearance ; ample, rustling, gravely voluminous ; always upright behind the proprieties. She might have been taken—had been taken—to the top of the Alps and the bottom of Herculaneum, without disarranging a fold in her dress, or displacing a pin. If her countenance and hair had rather a floury appearance, as though from living in some transcendently genteel Mill, it was rather because she was a chalky creation altogether, than because she mended her complexion with violet powder, or had turned gray.

If her eyes had no expression, it was probably because they had nothing to express. If she had few wrinkles, it was because her mind had never traced its name or any other inscription on her face. A cool, waxy, blown-out woman, who had never lighted well.

Mrs. General had no opinions. Her way of forming a mind was to prevent it from forming opinions. She had a little circular set of mental grooves or rails, on which she started little trains of other people's opinions, which never overtook one another, and never got anywhere. Even her propriety could not dispute that there was impropriety in the world; but Mrs. General's way of getting rid of it was to put it out of sight, and make believe that there was no such thing. This was another of her ways of forming a mind—to cram all articles of difficulty into cupboards, lock them up, and say they had no existence. It was the easiest way, and beyond all comparison, the properist.

Mrs. General was not to be told of any thing shocking. Accidents, miseries, and offenses, were never to be mentioned before her. Passion was to go asleep in the presence of Mrs. General, and blood was to change to milk and water. The little that was left in the world, when all these deductions were made, it was Mrs. General's province to varnish. In that formation process of hers, she dipped the smallest of brushes into the largest of pots, and varnished the surface of every object that came under consideration. The more cracked it was, the more Mrs. General varnished it.

There was varnish in Mrs. General's voice, varnish in Mrs. General's touch, an atmosphere of varnish round Mrs. General's figure. Mrs. General's dreams ought to have been varnish—if she had any—lying asleep in the arms of the good Saint Bernard, with the feathery snow falling on his house-top.

CHAPTER XXXIX.

ON THE ROAD.

THE bright morning sun dazzled the eyes, the snow had ceased, the mists had vanished, the mountain air was so clear and light that the new sensation of breathing it, was like the having entered on a new existence. To help the delusion, the solid ground itself seemed gone, and the mountain, a shining waste of immense white heaps and masses, to be a region of cloud floating between the blue sky above and the earth far below.

Some dark specks in the snow, like knots upon a little thread, beginning at the convent door and winding away down the descent in broken lengths which were not yet pieced together, showed where the Brethren were at work in several places clearing the track. Already the snow had begun to be foot-thawed again about the door. Mules were busily brought out, tied to the rings in the wall, and laden; strings of bells were buckled on, burdens were adjusted, the voices of drivers and riders sounded musically. Some of the earliest had even already resumed their journey; and, both on the level summit by the dark water near the convent, and on the downward way of yesterday's ascent, little moving figures of men and mules, reduced to miniatures by the immensity around, went with a clear tinkling of bells and a pleasant harmony of tongues.

In the supper-room of last night, a new fire, piled upon the feathery ashes of the old one, shone upon a homely breakfast of loaves, butter, and milk. It also shone on the courier of the Dorrit family, making tea for his party from a supply he had brought up with him, together with several other small stores, which were chiefly laid in for the use of the strong body of inconvenience. Mr. Gowan, and Blandois of Paris, had already breakfasted, and were walking up and down by the lake, smoking their cigars.

"Gowan, eh?" muttered Tip, otherwise Edward Dorrit, Esquire, turning over the leaves of the book, when the courier had left them to breakfast. "Then Gowan is the name of a puppy, that's all I have got to say! If it was worth my while, I'd pull his nose. But it isn't worth my while—fortunately for him. How's his wife, Amy? I suppose you know. You generally know things of that sort."

"She is better, Edward. But they are not going to-day."

"Oh! They are not going to-day! Fortunately for that fellow, too," said Tip, "or he and I might have come into collision."

"It is thought better here that she should lie quiet to-day, and not be fatigued and shaken by the ride down until to-morrow."

"With all my heart. But you talk as if you had been nursing her. You havn't been relapsing into (Mrs. General is not here) old habits, have you, Amy?"

He asked her the question with a sly glance of observation at Miss Fanny, and at his father too.

"I have only been in to ask her if I could do any thing for her, Tip," said Little Dorrit.

"You needn't call me Tip, Amy child," returned that young gentleman with a frown; "because that's an old habit, and one you may as well lay aside."

"I didn't mean to say so, Edward dear. I forgot. It was so natural once, that it seemed at the moment the right word."

"Oh yes!" Miss Fanny struck in. "Natural, and right word, and once, and all the rest of it! Nonsense, you little thing! I know perfectly well why you have been taking such an interest in this Mrs. Gowan. You can't blind *me*."

"I will not try to, Fanny. Don't be angry."

"Oh! angry!" returned that young lady with a flounce. "I have no patience" (which indeed was the truth).

"Pray, Fanny," said Mr. Dorrit, raising his eyebrows, "what do you mean? Explain yourself."

"Oh! Never mind, Pa," replied Miss Fanny, "it's no great matter. Amy will understand me. She knew, or knew of, this Mrs. Gowan before yesterday, and she may as well admit that she did."

"My child," said Mr. Dorrit, turning to his younger daughter, "has your sister—any—ha—authority for this curious statement?"

"However meek we are," Miss Fanny struck in before she could answer, "we don't go creeping into people's rooms on the tops of cold mountains, and sitting perishing in the frost with people, unless we know something about them beforehand. It's not very hard to divine whose friend Mrs. Gowan is."

"Whose friend?" inquired her father.

"Pa, I am sorry to say," returned Miss Fanny, who had by this time succeeded in goading herself into a state of much ill-usage and grievance, which she was often at great pains to do: "that I believe her to be a friend of that very objectionable and unpleasant person, who, with a total absence of all delicacy, which our experience might have led us to expect from him, insulted us and outraged our feelings in so public and willful a manner, on an occasion to which it is understood among us, that we will not more pointedly allude."

"Amy, my child," said Mr. Dorrit, tempering a bland severity with a dignified affection, "is this the case?"

Little Dorrit mildly answered, Yes it was.

"Yes it is!" cried Miss Fanny. "Of course! I said so! And now, Pa, I do declare once for all," this young lady was in the habit of declaring the same thing once for all, every day of her life, and even several times in a day, "that this is shameful! I do declare once for all that it ought to be put a stop to. Is it not enough that we have gone through what is only known to ourselves, but are we to have it thrown in our faces, perseveringly and systematically, by the very person who should spare our feelings most? Are we to be exposed to this unnatural conduct every moment of our lives? Are we never to be permitted to forget? I say again, it is absolutely infamous!"

"Well, Amy," observed her brother, shaking his head, "you know I stand by you whenever I can, and on most occasions But I must say, that upon my soul I do consider it rather an unaccountable mode of showing your sisterly affection, that you should back up a man who treated me in the most ungentlemanly way in which one man can treat another. And who," he added convincingly, "must be a low-minded thief, you know, or he never could have conducted himself as he did."

"And see," said Miss Fanny, "see what is involved in this! Can we ever hope to be respected by our servants? Never. Here are our two women, and Pa's valet, and a footman, and a courier, and all sorts of dependents, and yet, in the midst of these, we are to have one of ourselves rushing about with tumblers of cold water, like a menial! Why, a policeman," said Miss Fanny, "if a beggar had a fit in the street, could but go plunging about with tumblers, as this very Amy did in this very room before our very eyes last night!"

"I don't so much mind that, once in a way," remarked Mr. Edward; "but your Clennam, as he thinks proper to call himself, is another thing."

"He is a part of the same thing," returned Miss Fanny, "and of a piece with all the rest. He obtruded himself upon us in the first instance. We never wanted him. I always showed him, for one, that I could have dispensed with his company with the greatest pleasure. He then commits that gross outrage upon our feelings, which he never could or would have committed but for the delight he took in exposing us; and then we are to be demeaned for the service of his friends! Why, I don't wonder at this Mr. Gowan's conduct toward you. What else was to be expected when he was enjoying our past misfortunes—gloating over them at the moment!"

"Father—Edward—no indeed!" pleaded little Dorrit.—"Neither Mr. nor Mrs. Gowan had ever heard our name. They were, and they are, quite ignorant of our history."

"So much the worse," retorted Fanny, determined not to admit any thing in extenuation, "for then you have *no* excuse. If they had known about us, you might have felt yourself called upon to conciliate them. That would have been a weak and ridiculous mistake, but I can respect a mistake, whereas I can't respect a willful and deliberate debasing of those who should be nearest and dearest to us. No. I can't respect that. I can do nothing but denounce that."

"I never offend you willfully, Fanny," said Little Dorrit, "though you are so hard with me."

"Then you should be more careful, Amy," returned her sister. "If you do such things by accident, you should be more careful. If I happened to have been born in a peculiar place, and under peculiar circumstances that blunted my knowledge of propriety, I fancy I should think myself bound to consider at every step, 'Am I going, ignorantly, to compromise any near and dear relations?' That is what I fancy *I* should do, if it was *my* case."

Mr. Dorrit now interposed, at once to stop these painful subjects by his authority, and to point their moral by his wisdom.

"My dear," said he to his younger daughter, "I beg you to —ha—to say no more. Your sister Fanny expresses herself strongly, but not without considerable reason. You have now a—hum—a great position to support. That great position is not occupied by yourself alone, but by—ha—by me, and—ha hum—by us. Us. Now, it is incumbent upon all people in an exalted position, but it is particularly so on this family, for reasons which I—ha—will not dwell upon, to make themselves respected. To be vigilant in making themselves respected. Dependents, to respect us, must be—ha—kept at a distance and —hum—kept down. Down. Therefore, your not exposing yourself to the remarks of our attendants, by appearing to have at any time dispensed with their services and performed them yourself, is—ha—highly important."

"Why, who can doubt it?" cried Miss Fanny. "It's the essence of every thing!"

"Fanny," returned her father, grandiloquently, "give me leave, my dear. We then come to—ha—to Mr. Clennam. I am free to say that I do not, Amy, share your sister's sentiments—that is to say altogether—hum—altogether—in reference to Mr. Clennam. I am content to regard that individual in the light of—ha—generally—a well-behaved person. Hum. A well-behaved person. Nor will I inquire whether Mr. Clennam did, at any time, obtrude himself on—ha—my society. He knew my society to be—hum—sought, and his plea might be that he regarded me in the light of a public character. But there were circumstances attending my—ha—slight knowledge of Mr. Clennam (it was very slight), which," here Mr. Dorrit became extremely grave and impressive, "would render it highly indelicate in Mr. Clennam to—ha—to seek to renew communication with me or with any member of my family, under existing circumstances. If Mr. Clennam has sufficient delicacy to perceive the impropriety of any such attempt, I am bound as a responsible gentleman to—ha—defer to that delicacy on his part. If, on the other hand, Mr. Clennam has not that delicacy, I cannot for a moment—ha—hold any correspondence with so —hum—coarse a mind. In either case, it would appear that Mr. Clennam is put altogether out of the question, and that we have nothing to do with him or he with us. Ha—Mrs. General."

The entrance of the lady whom he announced, to take her place at the breakfast-table, terminated the discussion. Shortly afterward, the courier announced that the valet, and the footman, and the two maids, and the four guides, and the fourteen mules, were in readiness; so the breakfast party went out to the convent door to join the cavalcade.

Mr. Gowan stood aloof with his cigar and pencil, but Mr. Blandois was on the spot, to pay his respects to the ladies. When he gallantly pulled off his slouched hat to Little Dorrit, she thought he had even a more sinister look, standing swart and cloaked in the snow, than he had had in the fire-light over night. But, as both her father and her sister received his homage with some favor, she refrained from expressing any distrust of him, lest it should prove to be a new blemish derived from her prison-birth.

Nevertheless, as they wound down the rugged way while the convent was yet in sight, she more than once looked round, and descried Mr. Blandois, backed by the convent smoke which rose straight and high from the chimneys in a golden film, always standing on one jutting point looking down after them. Long after he was a mere black stick in the snow, she felt as though she could yet see that smile of his, that high nose, and those eyes that were too near it. And even after that, when the convent was gone and some light morning clouds vailed the pass below it, the ghastly skeleton arms by the wayside seemed to be all pointing up at him.

More treacherous than snow, perhaps, colder at heart, and harder to melt, Blandois of Paris by degrees passed out of her mind, as they came down into the softer regions. Again the sun was warm, again the streams descending from glaciers and snowy caverns were refreshing to drink at, again they came among the pine trees, the rocky rivulets, the verdant heights and dales, the wooden chalets and rough zigzag fences of Swiss country. Sometimes, the way so widened that she and her father could ride abreast. And then to look at him, handsomely clothed in his furs and broadcloths, rich, free, numerously served and attended, his eyes roving far away among the glories of the landscape, no miserable screen before them to darken his sight and cast its shadow on him, was enough.

Her uncle was so far rescued from that shadow of old, that he wore the clothes they gave him, and performed some ablutions as a sacrifice to the family credit, and went where he was taken, with a certain patient animal enjoyment, which seemed to express that the air and change did him good. In all other respects, save one, he shone with no light but such as was reflected from his brother. His brother's greatness, wealth, freedom, and grandeur, pleased him without any reference to himself. Silent and retiring, he had no use for speech when he could hear his brother speak; and no desire to be waited on, so that the servants devoted themselves to his brother. The only noticeable change he originated in himself, was an alteration in his manner to his younger niece. Every day it refined more and more into a marked respect, very rarely shown by age to youth, and still more rarely susceptible, one would have said, of the fitness with which he invested it. On those occasions when Miss Fanny did declare once for all, he would take the next opportunity of baring his gray head before his younger niece, and of helping her to alight, or handing her to the carriage, or showing her any other attention, with the profoundest deference. Yet it never appeared misplaced or forced, being always heartily simple, spontaneous, and genuine. Neither would he ever consent, even at his brother's request, to be helped to any place before her, or to take precedence of her in any thing. So jealous was he of her being respected, that on his very journey down from the Great Saint Bernard, he took sudden and violent umbrage at the footman's being remiss to hold her stirrup, though standing near when she dismounted; and unspeakably astonished the whole retinue by charging at him on a hard-headed mule, riding him into a corner, and threatening to trample him to death.

They were a goodly company, and the Innkeepers all but worshiped them. Wherever they went, their importance preceded them in the person of the courier riding before, to see that the rooms of state were ready. He was the herald of the family procession. The great traveling-carriage came next: containing, inside, Mr. Dorrit, Miss Dorrit, Miss Amy Dorrit, and Mrs. General; outside, some of the retainers, and (in fine weather) Edward Dorrit, Esquire, for whom the box was reserved. Then came the chariot containing Frederick Dorrit, Esquire, and an empty place occupied by Edward Dorrit, Esquire, in wet weather. Then came the fourgon with the rest of the retainers, the heavy baggage, and as much as it could carry of the mud and dust which the other vehicles left behind.

These equipages adorned the yard of the hotel at Martigny, on the return of the family from their mountain excursion. Other vehicles were there, much company being on the road, from the patched Italian Vettura—like the body of a swing from an English fair put upon a wooden tray on wheels, and having another wooden tray without wheels put atop of it—to the trim English carriage. But there was another adornment of the hotel which Mr. Dorrit had not bargained for. Two strange travelers embellished one of his rooms.

The Innkeeper, hat in hand in the yard, swore to the courier that he was blighted, that he was desolated, that he was profoundly afflicted, that he was the most miserable and unfortunate of beasts, that he had the head of a wooden pig. He ought never to have made the concession, he said, but the very genteel lady had so passionately prayed him for the accommodation of that room to dine in, only for a little half-hour, that he had been vanquished. The little half-hour was expired, the lady and gentleman were taking their little dessert and half-cup of coffee, the note was paid, the horses were ordered, they would depart immediately; but, owing to an unhappy destiny and the curse of Heaven, they were not yet gone.

Nothing could exceed Mr. Dorrit's indignation, as he turned at the foot of the staircase on hearing these apologies. He felt that the family dignity was struck at, by an assassin's hand. He had a sense of his dignity, which was of the most exquisite nature. He could detect a design upon it when nobody else had any perception of the fact. His life was made an agony by the number of fine scalpels that he felt to be incessantly engaged in dissecting his dignity.

"Is it possible, sir," said Mr. Dorrit, reddening excessively, "that you have—ha—had the audacity to place one of my rooms at the disposition of any other person?"

Thousands of pardons! It was the host's profound misfortune to have been overcome by that too genteel lady. He besought Monseigneur not to enrage himself. He threw himself on Monseigneur for clemency. If Monseigneur would have the distinguished goodness to occupy the other salon especially reserved for him, for but five minutes, all would go well.

"No, sir," said Mr. Dorrit. "I will not occupy any salon. I will leave your house without eating or drinking, or setting foot in it. How do you dare to act like this? Who am I that you—ha—separate me from other gentlemen?"

Alas! The host called all the universe to witness that Monseigneur was the most amiable of the whole body of nobility, the most important, the most estimable, the most honored. If he separated Monseigneur from others, it was only because he was more distinguished, more cherished, more generous, more renowned.

"Don't tell me so, sir," returned Mr. Dorrit, in a mighty heat. "You have affronted me. You have heaped insults upon me. How dare you? Explain yourself."

Ah, just Heaven, then, how could the host explain himself when he had nothing more to explain; when he had only to apologize, and confide himself to the so well-known magnanimity of Monseigneur!

"I tell you, sir," said Mr. Dorrit, panting with anger, "that you separate me—ha—from other gentlemen; that you make distinctions between me and other gentlemen of fortune and station. I demand of you, why? I wish to know on—ha—what authority, on whose authority. Reply, sir. Explain. Answer why."

Permit the landlord humbly to submit to Monsieur the Courier then, that Monseigneur, ordinarily so gracious, enraged himself without cause. There was no why. Monsieur the Courier would represent to Monseigneur, that he deceived himself in suspecting that there was any why, but the why his devoted servant had already had the honor to present to him. The very genteel lady——

"Silence!" cried Mr. Dorrit. "Hold your tongue! I will hear no more of the very genteel lady; I will hear no more of you. Look at this family—my family—a family more genteel than any lady. You have treated this family with disrespect; you have been insolent to this family. I'll ruin you. Ha—send for the horses, pack the carriages, I'll not set foot in this man's house again!"

No one had interfered in the dispute, which was beyond the French colloquial powers of Edward Dorrit, Esquire, and scarcely within the province of the ladies. Miss Fanny, however, now supported her father with great bitterness; declaring, in her native tongue, that it was quite clear there was something special in this man's impertinence; and that she considered it important that he should be, by some means, forced to give up his authority for making distinctions between that family and other wealthy families. What the reasons of his presumption could be, she was at a loss to imagine; but reasons he must have, and they ought to be torn from him.

All the guides, mule-drivers, and idlers in the yard, had made themselves parties to the angry conference, and were much impressed by the courier's now bestirring himself to get the carriages out. With the aid of some dozen people to each wheel, this was done at a great cost of noise; and then the loading was proceeded with, pending the arrival of the horses from the post-house.

But, the very genteel lady's English chariot being already horsed and at the inn-door, the landlord had slipped up-stairs to represent his hard case. This was notified to the yard by his now coming down the staircase in attendance on the gentleman and the lady, and by his pointing out the offended majesty of Mr. Dorrit to them with a significant motion of his hand.

"Beg your pardon," said the gentleman, detaching himself from the lady, and coming forward. "I am a man of few words and a bad hand at an explanation—but lady here is extremely anxious that there should be no Row. Lady—a mother of mine, in point of fact—wishes me to say that she hopes no Row."

Mr. Dorrit, still panting under his injury, saluted the gentleman, and saluted the lady, in a distant, final, and invincible manner.

"No, but really—here, old feller; you!" This was the gentleman's way of appealing to Edward Dorrit, Esquire, on whom he pounced as a great and providential relief. "Let you and I try to make this all right. Lady so very much wishes no Row."

Edward Dorrit, Esquire, led a little apart by the button, assumed a diplomatic expression of countenance in replying, "Why you must confess, that when you bespeak a lot of rooms beforehand and they belong to you, it's not pleasant to find other people in 'em."

"No," said the other, "I know it isn't. I admit it. Still, let you and I try to make it all right, and avoid Row. The fault is not this chap's at all, but my mother's. Being a remarkably fine woman with no bigodd nonsense about her—well educated, too—she was too many for this chap. Regularly pocketed him."

"If that's the case——" Edward Dorrit, Esquire, began.

"Assure you 'pon my soul 'tis the case. Consequently," said the other gentleman, retiring on his main position, "why Row?"

"Edmund," said the lady from the doorway, "I hope you have explained, or are explaining, to the satisfaction of this gentleman and his family, that the civil landlord is not to blame?"

"Assure you, ma'am," returned Edmund, "perfectly paralyzing myself with trying it on." He then looked stedfastly at Edward Dorrit, Esquire, for some seconds, and suddenly added, in a burst of confidence, "Old feller! *Is* it all right?"

"I don't know, after all," said the lady, gracefully advancing a step or two toward Mr. Dorrit, "but that I had better say myself, at once, that I assured this good man I took all the consequences on myself of occupying one of a stranger's suite of rooms during his absence, for just as much (or as little) time as I could dine in. I had no idea the rightful owner would

THE FAMILY DIGNITY IS AFFRONTED.

come back so soon, nor had I any idea that he had come back, or I should have hastened to make restoration of my ill-gotten chamber, and to have offered my explanation and apology. I trust, in saying this——"

For a moment the lady, with a glass at her eye, stood transfixed and speechless before the two Miss Dorrits. At the same moment Miss Fanny, in the foreground of a grand pictorial composition formed by the family, the family equipages, and the family servants, held her sister tight under one arm to detain her on the spot, and with the other arm fanned herself with a distinguished air, and negligently surveyed the lady from head to foot.

The lady, recovering herself quickly—for it was Mrs. Merdle and she was not easily dashed—went on to add that she trusted, in saying this, she apologized for her boldness, and restored this well-behaved landlord to the favor that was so very valuable to him. Mr. Dorrit, on the altar of whose dignity all this was incense, made a gracious reply; and said that his people should—ha—countermand his horses, and he would —hum—overlook what he had at first supposed to be an affront, but now regarded as an honor. Upon this, the bosom bent to him; and its owner, with a wonderful command of feature, addressed a winning smile of adieu to the two sisters, as young ladies of fortune in whose favor she was much prepossessed, and whom she had never had the gratification of seeing before.

Not so, however, Mr. Sparkler. This gentleman, becoming transfixed at the same moment as his lady-mother, could not by any means unfix himself again, but stood stiffly staring at the whole composition with Miss Fanny in the foreground. On his mother's saying, "Edmund, we are quite ready; will you give me your arm?" he seemed, by the motion of his lips, to reply with some remark comprehending the form of words in which his shining talents found the most frequent utterance, but he relaxed no muscle. So fixed was his figure, that it would have been matter of some difficulty to bend him sufficiently to get him in the carriage door, if he had not received the timely assistance of a maternal pull from within. He was no sooner within, than the pad of the little window in the back of the chariot disappeared, and his eye usurped its place. There it remained as long as so small an object was discernible, and probably much longer, staring (as though something inexpressibly surprising should happen to a cod-fish) like an ill-executed eye in a large locket.

This encounter was so highly agreeable to Miss Fanny, and gave her so much to think of with triumph afterward, that it softened her asperities exceedingly. When the procession was again in motion next day, she occupied her place in it with a new gayety; and showed such a flow of spirits indeed, that Mrs. General looked rather surprised.

Little Dorrit was glad to be found no fault with, and to see that Fanny was pleased; but her part in the procession was a musing part, and a quiet one. Sitting opposite her father in the traveling-carriage, and recalling the old Marshalsea room, her present existence was a dream. All that she saw was new and wonderful, but it was not real; it seemed to her as if those visions of mountains and picturesque countries might melt away at any moment, and the carriage, turning some abrupt corner, bring up with a jolt at the old Marshalsea gate.

To have no work to do was strange, but not half so strange as having glided into a corner where she had no one to think for, nothing to plan and contrive, no cares of others to load herself with. Strange as that was, it was far stranger yet to find a space between herself and her father, where others occupied themselves in taking care of him, and where she was never expected to be. At first, this was so much more unlike her old experience than even the mountains themselves, that she had been unable to resign herself to it, and had tried to retain her old place about him. But he had spoken to her alone, and had said that people—ha—people in an exalted position, my dear, must scrupulously exact respect from their dependents; and that for her, his daughter, Miss Amy Dorrit, of the sole remaining branch of the Dorrits of Dorsetshire, to be known to—hum—to occupy herself in fulfilling the functions of—ha hum—a valet, would be incompatible with that respect. Therefore, my dear, he—ha—he laid his parental injunctions upon her, to remember that she was a lady, who had now to conduct herself with—hum—a proper pride, and to preserve the rank of a lady; and consequently he requested her to abstain from doing what would occasion—ha—unpleasant and derogatory remarks. She had obeyed without a murmur. Thus it had been brought about that she now sat in her corner of the luxurious carriage with her little patient hands folded before her, quite displaced even from the last point of the old standing-ground in life on which her feet had lingered.

It was from this position that all she saw appeared unreal; the more surprising the scenes, the more they resembled the unreality of her own inner life as she went through its vacant places all day long. The gorges of the Simplon, its enormous depth and thundering water-falls, the wonderful road, the points of danger where a loose wheel or a faltering horse would have been destruction, the descent into Italy, the opening of that beautiful land, as the rugged mountain-chasm widened and let them out from a gloomy and dark imprisonment—all a dream—only the old mean Marshalsea a reality. Nay, even the old mean Marshalsea was shaken to its foundations, when she pictured it without her father. She could scarcely believe that the prisoners were still lingering in the close yard, that the mean rooms were still every one tenanted, and that the turnkey still stood in the Lodge letting people in and out, all just as she well knew it to be.

With a remembrance of her father's old life in prison hanging about her like the burden of a sorrowful tune, Little Dorrit would wake from a dream of her birth-place into a whole day's dream. The painted room in which she awoke, often a humbled state-chamber in a dilapidated palace, would begin it; with its wild red autumnal vine-leaves overhanging the glass, its orange trees on the cracked white terrace outside the window, a group of monks and peasants in the little street below, misery and magnificence wrestling with each other upon every rood of ground in the prospect, no matter how widely diversified, and misery throwing magnificence with the strength of fate. To this would succeed a labyrinth of bare passages and pillared galleries, with the family procession already preparing in the quadrangle below, through the carriages and luggage being brought together by the servants for the day's journey. Then, breakfast in another painted chamber, damp-stained and of desolate proportions; and then the departure, which, to her timidity and sense of not being grand enough for her place in the ceremonies, was always an uneasy thing. For, then the courier (who himself would have been a foreign gentleman of high mark in the Marshalsea) would present himself to report that all was ready; and then her father's valet would pompously induct him into his traveling cloak; and then Fanny's maid, and her own maid (who was a weight on Little Dorrit's mind —absolutely made her cry at first, she knew so little what to do with her), would be in attendance; and then her brother's man would complete his master's equipment; and then her father would give his arm to Mrs. General, and her uncle would give his to her, and, escorted by the landlord and Inn servants, they would swoop down stairs. There, a crowd would be collected to see them enter their carriages, which, amidst much bowing, and begging, and prancing, and lashing, and clattering, they would do; and so they would be driven madly through the narrow unsavory streets, and jerked out at the town gate.

Among the day's unrealities would be, roads where the bright red vines were looped and garlanded together on trees for many miles; woods of olives; white villages and towns on hill-sides, lovely without, but frightful in their dirt and poverty within; crosses by the way; deep blue lakes with fairy islands, and clustering boats with awnings of bright colors and sails of beautiful forms; vast piles of building mouldering to dust; hanging-gardens where the weeds had grown so strong that their stems, like wedges driven home, had split the arch and rent the wall; stone-terraced lanes, with the lizards running into and out of every chink; beggars of all sorts everywhere: pitiful, picturesque, hungry, merry: children beggars and aged beggars. Often at posting-houses, and other halting places, these miserable creatures would appear to her the only realities of the day; and many a time when the money she had brought to give them was all given away, she would sit with her folded hands, thoughtfully looking after some diminutive girl leading her gray father, as if the sight reminded her of something in the days that were gone.

Again, there would be places where they stayed the week together, in splendid rooms, had banquets every day, rode out among heaps of wonders, walked through miles of palaces, and rested in dark corners of great churches; where there were winking lamps of gold and silver among pillars and arches, kneeling figures dotted about at confessionals and on the pavements; where there was the mist and scent of incense; where there were pictures, fantastic images, gaudy altars, great heights and distances, all softly lighted through stained glass, and the massive curtains that hung in the door-ways. From these cities they would go on again, by the roads of vines and olives, through squalid villages where there was not a hovel without a gap in its filthy walls, not a window with a whole inch of glass or paper; where there seemed to be nothing to support life, nothing to eat, nothing to make, nothing to grow, nothing to hope, nothing to do but die.

Again they would come to whole towns of palaces, whose proper inmates were all banished, and which were all changed into barracks; troops of idle soldiers leaning out of the state-windows, where their accoutrements hung drying on the marble architecture, and showing to the mind like hosts of rats who were (happily) eating away the props of the edifices that supported them, and must soon, with them, be smashed on the heads of the other swarms of soldiers, and the swarms of priests, and the swarms of spies, who were all of the ill-looking population left to be ruined, in the streets below.

Through such scenes the family procession moved on to Venice. And here it dispersed for a time, as they were to live in Venice some few months, in a palace (itself six times as big as the whole Marshalsea) on the Grand Canal.

In this crowning unreality, where all the streets were paved with water, and where the death-like stillness of the days and nights was broken by no sound but the softened ringing of church-bells, the rippling of the current, and the cry of the gondoliers turning the corners of the flowing streets, Little Dorrit, quite lost by her task being done, sat down to muse. The family began a gay life, went here and there, and turned night into day; but she was timid of joining in their gayeties, and only asked leave to be left alone.

Sometimes she would step alone into one of the gondolas that were always kept in waiting, moored to painted posts at the door —when she could escape from the attendance of that oppressive maid who was her mistress, and a very hard one—and would be taken all over the strange city. Social people in other gondolas began to ask each other who the little solitary girl was whom they passed, sitting in her boat with folded hands, looking so pensively and wonderingly about her. Never thinking that it would be worth anybody's while to notice her or her doings, Little Dorrit, in her quiet, scared, lost manner, went about the city none the less.

But her favorite station was the balcony of her own room, overhanging the canal, with other balconies below, and none above. It was of massive stone darkened by ages, built in a wild fancy which came from the East to that collection of wild fancies; and Little Dorrit was little indeed, leaning on the broad-cushioned ledge, and looking over. As she liked no place of an evening half so well, she soon began to be watched for, and many eyes in passing gondolas were raised, and many people said, There was the little figure of the English girl who was always alone.

Such people were not realities to the little figure of the English girl; such people were all unknown to her. She would watch the sunset, in its long low lines of purple and red, and its burning flush high up into the sky; so glowing on the buildings, and so lightening their structure, that it made them look as if their strong walls were transparent, and they shone from within. She would watch those glories expire; and then, after looking at the black gondolas underneath, taking guests to music and dancing, would raise her eyes to the shining stars. Was there no party of her own, in other times, on which the stars had shone? To think of that old gate now!

She would think of that old gate, and of herself sitting at it in the dead of the night, pillowing Maggy's head; and of other places and of other scenes associated with those different times. And then she would lean upon her balcony, and look over at the water, as though they all lay underneath it. When she got to that, she would musingly watch its running, as if, in the general vision, it might run dry, and show her the prison again, and herself, and the old room, and the old inmates, and the old visitors; all lasting realities that had never changed.

CHAPTER XL.

A LETTER FROM LITTLE DORRIT.

Dear Mr. Clennam.

I write to you from my own room at Venice, thinking you will be glad to hear from me. But I know you cannot be so glad to hear from me, as I am to write to you; for every thing about you is as you have been accustomed to see it, and you miss nothing—unless it should be me, which can only be for a very little while together and very seldom—while every thing in my life is so strange, and I miss so much.

When we were in Switzerland, which appears to have been years ago, though it was only weeks, I met young Mrs. Gowan, who was on a mountain excursion like ourselves. She told me she was very well and very happy. She sent you the message by me, that she thanked you affectionately and would never forget you. She was quite confiding with me, and I loved her almost as soon as I spoke to her. But there is nothing singular in that; who could help loving so beautiful and winning a creature! I could not wonder at any one loving her. No, indeed.

It will not make you uneasy on Mrs. Gowan's account, I hope —for I remember that you said you had the interest of a true friend in her—if I tell you that I wish she could have married some one better suited to her. Mr. Gowan seems fond of her, and of course she is very fond of him, but I thought he was not earnest enough—I don't mean in that respect—I mean in any thing. I could not keep it out of my mind that if I was Mrs. Gowan (what a change that would be, and how I must alter to become like her!) I should feel that I was rather lonely and lost, for the want of some one who was stedfast and firm in purpose. I even thought she felt this want a little, almost without knowing it. But mind you are not made uneasy by this, for she was "very well and very happy." And she looked most beautiful.

I expect to meet her again before long, and indeed have been expecting for some days past to see her here. I will ever be as good a friend to her as I can for your sake. Dear Mr. Clenman, I dare say you think little of having been a friend to me when I had no other (not that I have any other now, for I have made no new friends), but I think much of it, and I never can forget it.

I wish I knew—but it is best for no one to write to me—how Mr. and Mrs. Plornish prosper in the business which my dear father bought for them, and that old Mr. Nandy lives happily with them and his two grandchildren, and sings all his songs over and over again. I cannot quite keep back the tears from my eyes when I think of my poor Maggy, and of the blank she must have felt at first, however kind they all are to her, without her Little Mother. Will you go and tell her, as a strict secret, with my love, that she never can have regretted our separation more than I have regretted it; and will you tell them all that I have thought of them every day, and that my heart is faithful to them everywhere? O, if you could know how faithful, you would almost pity me for being so far away and being so grand!

You will be glad, I am sure, to know that my dear father is very well in health, and that all these changes are highly beneficial to him, and that he is very different indeed from what he used to be when you used to see him. There is an improvement in my uncle too, I think, though he never complained of old, and never exults now. Fanny is very graceful, quick, and clever. It is natural to her to be a lady; she has adapted herself to our new fortunes with wonderful ease.

This reminds me that I have not been able to do so, and that I sometimes almost despair of ever being able to do so. I find that I cannot learn. Mrs. General is always with us, and we speak French and speak Italian, and she takes pains to form us in many ways. When I say we speak French and Italian I mean they do. As for me, I am so slow that I scarcely get on at all. As soon as I begin to plan and think, and try, all my planning, thinking, and trying go in old directions, and I begin to feel careful again about the expenses of the day, and about my dear father, and about my work, and then I remember with a start that there are no such cares left, and that in itself is so new and improbable that it sets me wandering again. I should not have the courage to mention this to any one but you.

It is the same with all these new countries and wonderful sights. They are very beautiful, and they astonish me, but I am not collected enough—not familiar enough with myself, if you can quite understand what I mean—to have all the pleasure in them that I might have. What I knew before them, blends with them, too, so curiously. For instance, when we were among the mountains, I often felt (I hesitate to tell such an idle thing, dear Mr. Clennam, even to you), as if the Marshalsea must be behind that great rock; or as if Mrs. Clennam's room where I have worked so many days, and where I first saw you, must be just beyond that snow. Do you remember one night when I came with Maggy to your lodging in Covent Garden? That room I have often and often fancied I have seen before me, traveling along for miles by the side of our carriage, when I have looked out of the carriage window after dark. We were shut out that night, and sat at the iron gate, and walked about till morning. I often look up at the stars, even from the balcony of this room, and believe that I am in the street again, shut out with Maggy. It is the same with people that I left in England. When I go about here in a gondola, I surprise myself looking into other gondolas as if I hoped to see them. It would overcome me with joy to see them, but I don't think it would surprise me much, at first. In my fanciful times, I fancy that they might be anywhere; and I almost expect to see their dear faces on the bridges or the quays.

Another difficulty that I have will seem very strange to you. It must seem very strange to any one but me, and does even to me: I often feel the old sad pity for—I need not write the word—for him. Changed as he is, and inexpressibly blest and thankful as I always am to know it, the old sorrowful feeling of compassion comes upon me sometimes with such strength, that I want to put my arms round his neck, tell him how I love him, and cry a little on his breast. I should be glad after that, and proud and happy. But I know that I must not do this; that he would not like it, that Fanny would be angry, that Mrs. General would be amazed; and so I quiet myself. Yet in doing so, I struggle with the feeling that I have come to be at a distance from him; and that even in the midst of all the servants and attendants, he is deserted, and in want of me.

Dear Mr. Clennam, I have written a great deal about myself, but I must write a little more still, or what I wanted most of all to say in this weak letter would be left out of it. In all these foolish thoughts of mine, which I have been so hardy as to confess to you because I know you will understand me if any body can, and will make more allowance for me than any body else would if you cannot—in all these thoughts, there is one thought scarcely ever—never—out of my memory, and that is, that I hope you sometimes, in a quiet moment, have a thought for me. I must tell you that as to this, I have felt ever since I have been away, an anxiety which I am very very anxious to relieve. I have been afraid that you may think of me in a new light, or a new character. Don't do that, I could not bear that—it would make me more unhappy than you can suppose. It would break my heart to believe that you thought of me in any way that would make me stranger to you, than I was when you was so good to me. What I have to pray and entreat of you is, that you will never think of me as the daughter of a rich person; that you will never think of me as dressing any better, or living any better than when you first knew me. That you will remember me only as the little shabby girl you protected with so much tenderness, from whose threadbare dress you have kept away the rain, and whose wet feet you have dried at your fire. That you will think of me (when you think of me at all), and of my true affection and devoted gratitude, always without change, as of

Your poor child,

LITTLE DORRIT.

P.S.—Particularly remember that you are not to be uneasy about Mrs. Gowan. Her words were, "Very well and very happy." And she looked most beautiful.

CHAPTER XLI.

SOMETHING WRONG SOMEWHERE.

The family had been a month or two at Venice, when Mr. Dorrit, who was much among Counts and Marquises, and had but scant leisure, set an hour of one day apart beforehand for the purpose of holding some conference with Mrs. General.

The time he had reserved in his mind arriving, he sent Mr. Tinkler, his valet, to Mrs. General's apartment (which would have absorbed about a third of the area of the Marshalsea), to present his compliments to that lady, and represent him as desiring the favor of an interview. It being that period of the forenoon when the various members of the family had coffee in their own chambers, some couple of hours before assembling at breakfast in a faded hall which had once been sumptuous but was now the prey of watery vapors and a settled melancholy, Mrs. General was accessible to the valet. That envoy found her on a little square of carpet so extremely diminutive in reference to the size of her stone and marble floor, that she looked as if she might have had it spread for the trying on of a ready-made pair of shoes, or as if she had come into possession of the enchanted piece of carpet bought for forty purses by one of the three princes in the Arabian Nights, and had that moment been transported on it, at a wish, into a palatial saloon with which it had no connection.

Mrs. General, replying to the envoy as she set down her empty coffee-cup, that she was willing at once to proceed to Mr. Dorrit's apartment, and spare him the trouble of coming to her (which, in his gallantry, he had proposed), the envoy threw open the door, and escorted Mrs. General to the presence. It was quite a walk, by mysterious staircases and corridors, from Mrs. General's apartment, hoodwinked by a narrow side street with a low gloomy bridge in it, and dungeon-like opposite tenements, their walls besmeared with a thousand downward stains and streaks, as if every crazy aperture in them had been weeping tears of rust into the Adriatic for centuries, to Mr. Dorrit's apartment: with a whole English house-front of window, a prospect of beautiful church-domes rising into the blue sky sheer out of the water which reflected them, and a hushed murmur of the Grand Canal laving the door-ways below, where his gondolas and gondoliers attended his pleasure, drowsily swinging in a little forest of piles.

Mr. Dorrit, in a resplendent dressing-gown and cap—the dormant grub that had so long bided its time among the Collegians had burst into a rare butterfly—rose to receive Mrs. General. A chair to Mrs. General. An easier chair, sir; what are you doing, what are you about, what do you mean? Now, leave us!"

"Mrs. General," said Mr. Dorrit, "I took the liberty—"

"By no means," Mrs. General interposed. "I was quite at your disposition. I had had my coffee."

"I took the liberty," said Mr. Dorrit again, with the magnificent placidity of one who was above correction, "to solicit the favor of a little private conversation with you, because I feel rather worried respecting my—ha—my younger daughter. You will have observed a great difference of temperament, madam, between my two daughters?"

Said Mrs. General in response, crossing her gloved hands (she was never without gloves, and they never creased and always fitted), "There is a great difference."

"May I ask to be favored with your view of it?" said Mr. Dorrit, with a deference not incompatible with majestic serenity.

"Fanny," returned Mrs. General, "has force of character and self-reliance. Amy, none."

None? Oh, Mrs. General, ask the Marshalsea stones and bars. Oh, Mrs. General, ask the milliner who taught her to work, and the dancing-master who taught her sister to dance. Oh, Mrs. General, Mrs. General, ask me, her father, what I owe to her, and hear my testimony touching the life of this slighted little creature, from her childhood up!

No such adjuration entered Mr. Dorrit's head. He looked at Mrs. General, seated in her usual erect attitude on her coach-box behind the proprieties, and he said, in a thoughtful manner, "True, madam."

"I would not," said Mrs. General, "be understood to say, observe, that there is nothing to improve in Fanny. But there is material there—perhaps, indeed, a little too much."

"Will you be kind enough, madam," said Mr. Dorrit, "to be—ha—more explicit? I do not quite understand my elder daughter's having—hum—too much material. What material?"

"Fanny," returned Mrs. General, "at present forms too many opinions. Perfect breeding forms none, and is never demonstrative."

Lest he himself should be found deficient in perfect breeding, Mr. Dorrit hastened to reply, "Unquestionably, madam, you are right." Mrs. General returned, in her emotionless and expressionless manner, "I believe so."

"But you are aware, my dear madam," said Mr. Dorrit, "that my daughters had the misfortune to lose their lamented mother when they were very young; and that, in consequence of my not having been until lately the recognized heir to my property, they have lived with me as a comparatively poor, though always proud, gentleman, in—ha hum—retirement!"

"I do not," said Mrs. General, "lose sight of the circumstance."

"Madam," pursued Mr. Dorrit, "of my daughter Fanny, under her present guidance, and with such an example constantly before her—"

(Mrs. General shut her eyes.)

—"I have no misgivings. There is adaptability of character in Fanny. But my younger daughter, Mrs. General, rather worries and vexes my thoughts. I must inform you that she has always been my favorite."

"There is no accounting," said Mrs. General, "for these partialities."

"Ha—no," assented Mr. Dorrit. "No. Now, madam, I am troubled by noticing that Amy is not, so to speak, one of ourselves. She does not care to go about with us; she is lost in the society we have here; our tastes are evidently not her tastes. Which," said Mr. Dorrit, summing up with judicial gravity, "is to say, in other words, that there is something wrong in—ha—Amy."

"May we incline to the supposition," said Mrs. General, with a little touch of varnish, "that something is referable to the novelty of the position?"

"Excuse me, madam," observed Mr. Dorrit, rather quickly. "The daughter of a gentleman, though—ha—himself at one time comparatively far from affluent—comparatively—and herself reared in—hum—retirement, need not of necessity find this position so very novel."

"True," said Mrs. General, "true."

"Therefore, madam," said Mr. Dorrit, "I took the liberty" (he laid an emphasis on the phrase and repeated it, as though he stipulated, with urbane firmness, that he must not be contradicted again), "I took the liberty of requesting this interview, in order that I might mention the topic to you and inquire how you would advise me."

"Mr. Dorrit," returned Mrs. General, "I have conversed with Amy several times since we have been residing here, on the general subject of the formation of a demeanor. She has expressed herself to me as wondering exceedingly at Venice. I have mentioned to her that it is better not to wonder. I have pointed out to her that the Rev. Mr. Eustace, the classical tourist, did not think much of it, and that he compared the Rialto, greatly to its disadvantage, with Westminster and Blackfriars Bridges. I need not add, after what you have said, that I have not yet found my arguments successful. You do me the honor to ask me what I advise. It always appears to me (if this should prove to be a baseless assumption I shall be pardoned), that Mr. Dorrit has been accustomed to exercise influence over the minds of others."

"Hum—madam," said Mr. Dorrit, "I have been at the head of—ha—of a considerable community. You are right in supposing that I am not unaccustomed to—an influential position."

"I am happy," returned Mrs. General, "to be so corroborated. I would therefore the more confidently recommend that Mr. Dorrit should speak to Amy himself, and make his observations and wishes known to her. Being his favorite besides, and no doubt attached to him, she is all the more likely to yield to his influence."

"I had anticipated your suggestion, madam," said Mr. Dorrit, "but—ha—was not sure that I might—hum—not encroach on—"

"On my province, Mr. Dorrit?" said Mrs. General, graciously. "Do not mention it."

"Then, with your leave, madam," resumed Mr. Dorrit, ringing his little bell to summon his valet, "I will send for her at once."

"Does Mr. Dorrit wish me to remain?"

"Perhaps, if you have no other engagement, you would not object for a minute or two—"

"Not at all."

So Tinkler the valet was instructed to find Miss Amy's maid, and to request that subordinate to inform Miss Amy that Mr. Dorrit wished to see her in his own room. In delivering this charge to Tinkler, Mr. Dorrit looked severely at him, and also kept a jealous eye upon him until he went out at the door, mistrusting that he might have something in his mind prejudicial to the family dignity—that he might have even got wind of some Collegiate joke before he came into the service, and might be derisively reviving its remembrance at the present moment. If Tinkler had happened to smile, however faintly and innocently, nothing would have persuaded Mr. Dorrit to the hour of his death but that this was the case. As Tinkler happened, however, very fortunately for himself, to be of a serious and composed countenance, he escaped the secret danger that threatened him. And as on his return—when Mr. Dorrit eyed him again—he announced Miss Amy as if she had come to a funeral, he left a vague impression on Mr. Dorrit's mind that he was a well-conducted young fellow, who had been brought up in the study of the Catechism by a widowed mother.

"Amy," said Mr. Dorrit, "you have just now been the subject of some conversation between myself and Mrs. General. We agree that you scarcely seem at home here. Ha—how is this?"

A pause.

"I think, father, I require a little time."

"Papa is a preferable mode of address," observed Mrs. Gene

ral. "Father is rather vulgar, my dear. The word Papa, besides, gives a pretty form to the lips. Papa, potatoes, poultry prunes, and prism, are all very good words for the lips. You will find it serviceable, in the formation of a demeanor, if you sometimes say to yourself in company—on entering a room, for instance—Papa, potatoes, poultry, prunes, and prism."

"Pray, my child," said Mr. Dorrit, "attend to the—hum—precepts of Mrs. General."

Poor Little Dorrit, with a rather forlorn glance at that eminent varnisher, promised to try.

"You say, Amy," pursued Mr. Dorrit, "that you think you require time. Time for what?"

Another pause.

"To become accustomed to the novelty of my life, was all I meant," said Little Dorrit, with her loving eyes upon her father, whom she had very nearly addressed as poultry, if not prunes and prism too, in her desire to submit herself to Mrs. General and please him.

Mr. Dorrit frowned, and looked any thing but pleased. "Amy," he returned, "it appears to me, I must say, that you have had abundance of time for that. Ha—you surprise me. You disappoint me. Fanny has conquered any such little difficulties, and—hum—why not you?"

"I hope I shall do better soon," said Little Dorrit.

"I hope so," returned her father. "I—ha—I most devoutly hope so, Amy. I sent for you, in order that I might say—hum—impressively say, in the presence of Mrs. General, to whom we are all so much indebted for obligingly being present among us, on—ha—on this or any other occasion," Mrs. General shut her eyes, "that I—ha hum—am not pleased with you. You make Mrs. General's a thankless task. You—ha—embarrass me very much. You have always (as I have informed Mrs. General) been my favorite child; I have always made you a—hum—a friend and companion; in return, I beg—I—ha—I *do* beg that you accommodate yourself better to—hum—circumstances, and dutifully do what becomes your—your station."

Mr. Dorrit was even a little more fragmentary than usual, being excited on the subject, and anxious to make himself particularly emphatic.

"I do beg," he repeated, "that this may be attended to, and that you will seriously take pains and try to conduct yourself in a manner both becoming your position as—ha—Miss Amy Dorrit, and satisfactory to myself and Mrs. General."

That lady shut her eyes again on being again referred to; then, slowly opening them and rising, added these words:

"If Miss Amy Dorrit will direct her own attention to, and will accept of my poor assistance in, the formation of a surface, Mr. Dorrit will have no further cause of anxiety. May I take this opportunity of remarking, as an instance in point, that it is scarcely delicate to look at vagrants with the attention which I have seen bestowed upon them by a very dear young friend of mine. They should not be looked at. Nothing disagreeable should ever be looked at. Apart from such a habit standing in the way of that graceful equanimity of surface which is so expressive of good breeding, it hardly seems compatible with refinement of mind. A truly refined mind will be ignorant of the existence of any thing that is not perfectly proper, placid, and pleasant." Having delivered this exalted sentiment, Mrs. General made a sweeping obeisance, and retired with an expression of mouth indicative of prunes and prism.

Little Dorrit, whether speaking or silent, had preserved her quiet earnestness and her loving look. It had not been clouded, except for a passing moment, until now. But now that she was left alone with him, the fingers of her lightly-folded hands were agitated, and there was repressed emotion in her face.

Not for herself. She might feel a little wounded, but her care was not for herself. Her thoughts still turned, as they always had turned, to him. A faint misgiving which had hung about her since their accession to fortune that even now she could never see him as he used to be before the prison days, had gradually begun to assume form in her mind. She felt that in what he had just now said to her, and in his whole bearing toward her, there was the well-known shadow of the Marshalsea wall. It took a new shape, but it was the old, sad shadow. She began with sorrowful unwillingness to acknowledge to herself that she was not strong enough to keep off the fear that no space in the life of man could overcome that quarter of a century behind the prison bars. She had no blame to bestow upon him, therefore; nothing to reproach him with, no emotions in her faithful heart, but great compassion and unbounded tenderness.

This is why it was that even as he sat before her on his sofa, in the brilliant light of a bright Italian day, the wonderful city without, and the splendors of an old palace within, she saw him at the moment in the long-familiar gloom of his Marshalsea lodging, and wished to take her seat beside him, and comfort him, and be again full of confidence with him, and of usefulness to him. If he divined what was in her thoughts, his own were not in tune with it. After some uneasy moving in his seat, he got up, and walked about, looking very much dissatisfied.

"Is there any thing else you wish to say to me, dear father?"

"No, no. Nothing else."

"I am sorry you have not been pleased with me, dear. I hope you will not think of me with displeasure now. I am going to try more than ever to adapt myself, as you wish, to what surrounds me—for indeed I have tried all along, though I have failed, I know."

"Amy," he returned, turning short upon her. "You—ha—habitually hurt me."

"Hurt you, father! I?"

"There is a—hum—a topic," said Mr. Dorrit, looking all about the ceiling of the room, and never at the attentive, uncomplainingly-shocked face, "a painful topic, a series of events which I wish—ha—altogether to obliterate. This is understood by your sister, who has already remonstrated with you in my presence; it is understood by your brother; it is understood by—ha, hum—by every one of delicacy and sensitiveness except yourself—ha—I am sorry to say except yourself. You, Amy—hum—you alone, and only you—constantly revive the topic, though not in words."

She laid her hand upon his arm. She did nothing more. She gently touched him. The trembling hand may have said, with some expression, "Think of me; think how I have worked; think of my many cares!" But she said not a syllable herself.

There was a reproach in the touch so addressed to him that

she had not foreseen, or she would have withheld her hand. He began to justify himself, in a heated, stumbling, angry manner, that made nothing of it.

"I was there all those years. I was—ha—universally acknowledged as the head of the place. I—hum—I caused you to be respected there, Amy. I—ha, hum—I gave my family a position there. I deserve a return. I claim a return. I say, sweep it off the face of the earth, and begin afresh. Is that much? I ask, is *that* much?"

He did not once look at her as he rambled on in this way, but gesticulated at and appealed to the empty air.

"I have suffered. Probably I know how much I have suffered better than any one—ha—I say than any one! If *I* can put that aside, if *I* can eradicate the marks of what I have endured, and can emerge before the world a—ha—gentleman unspoiled, unspotted—is it a great deal to expect—I say again, is it a great deal to expect—that my children should—hum—do the same, and sweep the accursed experience off the face of the earth?"

In spite of his flustered state, he made all these exclamations in a carefully suppressed voice, lest the valet should overhear any thing.

"Accordingly they do it. Your sister does it. Your brother does it. You alone, my favorite child, whom I made the friend and companion of my life when you were a mere—hum—baby, do not do it. You alone can say you can't do it. I provide you with valuable assistance to do it. I attach an accomplished and highly-bred lady—ha—Mrs. General, to you, for the purpose of doing it. Is it surprising that I should be displeased? Is it necessary that I should defend myself for expressing my displeasure? No!"

Notwithstanding which, he continued to defend himself, without any abatement of his flushed mood.

"I am careful to appeal to that lady for confirmation, before I express any displeasure at all. I—hum—I necessarily make that appeal within limited bounds, or—ha—should render legible, by that lady, what I desire to be blotted out. Am I selfish? Do I complain for my own sake? No. No. Principally for—ha hum—your sake, Amy."

This last consideration plainly appeared, from his manner of pursuing it, to have just that instant come into his head.

"I said I was hurt. So I am. So I—ha—am determined to be, whatever is advanced to the contrary. I am hurt that my daughter, seated in the—hum—lap of fortune, should mope and retire, and proclaim herself unequal to her destiny. I am hurt that she should—ha—systematically reproduce what the rest of us blot out, and seem—hum—I had almost said positively anxious—to announce to wealthy and distinguished society that she was born and bred in--ha hum—a place that I, myself, decline to name. But there is no inconsistency—ha—not the least in my feeling hurt, and yet complaining principally for your sake, Amy. I do; I say again, I do. It is for your sake that I wish you, under the auspices of Mrs. General, to form a—hum—a surface. It is for your sake that I wish you to have a—ha—truly refined mind, and (in the striking words of Mrs. General), to be ignorant of every thing that is not perfectly proper, placid, and pleasant."

He had been running down by jerks, during his last speech, like a sort of ill-adjusted alarum. The touch was still upon his arm. He fell silent, and after looking about the ceiling again for a little while, looked down at her. Her head drooped, and he could not see her face, but her touch was tender and quiet, and in the expression of her dejected figure there was no blame—nothing but love. He began to whimper just as he had done that night in the prison when she afterward sat at his bedside till morning, exclaimed that he was a poor ruin and a poor wretch in the midst of his wealth, and clasp her in his arms. "Hush, hush, my own dear! Kiss me!" was all she said to him. His tears were soon dried, much sooner than on the former occasion, and he was presently afterward very high with his valet, as a way of righting himself for having shed any.

With one remarkable exception, to be recorded in its place, this was the only time in his life of freedom and fortune, when he spoke to his daughter Amy of the old days.

But now the breakfast hour arrived, and with it Miss Fanny from her apartment, and Mr. Edward from his apartment. Both these young persons of distinction were something the worse for late hours. As to Miss Fanny, she had become the victim of an insatiate mania for what she called "going into society," and would have gone into it head-foremost fifty times between sunset and sunrise if so many opportunities had been at her disposal. As to Mr. Edward, he, too, had a large acquaintance, and was generally engaged (for the most part, in dicing circles, or others of a kindred nature) during the greater part of every night. For this gentleman, when his fortunes changed, had stood at the great advantage of being already prepared for the highest associates, and having little to learn; so much was he indebted to the happy accidents which had made him acquainted with horse-dealing and billiard-marking.

At breakfast, Mr. Frederick Dorrit likewise appeared. As the old gentleman inhabited the highest story of the palace, where he might have practiced pistol-shooting without much chance of discovery by the other inmates, his younger niece had taken courage to propose the restoration to him of his clarionet: which Mr. Dorrit had ordered to be confiscated, but which she had ventured to preserve. Notwithstanding some objections from Miss Fanny that it was a low instrument, and that she detested the sound of it, the concession had been made. But it was then discovered that he had had enough of it, and never played it, now that it was no longer his means of getting bread. He had insensibly acquired a new habit of shuffling into the picture-galleries, always with his twisted paper of snuff in his hand (much to the indignation of Miss Fanny, who had proposed the purchase of a gold box for him that the family might not be discredited, which he had absolutely refused to carry when it was bought), and of passing hours and hours before the portraits of renowned Venetians. It was never made out what his dazed eyes saw in them, whether he had an interest in them merely as pictures, or whether he confusedly identified them with a glory that was departed, like the strength of his own mind. But he paid his court to them with great exactness, and clearly derived pleasure from the pursuit. After the first few days, Little Dorrit happened one morning to assist at these attentions. It so evidently heightened his gratification that she often accompanied him afterward, and the greatest delight of which the old man had shown himself susceptible since his ruin, arose out of these excursions, when he would carry a chair about for her from picture to picture, and stand behind it, in spite of all her remonstrances, silently presenting her to the noble Venetians.

It fell out that at this family breakfast he referred to their having seen in a gallery, on the previous day, the lady and gentleman whom they had encountered on the Great Saint Bernard. "I forget the name," said he. "I dare say you remember them, William? I dare say you do, Edward."

"*I* remember 'em well enough," said the latter.

"I should think so, too," observed Miss Fanny, with a toss of her head, and a glance at her sister. "But they would not have been recalled to our remembrance, I suspect, if Uncle hadn't tumbled over the subject."

"My dear, what a curious phrase," said Mrs. General. "Would not inadvertently lighted upon, or accidentally referred to, be better?"

"Thank you very much, Mrs. General," returned the young lady, "no, I think not. On the whole, I prefer my own expression."

This was always Miss Fanny's way of receiving a suggestion from Mrs. General. But she always stored it up in her mind, and adopted it at another time.

"I should have mentioned our having met Mr. and Mrs. Gowan, Fanny," said Little Dorrit, "even if uncle had not. I have scarcely seen you since, you know. I meant to have spoken of it at breakfast, because I should like to pay a visit to Mrs. Gowan, and to become better acquainted with her, if papa and Mrs. General do not object."

"Well, Amy," said Fanny, "I am sure I am glad to find you, at last, expressing a wish to become better acquainted with any body in Venice. Though whether Mr. and Mrs. Gowan are desirable acquaintances, remains to be determined."

"Mrs. Gowan I spoke of, dear."

"No doubt," said Fanny. "But you can't separate her from her husband, I believe, without an Act of Parliament."

"Do you think, papa," inquired Little Dorrit, with diffidence and hesitation, "there is any objection to making this visit?"

"Really," he replied, "I—ha—what is Mrs. General's view?"

Mrs. General's view was, that not having the honor of any acquaintance with the lady and gentleman referred to, she was not in a position to varnish the present article. She could only remark, as a general principal observed in the varnishing trade, that much depended on the quarter from which the lady under consideration was accredited to a family so conspicuously niched in the social temple as the family of Mr. Dorrit.

At this remark the face of Mr. Dorrit gloomed considerably. He was about (connecting the accrediting with an obtrusive person of the name of Clennam, whom he imperfectly remembered in some former state of existence) to blackball the name of Gowan finally, when Edward Dorrit, Esquire, came into the conversation, with his glass in his eye, and the preliminary remark of "I say—you there! Go out, will you!" Which was addressed to a couple of men who were handing the dishes round, as a courteous intimation that their services could be temporarily dispensed with.

Those menials having obeyed the mandate, Edward Dorrit, Esquire, proceeded.

"Perhaps it's a matter of policy to let you all know that these Gowans—in whose favor, or at least the man's, I can't be supposed to be much prepossessed myself—are known to people of importance, if that makes any difference."

"That I would say," observed the fair varnisher, "makes the greatest difference. The connection in question, being really people of importance and consideration—"

"As to that," said Edward Dorrit, Esquire, "I will give you the means of judging for yourself. You are acquainted, perhaps, with the famous name of Merdle?"

"The great Merdle?" exclaimed Mrs. General.

"*The* Merdle," said Edward Dorrit, Esquire. "They are known to him. Mrs. Gowan—I mean the Dowager, my polite friend's mother—is intimate with Mrs. Merdle, and I know these two to be on their visiting-list."

"If so, a more undeniable guarantee could not be given," said Mrs. General to Mr. Dorrit, raising her gloves and bowing her head, as if she were doing homage to some visible graven image.

"I beg to ask my son, from motives of—ha—curiosity," Mr. Dorrit observed, with a decided change in his manner, "how he becomes possessed of this—hum—timely information?"

"It's not a long story, sir," returned Edward Dorrit, Esquire, "and you shall have it out of hand. To begin with, Mrs. Merdle is the lady you had the parley with, at what's-his-name place."

"Martigny," interposed Miss Fanny, with an air of infinite languor.

"Martigny," assented her brother, with a slight nod and a slight wink, in acknowledgment of which Miss Fanny looked surprised, and laughed and reddened.

"How can that be, Edward?" said Mr. Dorrit. "You informed me that the name of the gentleman with whom you conferred was—ha—Sparkler. Indeed, you showed me his card. Hum. Sparkler."

"No doubt of it, father; but it doesn't follow that his mother's name must be the same. Mrs. Merdle was married before, and he is her son. She is in Rome now, where probably we shall know more of her, as you decide to winter there. Sparkler is just come here. I passed last evening in company with Sparkler. Sparkler is a very good fellow on the whole, though rather a bore on one subject, in consequence of being tremendously smitten with a certain young lady." Here Edward Dorrit, Esquire, eyed Miss Fanny through his glass across the table. "We happened last night to compare notes about our travels, and I had the information I have given you from Sparkler himself." Here he ceased; continuing to eye Miss Fanny through his glass, with a face much twisted, and not ornamentally so, in part by the action of keeping his glass in his eye, and in part by the great subtlety of his smile.

"Under these circumstances," said Mr. Dorrit, "I believe I express the sentiments of—ha—Mrs. General, no less than my own, when I say that there is no objection, but—ha—hum—quite the contrary—to your gratifying your desire, Amy. I trust I may—ha—hail this desire," said Mr. Dorrit, in an encouraging and forgiving manner, "as an auspicious omen. It is quite right to know these people. It is a very proper thing. Mr. Merdle's is a name of—ha—world-wide repute. Mr. Merdle's undertakings are immense. They bring him in such vast sums of money that they are regarded as—hum—national benefits. Mr. Merdle is the man of this time. The name of Merdle is the name of the age. Pray do every thing on my behalf that is civil to Mr. and Mrs. Gowan, for we will—ha—we will certainly notice them."

This magnificent accordance of Mr. Dorrit's recognition settled the matter. It was not observed that uncle had pushed away his plate and forgotten his breakfast; but he was not much observed at any time, except by Little Dorrit. The servants were recalled, and the meal proceeded to its conclusion. Mrs. General rose and left the table. Little Dorrit rose and left the table. When Edward and Fanny remained whispering together across it, and when Mr. Dorrit remained eating figs and reading a French newspaper, uncle suddenly fixed the attention of all three, by rising out of his chair, striking his hand upon the table, and saying, "Brother! I protest against it!"

If he had made a proclmation in an unknown tongue, and given up the ghost immediately afterward, he could not have astounded his audience more. The paper fell from Mr. Dorrit's hand, and he sat petrified, with a fig half way to his mouth.

"Brother," said the old man, conveying a surprising energy into his trembling voice, "I protest against it! I love you; you know I love you dearly. In these many years I have never been untrue to you in a single thought. Weak as I am, I would at any time have struck any man who spoke ill of you. But, brother, brother, brother, I protest against it!"

It was extraordinary to see of what a burst of earnestness such a decrepit man was capable. His eyes became bright, his gray hair rose on his head, markings of purpose on his brow and face which had faded from them for five-and-twenty years, started out again, and there was an energy in his hand that made its action nervous once more.

"My dear Frederick!" exclaimed Mr. Dorrit, faintly. "What is wrong? What is the matter?"

"How dare you," said the old man, turning round on Fanny,

"how dare you do it? Have you no memory? Have you no heart?"

"Uncle!" cried Fanny, affrighted, and bursting into tears, "why do you attack Me in this cruel manner? What have I done?"

"Done?" returned the old man, pointing to her sister's place, "where's your affectionate, invaluable friend? Where's your devoted guardian? Where's your more than mother? How dare you set up superiorities against all these characters combined in your sister? For shame, you false girl, for shame!"

"I love Amy," cried Miss Fanny, sobbing and weeping, "as well as I love my life—better than I love my life. I don't deserve to be so treated. I am as grateful to Amy and as fond of Amy as it's possible for any human being to be. I wish I was dead. I never was so wickedly wronged. And only because I am anxious for the family credit."

"To the winds with the family credit!" cried the old man, with great scorn and indignation. "Brother, I protest against pride. I protest against ingratitude. I protest against any one of us here who have known what we have known, and have seen what we have seen, setting up any pretension that puts Amy at a moment's disadvantage, or to the cost of a moment's pain. We may know that it's a base pretension by its having that effect. It ought to bring a judgment on us. Brother, I protest against it, in the sight of God!"

As his hand went up above his head and came down on the table, it might have been a blacksmith's. After a few moments silence it had relaxed into its usual weak condition. He went round to his brother with his ordinary shuffling step, put the hand on his shoulder, and said, in a softened voice, "William, my dear, I felt obliged to say it; forgive me, for I felt obliged to say it!" and then went, in his bowed way, out of the palace hall, just as he might have gone out of the Marshalsea room.

All this time Fanny had been sobbing and crying, and still continued to do so. Edward, beyond opening his mouth in amazement, had not opened his lips, and had done nothing but stare. Mr. Dorrit also had been utterly discomfited, and quite unable to assert himself in any way. Fanny was now the first to speak.

"I never, never, never was so used!" she sobbed. "There never was any thing so harsh and unjustifiable, so disgracefully violent and cruel! Dear, kind, quiet little Amy, too, what would she feel if she could know that she had been innocently the means of exposing me to such treatment! But I'll never tell her! No, good darling, I'll never tell her!"

This helped Mr. Dorrit to break his silence.

"My dear," said he, "I—ha—approve of your resolution. It will be—ha hum—much better not to speak of this to Amy. It might—hum—it might distress her. Ha. No doubt it would distress her greatly. It is considerate and right to avoid doing so. We will—ha—keep this to ourselves."

"But the cruelty of uncle!" cried Miss Fanny. "Oh, I never can forgive the wanton cruelty of uncle!"

"My dear," said Mr. Dorrit, recovering his tone, though he remained unusually pale, "I must request you not to say so. You must remember that your uncle is—ha—not what he formerly was. You must remember that your uncle's state requires—hum—great forbearance from us, great forbearance."

"I am sure," cried Fanny, piteously, "it is only charitable to suppose that there must be something wrong in him somewhere, or he never could have so attacked Me, of all the people in the world."

"Fanny," returned Mr. Dorrit, in a deeply-fraternal tone, "you know, with his innumerable good points, what a—hum—wreck your uncle is, and I entreat you, by the fondness that I have for him, and by the fidelity that you know I have always shown him, to—ha—to draw your own conclusions, and to spare my brotherly feelings."

This ended the scene; Edward Dorrit, Esquire, saying nothing throughout, but looking, to the last, perplexed and doubtful. Miss Fanny awakened much affectionate uneasiness in her sister's mind that day, by passing the greater part of it in violent fits of embracing her, and in alternately giving her brooches, and wishing herself dead.

CHAPTER XLII.

SOMETHING RIGHT SOMEWHERE.

To be in the halting state of Mr. Henry Gowan; to have left one of two Powers in disgust; to want the necessary qualifications for finding promotion with another, and to be loitering moodily about on neutral ground, cursing both, is to be in a situation unwholesome for the mind, which time is not likely to improve. The worst class of sum worked in the every-day world is ciphered by the diseased arithmeticians who are always in the rule of Substraction as to the merits and successes of others, and never in Addition as to their own.

The habit, too, of seeking some sort of recompense in the discontented boast of being disappointed, is a habit fraught with degeneracy. A certain idle carelessness and recklessness of consistency soon come of it. To bring deserving things down by setting undeserving things up, is one of its perverted delights; and there is no playing fast and loose with the truth, in any game, without growing the worse for it.

In his expressed opinions of all performances in the Art of painting that were completely destitute of merit, Gowan was the most liberal fellow on earth. He would declare such a man to have more power in his little finger (provided he had none) than such another had (provided he had much) in his whole mind and body. If the objection were taken that the thing commended was trash, he would reply, on behalf of his art, "My good fellow, what do we all turn out but trash? *I* turn out nothing else, and I make you a present of the confession."

To make a vaunt of being poor was another of the incidents of his splenetic state, though this may have had the design in it of showing that he ought to be rich; just as he would publicly laud and decry the Barnacles, lest it should be forgotten that he belonged to the family. Howbeit, these two subjects were very often on his lips, and he managed them so well, that he might have praised himself by the month together, and not have made himself out half so important a man as he did by his light disparagement of his claims on any body's consideration.

Out of this same airy talk of his it always soon came to be understood, wherever he and his wife went, that he had married against the wishes of his exalted relations, and had had much ado to prevail on them to countenance her. He never made the representation, on the contrary seemed to laugh the idea to scorn, but it did happen that, with all his pains to depreciate himself, he was always in the superior position. From the days of their honeymoon, Minnie Gowan felt sensible of being usually regarded as the wife of a man who had made a descent in marrying her, but whose chivalrous love for her had canceled that inequality.

To Venice they had been accompanied by Monsieur Blandois of Paris, and at Venice Monsieur Blandois of Paris was very much in the society of Gowan. When they had first met this gallant gentleman at Geneva, Gowan had been undecided whether to kick him or encourage him, and had remained for about four-and-twenty hours so troubled to settle the point to his satisfaction, that he had thought of tossing up a five-franc piece on the terms "Tails, kick; heads, and encourage," and abiding by the voice of the oracle. It chanced, however, that his wife expressed a dislike to the engaging Blandois, and that the balance of feeling in the hotel was against him. Upon that, Gowan resolved to encourage him.

With this perversity, if it were not in a generous fit?—which it was not. Why should Gowan, very much the superior of Blandois of Paris, and very well able to pull that prepossessing gentleman to pieces, and find out the stuff he was made of, take up with such a man? In the first place, he opposed the first separate wish he observed in his wife, because her father had paid his debts, and it was desirable to take an early opportunity of asserting his independence. In the second place, he opposed the prevalent feeling, because, with many capacities of being otherwise, he was an ill-conditioned man. He found a pleasure in declaring that a courtier with the refined manners of Blandois ought to rise to the greatest distinction in any polished country. He found a pleasure in setting up Blandois as the type of elegance, and making him a satire upon others who piqued themselves on personal graces. He seriously protested that the bow of Blandois was perfect, that the address of Blandois was irresistible, and that the picturesque ease of Blandois would be cheaply purchased (if it were not a gift, and unpurchasable) for a hundred thousand francs. That exaggeration in the manner of the man, which has been noticed as appertaining to him and to every such man, whatever his original breeding, as certainly as the sun belongs to this system, was acceptable to Gowan as a caricature, which he found it a humorous resource to have at hand for the ridiculing of numbers of people who necessarily did more or less of what Blandois overdid. Thus he had taken up with him; and thus, negligently strengthening these inclinations with habit, and idly deriving some amusement from his talk, he had glided into a way of having him for a companion. This, though he supposed him to live by his wits at play-tables and the like; though he suspected him to be a coward, while he himself was daring and courageous; though he thoroughly knew him to be disliked by Minnie; and though he cared so little for him after all that if he had given her any personal cause to regard him with aversion, he would have had no compunction whatever in flinging him out of the highest window in Venice into the deepest water in the city.

Little Dorrit would have been glad to make her visit to Mrs. Gowan alone; but, as Fanny, who had not yet recovered from her uncle's protest, though it was four-and-twenty hours of age, pressingly offered her company, the two sisters stepped together into one of the gondolas under Mr. Dorrit's window, and, with the courier in attendance, were taken in high state to Mrs. Gowan's lodging. In truth, their state was rather too high for the lodging, which was, as Fanny complained, "fearfully out of the way," and which took them through a complexity of narrow streets of water, which the same lady disparaged as "mere ditches."

The house, on a little desert island, looked as if it had broken away from somewhere else, and had floated by chance into its present anchorage, in company with a vine almost as much in want of training as the poor wretches who were lying under its leaves. The features of the surrounding picture were, a church with boarding and scaffolding about it, which had been under supposititious repair so long that the means of repair looked a hundred years old, and had themselves fallen into decay; a quantity of washed linen spread to dry in the sun; a number of houses at odds with one another and grotesquely out of the perpendicular, like rotten pre-Adamite cheeses cut into fantastic shapes and full of mites; and a feverish bewilderment of windows, with their lattice blinds all hanging askew, and something draggled and dirty dangling out of most of them.

On the first floor of the house was a Bank—a surprising experience for any gentleman of commercial pursuits from a British city—here two spare clerks, like dried dragoons, in green velvet caps adorned with golden tassels, stood, bearded, behind a small counter in a small room containing no other visible objects than an empty iron safe with the door open, a jug of water, and a papering of garlands of roses; but who, on lawful requisition, by merely dipping their hands out of sight, could produce exhaustless mounds of five-franc pieces. Below the Bank was a suite of three or four rooms with barred windows, which had the appearance of a jail for criminal rats. Above the Bank was Mrs. Gowan's residence.

Notwithstanding that its walls were blotched as if missionary maps were bursting out of them to impart geographical knowledge; notwithstanding that its weird furniture was forlornly faded and musty, and that the prevailing Venetian odor of bilge-water and an ebb-tide on a weedy shore was very strong, the place was better within than it promised. The door was opened by a smiling man like a reformed assassin—a temporary servant—who ushered them into the room where Mrs. Gowan sat, with the announcement that two beautiful English ladies were come to see the mistress.

Mrs. Gowan, who was engaged in needlework, put her work aside in a covered basket, and rose, a little hurriedly. Miss Fanny was excessively courteous to her, and said the usual nothings with the skill of a veteran.

"Papa was extremely sorry," proceeded Fanny, "to be engaged to-day (he is so much engaged here, our acquaintance being so wretchedly large !), and particularly requested me to bring his card for Mr. Gowan. That I may be sure to acquit myself of a commission which he impressed upon me at least a dozen times, allow me to relieve my conscience by placing it on the table at once."

Which she did with veteran ease.

"We have been," said Fanny, "charmed to understand that you know the Merdles. We hope it may be another means of bringing us together."

"They are friends," said Mrs. Gowan, "of Mr. Gowan's family. I have not yet had the pleasure of a personal introduction to Mrs. Merdle, but I suppose I shall be presented to her at Rome."

"Indeed !" returned Fanny, with an appearance of amiably quenching her own superiority. "I think you'll like her."

"You know her very well ?"

"Why, you see," said Fanny, with a frank action of her pretty shoulders, "in London one knows every one. We met her on our way here, and, to say the truth, papa was at first rather cross with her for taking one of the rooms that our people had ordered for us. However, of course, that soon blew over, and we were all good friends again."

Although the visit had, as yet, given Little Dorrit no opportunity of conversing with Mrs. Gowan, there was a silent understanding between them, which did as well. She looked at Mrs. Gowan with keen and unabated interest; the sound of her voice was thrilling to her; nothing that was near her, or about her, or at all concerned her, escaped Little Dorrit. She was quicker to perceive the slightest matter here than in any other case—but one.

"You have been quite well," she now said, "since that night ?"

"Quite, my dear. And you ?"

"Oh ! I am always well," said Little Dorrit, timidly. "I—yes, thank you."

There was no reason for her faltering and breaking off, other than that Mrs. Gowan had touched her hand in speaking to her, and their looks had met. Something thoughtfully apprehensive in the large, soft eyes, had checked Little Dorrit in an instant.

"You don't know that you are a favorite of my husband's, and that I am almost bound to be jealous of you?" said Mrs. Gowan.

Little Dorrit, blushing, shook her head.

"He will tell you, if he tells you what he tells me, that you are quieter, and quicker of resource, than any one he ever saw."

"He speaks far too well of me," said Little Dorrit.

"I doubt that; but I don't at all doubt that I must tell him you are here. I should never be forgiven, if I were to let you —and Miss Dorrit—go without doing so. May I? You can excuse the disorder and discomfort of a painter's studio?"

The inquiries were addressed to Miss Fanny, who graciously replied that she would be beyond any thing interested and enchanted. Mrs. Gowan went to a door, looked in beyond it, and came back. "Do Henry the favor to come in," said she. "I knew he would be pleased!"

The first object that confronted Little Dorrit, entering first, was Blandois of Paris in a great cloak, and a furtive slouched hat, standing in a corner, as he had stood on the Great Saint Bernard, when the warning arms seemed to be all pointing up at him. She instinctively recoiled from this figure as it smiled at her.

"Don't be alarmed," said Gowan, coming from his easel behind the door. "It's only Blandois. He is doing duty as a model to-day. I am making a study of him. It saves me money to turn him to some use. We poor painters have none to spare."

Blandois of Paris pulled off his slouched hat, and saluted the ladies without coming out of his corner.

"A thousand pardons!" said he. "But the Professore here is so inexorable with me, that I am afraid to stir."

"Don't stir, then," said Gowan, coolly, as the sisters approached the easel. "Let the ladies at least see the original of the daub, that they may know what it's meant for. There he stands, you see. A bravo waiting for his prey, a distinguished noble waiting to save his country, the common enemy waiting to do somebody a bad turn, an angelic messenger waiting to do somebody a good turn—whatever you think he looks most like!"

"Say, Professore Mio, a poor gentleman waiting to do homage to elegance and beauty," remarked Blandois.

"Or say, Cattivo Soggetto Mio," returned Gowan, touching the painted face with his brush in the part where the real face had moved, "a murderer after the fact. Show that white hand of yours, Blandois. Put it outside the cloak. Keep it still."

Blandois' hand was unsteady; but he laughed, and that would naturally shake it.

"He was formerly in some scuffle with another murderer, or with a victim, you observe," said Gowan, putting in the markings of the hand with a quick, impatient, unskillful touch, "and these are the tokens of it. Outside the cloak, man!—Corpo di San Marco, what are you thinking of!"

Blandois of Paris shook with a laugh again, so that his hand shook more; now he raised it to twist his moustache, which had a damp appearance; and now he stood in the required position, with a little new swagger.

His face was so directed in reference to the spot where Little Dorrit stood by the easel, that throughout he looked at her. Once attracted by his peculiar eyes, she could not remove her own, and they looked at each other all the time. She trembled now; Gowan, feeling it, and supposing her to be alarmed by the large dog beside him, whose head she caressed in her hand, and who had just uttered a low growl, glanced at her to say, "He won't hurt you, Miss Dorrit."

"I am not afraid of him," she returned, in the same breath; "but will you look at him?"

In a moment Gowan had thrown down his brush and seized the dog with both hands by the collar.

"Blandois! How can you be such a fool as to provoke him! By Heaven and the other place too, he'll tear you to bits! Lie down, Lion! Do you hear my voice, you rebel!"

The great dog, regardless of being half-choked by his collar, was obdurately pulling with his dead weight against his master, resolved to get across the room. He had been crouching for a spring at the moment when his master caught him.

"Lion! Lion!" He was up on his hind legs, and it was a

INSTINCT STRONGER THAN TRAINING

wrestle between master and dog. "Get back! Down, Lion! Get out of his sight, Blandois! What devil have you conjured into the dog?"

"I have done nothing to him!"

"Get out of his sight, or I can't hold the wild beast. Get out of the room! By my soul he'll kill you!"

The dog, with a ferocious bark, made one other struggle as Blandois vanished; then, in the moment of the dog's submission, the master, little less angry than the dog, felled him with a blow on the head, and standing over him, struck him many times severely with the heel of his boot, so that his mouth was presently bloody.

"Now get you into that corner and lie down," said Gowan, "or I'll take you out and shoot you!"

Lion did as he was ordered, and lay down licking his mouth and chest. Lion's master stopped for a moment to take breath, and then, recovering his usual coolness of manner, turned to speak to his frightened wife and her visitors. Probably the whole occurrence had not occupied two minutes.

"Come, come, Minnie! You know he is always good humored and tractable. Blandois must have irritated him—made faces at him. The dog has his likings and dislikings, and Blandois is no great favorite of his; but I am sure you'll give him a character, Minnie, for never having been like this before."

Minnie was too much disturbed to say any thing connected in reply; Little Dorrit was already occupied in soothing her; Fanny, who had cried out twice or thrice, held Gowan's arm for protection; Lion, deeply ashamed of having caused them this alarm, came trailing himself along the ground to the feet of his mistress.

"You furious brute!" said Gowan, striking him with his foot again. "You shall do penance for this." And he struck him again, and yet again.

"Oh, pray don't punish him any more!" cried Little Dorrit. "Don't hurt him! See how gentle he is!" At her entreaty, Gowan spared him, and he deserved her intercession, for truly he was as submissive, and as sorry, and as wretched as a dog could be.

It was not easy to recover this shock and make the visit unrestrained, even though Fanny had not been, under the best of circumstances, the least trifle in the way. In such further communication as passed among them before the sisters took their departure, Little Dorrit fancied that it was revealed to her that Mr. Gowan treated his wife, even in his very fondness, too much like a beautiful child. He seemed so unsuspicious of the depths of feeling which she knew must lie below that surface, that she doubted if there could be any such depths in himself. She wondered whether his want of earnestness might be the natural result of his want of such qualities, and whether it was with people as with ships, that, in too shallow and rocky waters, their anchors had no hold, and they drifted any where.

He attended them down the staircase, jocosely apologizing for the poor quarters to which such poor fellows as himself were limited, and remarking that when the high and mighty Barnacles, his relatives, who would be dreadfully ashamed of them, presented him with better, he would live in better, to oblige them. At the water's edge they were saluted by Blandois, who looked pale enough after his late adventure, but who made very light of it, notwithstanding—laughed at the mention of Lion, in his ugliest manner.

Leaving the two together, under the scrap of vine upon the causeway, Gowan idly scattering the leaves from it into the water, and Blandois lighting a cigarette, the sisters were paddled away in state, as they had come. They had not glided on for many minutes, when Little Dorrit became aware that Fanny was more showy in manner than the occasion appeared to require, and, looking about for the cause, through the window and through the open door, saw another gondola evidently in waiting on them.

As this gondola attended their progress in various artful ways; sometimes shooting on ahead, and stopping to let them pass; sometimes, when the way was broad enough, skimming along side by side with them; and sometimes following close astern; and, as Fanny gradually made no disguise that she was playing off graces upon somebody within it, of whom she at the same time feigned to be unconscious, Little Dorrit at length asked who it was?

To which Fanny made the short answer, "That gaby."

"Who ?" said Little Dorrit.

"My dear child," returned Fanny (in a tone suggesting that before her uncle's protest she might have said, You little fool, instead), "how slow you are! Young Sparkler!"

She lowered the window on her side, and, leaning back and resting her elbow on it negligently, fanned herself with a rich Spanish fan of black and gold. The attendant gondola having skimmed forward again, with some swift trace of an eye in the window, Fanny laughed coquettishly, and said, "Did you ever see such a fool, my love?"

"Do you think he means to follow you all the way?" asked Little Dorrit.

"My precious child," returned Fanny, "I can't possibly answer for what an idiot in a state of desperation may do, but I should think it highly probable. It's not such an enormous distance. All Venice would scarcely be that, I imagine, if he's dying for a glimpse of me."

"And is he?" asked Little Dorrit, in perfect simplicity.

"Well, my love, that really is an awkward question for *me* to answer," said her sister. "I believe he is. You had better ask Edward. He tells Edward he is, I believe. I understand he makes a perfect spectacle of himself at the Casino, and that sort of places, by going on about me. But you had better ask Edward, if you want to know."

"I wonder he doesn't call," said Little Dorrit, after thinking a moment.

"My dear Amy, your wonder will soon cease, if I am rightly informed. I should not be at all surprised if he called to-day. The creature has only been waiting to get his courage up, I suspect."

"Will you see him?"

"Indeed, my darling," said Fanny, "that's just as it may happen. Here he is again. Look at him. Oh you simpleton!"

Mr. Sparkler had, undeniably, a weak appearance; with his eye in the window like a knot in the glass, and no reason on earth for stopping his bark suddenly, except the real reason.

"When you ask me if I will see him, my dear," said Fanny, almost as well composed in the graceful indifference of her attitude as Mrs. Merdle herself, "what do you mean?"

"I mean," said Little Dorrit—"I think I rather mean what you mean, dear Fanny?"

Fanny laughed again, in a manner at once condescending, arch, and affable; and said, putting her arm round her sister in a playfully affectionate way:

"Now tell me, my little pet. When we saw that woman at Martigny, how did you think she carried it off. Did you see what she decided on in a moment?"

"No, Fanny."

"Then I'll tell you, Amy. She settled with herself, Now I'll never refer to that meeting under such different circumstances, and I'll never pretend to have any idea that these are the same girls. That's *her* way out of a difficulty. What did I tell you when we came away from Harley Street that time? She is as insolent and false as any woman in the world. But in the first capacity, my love, she may find people who can match her."

A significant turn of the Spanish fan toward Fanny's bosom indicated, with great expression, where one of these people was to be found.

"Not only that," pursued Fanny, "but she gives the same charge to Young Sparkler, and doesn't let him come after me until she has got it thoroughly into his most ridiculous of all ridiculous noddles (for one really can't call it a head) that he is to pretend to have been first struck with me in that Inn Yard."

"Why?" asked Little Dorrit.

"Why? Good gracious, my love!" (again very much in the tone of You stupid little creature) "how can you ask? Don't you see that I may have become a rather desirable match for a noodle? And don't you see that she puts the deception upon us, and makes a pretense while she shifts it from her own shoulders (very good shoulders they are, too, I must say)," observed Miss Fanny, glancing complacently at herself, "of considering our feelings?"

"But we can always go back to the plain truth."

"Yes, but if you please we won't," retorted Fanny. "No; I am not going to have that done, Amy. The pretext is none of mine; it's her's, and she shall have enough of it."

In the triumphant exaltation of her feelings, Miss Fanny

using her Spanish fan with one hand, squeezed her sister's waist with the other, as if she were crushing Mrs. Merdle.

"No," repeated Fanny. "She shall find me go her way. She took it, and I'll follow it. And, with the blessing of fate and fortune, I'll go on improving that woman's acquaintance until I have given her maid, before her eyes, things from my dressmaker's ten times as handsome and expensive as she once gave me from hers!"

Little Dorrit was silent: sensible that she was not to be heard on any question affecting the family dignity; and unwilling to lose to no purpose her sister's newly and unexpectedly restored favor: she could not concur, but she was silent. Fanny well knew what she was thinking of—so well, that she soon asked her.

Her reply was, "Do you mean to encourage Mr. Sparkler, Fanny?"

"Encourage him, my dear?" said her sister, smiling contemptuously, "that depends upon what you call encourage. No, I don't mean to encourage him. But I'll make a slave of him."

Little Dorrit glanced seriously and doubtingly in her face, but Fanny was not to be so brought to a check. She furled her fan of black and gold, and used it to tap her sister's nose, with the air of a proud beauty and a great spirit who toyed with and playfully instructed a homely companion.

"I shall make him fetch and carry, my dear, and I shall make him subject to me. And if I don't make his mother subject to me too, it shall not be my fault."

"Do you think—dear Fanny, don't be offended, we are so comfortable together now—that you can quite see the end of that course?"

"I can't say I have so much as looked for it yet, my dear," answered Fanny, with supreme indifference; "all in good time. Such are my intentions. And really they have taken me so long to develop, that here we are at home. And Young Sparkler at the door inquiring who is within. By the merest accident of course!"

In effect, the swain was standing up in his gondola, card-case in hand, affecting to put the question to a servant. This conjunction of circumstances led to his immediately afterward presenting himself before the young ladies in a posture which in ancient times would not have been considered one of favorable augury for his suit; since the gondoliers of the young ladies having been put to some inconvenience by the chase, so neatly brought their own boat into the gentlest collision with the bark of Mr. Sparkler, as to tip that gentleman over like a large species of ninepin, and cause him to exhibit the soles of his shoes to the object of his dearest wishes, while the nobler portions of his anatomy struggled at the bottom of his boat in the arms of one of his men.

However, as Miss Fanny called out with much concern. Was the gentleman hurt, Mr. Sparkler rose more restored than might have been expected, and stammered for himself with blushes, "Not at all so." Miss Fanny had no recollection of having ever seen him before, and was passing on, with a distant inclination of her head, when he announced himself by name. Even then, she was in a difficulty from being unable to call it to mind, until he explained that he had the honor of seeing her at Martigny. Then she remembered him, and hoped his lady-mother was well.

"Thank you," stammered Mr. Sparkler; "she's uncommonly well—at least, poorly."

"In Venice?" said Miss Fanny.

"In Rome," Mr. Sparkler answered. "I am here by myself, myself. I came to call upon Mr. Edward Dorrit myself. Indeed, upon Mr. Dorrit likewise. In fact, upon the family."

Turning graciously to the attendants, Miss Fanny inquired whether her papa or brother was within? The reply being that they were both within, Mr. Sparkler humbly offered his arm. Miss Fanny accepting it, was squired up the great staircase by Mr. Sparkler, who, if he still believed (which there is not any reason to doubt) that she had no nonsense about her, rather deceived himself.

Arrived in a mouldering reception-room, where the faded hangings of a sad sea-green had worn and withered until they looked as if they might have claimed kindred with the waifs of sea-weed drifting under the windows, or clinging to the walls and weeping for their imprisoned relations, Miss Fanny dispatched emissaries for her father and brother. Pending whose

MR. SPARKLER UNDER A REVERSE OF CIRCUMSTANCES.

appearance, she showed to great advantage on a sofa, completing Mr. Sparkler's conquest with some remarks upon Dante—known to that gentleman as an eccentric man in the nature of an Old File, who used to put leaves round his head, and sit upon a stool for some unaccountable purpose, outside the cathedral at Florence.

Mr. Dorrit welcomed the visitor with his highest urbanity and most courtly manners. He inquired particularly after Mrs. Merdle. He inquired particularly after Mr. Merdle. Mr. Sparkler said, or rather twitched out of himself in small pieces by the shirt-collar, that Mrs. Merdle, having completely used up her place in the country, and also her house at Brighton, and being, of course, unable, don't you see, to remain in London when there wasn't a soul there, and not feeling herself this year quite up to visiting about at people's places, had resolved to have a touch at Rome, where a woman like herself, with a proverbially fine appearance and with no nonsense about her, couldn't fail to be a great acquisition. As to Mr. Merdle, he was so much wanted by the men in the city and the rest of those places, and was such a doosed extraordinary phenomenon in buying and banking and that, that Mr. Sparkler doubted if the monetary system of the country would be able to spare him: though that his work was occasionally too many for him, and that he would be all the better for a temporary shy at an entirely new scene and climate, Mr. Sparkler did not conceal. As to himself, Mr. Sparkler conveyed to the Dorrit family that he was going, on rather particular business, wherever they were going.

This immense conversational achievement required time, but was effected. Being effected, Mr. Dorrit expressed his hope that Mr. Sparkler would shortly dine with them. Mr. Sparkler received the idea so kindly, that Mr. Dorrit asked what he was going to do that day, for instance? As he was going to do nothing that day, (his usual occupation, and one for which he was particularly qualified,) he was secured without postponement, being further bound over to accompany the ladies to the opera in the evening.

At dinner-time Mr. Sparkler rose out of the sea, like Venus's son taking after his mother, and made a splendid appearance ascending the great staircase. If Fanny had been charming in the morning, she was now thrice charming, very becomingly dressed in her most suitable colors, and with an air of negligence upon her that doubled Mr. Sparkler's fetters, and riveted them.

"I hear you are acquainted, Mr. Sparkler," said his host, at dinner, "with—ha—Mr. Gowan. Mr. Henry Gowan?"

"Perfectly, sir," returned Mr. Sparkler. "His mother and my mother are cronies, in fact."

"If I had thought of it, Amy," said Mr. Dorrit, with a patronage as magnificent as that of Lord Decimus himself, "you should have dispatched a note to them, asking them to dine today. Some of our people could have—ha—fetched them and taken them home. We could have spared a—hum—gondola for that purpose. I am sorry to have forgotten this. Pray remind me of them to-morrow."

Little Dorrit was not without doubts how Mr. Henry Gowan might take their patronage; but she promised not to fail in the reminder.

"Pray, does Mr. Henry Gowan paint—ha—portraits?" inquired Mr. Dorrit.

Mr. Sparkler opined that he painted any thing, if he could get the job.

"He has no particular walk?" said Mr. Dorrit.

Mr. Sparkler, stimulated by love to brilliancy, replied that, for a particular walk, a man ought to have a particular pair of shoes; as, for example, shooting, shooting-shoes; cricket, cricket-shoes. Whereas, he believed that Henry Gowan had no particular pair of shoes.

"No speciality?" said Mr. Dorrit.

This being a very long word for Mr. Sparkler, and his mind being exhausted by his late effort, he replied, "No, thank you. I seldom take it."

"Well!" said Mr. Dorrit. "It would be very agreeable to me to present a gentleman so connected with some—ha—Testimonial of my desire to further his interests, and develop the—hum—germs of his genius. I think I must engage Mr. Gowan to paint my picture. If the result should be—ha—mutually satisfactory, I might afterward engage him to try his hand upon my family."

The exquisitely bold and original thought presented itself to

Mr. Sparkler that there was an opening here for saying there were some of the family (emphasizing "some" in a marked manner) to whom no painter could render justice. But for want of a form of words in which to express the idea, it returned to the skies.

This was the more to be regretted as Miss Fanny greatly applauded the notion of the portrait, and urged her papa to act upon it. She surmised, she said, that Mr. Gowan had lost better and higher opportunities by marrying his pretty wife; and Love in a cottage, painting pictures for dinner, was so delightfully interesting, that she begged her papa to give him the commission, whether he could paint a likeness or not; though indeed both she and Amy knew he could, from having seen a speaking likeness on his easel that day, and having had the opportunity of comparing it with the original. These remarks made Mr. Sparkler (as perhaps they were intended to do) nearly distracted; for while, on the one hand, they expressed Miss Fanny's susceptibility to the tender passion, she herself showed such an innocent unconsciousness of his admiration, that his eyes goggled in his head with jealousy of an unknown rival.

Descending into the sea again after dinner, and ascending out of it at the Opera staircase, preceded by one of their gondoliers, like an attendant Merman, with a great linen lantern, they entered their box, and Mr. Sparkler entered on an evening of agony. The theatre being dark, and the box light, several visitors lounged in during the representation; in whom Fanny was so interested, and in conversation with whom she fell into such charming attitudes, as she had little confidences with them, and little disputes concerning the identity of people in distant boxes, that the wretched Sparkler hated all mankind. But he had two consolations at the close of the performance. She gave him her fan to hold while she adjusted her cloak, and it was his blessed privilege to give her his arm down stairs again. These crumbs of encouragement, Mr. Sparkler thought, would just keep him going; and it is not impossible that Miss Dorrit thought so too.

The Merman with his light was ready at the box-door, and other Mermen with other lights were ready at all the doors. The Dorrit Merman held his lantern low, to show the steps, and Mr. Sparkler put another heavy set of fetters on over his former set, as he watched her radiant feet twinkling down the stairs beside him. Among the loiterers here was Blandois of Paris. He spoke, and moved forward beside Fanny.

Little Dorrit was in front, with her brother and Mrs. General (Mr. Dorrit had remained at home); but on the brink of the quay they all came together. She started again to find Blandois close to her, handing Fanny into the boat.

"Gowan has had a loss," he said, "since he was made happy to-day by a visit from fair ladies."

"A loss," repeated Fanny, relinquished by the bereaved Sparkler, and taking her seat.

"A loss," said Blandois. "His dog, Lion."

Little Dorrit's hand was in his as he spoke.

"He is dead," said Blandois.

"Dead?" echoed Little Dorrit. "That noble dog?"

"Faith, dear ladies!" said Blandois, smiling and shrugging his shoulders, "somebody has poisoned that noble dog. He is as dead as the Doges!"

CHAPTER XLIII.

PRUNES AND PRISM.

MRS. GENERAL, always on her coach-box, keeping the proprieties well together, took pains to form a surface on her very dear young friend, and Mrs. General's very dear young friend tried hard to receive it. Hard as she had tried in her laborious life to attain many ends, she had never tried harder than she did now to be varnished by Mrs. General. It made her anxious and unhappy to be operated upon by that smoothing hand, it is true; but she submitted herself to the family wants in its greatness as she had submitted herself to the family wants in its littleness, and yielded to her own inclinations in this thing no more than she had yielded to her hunger itself in the days when she had saved her dinner that her father might have his supper.

One comfort that she had under the Ordeal by General was more sustaining to her, and made her more grateful, than to a less devoted and affectionate spirit, not habituated to her struggles and sacrifices, might have seemed quite reasonable. And, indeed, it may often be observed in life, that spirits like Little Dorrit do not appear to reason half as carefully as the folks who get the better of them. The continued kindness of her sister was this comfort to Little Dorrit. It was nothing to her that the kindness took the form of tolerant patronage; she was used to that. It was nothing to her that it kept her in a tributary position, and showed her in attendance on the flaming car in which Miss Fanny sat on an exalted seat, exacting homage; she sought no better place. Always admiring Fanny's beauty, and grace, and readiness, and not now asking herself how much of her disposition to be strongly attached to Fanny was due to her own heart, and how much to Fanny's, she gave her all the sisterly fondness her great heart contained.

The wholesale amount of prunes and prism which Mrs. General infused into the family life, combined with the perpetual plunge made by Fanny into society, left but a very small residue of any natural deposit at the bottom of the mixture. This rendered confidences with Fanny doubly precious to Little Dorrit, and heightened the relief they afforded her.

"Amy," said Fanny to her one night, when they were alone, after a day so tiring that Little Dorrit was quite worn out, though Fanny would have taken another dip into society with the greatest pleasure in life, "I am going to put something into your little head. You won't guess what it is, I suspect."

"I don't think that's likely, dear," said Little Dorrit.

"Come, I'll give you a clue, child," said Fanny. "Mrs. General."

Prunes and prism, in a thousand combinations, having been wearily in the ascendant all day—every thing having been surface and varnish, and show without substance—Little Dorrit looked as if she had hoped that Mrs. General was safely tucked up in bed for some hours.

"*Now*, can you guess, Amy?" said Fanny.

"No, dear. Unless I have done any thing," said Little Dorrit, rather alarmed, and meaning any thing calculated to crack varnish and ruffle surface.

Fanny was so very much amused by the misgiving, that she took up her favorite fan (being then seated at her dressing-table with her armory of cruel instruments about her, most of them reeking from the heart of Sparkler), and tapped her sister frequently on the nose with it, laughing all the time.

"Oh, our Amy, our Amy!" said Fanny. "What a timid little goose our Amy is! But this is nothing to laugh at. On the contrary, I am very cross, my dear."

"As it is not with me, Fanny, I don't mind," returned her sister, smiling,

"Ah! But I do mind," said Fanny, "and so will you, Pet, when I enlighten you. Amy, has it never struck you that somebody is monstrously polite to Mrs. General?"

"Every body is polite to Mrs. General," said Little Dorrit. "Because—"

"Because she freezes them into it?" interrupted Fanny. "I don't mean that; quite different from that. Come! Has it never struck you, Amy, that pa is monstrously polite to Mrs. General?"

Amy, murmuring "No," looked quite confounded.

"No; I dare say not. But he is," said Fanny. "He is, Amy. And remember my words. Mrs. General has designs on pa!"

"Dear Fanny, do you think it possible that Mrs. General has designs on any one?"

"Do I think it possible?" retorted Fanny. "My love, I know it. I tell you she has designs on pa. And more than that, I tell you, pa considers her such a wonder, such a paragon of accomplishment, and such an acquisition in our family, that he is ready to get himself into a state of perfect infatuation with her at any moment. And that opens a pretty picture of things, I hope! Think of me with Mrs. General for a mamma!"

Little Dorrit did not reply. "Think of me with Mrs. General for a mamma!" but she looked anxious, and seriously inquired what had led Fanny to these conclusions.

"Lard, my darling," said Fanny, tartly. "You might as well ask me how I know when a man is struck with myself! But, of course, I do know. It happens often; but I always know it. I know this, in much the same way, I suppose. At all events, I know it."

"You never heard papa say any thing?"

"Say any thing?" repeated Fanny. "My dearest, darling child, what necessity has he had, yet a while, to say any thing!"

"And you have never heard Mrs. General say any thing?"

"My goodness me, Amy," returned Fanny, "is she the sort of woman to say any thing? Isn't it perfectly plain and clear that she has nothing to do at present but to hold herself upright, keep her aggravating gloves on, and go sweeping about? Say any thing! If she had the ace of trumps in her hand, at whist, she wouldn't say any thing, child. It would come out when she played it."

"At least, you may be mistaken, Fanny. Now may you not?"

"Oh yes, I *may* be," said Fanny, "but I am not. However, I am glad you can contemplate such an escape, my dear, and I am glad that you can take this for the present with sufficient coolness to think of such a chance. It makes me hope that you may be able to bear the connection. I should not be able to bear it, and I should not try. I'd marry young Sparkler first."

"Oh, you would never marry him, Fanny, under any circumstances."

"Upon my word, my dear," rejoined that young lady, with exceeding indifference, "I wouldn't positively answer even for that. There's no knowing what might happen. Especially as I should have many opportunities afterward of treating that woman, his mother, in her own style. Which I most decidedly should not be slow to avail myself of, Amy."

No more passed between the sisters then; but what had passed gave the two subjects of Mrs. General and Mr. Sparkler great prominence in Little Dorrit's mind, and thenceforth she thought very much of both.

Mrs. General, having long ago formed her own surface to such perfection that it hid whatever was below it (if any thing), no observation was to be made in that quarter. Mr. Dorrit was undeniably very polite to her, and had a high opinion of her; but Fanny, impetuous at most times, might easily be wrong for all that. Now, the Sparkler question was on the different footing that any one could see what was going on there, and Little Dorrit saw it, and pondered on it, with many doubts and uneasy wonderings as to the end of it all.

The devotion of Mr. Sparkler was only to be equalled by the caprice and cruelty of his enslaver. Sometimes she would prefer him to such distinction of notice that he would chuckle aloud with joy; next day, or next hour, she would overlook him so completely, and drop him into such an abyss of obscurity, that he would groan under a weak pretense of coughing. The constancy of his attendance never touched Fanny; though he was so inseparable from Edward, that when that gentleman wished for a change of society he was under the irksome necessity of gliding out like a conspirator, in disguised boats and by secret doors and back ways; though he was so solicitous to know how Mr. Dorrit was, that he called every other day to inquire, as if Mr. Dorrit were the prey of an intermittent fever; though he was so constantly being paddled up and down before the principal windows that he might have been supposed to have made a wager for a large stake to be paddled a thousand miles in a thousand hours; though whenever the gondola of his mistress left the gate, the gondola of Mr. Sparkler shot out from some watery ambush and gave chase, as if she were a fair smuggler and he a custom-house officer. It was probably owing to this fortification of the natural strength of his constitution with so much exposure to the air and the salt sea that Mr. Sparkler did not pine outwardly; but, whatever the cause, he was so far from having any prospect of moving his mistress by a languishing state of health, that he grew bluffer every day, and that peculiarity in his appearance of seeming rather a swelled boy than a young man became developed to an extraordinary degree of ruddy puffiness.

Blandois calling to pay his respects, Mr. Dorrit received him with affability as the friend of Mr. Gowan, and mentioned to him his idea of commissioning Mr. Gowan to transmit him to posterity. Blandois highly extolling it, it occurred to Mr. Dorrit that it might be agreeable to Blandois to communicate to his friend the great opportunity reserved for him. Blandois accepted the commission with his own free elegance of manner, and protested he would discharge it before he was an hour older. On his imparting the news to Gowan, that Master gave Mr. Dorrit to the Devil with great liberality some round dozen of times (for he resented patronage almost as much as he resented the want of it), and was inclined to quarrel with his friend for bringing him the message.

"It may be a defect in my mental vision, Blandois," said he, "but may I die if I see what you have to do with this."

"Death of my life," replied Blandois, "nor I neither, except that I thought I was serving my friend."

"By putting an upstart's money in his pocket?" said Gowan, frowning. "Do you mean that? Tell your other friend to get his head painted for the sign of some public-house, and to get it done by a sign-painter. Who am I, and who is he?"

"Professore," returned the ambassador, "and who is Blandois?"

Without appearing at all interested in the latter question, Gowan angrily whistled Mr. Dorrit away. But next day he resumed the subject by saying, in his off-hand manner, and with a slighting laugh, " Well, Blandois, when shall we go to this Mecænas of yours? We journeymen must take jobs when we can get them. When shall we go and look after this job?"

"When you will," said the injured Blandois, "as you please. What have I to do with it? What is it to me?"

"I can tell you what it is to me," said Gowan. "Bread and cheese. One must eat! So come along, my Blandois."

Mr. Dorrit received them in the presence of his daughters and of Mr. Sparkler, who happened, by some surprising accident, to be calling there. "How are you, Sparkler?" said Gowan, carelessly. "When you have to live by your mother wit, old boy, I hope you may get on better than I do."

Mr. Dorrit then mentioned his proposal. "Sir," said Gowan, laughing, after receiving it gracefully enough, "I am new to the trade, and not expert at the trade mysteries. I believe I ought to look at you in various lights, tell you you are a capital subject, and consider when I shall be sufficiently disengaged to devote myself with the necessary enthusiasm to the fine picture I mean to make of you. I assure you," and he laughed again, "I feel quite a traitor in the camp of those dear, gifted, good, noble fellows, my brother artists, by not doing the hocus-pocus better. But I have not been brought up to it, and it's too late to learn it. Now, the fact is, I am a very bad painter, but not much worse than the generality. If you are going to throw away a hundred guineas or so, I am as poor as a poor relation of great people usually is, and I shall be very much obliged to you, if you'll throw them away upon me. I'll do the best I can for the money, and if the best should be bad, why even then you may probably have a bad picture with a small name to it, instead of a bad picture with a large name to it."

This tone, though not what he had expected, on the whole suited Mr. Dorrit remarkably well. It showed that the gentleman highly connected, and not a mere workman, would be under an obligation to him. He expressed his satisfaction in placing himself in Mr. Gowan's hands, and trusted that he would have the pleasure, in their characters as private gentlemen, of improving his acquaintance.

"You are very good," said Gowan. "I have not foresworn

society since I joined the brotherhood of the brush (the most delightful fellows on the face of the earth), and am glad enough to smell the old fine gunpowder now and then, though it did blow me into mid-air and my present calling. You'll not think, Mr. Dorrit," and here he laughed again, in the easiest way, "that I am lapsing into the freemasonry of the craft—for it's not so; upon my life I can't help betraying it wherever I go, though, by Jupiter, I love and honor the craft with all my might —if I propose a stipulation as to time and place?"

Ha. Mr. Dorrit could erect no—hum—suspicion of that kind on Mr. Gowan's frankness.

"Again, you are very good," said Gowan. "Mr. Dorrit, I hear you are going to Rome. I am going to Rome, having friends there. Let me begin to do you the injustice I have conspired to do you, there—not here. We shall all be hurried during the rest of our stay here, and though there's not a poorer man with whole elbows in Venice than myself, I have not quite got all the Amateur out of me yet—compromising the trade again, you see!—and can't fall on to order, in a hurry, for the mere sake of the sixpences."

These remarks were not less favorably received by Mr. Dorrit than their predecessors. They were the prelude to the first reception of Mr. and Mrs. Gowan at dinner, and they skillfully placed Mr. Gowan on his usual ground in the new family.

His wife, too, they placed on her usual ground. Miss Fanny understood, with particular distinctness, that Mrs. Gowan's good looks had cost her husband dear; that there had been a great disturbance about her in the Barnacle family, and that the dowager Mrs. Gowan, nearly heartbroken, had resolutely set her face against the marriage, until overpowered by her maternal feelings. Mrs. General likewise clearly understood that the attachment had occasioned much family grief and dissension. Of honest Mr. Meagles no mention was made, except that it was natural enough that a person of that sort should wish to raise his daughter out of his own obscurity, and that no one could blame him for trying his best to do so.

Little Dorrit's interest in the fair subject of this easily accepted belief was too earnest and watchful to fail in accurate observation. She could see that it had its part in throwing upon Mrs. Gowan, the touch of shadow under which she lived, and she even had an instinctive knowledge that there was no truth in it. But it had an influence in placing obstacles in the way of her association with Mrs. Gowan, by making the prunes and prism school excessively polite to her, but not very intimate with her; and Little Dorrit, as an enforced sizar of that college, was obliged to submit herself humbly to its ordinances.

Nevertheless, there was a sympathetic understanding already established between the two, which would have carried them over greater difficulties, and made a friendship out of a more restricted intercourse. As though accidents were determined to be favorable to it, they had a new assurance of congeniality in the aversion which each perceived that the other felt for Blandois of Paris; an aversion amounting to the repugnance and horror of a natural antipathy toward an odious creature of the reptile kind.

And there was a passive congeniality between them besides this active one. To both of them Blandois behaved in exactly the same manner, and to both of them his manner had uniformly something in it which they both knew to be different from his bearing toward others. The difference was too minute in its expression to be perceived by others, but they knew it to be there. A mere trick of his evil eyes, a mere turn of his smooth white hand, a mere hair's-breadth of addition to the fall of his nose and the rise of his mustache in the worst movement of his face, conveyed to both of them equally a swagger personal to themselves. It was, as if he had said, "I have a secret power in this quarter. I know what I know."

This had never been felt by them both in so great a degree, and never by each so perfectly to the knowledge of the other, as on a day when he came to Mr. Dorrit's to take his leave before quitting Venice. Mrs. Gowan was herself there for the same purpose, and he came upon the two together, the rest of the family being out.

"A thousand pardons, sweet ladies," said Blandois of Paris. "Excuse me. Am I too many here?"

"You are welcome, sir," said Little Dorrit, greatly disconcerted. "Will you take a seat?"

The two had not been together five minutes, and the peculiar manner seemed to convey to them, "You were going to talk about me. Hah! Behold me here to prevent it!"

"Gowan is coming here?" said Blandois, with a smile.

Mrs. Gowan replied he was not coming.

"Not coming!" said Blandois. "Permit your devoted servant, then, when you leave here, to escort you home."

"Thank you; I am not going home."

"Not going home!" said Blandois. "Then I am forlorn."

That he might be; but he was not so forlorn as to roam away and leave them together. He sat entertaining them with his finest compliments, and choicest conversation; but he conveyed to them, all the time, "No, no, no, dear ladies. Behold me here expressly to prevent it."

He conveyed it to them with so much meaning, and he had such a diabolical persistency in him, that at length Mrs. Gowan rose to depart. "I had hoped," she said, "that I might have sat with you a little while when you had no visitors; but I know how difficult that is, your circle of acquaintance being so very comprehensive."

"Being so very comprehensive," repeated Blandois, with a bow. Her eyes had slightly turned toward him, as if she would have said, "I wonder it should comprehend this man," and he had spoken and bowed immediately. "Being," he now said again, rendering his softest homage to the Dorrit hospitality, "so very comprehensive."

"But I shall see you, my dear, at Rome," said Mrs. Gowan.

"I also," said Blandois, "aspire to the felicity of again seeing Miss Dorrit at Rome. Farewell! All happiness until we meet!"

He had carefully reserved this salutation until they had taken leave of one another. On his offering his hand to Mrs. Gowan to lead her down the staircase, she retained Little Dorrit's hand in hers with a cautious pressure, and said, "No, thank you. But if you will please to see if my boatman is there, I shall be obliged to you."

It left him no choice but to go down before them. As he did so, hat in hand, Mrs. Gowan whispered,

"He killed the dog."

"Does Mr. Gowan know it?" Little Dorrit whispered

"No one knows it. Don't look toward me; look toward him. He will turn his face in a moment. No one knows it, but I am sure he did. You are?"

"I—I think so," Little Dorrit answered.

"Henry likes him, and will not think ill of him; he is so generous and open himself. But we feel sure that we think of him as he deserves. He argued with Henry that the dog had been already poisoned when he changed so, and sprung at him. Henry believes it, but we do not. I see he is listening, but can't hear. Good-by, my dear! Good-by!"

The last words were spoken aloud, as the vigilant Blandois stopped, turned his head, and looked at them from the bottom of the staircase. Assuredly he did look then, though he looked his politest, as if any real philanthropist could have desired no better employment than to lash a great stone to his neck and drop him into the water flowing beyond the dark arched gateway in which he stood. No such benefactor to mankind being on the spot, he handed Mrs. Gowan to her boat, stood there until it had shot out of the narrow view; when he handed himself into his own boat and followed it.

Little Dorrit had sometimes thought, and now thought again as she retraced her steps up the staircase, that he had made his way too easily into her father's house. But so many and such varieties of people did the same, through Mr. Dorrit's participation in his elder daughter's society mania, that it was hardly an exceptional case. A perfect fury for making acquaintances on whom to impress their riches and importance, had seized the House of Dorrit.

It appeared on the whole to Little Dorrit herself that this same society in which they lived greatly resembled a superior sort of Marshalsea. Numbers of people seemed to come abroad, pretty much as people had come into the prison; through debt, through idleness, relationship, curiosity, and general unfitness for getting on at home. They were brought into these foreign towns in the custody of couriers and local followers, just as the debtors had been brought into the prison. They prowled about the churches and picture-galleries much in the old, dreary, prison-yard manner. They were usually going away again to-morrow or next week, and rarely knew their own minds, and seldom did what they said they would do, or went where they said they would go: in all this again very like the prison debtors. They paid high for poor accommodation, and disparaged a place while they pretended to like it; which was exactly the Marshalsea custom. They were envied when they went away, by people left behind feigning not to want to go; and that again was the Marshalsea habit invariably. A certain set of words and phrases, as much belonging to tourists as the College and the Snuggery belonged to the jail, was always in their mouths. They had precisely the same incapacity for settling down to any thing as the prisoners used to have; they rather deteriorated one another, as the prisoners used to do; and they wore untidy dresses, and fell into a slouching way of life; still always like the people in the Marshalsea.

The period of the family's stay at Venice, came, in its course, to an end, and they moved, with their retinue, to Rome. Through a repetition of the former Italian scenes, growing more dirty and more wretched as they went on, and bringing them at length to where the very air was contaminated and diseased, they passed to their destination. A fine residence had been taken for them on the Corso, and there they took up their abode in a city where every thing seemed to be trying to stand still forever on the ruins of something else, except the water, which, following eternal laws, tumbled and rolled from its multitude of fountains.

Here, it seemed to Little Dorrit that a change came over the Marshalsea spirit, and that Prunes and Prism got the upper hand. Every body was walking about St. Peter's and the Vatican on somebody else's cork legs, and straining every visible object through somebody else's sieve. No body said what any thing was, but every body said what the Reverend Mr. Eustace somebody else said it was. The whole body of travelers seemed to be a collection of voluntary human sacrifices, bound hand and foot, and delivered over to the Reverend Mr. Eustace and his attendants, to have the entrails of their intellects arranged according to the taste of that sacred priesthood. Through the rugged remains of temples, and tombs, and palaces, and senate-halls, and theatres, and amphitheatres of ancient days, hosts of tongue-tied and blindfolded moderns were carefully feeling their way, incessantly repeating Prunes and Prism, in the endeavor to set their lips according to the received form. Mrs. General was in her pure element. Nobody had an opinion. There was a formation of surface going on around her on an amazing scale, and it had not a flaw of free speech in it.

Another modification of Prunes and Prism insinuated itself on Little Dorrit's notice, very shortly after their arrival. They received an early visit from Mrs. Merdle, who led that extensive department of life in the Eternal City that winter; and the skillful manner in which she and Fanny fenced with one another on the occasion almost made her quiet sister wink, like the glittering of small-swords.

"So delighted," said Mrs. Merdle, "to resume an acquaintance so inauspiciously begun—at Martigny."

"At Martigny, of course," said Fanny. "Charmed, I am sure!"

"I understand," said Mrs. Merdle, "from my son Edmund Sparkler, that he has already improved that chance occasion. He has returned quite transported with Venice."

"Indeed!" returned Fanny. "Was he there long?"

"I might refer that question to Mr. Dorrit," said Mrs. Merdle, turning the bosom toward that gentleman; "Edward having been so much obliged to him for rendering his stay agreeable."

"Oh, pray don't speak of it," returned Fanny. "I believe papa had the pleasure of inviting Mr. Sparkler twice or thrice—but it was nothing. We had so many people about us, and kept such open house, that if he had that pleasure it was less than nothing."

"Except," my dear," said Mr. Dorrit, "except—ha—as it afforded me unusual gratification to—hum—show by any means, however slight and worthless, the—ha, hum—high estimation in which, in—ha—common with the rest of the world, I hold so distinguished and princely a character as Mr. Merdle's."

The bosom received the tribute in its most engaging manner. "Mr. Merdle," observed Fanny, as a means of dismissing Mr. Sparkler into the background, "is quite a theme of papa's, you must know, Mrs. Merdle."

"I have been—ha—disappointed, madam," said Mr. Dorrit, "to understand from Mr. Sparkler that there is no great—hum—probability of Mr. Merdle's coming abroad."

"Why, indeed," said Mrs. Merdle, "he is so much engaged, and in such request, that I fear not. He has not been able to get abroad for some years now. You, Miss Dorrit, I believe, have been almost continually abroad for a long time."

"Oh dear yes," drawled Fanny, with the greatest hardihood. "An immense number of years."

"So I should have inferred," said Mrs. Merdle.

"Exactly," said Fanny.

"I trust, however," resumed Mr. Dorrit, "that if I haven ot the—hum—great advantage of becoming known to Mr. Merdle on this side of the Alps or Mediterranean, I shall have that honor on returning to England. It is an honor I shall particularly esteem."

"Mr. Merdle," said Mrs. Merdle, who had been looking admiringly at Fanny through her eye-glass, "will esteem it, I am sure, no less."

Little Dorrit, thoughtful and still solitary, though no longer alone, at first supposed this to be mere Prunes and Prism. But as her father when they had been to a brilliant reception at Mrs. Merdle's, harped, at their own family breakfast-table, on his desire to know Mr. Merdle, with the contingent view of benefiting by the advice of that wonderful man in the disposal of his fortune, she began to think it had a real meaning, and to entertain a wish, on her own part, to see the shining light of the time

CHAPTER XLIV.

THE DOWAGER MRS. GOWAN IS REMINDED THAT "IT NEVER DOES."

WHILE the waters of Venice and the ruins of Rome were sunning themselves for the pleasure of the Dorrit family, and were daily being sketched out of all earthly proportion, lineament, and likeness, by traveling pencils innumerable, the firm of Doyce and Clennam hammered away in Bleeding Heart Yard, and the vigorous clink of iron upon iron was heard there through the working hours.

The younger partner had by this time brought the business into sound trim; and the elder, left free to follow his own ingenious devices, had done much to enhance the character of the factory. As an ingenious man he had necessarily to encounter every discouragement that the ruling powers for a length of time had been able, by any means, to put in the way of his class of culprits, but that was only reasonable self-defense in the powers, since How to do it must obviously be the natural and mortal enemy of How not to do it. In this was to be found the basis of the wise system, by tooth and nail upheld by the Circumlocution Office, of warning every ingenious British subject to be ingenious at his peril: of harassing him, obstructing him, inviting robbers (by making his remedy uncertain, difficult, and expensive) to plunder him, and at the best of confiscating his property, after a short term of enjoyment, as though invention were on a par with felony. The system had uniformly found great favor with the Barnacles, and that was only reasonable, too; for one who worthily invents must be in earnest, and the Barnacles abhorred and dreaded nothing half so much. That again was very reasonable, since in a country suffering under the affliction of a great amount of earnestness, there might, in an exceeding short space of time, be not a single Barnacle left sticking to a post.

Daniel Doyce faced his condition with its pains and penalties attached to it, and soberly worked on for the work's sake. Clennam cheering him with a hearty co-operation, was a moral support to him, besides doing good service in his business relation. The concern prospered, and the partners were fast friends.

But Daniel could not forget the old design of so many years. It was not in reason to be expected that he should ; if he could have lightly forgotten it, he could never have conceived it, or had the patience and the perseverance to work it out! So Clennam thought, when he sometimes observed him of an evening looking over the models and drawings, and consoling himself by muttering with a sigh as he put them away again, that the thing was as true as it ever was.

To show no sympathy with so much endeavor and so much disappointment, would have been to fail in what Clennam regarded as among the implicit obligations of his partnership. A revival of the passing interest in the subject which had been by chance awakened at the door of the Circumlocution Office, originated in this feeling. He asked his partner to explain the invention to him ; "having a lenient consideration," he stipulated, "for my being no workman, Doyce."

"No workman?" said Doyce. "You would have been a thorough workman if you had given yourself to it. You have as good a head for understanding such things as I have met with."

"A totally uneducated one, I am sorry to add," said Clennam.

"I don't know that," returned Doyce, "and I wouldn't have you say that. No man of sense who has been generally improved, and has improved himself, can be called quite uneducated as to any thing. I don't particularly favor mysteries. I would as soon, on a fair and clear explanation, be judged by one class of man as another, provided he had the qualification I have named."

"At all events," said Clennam—"this sounds as if we were exchanging compliments, but you know it's not so—I shall have the advantage of as plain an explanation as can be given."

"Well!" said Daniel, in his steady, even way, "I'll try to make it so."

He had the power often to be found in union with such a character, of explaining what he himself perceived and meant with the direct force and distinctness with which it struck his own mind. His manner of demonstration was so orderly and neat and simple, that it was not easy to mistake him. There was something almost ludicrous in the complete irreconcilability of a vague, conventional notion that he must be a visionary man, with the precise, sagacious traveling of his eye and thumb over the plans, their patient stoppages at particular points, their careful returns to other points whence little channels of explanation had to be traced up, and his steady manner of making every thing good and every thing sound, at each important stage, before taking his hearer on a line's-breadth further. His dismissal of himself from his description, was hardly less remarkable. He never said, I discovered this adaptation or invented that combination; but showed the whole thing as if the Divine artificer had made it, and he had happened to find it. So modest was he about it, such a pleasant touch of respect was mingled with his quiet admiration of it, and so calmly convinced he was that it was established on great universal aws.

Not only that evening, but for several succeeding evenings, Clennam was quite charmed by this investigation. The more he pursued it, and the oftener he glanced at the gray head bending over it, and the shrewd eye kindling with pleasure in it and love of it—instrument for probing his heart though it had been made his own twelve long years—the less he could reconcile it to his younger energy to let it go without one effort more. At length he said,

"Doyce, it came to this at last—that the business was to be sunk with Heaven knows how many more wrecks, or begun all over again?"

"Yes," returned Doyce, "that's what the noblemen and gentlemen made of it after a dozen years."

"And pretty fellows, too!" said Clennam, bitterly.

"The usual thing!" observed Doyce. "I must not make a martyr of myself, when I am one of so large a company."

"Relinquish it, or begin it all over again?" mused Clennam.

"That was exactly the long and the short of it," said Doyce.

"Then, my friend," cried Clennam, starting up and taking his work-roughened hand, "it shall be begun all over again!"

Doyce looked alarmed, and replied, in a hurry for him, "No, no. Better put it by. Far better put it by. It will be heard of one day. I can put it by. You forget, my good Clennam; I *have* put it by. It's all at an end."

"Yes, Doyce," returned Clennam, "at an end as far as your efforts and rebuffs are concerned, I admit, but not as far as mine are. I am younger than you, I have only once set foot in that precious office, and I am fresh game for them. Come! I'll try them. You shall do exactly as you have been doing since we have been together. I will add (as I easily can) to what I have been doing, the attempt to get justice done to you by the government; and, unless I have some success to report, you shall hear no more of it."

Daniel Doyce was still reluctant to consent, and again and again urged that they had better put it by. But it was natural enough that he should gradually allow himself to be over-persuaded by Clennam, and should yield. Yield he did. So Arthur resumed the long and hopeless labor of striving to make way with the Circumlocution Office.

The waiting-rooms of that Department soon began to be familiar with his presence, and he was usually ushered into them by its janitors much as a pickpocket might be shown into a police office; the principal difference being that the object of the latter class of public business is to keep the pickpocket, while the Circumlocution object was to get rid of Clennam. However, he was resolved to stick to the great Department, and so the work of form-filling, corresponding, minuting, memorandum-making, signing, counter-signing, counter-counter-signing, referring backward and forward, and referring sideways, crosswise, and zigzag recommenced.

Here arises a feature of the Circumlocution Office, not previously mentioned in the present record. When that admirable Department got into trouble, and was, by some infuriated member of Parliament, whom the smaller Barnacles almost suspected of laboring under diabolic possession, attacked, on the merits of no individual case, but as an Institution wholly abominable and Bedlamite; then the noble or right honorable Barnacle who represented it in the House, would smite that member, and cleave him asunder with a statement of the quantity of business (for the prevention of business) done in the Circumlocution Office. Then would that noble or right honorable Barnacle hold in his hand a paper containing a few figures, to which, with the permission of the House, he would entreat its attention. Then would the inferior Barnacles exclaim, following orders, "Hear, Hear, Hear!" and "Read!" Then would the noble or right honorable Barnacle perceive, sir, from this little document, which he thought might carry conviction even to the perversest mind (Derisive laughter and cheering from the Barnacle fry), that within the short compass of the last financial half-year, this much maligned Department (Cheers) had written and received fifteen thousand letters (Loud cheers), twenty-four thousand minutes (Louder cheers), and thirty-two thousand five hundred and seventeen memoranda (Vehement cheering). Nay, an ingenious gentleman connected with the Department, and himself a valuable public servant, had done him the favor to make a curious calculation of the amount of stationery consumed in it during the same period. It formed a part of this same short document, and he derived from it a remarkable fact, that the sheets of foolscap paper it had devoted to the public service would pave the footways on both sides of Oxford Street from end to end, and leave nearly a quarter of a mile to spare for the park (Immense cheering and laughter); while of tape—red tape—it had used enough to stretch in graceful festoons from Hyde Park Corner to the General Post-office. Then, amidst a burst of saved exultations, would the noble or right honorable Barnacle sit down, leaving the mutilated fragments of the Member on the field. No one, after that exemplary demolition of him, would have the hardihood to hint that the more the Circumlocution Office did, the less was done, and that the greatest blessing it could confer on an unhappy public would be to do nothing at all.

With sufficient occupation on his hands, now that he had this additional task—such a task had many and many a serviceable man died of before his day—Arthur Clennam led a life of slight variety. Regular visits to his mother's dull sick room, and visits scarcely less regular to Mr. Meagles at Twickenham, were its only changes during many months.

He sadly and sorely missed Little Dorrit. He had been prepared to miss her very much, but not so much. He knew to the full extent only through experience what a large place in his life was left blank when her familiar little figure went out of it. He felt, too, that he must relinquish the hope of its return, knowing the family character sufficiently well to be assured that he and she were divided by a broad ground of separation. The old interest he had had in her, and her old trusting reliance on him, were tinged with melancholy in his mind: so soon had change stolen over them, and so soon had they glided into the past with other secret tendernesses.

When he received her letter he was greatly moved, but did not the less sensibly feel that she was far divided from him by more than distance. It helped him to a clearer and keener perception of the place assigned him by the family. He saw that he was cherished in her grateful remembrance secretly, and that they resented him with the jail and the rest of its belongings.

Through all these meditations which every day of his life crowded about her, he thought of her otherwise in the old way. She was his innocent friend, his delicate child, his dear Little Dorrit. This very change of circumstances fitted curiously in with the habit, begun on the night when the roses floated away, of considering himself a much older man than his years really made him. He regarded her from a point of view which in its remoteness, tender as it was, he little thought would have been unspeakable agony to her. He speculated about her future destiny, and about the husband she might have, with an affection for her which would have drained her heart of its dearest drop of hope, and broken it.

Every thing about him tended to confirm him in the custom of looking on himself as an elderly man, from whom such aspirations as he had combated in the case of Minnie Gowan (though that was not so long ago either, reckoning by months and seasons), were finally departed. His relations with her father and mother were like those on which a widower son-in-law might have stood. If the twin sister, who was dead, had lived to pass away in the bloom of womanhood, and he had been her husband, the nature of his intercourse with Mr. and Mrs. Meagles would probably have been just what it was. This imperceptibly helped to render habitual the impression within him that he had done with and dismissed that part of life.

He invariably heard of Minnie from them, as telling them in her letters how happy she was, and how she loved her husband; but inseparably from that subject, he invariably saw the old cloud on Mr. Meagles's face. Mr. Meagles had never been quite so radiant since the marriage as before. He had never quite overcome the separation from Pet. He was the same good-humored, open creature; but, as if his face, from being much turned toward the pictures of his two children which could show him only one look, unconsciously adopted a characteristic from them, it always had now, through all its changes of expression, a look of loss in it.

One wintry Saturday when Clennam was at the cottage, the Dowager Mrs. Gowan drove up in the Hampton Court equipage which pretended to be the exclusive equipage of so many individual proprietors. She descended, in her shady ambuscade of a green fan, to favor Mr. and Mrs. Meagles with a call.

"And how do you both do, Papa and Mamma Meagles?" said she, encouraging her humble connections; "and when did you last hear from or about my poor fellow?"

My poor fellow was her son, and this mode of speaking of him politely kept alive, without any offense in the world, the pretense that he had fallen a victim to the Meagles' wiles.

"And the dear pretty one," said Mrs. Gowan. "Have you later news of her than I have?"

Which also delicately implied that her son had been captured by mere beauty, and under its fascination had foregone all sorts of worldly advantages.

"I am sure," said Mrs. Gowan, without straining her attention on the answers she received, "it's an unspeakable comfort to know they continue happy. My poor fellow is of such a restless disposition, and has been so used to roving about, and to being inconstant and popular among all manner of people, that it's the greatest comfort in life. I suppose they're as poor as mice, Papa Meagles ?"

Mr. Meagles, fidgetty under the question, replied, "I hope not, ma'am. I hope they will manage their little income."

"Oh, my dearest Meagles !" returned that lady, tapping him on the arm with the green fan, and then adroitly interposing it between a yawn and the company, "how can you, as a man of the world, and one of the most business-like of human beings—for you know you are business-like, and a great deal too much for us who are not—"

(Which went to the former purpose by making Mr. Meagles out to be an artful schemer.)

"—How can you talk about their managing their little means ? My poor dear fellow ! The idea of his managing mere hundreds ! And the sweet pretty creature too. The notion of her managing ! Papa Meagles ! Don't !"

"Well, ma'am," said Mr. Meagles, gravely, "I am sorry to admit, then, that Henry certainly does anticipate his means."

"My dear good man—I use no ceremony with you, because we are a kind of relations positively, Mamma Meagles," exclaimed Mrs. Gowan, cheerfully, as if the absurd coincidence then flashed upon her for the first time—"a kind of relations ! My dear good man, in this world none of us can have *every thing* our own way."

This again went to the former point, and showed Mr. Meagles with all good breeding that, so far, he had been brilliantly successful in his deep designs. Mrs. Gowan thought the hit so good a one that she dwelt upon it ; repeating, "Not *every thing*. No, no ; in this world we must not expect *every thing*, Papa Meagles."

"And may I ask, ma'am," retorted Mr. Meagles, a little heightened in color, "who does expect every thing ?"

"Oh, nobody, nobody !" said Mrs. Gowan. "I was going to say—but you put me out. You interrupting papa, what was I going to say !"

Drooping her large green fan, she looked musingly at Mr. Meagles while she thought about it—a performance not tending to the cooling of that gentleman's rather heated spirits.

"Ah ! Yes, to be sure !" said Mrs. Gowan. "You must

remember that my poor fellow has always been accustomed to expectations. They may have been realized, or they may not have been realized—"

"Let us say, then, may not have been realized," observed Mr. Meagles.

The Dowager for a moment gave him an angry look, but tossed it off with her head and her fan, and pursued the tenor of her way in her former manner.

"It makes no difference. My poor fellow has been accustomed to that sort of thing, and of course you knew it, and were prepared for the consequences. I myself always clearly foresaw the consequences, and am not surprised. And you must not be surprised. In fact, can't be surprised. Must have been prepared for it."

Mr. Meagles looked at his wife, and at Clennam; bit his lip, and coughed.

"And now here's my poor fellow," Mrs. Gowan pursued, "receiving notice that he is to hold himself in expectation of a baby, and all the expenses attendant on such an addition to his family! Poor Henry! But it can't be helped now: it's too late to help it now. Only don't talk of anticipating means, papa Meagles, as a discovery; because that would be too much."

"Too much, ma'am?" said Mr. Meagles, as seeking an explanation.

"There, there!" said Mrs. Gowan, putting him in his inferior place with an expressive action of her hand. "Too much for my poor fellow's mother to bear at this time of day. They are fast married, and can't be unmarried. There, there! I know that! You needn't tell me that, Papa Meagles. I know it very well. What was it I said just now? That it was a great comfort they continued happy. It is to be hoped they will still continue happy. It is to be hoped Pretty One will do every thing she can to make my poor fellow happy, and keep him contented. Papa and Mamma Meagles, we had better say no more about it. We never did look at this subject from the same side, and we never shall. There, there! Now I am good."

Truly, having by this time said every thing she could say in maintenance of her wonderfully mythical position, and in admonition to Mr. Meagles that he must not expect to bear his honors of alliance too cheaply, Mrs. Gowan was disposed to forego the rest. If Mr. Meagles had submitted to a glance of entreaty from Mrs. Meagles, and an expressive gesture from Mr. Clennam, he would have left her in the undisturbed enjoyment of this state of mind. But Pet was the darling and pride of his heart; and if he could ever have championed her more devotedly, or loved her better, than in the days when she was the sunlight of his house, it would have been now, when, in its daily grace and delight, she was lost to it.

"Mrs. Gowan, ma'am," said Mr. Meagles, "I have been a plain man all my life. If I was to try—no matter whether on myself, or somebody else, or both— any genteel mystifications, I should probably not succeed in them."

"Papa Meagles," returned the Dowager, with an affable smile, but with the bloom on her cheeks standing out a little more vividly than usual, as the neighboring surface became paler, "probably not."

"Therefore, my good madam," said Mr. Meagles, at great pains to restrain himself, "I hope I may, without offense, ask to have no such mystifications played off upon me."

"Mamma Meagles," observed Mrs. Gowan, "your good man is incomprehensible."

Her turning to that worthy lady was an artifice to bring her into the discussion, quarrel with her, and vanquish her. Mr. Meagles interposed to prevent that consummation.

"Mother," said he, "you are inexpert, my dear, and it is not a fair match. Let me beg of you to remain quiet. Come, Mrs. Gowan, come! Let us try to be sensible; let us try to be good-natured; let us try to be fair. Don't you pity Henry, and I won't pity Pet. And don't be one-sided, my dear madam; it's not considerate, it's not kind. Don't let us say that we hope Pet will make Henry happy, or even that we hope Henry will make Pet happy"—(Mr. Meagles himself did not look happy as he spoke the words)—"but let us hope that they will make each other happy."

"Yes, sure, and there leave it, Father," said Mrs. Meagles, the kind-hearted and comfortable.

"Why, Mother, no," returned Mr. Meagles, "not exactly

there. I can't quite leave it there; I must say just half-a-dozen words more. Mrs. Gowan, I hope I am not oversensitive. I dare say I don't look it."

"Indeed you do not," said Mrs. Gowan, shaking her head and the great green fan together, for emphasis.

"Thank you, ma'am; that's well. Notwithstanding which, I feel a little—I don't want to use a strong word—now shall I say hurt?" asked Mr. Meagles, at once with frankness and moderation, and with a conciliatory appeal in his tone.

"Say what you like," answered Mrs. Gowan. "It is perfectly indifferent to me."

"No, no, don't say that," urged Mr. Meagles; "because that's not responding amicably. I feel a little hurt when I hear reference made to consequences having been foreseen, and to its being too late now, and so forth."

"*Do* you, Papa Meagles?" said Mrs. Gowan. "I am not surprised."

"Well, ma'am," reasoned Mr. Meagles; "I was in hopes you would have been at least surprised, because to hurt me willfully on so tender a subject is surely not generous."

"I am not responsible," said Mrs. Gowan, "for your conscience, you know."

Poor Mr. Meagles looked aghast with astonishment.

"If I am unluckily obliged to carry a cap about with me which is yours and fits you," pursued Mrs. Gowan, "don't blame *me* for its pattern, Papa Meagles, I beg!"

"Why, good Lord, ma'am!" Mr. Meagles broke out, "that's as much as to state—"

"Now, Papa Meagles, Papa Meagles," said Mrs. Gowan, who became extremely deliberate and prepossessing in manner whenever that gentleman became at all warm, "perhaps, to prevent confusion, I had better speak for myself than trouble your kindness to speak for me. It's as much as to state, you begin. If you please, I will finish the sentence. It is as much as to state—not that I wish to press it, or even recall it, for it is of no use now, and my only wish is to make the best of existing circumstances—that from the first to the last I always objected to this match of yours, and at a very late period yielded a most unwilling consent to it."

"Mother!" cried Mr. Meagles. "Do you hear this? Arthur! Do you hear this?"

"The room being of a convenient size," said Mrs. Gowan, looking about as she fanned herself, "and quite charmingly adapted in all respects to conversation, I should imagine that I am audible in any part of it."

Some moments passed in silence before Mr. Meagles could hold himself in his chair with sufficient security to prevent his breaking out of it at the next word he spoke. At last he said: "Ma'am, I am very unwilling to revive them, but I must remind you what my opinions and my course were, all along, on that unfortunate subject."

"Oh, my dear sir!" said Mrs. Gowan, smiling and shaking her head with accusatory intelligence; "they were well understood by me, I assure you."

"I never, ma'am," said Mr. Meagles, "knew unhappiness before that time, I never knew anxiety before that time. It was a time of such distress to me, that—" That Mr. Meagles really could say no more about it, in short, but passed his handkerchief before his face.

"I understood the whole affair," said Mrs. Gowan, composedly looking over her fan. "As you have appealed to Mr. Clennam, I may appeal to Mr. Clennam, too. He knows whether I did or not."

"I am very unwilling," said Clennam, "to take any part in this discussion, more especially because I wish to preserve the best understanding and the clearest relations with Mr. Henry Gowan. I have very strong reasons indeed for entertaining that wish. Mrs. Gowan attributed certain views of furthering the marriage to my friend here, in conversation with me before it took place, and I endeavored to undeceive her. I represented that I knew him (as I did and do) to be strenuously opposed to it, both in opinion and action."

"You see," said Mrs. Gowan, turning the palms of her hands toward Mr. Meagles, as if she were Justice herself, representing to him that he had better confess, for he had not a leg to stand on. "You see! Very good! Now, Papa and Mamma Meagles both!" Here she rose; "allow me to take the liberty of putting an end to this rather formidable controversy. I will not say another word upon its merits. I will only say that it is an additional proof of what one knows from all experience; that this kind of thing never answers—as my poor fellow himself would say, that it never pays—in one word, that it never does."

Mr. Meagles asked, What kind of thing!

"It is in vain," said Mrs. Gowan, "for people to attempt to get on together who have such extremely different antecedents, who are jumbled against each other in this accidental, matrimonial sort of way, and who can not look at the untoward circumstances which has shaken them together in the same light. It never does."

Mr. Meagles was beginning, "Permit me to say, ma'am—"

"No, don't!" returned Mrs. Gowan. "Why should you! It is an ascertained fact. It never does. I will, therefore, if you please, go my way, leaving you to yours. I shall at all times be happy to receive my poor fellow's pretty wife, and I shall always make a point of being on the most affectionate terms with her. But as to these terms, semi-family and semi-stranger, semi-goring and semi-boring, they form a state of things quite amusing in its impracticability. I assure you it never does."

The Dowager here made a smiling obeisance, rather to the room than to any one in it, and therewith took a final farewell of Papa and Mamma Meagles. Clennam stepped forward to hand her to the Pill-Box which was at the service of all the Pills in Hampton Court Palace, and she got into that vehicle with distinguished serenity and was driven away.

Thenceforth the Dowager with a light and careless humor often recounted to her particular acquaintance how, after a hard trial, she had found it impossible to know those people who belonged to Henry's wife, and who had made that desperate set to catch him; whether she had come to the conclusion beforehand that to get rid of them would give her favorite pretense a better air, might save her some occasional inconvenience, and could risk no loss, (the pretty creature being fast married, and her father devoted to her,) was best known to herself. Though this history has its opinion on that point, too, and decidedly in the affirmative.

CHAPTER XLV.

APPEARANCE AND DISAPPEARANCE.

"ARTHUR, my dear boy," said Mr. Meagles, on the evening of the following day, "Mother and I have been talking this over, and we don't feel comfortable in remaining as we are. That elegant connection of ours—that dear lady who was here yesterday—"

"I understand," said Arthur.

"Even that affable and condescending ornament of society," pursued Mr. Meagles, "may misrepresent us, we are afraid. We could bear a great deal, Arthur, for her sake; but we think we would rather not submit to that, if it was all the same to her."

"Good," said Arthur. "Go on."

"You see," proceeded Mr. Meagles, "it might put us wrong with our son-in-law, it might even put us wrong with our daughter, and it might lead to a great deal of domestic trouble. You see, don't you?"

"Yes, indeed," returned Arthur, "there is much reason in what you say." He had glanced at Mrs. Meagles, who was always on the good and sensible side, and a petition had shone out of her honest face that he would support Mr. Meagles in his present inclinings.

"So we are very much disposed, are Mother and I," said Mr. Meagles, "to pack up bag and baggage, and go among the Allongers and Marshongers once more. I mean, we are very much disposed to be off; strike right through France into Italy, and see our Pet."

"And I don't think," replied Arthur, touched by the motherly anticipation in the bright face of Mrs. Meagles (she must have been very like her daughter once), "that you could do better. And if you ask me for my advice, it is that you set off to-morrow."

"Is it really, though?" said Mr. Meagles. "Mother, this is being backed in an idea!"

Mother, with a look which thanked Clenman in a manner very agreeable to him, answered that it was indeed.

"The fact is, besides, Arthur," said Mr. Meagles, the old cloud coming over his face, "that my son-in-law is already in debt again, and that I suppose I must clear him again. It may be as well, even on this account, that I should step over there, and look him up in a friendly way. Then again, here's Mother foolishly anxious (and yet naturally, too) about Pet's state of health, and that she should not be left to feel lonesome at the present time. It's undeniably a long way off, Arthur, and a strange place for the poor love under all the circumstances. Let her be as well cared for as any lady in that land, still it is a long way off. Just as Home is Home though it's never so homely, why you see," said Mr. Meagles, adding a new version to the proverb, "Rome is Rome though it's never so Romely."

"All perfectly true," observed Arthur, "and all sufficient reasons for going."

"I am glad you think so; it decides me. Mother, my dear, you may get ready. We have lost our pleasant interpreter (she spoke three foreign languages beautifully, Arthur; you have heard her many a time), and you must pull me through it, Mother, as well as you can. I require a deal of pulling through, Arthur," said Mr. Meagles, shaking his head, "a deal of pulling through. I stick at every thing beyond a noun-substantive—and I stick at him, if he's at all a tight one."

"Now I think of it," returned Clennam, "there's Cavalletto. He shall go with you if you like. I could not afford to lose him, but you will bring him safe back."

"Well! I am much obliged to you, my boy," said Mr. Meagles, turning it over, "but I think not. No, I think I'll just be pulled through by Mother. Caval-looro (I stick at his very name to start with, and it sounds like the chorus to a comic song), is so necessary to you, that I don't like the thought of taking him away. More than that, there's no saying when we may come home again; and it would never do to take him away for an indefinite time. The cottage is not what it was. It only holds two little people less than it ever did, Pet, and her poor unfortunate maid, Tattycoram; but it seems empty now. Once out of it, there's no knowing when we may come back to it. No, Arthur, I'll be pulled through by Mother."

They would do best by themselves, perhaps, after all, Clennam thought, therefore did not press his proposal.

"If you would come down and stay here for a change, when it wouldn't trouble you," Mr. Meagles resumed, "I should be glad to think—and so would Mother, too, I know—that you were brightening up the old place with a bit of life it was used to when it was full, and that the Babies on the wall there, had a kind eye upon them sometimes. You so belong to the spot, and to them, Arthur; and we should every one of us have been so happy if it had fallen out—but, let us see—how's the weather for traveling now?"—Mr. Meagles broke off, cleared his throat, and got up to look out of window.

They agreed that the weather was of high promise, and Clennam kept the tack in that safe direction until it had become easy again, when he gently diverted it to Henry Gowan, and his quick sense and agreeable qualities when he was delicately dealt with; he likewise dwelt on the indisputable affection he entertained for his wife. Clennam did not fail of his effect upon good Mr. Meagles, whom these commendations greatly cheered, and who took Mother to witness that the single and cordial desire of his heart in reference to their daughter's husband, was harmoniously to exchange friendship for friendship, and to confide and be confided in. Within a few hours the cottage furniture began to be wrapped up for preservation in the family absence—or, as Mr. Meagles expressed it, the house began to put its hair in papers—and within a few days Father and Mother were gone, Mrs. Tickit and Dr. Buchan were posted, as of yore, behind the parlor blind, and Arthur's solitary feet were rustling among the dry fallen leaves in the garden walks.

As he had a liking for the spot, he seldom let a week pass without paying it a visit. Sometimes, he went down alone from Saturday to Monday; sometimes, his partner accompanied him; sometimes, he merely strolled for an hour or two about the house and garden, saw that all was right, and returned to London again. At all times and under all circumstances Mrs. Tickit, with her dark row of curls and Dr. Buchan, sat in the parlor window, looking out for the family return.

On one of his visits Mrs. Tickit received him with the words, "I have something to tell you, Mr. Clennam, that will surprise you." So surprising was the something in question, that it actually brought Mrs. Tickit out of the parlor window, and produced her in the garden walk when Clennam went in at the gate on its being opened for him.

"What is it, Mrs. Tickit?" said he.

"Sir," returned that faithful housekeeper, having taken him into the parlor and closed the door; "if ever I saw the led away and deluded child in my life, I saw her identically in the dusk of yesterday evening."

"You don't mean Tatty—"

"Coram, yes I do!" quoth Mrs. Tickit, clearing the disclosure at a leaf.

"Where?"

"Mr. Clennam," returned Mrs. Tickit, "I was a little heavy in my eyes, being that I was waiting longer than customary for my cup of tea which was then preparing by Mary Jane. I was not sleeping, nor what a person would term correctly, dozing. I was more what a person would strictly call watching with my eyes shut."

Without entering upon an inquiry into this curious abnormal condition, Clennam said, "Exactly. Well?"

"Well, sir," proceeded Mrs. Tickit, "I was thinking of one thing and thinking of another. Just as you yourself might. Just as any body might."

"Precisely so," said Clennam. "Well?"

"And when I do think of one thing and do think of another," pursued Mrs. Tickit, "I hardly need to tell you, Mr. Clennam, that I think of the family. Because, dear me! a person's thoughts"—Mrs. Tickit said this with an argumentative and philosophic air—"however they may stray will go more or less on what is uppermost in their minds. They *will* do it, sir, and a person can't prevent them."

Arthur subscribed to this discovery with an emphatic nod.

"You find it so yourself, sir, I'll be bold to say," said Mrs. Tickit, "and we all find it so. It an't our stations in life that changes us, Mr. Clennam; thoughts is free! As I was saying, I was thinking of one thing, and thinking of another, and thinking very much of the family. Not of the family in the present times only, but in the past times too. For when a person does begin thinking of one thing and thinking of another, in that manner as it's getting dark, what I say is that all times seem to be present, and a person must get out of that state and consider before they can say which is which."

He nodded again; afraid to utter a word, lest it should present any new opening to Mrs. Tickit's conversational powers.

"In consequence of which," said Mrs. Tickit, "when I quivered my eyes and saw her actual form and figure looking in at the gate, I let them close again without so much as starting, for that actual form and figure came so pat to the time when it belonged to the house as much as mine or your own, that I never thought at the moment of its having gone away. But, sir, when I quivered my eyes again and saw that it wasn't there, then it all flooded upon me with a fright, and I jumped up."

"You ran out directly?" said Clennam.

"I ran out," assented Mrs. Tickit, "as fast as ever my feet would carry me; and if you'll credit it, Mr. Clennam, there wasn't in the whole shining heavens, no not so much as a finger of that young woman."

Passing over the absence from the firmament of this novel constellation, Arthur inquired of Mrs. Tickit if she herself went beyond the gate?

"Went to and fro, and high and low," said Mrs. Tickit, "and saw no sign of her!"

He then asked Mrs. Tickit how long a space of time she supposed there might have been between the two sets of ocular quiverings she had experienced? Mrs. Tickit, though minutely circumstantial in her reply, had no settled opinion between five seconds and ten minutes. She was so plainly at sea on this point of the case, and had so clearly been startled out of slumber, that Clennam was much disposed to regard the appearance as a dream. Without hurting Mrs. Tickit's feelings with that improbable solution of her mystery, he took it away from the cottage with him; and probably would have retained it ever afterward, if a circumstance had not soon happened to change his opinion.

He was passing at nightfall along the Strand, and the lamp-lighter was going on before him, under whose hand the street-lamps, blurred by the foggy air, burst out one after another, like so many blazing sunflowers coming into full-blow all at once; when a stoppage on the pavement, caused by a train of coal-wagons toiling up from the wharves at the river-side, brought him to a stand-still. He had been walking quickly, and going with some current of thought, and the sudden check given to both operations caused him to look freshly about him, as people under such circumstances usually do.

Immediately, he saw in advance—a few people intervening, but still so near to him that he could have touched them by stretching out his arm—Tattycoram and a strange man of a very remarkable appearance: a swaggering man, with a high nose, and black mustache as false in its color as his eyes were false in their expression, who wore his heavy cloak with the air of a foreigner. His dress and general appearance were those of a man on travel, and he seemed to have very recently joined the girl. In bending down (being much taller than she was), listening to whatever she said to him, he looked over his shoulder with the suspicious glance of one who was not unused to be mistrustful that his footsteps were dogged. It was then that Clennam saw his face, as his eyes lowered on the people behind him in the aggregate, without particularly resting on Clennam's face or any other.

He had scarcely turned his head about again, and it was still bent down, listening to the girl, when the stoppage ceased, and the obstructed stream of people flowed on. Still bending his head and listening to the girl, he went on at her side, and Clennam followed them, resolved to play this unexpected play out, and see where they went to.

He had hardly made the determination (though he was not long about it), when he was again as suddenly brought up as he had been by the stoppage. They turned short into the Adelphi—the girl evidently leading—and went straight on, as if they were going to the terrace which overhangs the river.

There is always, to this day, a sudden pause in that place to the roar of the great thoroughfare. The many sounds become so deadened that the change is like putting cotton in the ears, or having the head thickly muffled. At that time the contrast was far greater; there being no small steamboats on the river, no landing places but slippery stairs and foot-causeways, no railroad on the opposite bank, no hanging-bridge or fish-market near at hand, no traffic on the nearest bridge of stone, nothing moving on the stream but watermen's wherries and coal lighters. Long and broad black tiers of the latter, moored fast in the mud as if they were never to move again, made the shore funereal and silent after dark, and kept what little water movement there was far out toward mid-stream. At any hour later than sunset, and not least at that hour when most of the people who have any thing to eat at home are going home to eat it, and when most of those who have nothing have hardly yet slunk out to beg or steal, it was a deserted place and looked on a deserted scene.

Such was the hour when Clennam stopped at the corner, observing the girl and the strange man as they went down the street. The man's footsteps were so noisy on the echoing stones that he was unwilling to add the sound of his own. But when they had passed the turning and were in the darkness of the dark corner leading to the terrace, he made after them with such indifferent appearance of being a casual passenger on his way, as he could assume.

When he rounded the dark corner, they were walking along the terrace, toward a figure which was coming toward them. If he had seen it by itself, under such conditions of gas-lamp, mist, and distance, he might not have known it at first sight; but with the figure of the girl to prompt him, he at once recognized Miss Wade.

He stopped at the corner, seeming to look expectantly up the street, as if he had made an appointment with some one to meet him there; but kept a careful eye on the three. When they came together, the man took off his hat, and made Miss Wade a bow. The girl appeared to say a few words as though she presented him, or accounted for his being late, or early, or what not, and then fell a pace or so behind by herself. Miss

Wade and the man then began to walk up and down; the man having the appearance of being extremely courteous and complimentary in his manner; Miss Wade having the appearance of being extremely haughty.

When they came down to the corner and turned, she was saying: "If I pinch myself for it, that is my business. Confine yourself to yours, and ask me no questions."

"By Heaven, ma'am!" he replied, making her another bow, "it was my profound respect for the strength of your character, and my admiration of your beauty."

"I want neither the one nor the other from any one," said she, "and certainly not from you of all creatures. Go on with your report."

"Am I pardoned?" he asked, with an air of half-abashed gallantry.

"You are paid," she said, disdainfully, "and that is all you want."

Whether the girl hung behind because she was not to hear the business, or as already knowing enough about it, Clennam could not determine. They turned and she turned. She looked away at the river, as she walked with her hands folded before her, and that was all he could make of her without showing his face. There happened, by good fortune, to be a lounger really waiting for some one, and he sometimes looked over the railing at the water, and sometimes came to the dark corner and looked up the street, rendering Arthur less conspicuous.

When Miss Wade and the man came back again, she was saying, "You must wait until to-morrow."

"A thousand pardons!" he returned. "My faith! Then it's not convenient to-night?"

"No. I must get it before I can give it to you."

She stopped in the roadway, as if to put an end to the conference. He of course stopped too. And the girl stopped.

"It's a little inconvenient," said the man. "A little. But, Holy Blue! that's nothing in such a service. I am without money to-night by chance. I *have* a good banker in this city—ha, ha!—but I would not wish to draw upon the house until the time when I shall draw for a round sum."

"Harriet," said Miss Wade, "arrange with him—this gentleman here—for sending him some money to-morrow." She said it with a slur of the word gentleman which was more contemptuous than any emphasis, and walked slowly on.

The man bent his head again, and the girl spoke to him as they both followed her. Clennam ventured to look at the girl as they moved away. He could note that her rich black eyes were fastened upon the man with a scrutinizing expression, and that she kept at a little distance from him as they walked side by side to the further end of the terrace.

A loud and altered clank upon the pavement warned him, before he could discern what was passing there, that the man was coming back alone. Clennam lounged into the road, toward the railing, and the man passed at a quick swing, with the end of his cloak thrown over his shoulder, singing a scrap of a French song.

The whole vista had no one in it now but himself. The lounger had lounged out of view, and Miss Wade and Tattycoram were gone. More than ever bent on seeing what became of them, and on having some information to give his good friend Mr. Meagles, he went out at the further end of the terrace, looking cautiously about him. He rightly judged that, at first at all events, they would go in a contrary direction from their late companion. He soon saw them in a neighboring by-street, which was not a thoroughfare, evidently allowing time for the man getting well out of their way. They walked leisurely arm-in-arm down one side of the street, and returned upon the opposite side. When they came back to the street-corner, they changed their pace for the pace of people with an object and a distance before them, and walked steadily away. Clennam, no less steadily, kept them in view.

They crossed the Strand, and passed through Covent Garden (under the windows of his old lodging, where dear Little Dorrit had come that night), and slanted away north-east, until they passed the great building whence Tattycoram derived her name, and turned into the Gray's Inn Road. Clennam was quite at home here, in sight of Flora, not to mention the Patriarch and Pancks, and kept them in sight with ease. He was beginning to wonder where they might be going next, when that wonder was lost in the greater wonder with which he saw them turn into the Patriarchal street. That wonder was in its turn swallowed up in the greater wonder with which he saw them stop at the Patriarchal door. A low double knock at the bright brass knocker, a gleam of light into the road from the opened door, a brief pause for inquiry and answer, and the door was shut, and they were housed.

After looking at the surrounding objects for assurance that he was not in a dream, and after pacing a little while before the house, Arthur knocked at the door. It was opened by the usual maid-servant, and she showed him up at once, with her usual alacrity, to Flora's sitting-room.

There was no one with Flora but Mr. F.'s Aunt, which respectable gentlewoman, basking in a balmy atmosphere of tea and toast, was ensconced in an easy chair by the fireside, with a little table at her elbow, and a clean white handkerchief spread over her lap, on which two pieces of toast at that moment awaited consumption. Bending over a steaming vessel of tea, and looking through steam, and breathing forth steam, like a malignant Chinese enchantress engaged in the performance of unholy rites, Mr. F.'s Aunt put down the great tea-cup, and exclaimed, "Drat him, if he an't come back again!"

It would seem from the foregoing exclamation that this uncompromising relative of the lamented Mr. F., measuring time by the acuteness of her sensations, and not by the clock, supposed Clennam to have lately gone away; whereas at least a quarter of a year had elapsed since he had had the temerity to present himself before her.

"My goodness Arthur!" cried Flora, rising to give him a cordial reception, "Doyce and Clennam what a start and a surprise for though not far from the machinery and foundry business and surely might be taken sometimes if at no other time about mid-day when a glass of sherry and a humble sandwich of whatever cold meat in the larder might not come amiss nor taste the worse for being from it you know you buy it somewhere and wherever bought a profit must be made or they would never keep the place it stands to reason without a motive still never seen and learned now not to be expected, for as Mr. F. himself said if seeing is believing not seeing is believing too and when you don't see you may fully believe you're not remem-

RIGOUR OF MR. F'S AUNT.

bered, not that I expect you Arthur Doyce and Clennam to remember me why should I for the days are gone but bring another tea-cup here directly and tell her fresh toast and pray sit near the fire."

Arthur was in the greatest anxiety to explain the object of his visit; but was put off for the moment, in spite of himself, by what he understood of the reproachful purport of these words, and by the genuine pleasure she testified in seeing him.

"And now pray tell me something all you know," said Flora, drawing her chair near to his, "about the good dear quiet little thing, and all the changes of her fortunes carriage people now no doubt and horses without number most romantic! a coat-of-arms of course and wild beasts on their hind legs showing it as if it was a copy they had done with mouths from ear to ear good gracious! and has she her health which is the first consideration after all, for what is wealth without it Mr. F. himself so often saying when his twinges came that sixpence a day and find yourself and no gout so much preferable, not that he could have lived on any thing like it being the last man or that the precious little thing though far too familiar an expression now had any tendency of that sort much too slight and small but looked so fragile bless her!"

Mr. F.'s Aunt, who had eaten a piece of toast down to the crust, here solemnly handed the crust to Flora, who ate it for her as a matter of business. Mr. F.'s Aunt then moistened her ten fingers in slow succession at her lips, and wiped them in exactly the same order on the white handkerchief; then took the other piece of toast, and fell to work upon it. While pursuing this routine, she looked fixedly at Clennam with an expression of such intense severity that he felt obliged to look at her in return, against his personal inclinations.

"She is in Italy, with all her family, Flora," he said, when the dread lady was occupied again.

"In Italy, really," said Flora, "with the grapes and figs growing every where and lava necklaces and bracelets too that land of poetry with burning mountains picturesque beyond belief though if the organ-boys come away from the neighborhood not to be scorched nobody can wonder being so young and bringing their white mice with them most humane! and is she really in that favored land with nothing but blue about her and dying gladiators and Belvideras though Mr. F. himself did not believe for his objection when in spirits was that the images could not be true there being no medium between expensive quantities of linen badly got up and all in creases and none at all, which certainly does not seem probable though perhaps in consequence of the extremes of rich and poor, which may account for it."

Arthur tried to edge a word in, but Flora hurried on again.

"Venice Preserved too," said she, "I think you have been there is it well or ill preserved for people differ so, and Maccaroni if they really eat it like the conjurers why not cut it shorter, you are acquainted Arthur—dear Doyce and Clennam at least not dear and most assuredly not Doyce for I have not the pleasure but pray excuse me—acquainted I believe with Mantua, what *has* it got to do with mantua-making for I never have been able to conceive?"

"I believe there is no connection, Flora, between the two—" Arthur was beginning, when she caught him up again.

"Upon your word no isn't there I never did but that's like me I run away with an idea and having none to spare I keep it, alas there was a time dear Arthur that is to say decidedly not dear nor Arthur neither but you understand me when one bright idea gilded the what's-his-name horizon of et cetera but it is darkly clouded now and all is over."

Arthur's increasing wish to speak of something very different was by this time so plainly written on his face, that Flora stopped in the beginning of a tender look and asked him what it was.

"I have the greatest desire, Flora, to speak to some one who is now in this house—with Mr. Casby no doubt—some one whom I saw come in, and who, in a misguided and deplorable way, has deserted the house of a friend of mine."

"Papa sees so many and such odd people," said Flora, rising, "that I shouldn't venture to go down for any one but you Arthur, but for you I would willingly go down in a diving-bell much more a dining-room and will come back directly if you'll mind and at the same time *not* mind Mr. F.'s Aunt while I'm gone."

With those words and a parting glance, Flora bustled out,

leaving Clennam under dreadful apprehensions of his terrible charge.

The first variation which manifested itself in Mr. F.'s Aunt's demeanor when she had finished her piece of toast, was a loud and prolonged sniff, sustained with such uncommon power that it rendered her whole form rigid. Finding it impossible to avoid construing this demonstration into a defiance of himself, Clennam looked plaintively at the excellent though prejudiced lady from whom it emanated, in the hope that she might be disarmed by a meek submission.

"None of your eyes at me," said Mr. F.'s Aunt, shivering with hostility. "Take that."

"That" was the crust of the piece of toast. Clennam accepted the boon with a look of gratitude, and held it in his hand under the pressure of a little embarrassment, which was not relieved when Mr. F.'s Aunt, elevating her voice into a cry of considerable power, exclaimed, "He's a proud stomach, this chap! He's too proud a chap to eat it!" and, coming out of her chair, shook her venerable fist so very close to his nose as to tickle the surface. But for the timely return of Flora to find him in this difficult situation, further consequences might have ensued. Flora, without the least discomposure or surprise, but congratulating the old lady in an approving manner on being "very lively to-night," handed her back to her chair.

"He's a proud stomach, this chap," said Mr. F.'s relation, on being reseated. "Give him a meal of chaff!"

"Oh! I don't think he would like that, aunt," returned Flora.

"Give him a feed of chaff, I tell you," said Mr. F.'s Aunt, glaring round Flora on her enemy. "It's the only thing for a proud stomach. Let him eat it up every morsel. Drat him, give him a meal of chaff!"

Under a general pretense of keeping him to this refreshment, Flora got him out on the stair-case; Mr. F.'s Aunt even then constantly reiterating, with inexpressible bitterness, that he was "a chap," and had "a proud stomach," and over and over again insisting on that equine provision being made for him which she had already so strongly recommended.

"Such an inconvenient staircase, and so many corner stairs,

Arthur," whispered Flora, "would you object to putting your arm round me, under my pelerine?"

With a sense of going down stairs in a highly ridiculous manner, Clennam descended in the required attitude, and only released his fair burden at the dining-room door; indeed, even there she was rather difficult to get rid of, remaining in his embrace to murmur, "Arthur, for mercy's sake, don't breathe it to papa!"

She accompanied Arthur into the room, where the Patriarch sat alone, with his list shoes on the fender, twirling his thumbs as if he had never left off. The youthful Patriarch, aged ten, looked out of his picture-frame above him, with no calmer air. Both smooth heads were alike beaming, blundering, and bumpy.

"Mr. Clennam, I am glad to see you. I hope you are well, sir, I hope you are well. Please to sit down, please to sit down."

"I had hoped, sir," said Clennam, doing so, and looking round with a face of extreme disappointment, "not to find you alone."

"Ah, indeed?" said the Patriarch, sweetly, "ah, indeed?"

"I told you so, you know, papa," cried Flora.

"Ah, to be sure!" returned the Patriarch. "Yes, just so. Ah, to be sure!"

"Pray, sir," demanded Clennam, anxiously, "is Miss Wade gone?"

"Miss ——? Oh, you call her Wade," returned Mr. Casby. "Highly proper."

Arthur quickly returned, "What do you call her, then?"

"Wade," said Mr. Casby. "Oh, always Wade."

After looking at the philanthropic visage, and the long silky white hair for a few seconds, during which Mr. Casby twirled his thumbs, and smiled at the fire as if he were benevolently wishing it to burn him that he might forgive it, Arthur began:

"I beg your pardon, Mr. Casby—"

"Not so, not so," said the Patriarch, "not at all."

"—But Miss Wade had an attendant with her—a young woman brought up by friends of mine, over whom her influence is not considered very salutary, and to whom I should be glad to have the opportunity of giving the assurance that she has not yet forfeited the interest of those protectors or lost them."

"Truly, truly ?" returned the Patriarch.

"Will you therefore be so good as to give me the address of Miss Wade ?"

"Dear, dear, dear !" said the Patriarch, "how very unfortunate ! If you had only sent in to me when they were here ! I observed the young woman, Mr. Clennam. A fine, full-colored young woman, Mr. Clennam, with very dark hair and very dark eyes. If I mistake not, if I mistake not ?"

Arthur assented, and said once more with new expression, "If you will be so good as to give me the address."

"Dear, dear, dear !" exclaimed the Patriarch, in sweet regret. "Tut, tut, tut ! what a pity, what a pity ! I have no address, sir. She mostly lives abroad, Mr. Clennam; she has done so for some years, and she is (if I may say so of a fellow-creature and a lady) fitful and uncertain to a fault, Mr. Clennam. I may not see her again for a long, long time. I may never see her again. What a pity, what a pity !"

Clennam saw, now, that he had as much hope of getting assistance out of the Portrait as out of the Patriarch, but he said, nevertheless :

"Mr. Casby, could you, for the satisfaction of my friends, and under any obligation of secrecy that you may consider it your duty to impose, give me any information at all touching Miss Wade ? I have seen her abroad, and I have seen her at home, but I know nothing of her. Could you give me any account of her whatever ?"

"None," returned the Patriarch, shaking his big head with his utmost benevolence. "None at all. Dear, dear, dear ! What a real pity that she staid so short a time, and you delayed ! As confidential agency business, I have occasionally paid this lady money ; but what satisfaction is it to you, sir, to know that ?"

"Truly, none at all," said Clennam.

"Truly," assented the Patriarch, with a shining love of all his species as he philanthropically smiled at the fire, "none at all, sir. You hit the wise answer, Mr. Clennam. Truly, none at all."

His turning of his smooth thumbs over one another as he sat there, was so typical to Clennam of the way in which he would make the subject revolve if it were pursued, never showing any new part of it nor allowing it to make the smallest advance, that it did much to help to convince him of his labor having been in vain. He might have taken any time to think about it, for Mr. Casby, well accustomed to get on any where by leaving every thing to his bumps and his white hair, knew his strength to lie in silence. So there Casby sat, twirling and twirling, and making his great polished head and forehead look as Christian in every knob as if he had got baptismal water on the brain.

With this hopeless spectacle before him, Arthur had risen to go, when from the inner Dock where the good ship Pancks was hove down when out in no cruising ground, the noise was heard of that steamer laboring toward them. It struck Arthur that the noise began demonstratively far off, as though Mr. Pancks sought to impress on any one who might happen to think about it, that he was working on from out of hearing.

Mr. Pancks and he shook hands, and the former brought his employer a letter or two to sign. Mr. Pancks in shaking hands merely scratched his eyebrow with his left forefinger and snorted once, but Clennam, who understood him better now than of old, comprehended that he had almost done for the evening, and wished to say a word to him outside. Therefore, when he had taken his leave of Mr. Casby, and (which was a more difficult process) of Flora, he sauntered in the neighborhood on Mr. Pancks' line of road.

He had waited but a short time when Mr. Pancks appeared. Mr. Pancks shaking hands again with another expressive snort, and taking off his hat to put his hair up, Arthur thought he received his cue to speak to him as one who knew pretty well what had just now passed. Therefore he said, without any preface,

"I suppose they were really gone, Pancks?"

"Yes," replied Pancks. "They were really gone."

"Does he know where to find that lady?"

"Can't say. I should think so."

Mr. Pancks did not? No, Mr. Pancks did not. Did Mr. Pancks know any thing about her?

"I expect," rejoined the worthy, evading Clennam's question; "I know as much about her as she knows about herself. She is somebody's child—any body's—nobody's. Put her in a room in London here with any six people old enough to be her parents, and her parents may be there for any thing she knows. They may be in any house she sees, they may be in any church-yard she passes, she may run against 'em in any street, she may make chance acquaintances of 'em at any time, and never know it. She knows nothing about 'em. She knows nothing about any relative whatever. Never did. Never will."

"Mr. Casby could enlighten her, perhaps?"

"Maybe," said Pancks. "I expect so, but don't know. He has long had money (not overmuch as I make out) in trust to dole out to her when she can't do without it. Sometimes she's proud and won't touch it; sometimes she's so poor that she must have it. She writhes under her life. A woman more angry, passionate, reckless, and revengeful never lived. She came for money to-night. Said she had peculiar occasion for it."

"I think," observed Clennam, musing, "I by chance know what occasion—I mean into whose pocket the money is to go."

"Indeed?" said Pancks. "If it's a compact, I'd recommend that party to be exact in it. I wouldn't trust myself to that woman, young and handsome as she is, if I had wronged her; no, not for twice my proprietor's money! Unless," Pancks added as a saving clause, "I had a lingering illness on me, and wanted to get it over."

Arthur, hurriedly reviewing his own observation of her, found it to tally pretty nearly with Mr. Pancks' view.

"The wonder is to me," pursued Pancks, "that she has never done for my proprietor, as the only person connected with her story she can lay hold of. Mentioning that, I may tell you, between ourselves, that I am sometimes tempted to do for him myself."

Arthur started, and said, "Good Heaven, Pancks, don't say that!"

"Understand me," said Pancks, extending five cropped, coally finger-nails on Arthur's arm; "I don't mean, cut his throat. But, by all that's precious, if he goes too far, I'll cut his hair!"

Having exhibited himself in the new light of enunciating this tremendous threat, Mr. Pancks, with a countenance of grave import, snorted several times and steamed away.

CHAPTER XLVI.

THE DREAMS OF MRS. FLINTWINCH THICKEN.

THE shady waiting-rooms of the Circumlocution Office, where he passed a good deal of time in company with various troublesome Convicts who were under sentence to be broken on that wheel, had afforded Arthur Clennam ample leisure, in three or four successive days, to exhaust the subject of his late glimpse of Miss Wade and Tattycoram. He had been able to make no more of it and no less of it, and in this unsatisfactory condition he was fain to leave it.

During this space he had not been to his mother's dismal old house. One of his customary evenings for repairing thither now coming round, he left his dwelling and his partner at nearly nine o'clock, and slowly walked in the direction of that grim home of his youth.

It always affected his imagination as wrathful, mysterious, and sad; and his imagination was sufficiently impressible to see the whole neighborhood under some tinge of its dark shadow. As he went along, upon a dreary night, the dim streets by which he went seemed all depositories of oppressive secrets. The deserted counting-houses, with their secrets of books and papers locked up in chests and safes; the banking-houses, with their secrets of strong rooms and wells, the keys of which were in a very few secret pockets and a very few secret breasts; the secrets of all the dispersed grinders in the vast mill—among whom there were, doubtless, plunderers, forgers, trust-betrayers of many sorts, whom the light of any day that dawned might reveal; he could have fancied that these things in hiding imparted a heaviness to the air. The shadow thickening and thickening as he approached its source, he thought of the secrets of the lonely church-vaults where the people who had hoarded and secreted in iron coffers were in their turn similarly hoarded, not yet at rest from doing harm; and then of the secrets of the river, as it rolled its turbid tide between two frowning wildernesses of secrets—far extending, thick and dense, for many miles, and warding off the free air and the free country swept by winds and wings of birds.

The shadow still darkening as he drew near the house, the melancholy room which his father had once occupied, picture-haunted by the appeal he had himself seen fade away with him when there was no other watcher by the bed, arose before his mind. Its close air was secret. The gloom, and must, and dust of the whole tenement, were secret. At the heart of it his mother presided, inflexible of face, indomitable of will, firmly holding all the secrets of her own and his father's life, and austerely opposing herself, front to front, to the great final secret of all life.

He had turned into the narrow and steep street from which the court or inclosure wherein the house stood opened, when another footstep turned into it behind him, and so close upon his own, that he was jostled to the wall. As his mind was teeming with these thoughts the encounter took him altogether unprepared, so that the other passenger had had time to say, boisterously, "Pardon! Not my fault!" and to pass on before the instant had elapsed which was requisite to his recovery of the realities about him.

When that moment had flashed away, he saw that the man striding on before him was the man who had been so much in his mind during the last few days. It was no casual resemblance, helped out by the force of the impression the man had made upon him. It was the man—the man he had followed in company with the girl, and whom he had overheard talking to Miss Wade.

The street was a sharp descent, and was crooked too, and the man (who, although not drunk, had the air of being flushed with some strong drink) went down it so fast that Clennam lost him as he looked at him. With no defined intention of following him again, but with an impulse to keep the figure in view a little longer, Clennam quickened his pace to pass the twist in the street which hid him from his sight. Turning it, he saw the man no more.

Standing now, close to the gateway of his mother's house, he looked down the street; but it was empty. There was no projecting shadow large enough to obscure the man; there was no turning near that he could have taken; nor had there been any audible sound of the opening and closing of a door. Nevertheless, he concluded that the man must have had a key in his hand, and must have opened one of the many house-doors and gone in.

Ruminating on this strange chance and strange glimpse, he turned into the court-yard. As he looked by mere habit toward the feebly-lighted windows of his mother's room, his eyes encountered the figure he had just lost, standing against the iron railings of the little waste enclosure looking up at those windows and laughing to himself. Some of the many vagrant cats who were always prowling about there by night, and who had taken fright at him, appeared to have stopped when he had stopped, and were looking at him with eyes by no means unlike his own from tops of walls and porches, and other safe points of pause. He had only halted for a moment to amuse himself thus; he immediately went forward, throwing the end of his cloak off his shoulder as he went, ascended the unevenly-sunken steps, and knocked a sounding knock at the door.

Clennam's amazement was not so absorbing but that he took his resolution without any incertitude. He went up to the door too, and ascended the steps too. His friend looked at him with a braggart air and sang to himself,

"Who passes by this road so late?
Compagnon de la Majolaine;
Who passes by this road so late?
Always gay!"

After which he knocked again.

"You are impatient, sir," said Arthur.

"I am, sir. Death of my life, sir," returned the stranger, "it's my character to be impatient."

The sound of Mistress Affery cautiously chaining the door before she opened it, caused them both to look that way. Affery opened it a very little, with a flaring candle in her hands, and asked who was that at that time of night with that knock? "Why, Arthur," she added, with astonishment, seeing him first.

"Not you, sure? Ah, Lord save us! No," she cried out, seeing the other. "Him again!"

"It's true! Ha, ha! Him again, dear Mrs. Flintwinch," cried the stranger. "Open the door, and let me take my dear friend Jeremiah to my arms! Open the door, and let me hasten myself to embrace my Flintwinch!"

"He's not at home," said Affery.

"Fetch him!" cried the stranger. "Fetch my Flintwinch! Tell him that it is his old Blandois, who comes from arriving in England; tell him that it is his little boy who is here, his cabbage, his well-beloved! Open the door, beautiful Mrs. Flintwinch, and in the mean time let me pass up stairs, to present my compliments—homage of Blandois—to my lady!—My lady lives always! It is well. Open then!"

To Arthur's increased surprise, Mistress Affery, opening her eyes wide at himself, as if in warning that this was not a gentleman for him to interfere with, drew back the chain, and opened the door. The stranger, without any ceremony, walked into the hall, leaving Arthur to follow him.

"Dispatch then! Achieve then! Bring my Flintwinch! Announce me to my lady!" cried the stranger, clanking about the stone floor.

"Pray tell me, Affery," said Arthur, aloud and sternly, as he surveyed him from head to foot with unutterable indignation, "who is this gentleman?"

"Pray tell me, Affery," the stranger repeated in his turn, "who—ha, ha, ha!—who is this gentleman?"

The voice of Mrs. Clennam opportunely called from her chamber above, "Affery, let them both come up. Arthur, come straight to me!"

"Arthur?" exclaimed Blandois, taking off his hat at arm's length, and bringing his heels together from a great stride in making him a flourishing bow. "The son of my lady? I am the all-devoted of the son of my lady."

Arthur looked at him again in no more flattering manner than before, and, turning on his heel without acknowledgment, went up stairs. The visitor followed him up stairs. Mistress Affery took the key from behind the door, and deftly slipped out to fetch her lord.

A by-stander, informed of the previous appearance of Monsieur Blandois in that room, would have observed a difference in Mrs. Clennam's present reception of him. Her face was not one to betray it, and her suppressed manner, and her set voice were equally under her control. It wholly consisted in her never taking her eyes off his face from the moment of his entrance, and in her twice or thrice, when he was becoming noisy, swaying herself a very little forward in the chair in which she sat upright, with her hands immovable upon its elbows; as if she gave him the assurance that he should be presently heard at any length he would. Arthur did not fail to observe this; though the difference between the present occasion and the former was not within his power of observation.

"Madame," said Blandois, "do me the honor to present me to Monsieur, your son. It appears to me, madame, that Monsieur, your son, is disposed to complain of me. He is not polite."

"Sir," said Arthur, striking in expeditiously, "whoever you are, and however you come to be here, if I were the master of this house I would lose no time in placing you on the outside of it."

"But you are not," said his mother, without looking at him. "Unfortunately, for the gratification of your unreasonable temper, you are not the master, Arthur."

"I make no claim to be, mother. If I object to this person's manner of conducting himself here, and object to it so much, that if I had any authority here I certainly would not suffer him to remain a minute, I object on your account, and in your name."

"In the case of objection being necessary," she returned, "I could object for myself. And of course I should."

The subject of their dispute, who had seated himself, laughed loud, and rapped his leg with his hand.

"You have no right," said Mrs. Clennam, always intent on Blandois, however directly she addressed her son, "to speak to the prejudice of any gentleman (and least of all a gentleman from another country) because he does not conform to your standard, or square his behavior by your rules. It is possible that the gentleman may, on similar grounds, object to you."

"I hope so," returned Arthur. "I sincerely hope so."

"The gentleman," pursued Mrs. Clennam, "on a former occasion brought a letter of recommendation to us from highly esteemed and responsible correspondents. I am perfectly unacquainted with the gentleman's object in coming here at present; I am entirely ignorant of it, and can not be supposed likely to be able to form the remotest guess at its nature;" her habitual frown became stronger as she very slowly and weightily emphasized those words; "but, when the gentleman proceeds to explain his object, I shall beg him to have the goodness to do to myself and Flintwinch, when Flintwinch returns just now, it will prove, no doubt, to be one more or less in the usual way of our business, which it will be both our business and our pleasure to advance. It can be nothing else."

"We shall see, madame!" said the man of business.

"We shall see," she asserted. "The gentleman is acquainted with Flintwinch; and when the gentleman was in London last, I remember to have heard that he and Flintwinch had some entertainment or good-fellowship together. I am not in the way of knowing much that passes outside this room, and the jingle of little worldly things beyond it does not much interest me; but I remember to have heard that."

"Right, madame. It is true." He laughed again, and whistled the burden of the tune he had sung at the door.

"Therefore, Arthur," said his mother, "the gentleman comes here as an acquaintance, and no stranger; and it is much to be regretted that your unreasonable temper should have found offense in him. I regret it. I say so to the gentleman. You will not say so, I know; therefore I say it for myself and Flintwinch, since with us two the gentleman's business lies."

The key of the door below was now heard in the lock, and the door was heard to open and close. In due sequence Mr. Flintwinch appeared; on whose entrance the visitor rose from his chair laughing, and folded him in a close embrace.

"How goes it, my cherished friend?" said he. "How goes the world, my Flintwinch? Rose-colored? So much the better! So much the better! Ah, but you look charming! Ah, but you look young and fresh as the flowers of Spring! Ah, good little boy! Brave child, brave child!"

MR. FLINTWINCH RECEIVES THE EMBRACE OF FRIENDSHIP.

While heaping these compliments on Mr. Flintwinch, he rolled him about with a hand on each of his shoulders, until the staggerings of that gentleman, who under the circumstances was dryer and more twisted than ever, were like those of a tee-totum nearly spent.

"I had a presentiment last time that we should be better and more intimately acquainted. Is it coming on you, Flintwinch? Is it yet coming on?"

"Why, no, sir," retorted Mr. Flintwinch. "Not unusually. Hadn't you better be seated? You have been calling for some more of that port, sir, I guess?"

"Ah! Little joker! Little pig!" cried the visitor. "Ha ha, ha ha!" And throwing Mr. Flintwinch away, as a closing piece of raillery, he sat down again.

The amazement, suspicion, resentment, and shame, with which Arthur looked on at all this, struck him dumb. Mr. Flintwinch, who had spun backward some two or three yards, under the impetus last given to him, brought himself up with a face completely unchanged in its stolidity, except as it was affected by shortness of breath, and looked hard at Arthur. Not a whit less reticent and wooden was Mr. Flintwinch outwardly than in the usual course of things; the only perceptible difference in him being that the knot of cravat, which was generally under his ear, had worked round to the back of his head, where it formed an ornamental appendage, not unlike a bag-wig, and gave him something of a courtly appearance.

As Mrs. Clennam never removed her eyes from Blandois (on whom they had some effect, as a steady look has on a lower sort of dog), so Jeremiah never removed his from Arthur. It was as if they had tacitly agreed to take their different provinces. Thus, in the ensuing silence, Jeremiah stood scraping his chin, and looking at Arthur, as though he were trying to screw his thoughts out of him with an instrument.

After a little, the visitor, as if he felt the silence irksome, rose, and impatiently put himself with his back to the sacred fire which had burned through so many years. Thereupon Mrs. Clennam said, moving one of her hands for the first time, and moving it very slightly with an action of dismissal:

"Please to leave us to our business, Arthur."

"Mother, I do so with great reluctance."

"Never mind with what," she returned, "or with what not. Please to leave us. Come back at any other time when you may consider it as a duty to bury half an hour wearily here. Good-night."

She held up her muffled fingers that he might touch them with his, according to their usual custom, and he stood over her wheeled chair to touch her face with his lips. He thought, then, that her cheek was more strained than usual, and that it was colder. As he followed the direction of her eyes, in rising again, toward Mr. Flintwinch's good friend, Mr. Blandois, Mr. Blandois snapped his finger and thumb with one loud, contemptuous snap.

"I leave your—your business acquaintance in my mother's room, Mr. Flintwinch," said Clennam, "with a great deal of surprise and a great deal of unwillingness."

The person referred to snapped his finger and thumb again.

"Good-night, mother."

"Good-night."

"I had a friend once, my good comrade Flintwinch," said Blandois, standing astride before the fire, and so evidently saying it to arrest Clennam's retreating steps, that he lingered near the door; "I had a friend once, who had heard so much of the dark side of this city and its ways, that he wouldn't have confided himself alone by night with two people who had an interest in getting him under the ground—my faith! not even in a respectable house like this—unless he was bodily too strong for them. Bah! What a poltroon, my Flintwinch! Eh?"

"A cur, sir."

"Agreed! A cur. But he wouldn't have done it, my Flintwinch, unless he had known them to have the will to silence him without the power. He wouldn't have drunk from a glass of water, under such circumstances—not even in a respectable house like this, my Flintwinch—unless he had seen one of them drink first—and swallow too."

Disdaining to speak, and indeed not very well able, for he was half choking, Clennam only glanced at the visitor as he passed out. The visitor saluted him with another parting snap, and his nose came down over his mustache, and his mustache went up under his nose, in an ominous and ugly smile.

"For God's sake, Affery," whispered Clennam, as she opened the door for him in the dark hall, and he groped his way to the sight of the night sky, "what is going on here?"

Her own appearance was sufficiently ghastly, standing in the dark with her apron thrown over her head and face, and speaking behind it in a low deadened voice.

"Don't ask me any thing, Arthur. I've been in a dream for ever so long. Go away!"

He went out, and she shut the door upon him. He looked up at the windows of his mother's room, and the dim light deadened by the yellow blinds, seemed to say a response after Affery, and to mutter, "Don't ask me any thing. Go away!"

CHAPTER XLVII.

A LETTER FROM LITTLE DORRIT.

DEAR MR. CLENNAM,—As I said in my last that it was best for nobody to write to me, and as my sending you another little letter can therefore give you no other trouble than the trouble of reading it (perhaps you may not find leisure for even that, though I hope you will some day), I am now going to devote an hour to writing to you again. This time I write from Rome.

We left Venice before Mr. and Mrs. Gowan did, but they were not so long upon the road as we were, and did not travel by the same way; and so, when we arrived, we found them in a lodging here in a place called the Via Gregoriana. I dare say you know it.

Now, I am going to tell you all I can about them, because I know that it is what you most want to hear. Theirs is not a very comfortable lodging, but perhaps I thought it less so when I first saw it than you would have done, because you have been in many countries, and have seen many different customs. Of course it is a far, far better place—millions of times—than any I have ever been used to until lately, and I fancy I don't look at it with my own eyes, but with hers. For it would be easy to see that she has always been brought up in a tender and happy home, even if she had not told me so with tears of love for it.

Well, it is a rather bare lodging, up a rather dark common staircase, and it is nearly all a large, dull room where Mr. Gowan paints. The windows are blocked up where any one could look out, and the walls have been all drawn over with chalk and charcoal by others who have lived there before—oh, I should think, for years! There is a curtain more dust-colored than red, which divides it, and the part behind the curtain makes the private sitting-room. When I first saw her there she was alone, and her work had fallen out of her hand, and she was looking up at the sky shining through the tops of the windows. Pray do not be uneasy when I tell you, but it was not quite so airy, nor so bright, nor so cheerful, nor so happy and youthful altogether as I should have liked it to be.

On account of Mr. Gowan painting papa's picture (which I am not quite convinced I should have known from the likeness if I had not seen him doing it), I have had more opportunities of being with her since then, that I might have had without this fortunate chance. She is very much alone. Very much alone indeed.

Shall I tell you about the second time I saw her? I went one day, when it happened that I could run round by myself, at four or five o'clock in the afternoon. She was then dining alone, and her solitary dinner had been brought in from somewhere, over a kind of brazier with a fire in it, and she had no company, or prospect of company, that I could see, but the old man who had brought it. He was telling her a long story of robbers outside the walls, being taken up by a stone statue of a saint, to entertain her—as he said to me when I came out, "because he had a daughter of his own, though she was not so pretty."

I ought now to mention Mr. Gowan, before I say what little more I have to say about her. He must admire her beauty, and he must be proud of her, for every body praises it, and he must be fond of her; and I do not doubt that he is—but in his way. You know his way, and if it appears as careless and discontented in your eyes as it does in mine, I am not wrong in thinking that it might be better suited to her. If it does not seem so to you, I am quite sure I am wholly mistaken; for your unchanged poor child confides in your knowledge and goodness more than she could ever tell you, if she was to try. But don't be frightened, I am not going to try.

Owing (as I think, if you think so, too) to Mr. Gowan's unsettled and dissatisfied way, he applies himself to his profession very little. He does nothing steadily or patiently, but equally takes things up and throws them down, and does them, or leaves them undone, without caring about them. When I have heard him talking to papa during the sittings for the picture, I have sat wondering whether it could really be that he has no belief in any body else, because he has no belief in himself to begin with. Is it so? I wonder what you will say when you come to this! I know how you will look, and I can almost hear the voice in which you would tell me on the Iron Bridge.

Mr. Gowan goes out a good deal among what is considered the best company here—though he does not look as if he liked it when he is with it—and she sometimes accompanies him, but lately she has gone out very little. I think I have noticed that they have an inconsistent way of speaking about her, as if she had made some great self-interested success in marrying Mr. Gowan, though, at the same time, the very same people would not have dreamed of taking him for themselves or their daughters. Then he goes into the country besides, to think about making sketches, and in all places where there are visitors he has a large acquaintance and is very well known. Besides all this, he has a friend who is much in his society, both at home and away from home, though he treats this friend very coolly, and is very uncertain in his behavior to him. I am quite sure (because she has told me so), that she does not like this friend. He is so revolting to me, too, that his being away from here, at present, is quite a relief to my mind. How much more to hers!

But what I particularly want you to know, and why I have resolved to tell you so much, even while I am afraid it may make you a little uncomfortable without occasion, is this. She is so true and so devoted, and knows so completely that all her love and duty are his forever, that you may be certain she will love him, admire him, praise him, and conceal all his faults, until she dies. I believe she conceals them, and always will conceal them, even from herself. She has given him a heart that can never be taken back, and however much he may try it, he will never wear out its affection. You know the truth of this, as you know every thing far, far better than I, but I can not help telling you what a nature she shows, and that you can never think too well of her.

I have not yet called her by name in this letter, but we are such friends now that I do so when we are quietly together, and she speaks to me by my name—I mean, not my Christian name, but the name you gave me. When she began to call me

Amy, I told her my short story, and that you had always called me Little Dorrit. I told her that the name was much dearer to me than any other, and so she calls me Little Dorrit, too.

Perhaps you have not heard from her father or mother yet, and may not know that she has a baby son. He was born only two days ago, and just a week after they came. It has made them very happy. However, I must tell you, as I am to tell you all, that I fancy they are under a constraint with Mr. Gowan, and that they feel as if his mocking way with them was sometimes a slight given to their love for her. It was but yesterday when I was there, that I saw Mr. Meagles change color, and get up and go out, as if he was afraid that he might say as much, unless he prevented himself by that means. Yet, I am sure they are both so considerate, good-humored, and reasonable, that he might spare them. It is hard of him not to think of them a little more.

I stopped at the last full stop to read all this over. It looked at first as if I was taking on myself to understand and explain so much, that I was half inclined not to send it. But when I had thought it over a little, I felt more hopeful of your knowing at once that I had only been watchful for you, and had only noticed what I think I have noticed, because I was quickened by your interest in it. Indeed, you may be sure that is the truth.

And now I have done with the subject in the present letter, and have little left to say.

We are all quite well, and Fanny improves every day. You can hardly think how kind she is to me, and what pains she takes with me. She has a lover who has followed her, first all the way from Switzerland, and then all the way from Venice, and who has just confided to me that he means to follow her every where. I was very much confused by his speaking to me about it, but he would. I did not know what to say, but at last I told him that I thought he had better not. For Fanny (but I did not tell him this) is much too spirited and clever to suit him. Still, he said he would, all the same. I have no lover, of course.

If you should ever get so far as this in this long letter, you will perhaps say, "Surely Little Dorrit will not leave off without telling me something about her travels, and surely it is time she did." I think it is, indeed, but I don't know what to tell you. Since we left Venice we have been in a great many wonderful places, Genoa and Florence among them, and have seen so many wonderful sights, that I am almost giddy when I think what a crowd they make. But you could tell me so much more about them than I can tell you, that why should I tire you with my accounts and descriptions!

Dear Mr. Clennam, as I had the courage to tell you what the familiar difficulties in my traveling mind were before, I will not be a coward now. One of my frequent thoughts is this: Old as these cities are, their age itself is hardly so curious to my reflections as that they should have been in their places all through those days when I did not even know of the existence of more than two or three of them, and when I scarcely knew of any thing outside our old walls. There is something very melancholy in it, and I don't know why. When we went to see the famous leaning tower at Pisa, it was a bright sunny day, and it and the buildings near it looked so old, and the earth and sky looked so young, and its shadow on the ground was so soft and retired. I could not at first think how beautiful it was, or how curious; but I thought, "Oh how many times when the shadow of the wall was falling on our room, and when that weary tread of feet was going up and down the yard—Oh how many times this place was just as quiet and lovely as it is this day!" It quite overpowered me. My heart was so full, that tears burst out of my eyes, though I did what I could to restrain them. And I have the same feeling often—often.

Do you know that since the change in our fortunes, though I appear to myself to have dreamed more than before, I have always dreamed of myself as very young indeed? I am not very old, you may say. No, but that is not what I mean. I have always dreamed of myself as a child learning to do needlework. I have often dreamed of myself as back there, seeing faces in the yard, little known, and which I should have thought I had quite forgotten; but, as often as not, I have been abroad here—in Switzerland, or France, or Italy—somewhere where we have been—yet always as that little child. I have dreamed of going down to Mrs. General with the patches on my clothes in which I can first remember myself. I have over and over again dreamed of taking my place at dinner at Venice, when we have had a large company, in the mourning for my poor mother which I wore when I was eight years old, and wore long after it was threadbare and would mend no more. It has been a great distress to me to think how irreconcilable the company would consider it with my father's wealth, and how I should displease and disgrace him and Fanny and Edward by so plainly disclosing what they wished to keep secret. But I have not grown out of the little child in thinking of it, and at the self-same moment I have dreamed that I sat with the heart-ache at the table, calculating the expenses of the dinner, and quite distracting myself with thinking how they were ever to be made good. I have never dreamed of the change in our fortunes itself, I have never dreamed of your coming back with me that memorable morning to break it, I have never even dreamed of you.

Dear Mr. Clennam, it is possible I have thought of you—and others—so much by day, that I have no thoughts left to wander around you by night. For I must now confess to you that I suffer from home-sickness—that I long so ardently and earnestly for home, as sometimes, when no one sees me, to grieve for it. I can not bear to turn my face further away from it. My heart is a little lightened when we turn toward it, even for a few miles, and with the knowledge that we are soon to turn away again. So dearly do I love the scene of my poverty and your kindness. Oh, so dearly, oh, so dearly!"

Heaven knows when your poor child will see England again. We are all fond of the life here, except me, and there are no plans for our return. My dear father talks of a visit to London late next spring, on some affairs connected with the property, but I have no hope that he will bring me with him.

I have tried to get on a little better under Mrs. General's instruction, and I trust I am not quite so dull as I used to be. I have begun to speak and understand, almost easily, the hard languages I told you about. I did not remember, at the moment when I wrote last, that you know them both, but I remembered it afterward, and it helped me on. God bless you, dear Mr. Clennam. Do not forget

Your ever grateful and affectionate

Little Dorrit.

P. S. Particularly remember that Minnie Gowan deserves the best remembrances in which you can hold her. You cannot think too generously or too highly of her. I forgot Mr. Pancks last time. Please, if you should see him, give him your Little Dorrit's regard. He was very good to Little D.

CHAPTER XLVIII.

IN WHICH A GREAT PATRIOTIC CONFERENCE IS HOLDEN.

THE famous name of Merdle became, every day, more famous in the land. Nobody knew that the Merdle of such high renown had ever done any good to any one, alive or dead, or to any earthly thing; nobody knew that he had any capacity or utterance of any sort in him, which had ever thrown, for any creature, the feeblest farthing-candle ray of light on any path of duty or diversion, pain or pleasure, toil or rest, fact or fancy, among the multiplicity of paths in the labyrinth trodden by the sons of Adam; nobody had the smallest reason for supposing the clay of which this object of worship was made to be other than the commonest clay, with as clogged a wick smouldering inside of it as ever kept an image of humanity from tumbling to pieces. All people knew (or thought they knew) that he had made himself immensely rich; and, for that reason alone, prostrated themselves before him, more degradedly and less excusably than the darkest savage creeps out of his hole in the ground to propitiate, in some log or reptile, the Deity of his benighted soul.

Nay, the high priests of this worship had the man before them as a protest against their meanness. The multitude worshiped on trust—though always distinctly knowing why—but the officiators at the altar had the man habitually in their view. They sat at his feasts, and he sat at theirs. There was a spectre always attendant on him, saying to these high priests, "Are such the signs you trust, and love to honor; this head, these eyes, this mode of speech, the tone and manner of this man? You are the levers of the Circumlocution Office, and the rulers of men. When half a dozen of you fall out by the ears, it seems that mother earth can give birth to no other rulers. Does your qualification lie in the superior knowledge of men, which accepts, courts, and puffs this man? Or, if you are competent to judge aright the signs I never fail to show you when he appears among you, is your superior honesty your qualification?" Two rather ugly questions these, always going about town with Mr. Merdle; and there was a tacit agreement that they must be stifled.

In Mrs. Merdle's absence abroad, Mr. Merdle still kept the great house open, for the passage through it of a stream of visitors. A few of these took affable possession of the establishment. Three or four ladies of distinction and liveliness used to say to one another, "Let us dine at our dear Merdle's next Thursday. Whom shall we have?" Our dear Merdle would then receive his instructions; and would sit heavily among the company at table and wander lumpishly about his drawing-rooms afterward, only remarkable for appearing to have nothing to do with the entertainment beyond being in its way.

The Chief Butler, the Avenging-Spirit of this great man's life, relaxed nothing of his severity. He looked on at these dinners when the bosom was not there, as he looked on at other dinners when the bosom was there; and his eye was a basilisk to Mr. Merdle. He was a hard man, and would never bate an ounce of plate or a bottle of wine. He would not allow a dinner to be given, unless it was up to his mark. He set forth the table for his own dignity. If the guests chose to partake of what was served, he saw no objection; but it was served for the maintenance of his rank. As he stood by the side-board he seemed to announce, "I have accepted office to look at this which is now before me, and to look at nothing less than this." If he missed the presiding bosom, it was as a part of his own state of which he was, from unavoidable circumstances, temporarily deprived. Just as he might have missed a centre-piece, or a choice wine-cooler, which had been sent to the banker's.

Mr. Merdle issued invitations for a Barnacle dinner. Lord Decimus was to be there, Mr. Tite Barnacle was to be there, the pleasant young Barnacle was to be there; and the Chorus of Parliamentary Barnacles who went about the provinces when the House was up, warbling the praises of their Chief, were to be represented there. It was understood to be a great occasion. Mr. Merdle was going to take up the Barnacles. Some delicate little negotiations had occurred between him and the noble Decimus—the young Barnacle of engaging manners acting as negotiator—and Mr. Merdle had decided to cast the weight of his great probity and great riches into the Barnacle scale. Jobbery was suspected by the malicious; perhaps because it was indisputable that if the adherence of the immortal Enemy of Mankind could have been secured by a job, the Barnacles would have jobbed him—for the good of the country, for the good of the country.

Mrs. Merdle had written to this magnificent spouse of hers, whom it was heresy to regard as any thing less than all the British Merchants since the days of Whittington rolled into one, and gilded three feet deep all over—had written to this spouse of hers several letters from Rome, in quick succession, urging upon him with importunity that now or never was the time to provide for Edmund Sparkler. Mrs. Merdle had shown him that the case of Edmund was urgent, and that infinite advantages might result from his having some good thing directly. In the grammar of Mrs. Merdle's verbs on this momentous subject, there was only one Mood, the Imperative; and that Mood has only one Tense, the Present. Mrs. Merdle's verbs were so pressingly presented to Mr. Merdle to conjugate, that his sluggish blood and his long coat-cuffs became quite agitated.

In which state of agitation, Mr. Merdle, evasively rolling his eyes round the Chief Butler's shoes without raising them to the index of that stupendous creature's thoughts, had signified to him his intention of giving a special dinner: not a very large dinner, but a very special dinner. The Chief Butler had signified, in return, that he had no objection to look on at the most expensive thing in that way that could be done: and the day of the dinner was now come.

Mr. Merdle stood in one of his drawing-rooms, with his back to the fire, waiting for the arrival of his important guests. He seldom or never took the liberty of standing with his back to his fire, unless he was quite alone. In the presence of the Chief Butler he could not have done such a deed. He would have clasped himself by the wrists in that constabulary manner of his, and have paced up and down the hearth-rug, or gone creeping about among the rich objects of furniture, if his oppressive retainer had appeared in the room at that very moment. The sly shadows which seemed to dart out of hiding when the fire rose, and to dart back into it when the fire fell, were sufficient witnesses of his making himself so easy. They were even more than sufficient, if his uncomfortable glances at them might be taken to mean any thing.

Mr. Merdle's right hand was filled with the evening paper, and the evening paper was full of Mr. Merdle. His wondertul enterprise, his wonderful wealth, his wonderful Bank, were the fattening food of the evening paper that night. The wonderful Bank, of which he was the chief projector, establisher, and manager, was the latest of the many Merdle wonders. So modest was Mr. Merdle withal, in the midst of these splendid achievements, that he looked far more like a man in possession of his house under a distraint, than a commercial Colossus bestriding his own hearth-rug, while the little ships were sailing in to dinner.

Behold the vessels coming into port! The engaging young Barnacle was the first arrival; but Bar overtook him on the stair-case. Bar, strengthened as usual with his double eye-glass, and his little jury droop, was overjoyed to see the engaging young Barnacle; and opined that we were going to sit *in Banco*, as we lawyers called it, to take a special argument?

"Indeed," said the sprightly young Barnacle, whose name was Ferdinand: "how so?"

"Nay," smiled Bar. "If *you* don't know, how can *I* know? *You* are in the innermost sanctuary of the temple; *I* am one of the admiring concourse on the plain without."

Bar could be light in hand, or heavy in hand, according to the customer he had to deal with. With Ferdinand Barnacle he was gossamer. Bar was likewise always modest and self-depreciatory—in his way. Bar was a man of great variety; but one leading thread ran through the woof of all his patterns. Every man with whom he had to do was, in his eyes, a juryman; and he must get that juryman over, if he could.

"Our illustrious host and friend," said Bar; "our shining mercantile star; going into politics?"

"Going? He has been in Parliament some time, you know," returned the engaging young Barnacle.

"True," said Bar, with his light-comedy laugh for special jurymen; which was a very different thing from his low-comedy laugh for comic tradesmen on common juries: "he has been in Parliament for some time. Yet hitherto our star has been a vacillating and wavering star? Humph?"

An average witness would have been seduced by the Humph? into an affirmative answer. But Ferdinand Barnacle looked knowingly at Bar as they strolled up stairs, and gave him no answer at all.

"Just so, just so," said Bar, nodding his head, for he was not to be put off in that way, "and therefore I spoke of our sitting *in Banco* to take a special argument—meaning this to be a high and solemn occasion, when, as Captain Macheath says, 'the Judges are met; a terrible show!' We lawyers are sufficiently liberal, you see, to quote the Captain, though the Captain is severe upon us. Nevertheless, I think I could put in evidence an admission of the Captain's," said Bar, with a little jocose roll of his head; for, in his legal current of speech, he always assumed the air of rallying himself with the best grace in the world: "an admission of the Captain's that Law, in the gross, is at least intended to be impartial. For, what says the Captain, if I quote him correctly—and if not," with a light-comedy touch of his double eye-glass on his companion's shoulder, "my learned friend will set me right:

"'Since laws were made for every degree,
To curb vice in others as well as in me,
I wonder we ha'n't better company
Upon Tyburn Tree!'"

These words brought them to the drawing-room, where Mr. Merdle stood before the fire. So immensely astounded was Mr. Merdle by the entrance of Bar with such a reference in his mouth, that Bar explained himself to have been quoting Gray. "Assuredly not one of our Westminster Hall authorities," said he, with the jury droop, "but still no despicable one to a man possessing the largely-practical Mr. Merdle's knowledge of the world."

Mr. Merdle looked as if he thought he would say something, but subsequently looked as if he thought he wouldn't. The interval afforded time for Bishop to be announced.

Bishop came in with meekness, and yet with a strong and rapid step, as if he wanted to get his seven-league dress-shoes on, and go round the world to see that every body was in a satisfactory state. Bishop had no idea that there was any thing significant in the occasion. That was the most remarkable trait in his demeanor. He was crisp, fresh, cheerful, affable, bland; but so surprisingly innocent!

Bar slided up to prefer his politest inquiries in reference to the health of Mrs. Bishop. Mrs. Bishop had been a little unfortunate in the article of taking cold at a Confirmation, but otherwise was well. Young Mr. Bishop was also well. He was down, with his young wife and little family, at his Cure of Souls—and it is to be hoped was curing largely.

The representatives of the Barnacle Chorus dropped in next, and Mr. Merdle's physician dropped in next. Bar, who had a bit of one eye and a bit of his double eye-glass for every one who came in at the door, no matter with whom he was conversing or what he was talking about, got among them all by some skillful means, without being seen to get at them, and touched each individual gentleman of the jury on his own individual favorite spot. With some of the Chorus, he laughed about the sleepy member who had gone out into the lobby the other night, and voted the wrong way: with others, he deplored that innovating spirit in the time which could not even be prevented from taking an unnatural interest in the public service and the public money: with the physician he had a word to say about the general health; he had also a little information to ask him for, concerning a professional man, of unquestioned erudition and polished manners—but those credentials in their highest development he believed were the possession of other professors of the healing art (jury droop)—whom he had happened to have in the witness-box the day before yesterday, and from whom he had elicited in cross-examination that he claimed to be one of the exponents of this new mode of treatment which appeared to Bar to—eh?—well, Bar thought so; Bar had thought, and hoped, Physician would tell him so. Without presuming to decide where doctors disagreed, it did appear to Bar, viewing it as a question of common sense and not of so-called legal penetration, that this new system was—might be, in the presence of so great an authority—say, Humbug? Ah! Fortified by such encouragement, he could venture to say Humbug; and now Bar's mind was relieved.

Mr. Tite Barnacle, who, like Dr. Johnson's celebrated acquaintance, had only one idea in his head, and that was a wrong one, had appeared by this time. This eminent gentleman and Mr. Merdle, seated diverse ways and with ruminating aspects, on a yellow ottoman in the light of the fire, holding no verbal communication with each other, bore a strong general resemblance to the two cows in the Cuyp picture over against them.

But, now, Lord Decimus arrived. The Chief Butler, who up to this time had limited himself to a branch of his usual function by looking at the company as they entered, (and that, with more of defiance than favor,) put himself so far out of his way as to come up stairs with him and announce him. Lord Decimus being an overpowering peer, a bashful young member of the Lower House, who was the last fish but one caught by the Barnacles, and who had been invited on this occasion to commemorate his capture, shut his eyes when his Lordship came in.

Lord Decimus nevertheless was glad to see the Member. He was also glad to see Mr. Merdle, glad to see Bishop, glad to see Bar, glad to see Physician, glad to see Tite Barnacle, glad to see Chorus, glad to see Ferdinand his private secretary. Lord Decimus, though one of the greatest of the earth, was not personally remarkable for ingratiatory manners, and Ferdinand had coached him up to the point of noticing all the fellows he might find there, and saying he was glad to see them. When he had achieved this rush of vivacity and condescension, his Lordship composed himself into the picture after Cuyp, and made a third cow in the group.

Bar, who felt that he had got all the rest of the jury and must now lay hold of the Foreman, soon came sliding up, double eye-glass in hand. Bar tendered the weather, as a subject neatly aloof from official reserve, for the Foreman's consideration. Bar said that he was told (as every body always is told, though who tells them, and why, will for ever remain a mystery), that there was to be no wall-fruit this year. Lord Decimus had not heard any thing amiss of his peaches, but rather believed, if his people were correct, he was to have no apples. No apples? Bar was lost in astonishment and concern. It would have been all one to him, in reality, if there had not been a pippin on the surface of the earth, but his show of interest in this apple question was positively painful. Now, to what, Lord Decimus—for we troublesome lawyers loved to gather information, and could never tell how useful it might prove to us—to what, Lord Decimus, was this to be attributed? Lord Decimus could not undertake to propound any theory about it. This might have stopped another man; but Bar, sticking to him fresh as ever, said, "As to pears, now?"

Long after Bar got made Attorney-General, this was told of him as a master-stroke. Lord Decimus had a reminiscence about a pear-tree, formerly growing in a garden near the back of his dame's house at Eton, upon which pear-tree the only joke of his life perennially bloomed. It was a joke of a compact and portable nature, turning on the difference between Eton pears and Parliamentary pairs; but it was a joke, a refined relish of which would seem to have appeared to Lord Decimus impossible to be had, without a thorough and intimate acquaintance with the tree. Therefore, the story at first had no idea of such a tree, sir, then gradually found it in winter, carried it through the changing seasons, saw it bud, saw it blossom, saw it bear fruit, saw the fruit ripen, in short cultivated the tree in that diligent and minute manner before it got out of the bed-room window to steal the fruit, that many thanks had been offered up by belated listeners for the tree's having been planted and grafted prior to Lord Decimus's time. Bar's interest in apples was so overtopped by the wrapt suspense in which he pursued the changes of these pears, from the moment when Lord Decimus solemnly opened with "Your mentioning pears recalls to my remembrance a pear-tree," down to the rich conclusion, "And so we pass, through the various changes of life, from Eton pears to Parliamentary pairs," that he had to go down stairs with Lord Decimus, and even then to be seated next him at table, in order that he might hear the anecdote out.

By that time, Bar felt that he had secured the Foreman, and might go to dinner with a good appetite.

It was a dinner to provoke an appetite, though he had not had one. The rarest dishes, sumptuously cooked and sumptuously served; the choicest fruits; the most exquisite wines; marvels of workmanship in gold and silver, china and glass; innumerable things delicious to the senses of taste, smell, and sight, were insinuated into its composition. Oh, what a wonderful man this Merdle, what a great man, what a master man, how blessedly and enviably endowed—in one word, what a rich man!

He took his usual poor eighteenpennyworth of food, in his usual indigestive way, and had as little to say for himself as ever a wonderful man had. Fortunately Lord Decimus was one of these sublimities who have no occasion to be talked to, for they can be at any time sufficiently occupied with the contemplation of their own greatness. This enabled the bashful young member to keep his eyes open long enough at a time to see his dinner. But, whenever Lord Decimus spoke, he shut them again.

The agreeable young Barnacle, and Bar, were the talkers of the party. Bishop would have been exceedingly agreeable also, but that his innocence stood in his way. He was soon left behind. When there was any little hint of any thing being in the wind, he got lost directly. Worldly affairs were too much for him; he couldn't make them out at all.

This was observable when Bar said, incidentally, that he was happy to have heard that we were soon to have the advantage of enlisting on the good side, the sound and plain sagacity—not demonstrative or ostentatious, but thoroughly sound and practical—of our friend Mr. Sparkler.

Ferdinand Barnacle laughed, and said, Oh, yes, he believed so. A vote was a vote, and always acceptable.

Bar was sorry to miss our good friend Mr. Sparkler to-day, Mr. Merdle.

"He is away with Mrs. Merdle," returned that gentleman, slowly coming out of a long abstraction, in the course of which he had been fitting a table-spoon up his sleeve. "It is not indispensable for him to be on the spot."

"The magic name of Merdle," said Bar, with the jury droop, "no doubt will suffice for all."

"Why—yes—I believe so," assented Mr. Merdle, putting the spoon aside, and clumsily hiding each of his hands in the coat-cuff of the other hand. "I believe the people in my interest down there, will not make any difficulty."

"Model people!" said Bar.

"I am glad you approve of them," said Mr. Merdle.

"And the people of those other two places, now," pursued Bar, with a bright twinkle in his keen eye, as it slightly turned in the direction of his magnificent neighbor; "we lawyers are always curious, always inquisitive, always picking up odds and ends for our patch-work minds, since there is no knowing when and where they may fit into some corner; the people of those other two places now? Do they yield so laudably to the vast and cumulative influence of such enterprise and such renown; do those little rills become absorbed so quietly and easily, and, as it were, by the influence of natural laws, so beautifully, in the swoop of the majestic stream as it flows upon its wondrous way enriching the surrounding lands, that their course is perfectly to be calculated, and distinctly to be predicated?"

Mr. Merdle, a little troubled by Bar's eloquence, looked fitfully about the nearest salt-cellar for some moments, and then said, hesitating:

"They are perfectly aware, sir, of their duty to Society They will return any body I send to them for that purpose."

"Cheering to know," said Bar. "Cheering to know."

The three places in question were three little rotten holes in this Island, containing three little ignorant, drunken, guzzling, dirty, out-of-the-way constituencies, that had reeled into Mr. Merdle's pocket. Ferdinand Barnacle laughed in his easy way, and airily said they were a nice set of fellows. Bishop, mentally perambulating among paths of peace, was altogether swallowed up in absence of mind.

"Pray," asked Lord Decimus, casting his eyes around the table, "what is this story I have heard of a gentleman long confined in a debtor's prison, proving to be of a wealthy family, and having come into the inheritance of a large sum of money?

I have met with a variety of allusions to it. Do you know any thing of it, Ferdinand?"

"I only know this much," said Ferdinand, "that he has given the Department with which I have the honor to be associated;" this sparkling young Barnacle threw off the phrase sportively, as who should say, We know all about these forms of speech, but we must keep it up, we must keep the game alive; "no end of trouble, and has put us into innumerable fixes."

"Fixes?" repeated Lord Decimus, with a majestic pausing and pondering on the word that made the bashful member shut his eyes quite tight. "Fixes."

"A very perplexing business indeed," observed Mr. Tite Barnacle, with an air of grave resentment.

"What," said Lord Decimus, "was the character of his business; what was the nature of these—a—fixes, Ferdinand?"

"Oh, it's a good story, as a story," returned that gentleman; "as good a thing of its kind as need be. This Mr. Dorrit (his name is Dorrit) had incurred a responsibility to us, ages before the fairy came out of the Bank and gave him his fortune, under a bond he had signed for the performance of a contract which was not at all performed. He was partner in a house in some large way—spirits, or buttons, or wine, or blacking, or oatmeal, or woolen, or pork, or hooks-and-eyes, or iron, or treacle, or shoes, or something or other that was wanted for troops, or seamen, or sombody—and the house burst, and we being among the creditors, detainers were lodged on the part of the Crown in a scientific manner, and all the rest of it. When the fairy had appeared, and he wanted to pay us off, egad we had got into such an exemplary state of checking and counter-checking, signing and counter-signing, that it was six months before we knew how to take the money, or how to give a receipt for it. It was a triumph of public business," said this handsome young Barnacle, laughing heartily. "You never saw such a lot of forms in your life. 'Why,' the attorney said to me one day, 'if I wanted this office to give me two or three thousand pounds, instead of take it, I couldn't have more trouble about it.' 'You are right, old fellow,' I told him, 'and in future you'll know that we have something to do here.'" The pleasant young Barnacle finished by once more laughing heartily. He was a very easy, pleasant fellow indeed, and his manners were exceedingly winning.

Mr. Tite Barnacle's view of the business was of a less airy character. He took it ill that Mr. Dorrit had troubled the Department by wanting to pay the money, and considered it a grossly informal thing to do after so many years. But Mr. Tite Barnacle was a buttoned-up man, and consequently a weighty one. All buttoned-up men are weighty. All buttoned-up men are believed in. Whether or no the reserved and never-exercised power of unbuttoning, fascinates mankind; whether or no wisdom is supposed to condense and augment when buttoned up, and to evaporate when unbuttoned; it is certain that the man to whom importance is accorded is the buttoned-up man. Mr. Tite Barnacle never would have passed for half his current value, unless his coat had been always buttoned up to his white cravat.

"May I ask," said Lord Decimus, "if Mr. Darrit—or Dorrit—has any family?"

Nobody else replying, the host said, "He has two daughters, my lord."

"Oh! you are acquainted with him?" asked Lord Decimus.

"Mrs. Merdle is. Mr. Sparkler is, too. In fact," said Mr. Merdle, "I rather believe that one of the young ladies has made an impression on Edmund Sparkler. He is susceptible, and—I—think—the conquest—" Here Mr. Merdle stopped, and looked at the table-cloth: as he usually did when he found himself observed or listened to.

Bar was uncommonly pleased to find that the Merdle family and this family had already been brought into contact. He submitted, in a low voice across the table to Bishop, that it was a kind of analogical illustration of those physical laws, in virtue of which Like flies to Like. He regarded this power of attraction in wealth to draw wealth to it, as something remarkably interesting and curious—something indefinably allied to the loadstone and gravitation. Bishop, who had ambled back to earth again when the present theme was broached, acquiesced. He said it was indeed highly important to Society that one in the trying situation of unexpectedly finding himself invested with a power for good or for evil in Society, should become, as it were, merged in the superior power of a more legitimate and more gigantic growth, the influence of which (as in the case of our friend, at whose board we sat) was habitually exercised in harmony with the best interests of Society. Thus, instead of two rival and contending flames, a larger and a lesser, each burning with a lurid and uncertain glare, we had a blended and a softened light, whose genial ray diffused an equable warmth throughout the land. Bishop seemed to like his own way of putting the case very much, and rather dwelt upon it; Bar, meanwhile (not to throw away a juryman), making a show of sitting at his feet and feeding on his precepts.

The dinner and dessert being three hours long, the bashful member cooled in the shadow of Lord Decimus faster than he warmed with food and drink, and had but a chilly time of it. Lord Decimus, like a tall tower in a flat country, seemed to project himself across the table-cloth, hide the light from the honorable member, cool the honorable member's marrow, and give him a woeful idea of distance. When he asked this unfortunate traveler to take wine, he encompassed his faltering steps with the gloomiest of shades; and when he said, "Your health, sir!" all around him was barrenness and desolation.

At length Lord Decimus, with a coffee-cup in his hand, began to hover about among the pictures, and to cause an interesting speculation to arise in all minds as to the probabilities of his ceasing to hover, and enabling the smaller birds to flutter up stairs; which could not be done until he had urged his noble pinions in that direction. After some delay, and several stretches of his wings which came to nothing, he soared to the drawing-rooms.

And here a difficulty arose, which always does arise when two people are specially brought together at a dinner to confer with one another. Every body (except Bishop, who had no suspicion of it) knew perfectly well that this dinner had been eaten and drunk, specifically to the end that Lord Decimus and Mr. Merdle should have five minutes' conversation together. The opportunity so elaborately prepared was now arrived, and it seemed from that moment that no merely human ingenuity could so much as get the two chieftains into the same room. Mr. Merdle and his noble guest persisted in prowling about at opposite ends of the perspective. It was in vain for the engaging Ferdinand to bring Lord Decimus to look at the bronze horses near Mr. Merdle. Then Mr. Merdle evaded, and wandered away. It was in vain for him to bring Mr. Merdle to Lord Decimus, to tell him the history of the unique Dresden vases. Then Lord Decimus evaded, and wandered away, while he was getting his man up to the mark.

"Did you ever see such a thing as this?" said Ferdinand to Bar, when he had been baffled twenty times.

"Often," returned Bar.

"Unless I butt one of them into an appointed corner, and you butt the other," said Ferdinand, "it will not come off at all."

"Very good," said Bar. "I'll butt Merdle, if you like; but, not my lord."

Ferdinand laughed, in the midst of his vexation. "Confound them both?" said he, looking at his watch. I want to get away. Why the deuce can't they come together! They both know what they want and mean to do. Look at them!"

They were still looming at opposite ends of the perspective, each with an absurd pretense of not having the other on his mind, which could not have been more transparently ridiculous though his real mind had been chalked on his back. Bishop, who had just now made a third with Bar and Ferdinand, but whose innocence had again cut him out of the subject and washed him in sweet-oil, was seen to approach Lord Decimus and glide into conversation.

"I must get Merdle's doctor to catch and secure him, I suppose," said Ferdinand; "and then I must lay hold of my illustrious kinsman, and decoy him if I can—drag him if I can't—to the conference."

"Since you do me the honor," said Bar, with his slyest smile, "to ask for my poor aid, it shall be yours with the greatest pleasure. I don't think this is to be done by one man. But, if you will undertake to pen my lord into that farthest drawing-room where he is now so profoundly engaged, I will undertake to bring our dear Merdle into the presence, without the possibility of getting away.

"Done!" said Ferdinand. "Done!" said Bar.

Bar was a sight wondrous to behold, and full of matter, when, jauntily waving his double eye-glass by its ribbon, and jauntily drooping to a Universe of Jurymen, he, in the most accidental manner ever seen, found himself at Mr. Merdle's shoulder, and embraced that opportunity of mentioning a little point to him, on which he particularly wished to be guided by the light of his practical knowledge. (Here he took Mr. Merdle's arm, and walked him gently away.) A banker, whom he would call A. B., advanced a considerable sum of money, which we would call fifteen thousand pounds, to a client or customer of his, whom we would call P. Q. (Here, as they were getting toward Lord Decimus, he held Mr. Merdle tight.) As a security for the repayment of this advance to P. Q., whom we would call a widow lady, there were placed in A. B.'s hands the title-deeds of a freehold estate, which we would call Blinkiter Doddles. Now, the point was this. A limited right of felling and lopping in the woods of Blinkiter Doddles lay in the son of P. Q., then past his majority, and whom we would call X. Y.—but really this was too bad! In the presence of Lord Decimus, to detain the host with chopping our dry chaff of law, was really too bad! Another time! Bar was truly repentant, and would not say another syllable. Would Bishop favor him with half a dozen words? (He had now set Merdle down on a couch, side by side with Lord Decimus, and to it they must go now, or never.)

And now the rest of the company, highly excited and interested, always excepting Bishop, who had not the slightest idea that any thing was going on, formed in one group round the fire in the next drawing-room, and pretended to be chatting easily on an infinite variety of small topics, while every body's thoughts and eyes were secretly straying toward the secluded pair. The Chorus were excessively nervous, perhaps as laboring under the dreadful apprehension that some good thing was going to be diverted from them. Bishop alone talked steadily and evenly. He conversed with the great Physician on that relaxation of the throat with which young curates were too frequently afflicted, and on the means of lessening the great prevalence of that disorder in the church. Physician, as a general rule, was of opinion that the best way to avoid it was to know how to read, before you made a profession of reading. Bishop said dubiously, did he really think so? And Physician said, decidedly, yes he did.

Ferdinand, meanwhile, was the only one of the party who skirmished on the outside of the circle; he kept about midway between it and the two, as if some sort of surgical operation were being performed by Lord Decimus on Mr. Merdle, or by Mr. Merdle on Lord Decimus, and his services might at any moment be required as Dresser. In fact, within a quarter of an hour, Lord Decimus called to him "Ferdinand!" and he went and took his place in the conference for some five minutes more. Then a half-suppressed gasp broke out among the Chorus; for Lord Decimus rose to take his leave. Again coached up by Ferdinand to the point of making himself popular, he shook hands in the most brilliant manner with the whole company, and even said to Bar, "I hope you were not bored by my pears?" To which Bar retorted, "Eton, my lord, or Parliamentary?" neatly showing that he had mastered the joke, and delicately insinuating that he could never forget it while life remained.

All the grave importance that was buttoned up in Mr. Tite Barnacle took itself away next; and Ferdinand took himself away next, to the opera. Some of the rest lingered a little, marrying golden liqueur glasses to Buhl tables with sticky rings; on the desperate chance of Mr. Merdle's saying something. But Mr. Merdle, as usual, oozed sluggishly and muddily about his drawing-room, saying never a word.

In a day or two, it was announced to all the town that Edmund Sparkler, Esquire, son-in-law of the eminent Mr. Merdle of world-wide renown, was made one of the Lords of the Circumlocution Office; and proclamation was issued, to all true believers, that this admirable appointment was to be hailed as a graceful and gracious mark of homage, rendered by the graceful and gracious Decimus, to that commercial interest which must ever in a great commercial country—and all the rest of it, with blast of trumpet. So, bolstered by this mark of Government homage, the wonderful Bank and all the other wonderful undertakings went on and went up; and gapers came to Harley

THE PATRIOTIC CONFERENCE.

Street, Cavendish Square, only to look at the house where the golden wonder lived.

And when they saw the Chief Butler looking out at the hall door in his moments of condescension, the gapers said how rich he looked, and wondered how much money he had in the wonderful Bank. But if they had known that respectable Nemesis better, they would not have wondered about it, and would have stated the amount with the utmost precision.

CHAPTER XLIX.

THE PROGRESS OF AN EPIDEMIC.

THAT it is at least as difficult to stay a moral infection as a physical one; that such a disease will spread with the malignity and rapidity of the Plague; that the contagion, when it has once made head, will spare no pursuit or condition, but will lay hold on people in the soundest health, and become developed in the most unlikely constitutions; is a fact as firmly established by experience as that we human creatures breathe an atmosphere. A blessing beyond appreciation would be conferred upon mankind, if the tainted, in whose weakness or wickedness these virulent disorders are bred, could be instantly seized and placed in close confinement (not to say summarily smothered) before the poison is communicable.

As a vast fire will fill the air to a great distance with its roar, so the sacred flame which the mighty Barnacles had fanned caused the air to resound more and more with the name of Merdle. It was deposited on every lip, and carried into every ear. There never was, there never had been, there never again should be, such a man as Mr. Merdle. Nobody, as aforesaid, knew what he had done; but every body knew him to be the greatest that had appeared.

Down in Bleeding Heart Yard, where there was not one unappropriated half-penny, as lively an interest was taken in this paragon of men as on the Stock Exchange. Mrs. Plornish, now established in the small grocery and general trade in a snug little shop at the crack end of the Yard, at the top of the steps, with her little old father and Maggy acting as assistants, habitually held forth about him over the counter, in conversation with her customers. Mr. Plornish, who had a small share in a small builder's business in the neighborhood, said, trowel in hand, on the tops of scaffolds and on the tiles of houses, that people did tell him as Mr. Merdle was *the* one, mind you, to put us all to rights in respects of that which all on us looked to, and to bring us all safe home as much we needed, mind you, for toe be brought. Mr. Baptist, sole lodger of Mr. and Mrs. Plornish, was reputed in whispers to lay by the savings which were the result of his simple and moderate life, for investment in one of Mr. Merdle's certain enterprises. The female Bleeding Hearts, when they came for ounces of tea and hundredweights of talk, gave Mrs. Plornish to understand, That how, ma'am, they had heard from their cousin Mary Anne, which worked in the line, that his lady's dresses would fill three wagons. That how she was as handsome a lady, ma'am, as lived, no matter wheres, and a busk like marble itself. That how, according to what they was told, ma'am, it was her son by a former husband as was took into the Government; and a General he had been, and armies he had marched again and victory crowned, if all you heard was to be believed. That how it was reported Mr. Merdle's words had been, that if they could have made it worth his while to take the whole government he would have took it without a profit, but that take it he could not and stand a loss. That how it was not to be expected, ma'am, that he should lose by it, his ways being, as you might say and utter no falsehood, paved with gold; but that how it was to be much regretted that something handsome hadn't been got up to make it worth his while; for it was such and only such that knowed the heighth to which the bread and butchers' meat had rose, and it was such and only such that both could and would bring that heighth down.

So rife and potent was the fever in Bleeding Heart Yard, that Mr. Pancks' rent days caused no interval in the patients. The disease took the singular form, on those occasions, of causing the infected to find an unfathomable excuse and consolation in allusions to the magic name.

"Now, then!" Mr. Pancks would say to a defaulting lodger, "Pay up! Come on!"

"I haven't got it, Mr. Pancks," Defaulter would reply. "I tell you the truth, sir, when I say I haven't got so much as a single sixpence of it to bless myself with."

"Well! This won't do, you know," Mr. Pancks would retort. "You don't expect it *will* do, do you?"

Defaulter would admit, with a low-spirited "No, sir," having no such expectation.

"My proprietor isn't going to stand this, you know," Mr. Pancks would proceed. "He don't send me here for this. Pay up! Come!"

The Defaulter would make answer, "Ah, Mr. Pancks. If I was the rich gentleman whose name is in every body's mouth—if my name was Merdle, sir—I'd soon pay up, and be glad to do it."

Dialogues on the rent-question usually took place at the house-doors or in the entries, and in the presence of several deeply-interested Bleeding Hearts. They always received a reference of this kind with a low murmur of response, as if it were convincing; and the Defaulter, however blank and discomfited before, always cheered up a little in making it.

"If I was Mr. Merdle, sir, you wouldn't have cause to complain of me then. No, believe me!" the Defaulter would proceed, with a shake of the head. "I'd pay up so quick, then, Mr. Pancks, that you shouldn't have to ask me."

The response would be heard again here, implying that it was impossible to say any thing fairer, and that this was the next thing to paying the money down.

Mr. Pancks would be now reduced to saying, as he booked the case, "Well! You'll have the broker in, and be turned out; that's what'll happen to you. It's no use talking to me about Mr. Merdle. You are not Mr. Merdle, any more than I am."

"No, sir," the Defaulter would reply. "I only wish you *were* him, sir."

The response would take up this quickly: replying with great feeling, "Only wish you *were* him, sir."

"You'd be easier with us if you were Mr. Merdle, sir," the Defaulter would go on, with rising spirits, "and it would be better for all parties. Better for our sakes, and better for yours, too. You wouldn't have to worry no one then, sir. You wouldn't have to worry us, and you wouldn't have to worry yourself. You'd be easier in your own mind, sir, and you'd leave others easier, too, you would, if you were Mr. Merdle."

Mr. Pancks, in whom these impersonal compliments produced

an irresistible sheepishness, never rallied after such a charge. He could only bite his nails and puff away to the next Defaulter. The responsive Bleeding Hearts would then gather round the Defaulter whom he had just abandoned, and the most extravagant rumors would circulate among them, to their great comfort, touching the amount of Mr. Merdle's ready money.

From one of the many such defeats of one of many rent days, Mr. Pancks, having finished his day's collection, repaired, with his note-book under his arm, to Mrs. Plornish's corner. Mr. Pancks' object was not professional, but social. He had had a trying day, and wanted a little brightening. By this time he was on friendly terms with the Plornish family, having often looked in upon them, at similar seasons, and borne his part in recollections of Miss Dorrit.

Mrs. Plornish's shop-parlor had been decorated under her own eye, and presented, on the side toward the shop, a little fiction in which Mrs. Plornish unspeakably rejoiced. This poetical heightening of the parlor consisted in the wall being painted to represent the exterior of a thatched cottage; the artist having introduced (in as effective a manner as he found compatible with their highly disproportionate dimensions) the real door and window. The modest sun-flower and hollyhock were depicted as flourishing with great luxuriance on this rustic dwelling, while a quantity of dense smoke issuing from the chimney indicated good cheer within, and also, perhaps, that it had not been lately swept. A faithful dog was represented as flying at the legs of the friendly visitor, from the threshold; and a circular pigeon-house, enveloped in a cloud of pigeons, arose from behind the garden-paling. On the door (when it was shut,) appeared the semblance of a brass-plate, presenting the inscription, Happy Cottage, T. and M. Plornish; the partnership expressing man and wife. No Poetry and no Art ever charmed the imagination more than the union of the two in this counterfeit cottage charmed Mrs. Plornish. It was nothing to her that Plornish had a habit of leaning against it as he smoked his pipe after work, when his hat blotted out the pigeon-house and all the pigeons, when his back swallowed up the dwelling, when his hands in his pockets uprooted the blooming garden, and laid waste the adjacent country. To Mrs.

Plornish it was still a most beautiful cottage, a most wonderful deception; and it made no difference that Mr. Plornish's eye was some inches above the level of the gable bed-room in the thatch. To come out into the shop after it was shut, and hear her father sing a song inside this cottage, was a perfect Pastoral to Mrs. Plornish, the Golden Age revived. And truly if that famous period had been revived, or had ever been at all, it may be doubted whether it would have produced many more heartily admiring daughters than this poor woman.

Warned of a visitor by the tinkling bell at the shop-door, Mrs. Plornish came out of Happy Cottage to see who it might be. "I guessed it was you, Mr. Pancks," said she, "for it's quite your regular night; ain't it? Here's father, you see, come out to serve at the sound of the bell, like a brisk young shopman. Ain't he looking well? Father's more pleased to see you than if you was a customer, for he dearly loves a gossip; and when it turns upon Miss Dorrit, he loves it all the more. You never heard father in such voice as he is in at present," said Mrs. Plornish, her own voice quavering, she was so proud and pleased. "He gave us Strephon last night, to that degree that Plornish gets up and makes him this speech across the table. 'John Edward Nandy,' says Plornish to father, 'I never heard you come the warbles as I have heard you come the warbles this night.' An't it gratifying, Mr. Pancks, though; really?"

Mr. Pancks, who had snorted at the old man in his friendliest manner, replied in the affirmative, and casually asked whether that lively Altro chap had come in yet? Mrs. Plornish answered no, not yet, though he had gone to the West-End with some work, and had said he should be back by tea-time. Mr. Pancks was then hospitably pressed into Happy Cottage, where he encountered the elder Master Plornish just come home from school. Examining that young student, lightly, on the educational proceedings of the day, he found that the more advanced pupils who were is large text and the letter M, had been set the copy, "Merdle, Millions."

"And how are *you* getting on, Mrs. Plornish," said Pancks, "since we're mentioning millions?"

"Very steady indeed, sir," returned Mrs. Plornish. "Father

dear, would you go into the shop and tidy the window a little bit before tea, your taste being so beautiful?"

John Edward Nandy trotted away, much gratified, to comply with his daughter's request. Mrs. Plornish, who was always in mortal terror of mentioning pecuniary affairs before the old gentleman, lest any disclosure she made might rouse his spirit and induce him to run away to the workhouse, was thus left free to be confidential with Mr. Pancks.

"It's quite true that the business is very steady indeed," said Mrs. Plornish, lowering her voice; "and has a excellent connection. The only thing that stands in its way, sir, is the Credit."

This drawback, rather severely felt by most people who engaged in commercial transactions with the inhabitants of Bleeding Heart Yard, was a large stumbling-block in Mrs. Plornish's trade. When Mr. Dorrit had established her in the business, the Bleeding Hearts had shown an amount of emotion and a determination to support her in it, that did honor to human nature. Recognizing her claim upon their generous feelings as one who had long been a member of their community, they pledged themselves, with great feeling, to deal with Mrs. Plornish, come what would, and bestow their patronage on no other establishment. Influenced by these noble sentiments, they had even gone out of their way to purchase little luxuries in the grocery and butter line to which they were unaccustomed; saying to one another, that if they did stretch a point, was it not for a neighbor and a friend, and for whom ought a point to be stretched if not for such? So stimulated, the business was extremely brisk, and the articles in stock went off with the greatest celerity. In short, if the Bleeding Hearts had but paid, the undertaking would have been a complete success; whereas, by reason of their exclusively confining themselves to owing, the profits actually realized had not yet begun to appear in the books.

Mr. Pancks was making a very porcupine of himself by sticking his hair up, in the contemplation of this state of accounts, when old Mr. Nandy, re-entering the cottage with an air of mystery, entreated them to come and look at the strange behavior of Mr. Baptist, who seemed to have met with something that had scared him. All three going into the shop, and watching through the window, then saw Mr. Baptist, pale and agitated, go through the following extraordinary performances. First, he was observed hiding at the top of the steps leading down into the Yard, and peeping up and down the street, with his head cautiously thrust out close to the side of the shop door. After very anxious scrutiny, he came out of his retreat, and went briskly down the street as if he were going away altogether; then, suddenly turned about, and went, at the same pace and with the same feint, up the street. He had gone no further up the street than he had gone down, when he crossed the road and disappeared. The object of this last manœuvre was only apparent when his entering the shop with a sudden twist, from the steps again, explained that he had made a wide and obscure circuit round to the other, or Doyce and Clennam, end of the Yard, and had come through the Yard and bolted in. He was out of breath by that time, as he might well be: and his heart seemed to jerk faster than the little shop-bell, as it quivered and jingled behind him with his hasty shutting of the door.

"Hallo, old chap!" said Mr. Pancks. "Altro, old boy! What's the matter?"

Mr. Baptist, or Signor Cavalletto, understood English now almost as well as Mr. Pancks himself, and could speak it very well to. Nevertheless, Mrs. Plornish, with pardonable vanity in that accomplishment of hers which made her all but Italian, stepped in as interpreter.

"E ask know," said Mrs. Plornish, "what go wrong?"

"Come into the happy little cottage, Padrona," returned Mr. Baptist, imparting great stealthiness to his flurried back-handed shake of his right fore-finger. "Come there?"

Mrs. Plornish was proud of the title Padrona, which she regarded as signifying: not so much Mistress of the house, as Mistress of the Italian tongue. She immediately complied with Mr. Baptist's request, and they all went into the cottage.

"E ope you no fright," said Mrs. Plornish, then, interpreting Mr. Pancks in a new way, with her usual fertility of resource. "What appen? Peaka Padrona?"

MR. BAPTIST IS SUPPOSED TO HAVE SEEN SOMETHING.

"I have seen some one," returned Baptist. "I have rincontrato him."

"Im? Oo him?" asked Mrs. Plornish.

"A bad man. A baddest man. I have hoped that I should never see him again."

"Ow you know im bad?" asked Mrs. Plornish.

"It does not matter, Padrona. I know it too well."

"E see you?" asked Mrs. Plornish.

"No. I hope not. I believe not."

"He says," Mrs. Plornish then interpreted, addressing her father and Pancks with mild condescension, "that he has met a bad man, but he hopes the bad man didn't see him.—Why," inquired Mrs. Plornish, reverting to the Italian language, "why ope bad man no see?"

"Padrona, dearest," returned the little foreigner, whom she so considerately protected, "do not ask, I pray. Once again, I say it matters not. I have fear of this man. I do not wish to see him, I do not wish to be known of him—never again! Enough, most beautiful. Leave it there!"

The topic was so disagreeable to him, and so put his usual liveliness to the rout, that Mrs. Plornish forbore to press him further; the rather as the tea had been drawing for some time on the hob. But she was not the less surprised and curious for asking no more questions; neither was Mr. Pancks whose expressive breathing had been laboring hard, since the entrance of the little man, like a locomotive engine with a great load getting up a steep incline. Maggy, now better dressed than of yore, though still faithful to the monstrous character of her cap, had been in the background from the first with open mouth and eyes, which staring and gaping features were not diminished in breadth by the untimely suppression of the subject. However, no more was said about it, though much appeared to be thought on all sides; by no means excepting the two young Plornishes, who partook of the evening meal as if their eating the bread and butter were rendered almost superfluous by the painful probability of the worst of men shortly presenting himself for the purpose of eating them. Mr. Baptist, by degrees, began to chirp a little; but never stirred from the seat he had taken behind the door and close to the window, though it was not his usual place. As often as the little bell rang, he started and peeped out secretly, with the end of the little curtain in his hand, and the rest before his face ; evidently not at all satisfied but that the man he dreaded had tracked him through all his doublings and turnings, with the certainty of a terrible bloodhound.

The entrance, at various times, of two or three customers and of Mr. Plornish, gave Mr. Baptist just enough of this employment to keep the attention of the company fixed upon him. Tea was over, and the children were abed, and Mrs. Plornish was feeling her way to the dutiful proposal that her father should favor them with Chloe, when the bell again rang, and Mr. Clennam came in.

Clennam had been poring late over his books and letters ; for the waiting-rooms of the Circumlocution Office ravaged his time sorely. Over and above that, he was depressed and made uneasy by the late occurrence at his mother's. He looked worn and solitary. He felt so, too ; but, nevertheless, was returning home from his counting-house by that end of the Yard, to give them the intelligence that he had received another letter from Miss Dorrit.

The news made a sensation in the cottage which drew off the general attention from Mr. Baptist. Maggy, who pushed her way into the foreground immediately, would have seemed to draw in the tidings of her Little Mother, equally at her ears, nose, mouth, and eyes, but that the last were obstructed by tears. She was particularly delighted when Clennam assured her that there were hospitals, and very kindly conducted hospitals in Rome. Mr. Pancks rose into new distinction in virtue of being specially remembered in the letter. Every body was pleased and interested, and Clennam was well repaid for his trouble.

"But you are tired, sir. Let me make you a cup of tea," said Mrs. Plornish, "if you'll condescend to take such a thing in the cottage ; and many thanks to you, too, I am sure, for bearing us in mind so kindly."

Mr. Plornish deeming it incumbent on him, as host, to add his personal acknowledgments, tendered them in the form which always expressed his highest ideal of a combination of ceremony with sincerity.

"John Edward Nandy," said Mr. Plornish, addressing the old gentleman. "Sir. It's not too often that you see unpretending actions without a spark of pride, and therefore when you see them give grateful honor unto the same, being that if you don't and live to want 'em it follows serve you right."

To which Mr. Nandy replied:

"I am heartily of your opinion, Thomas, and which your opinion is the same as mine, and therefore no more words and not being backward with that opinion, which opinion giving it as yes, Thomas, yes, is the opinion which yourself and me must ever be unanimously jined by all, and where there is no difference of opinion there can be none but one opinion, which fully no, Thomas, Thomas, no!"

Arthur, with less formality, expressed himself gratified by their high appreciation of so very slight an attention on his part; and explained as to the tea that he had not yet dined, and was going straight home to refresh after a long day's labor, or he would readily have accepted the hospitable offer. As Mr. Pancks was somewhat noisily getting his steam up for departure, he concluded by asking that gentleman if he would walk with him? Mr. Pancks said he wanted no better engagement, and the two took leave of Happy Cottage.

"If you will come home with me, Pancks," said Arthur, when they got into the street, "and will share what dinner or supper there is, it will be next door to an act of charity; for I am weary and out of sorts to-night."

"Ask me to do a greater thing than that," said Pancks, "when you want it done, and I'll do it."

Between this eccentric personage and Clennam, a tacit understanding and accord had been always improving since Mr. Pancks flew over Mr. Rugg's back in the Marshalsea Yard. When the carriage drove away on the memorable day of the family's departure, these two had looked after it together, and had walked slowly away together. When the first letter came from Little Dorrit, nobody was more interested in hearing of her than Mr. Pancks. The second letter, at that moment in Clennam's breast-pocket, particularly remembered him by name.

Though he had never before made any profession or protestation to Clennam, and though what he had just said was little enough as to the words in which it was expressed, Clennam had long had a growing belief that Mr. Pancks, in his own odd way, was becoming attached to him. All these strings intertwining, made Pancks a very cable of anchorage that night.

"I am quite alone," Arthur explained as they walked on. "My partner is away, busily engaged at a distance on his branch of our business, and you shall do just as you like."

"Thank you. You didn't take particular notice of little Altro just now; did you?" said Pancks.

"No. Why?"

"He's a bright fellow, and I like him," said Pancks. "Something has gone amiss with him to-day. Have you any idea of any cause that can have overset him?"

"You surprise me; none whatever."

Mr. Pancks gave his reasons for the inquiry. Arthur was quite unprepared for them, and quite unable to suggest an explanation of them.

"Perhaps you'll ask him," said Pancks, "as he's a stranger?"

"Ask him what?" returned Clennam.

"What he has on his mind."

"I ought first to see for myself that he has something on his mind, I think," said Clennam. "I have found him in every way so diligent, so grateful (for little enough), and so trustworthy, that it might look like suspecting him. And that would be very unjust."

"True," said Pancks. "But, I say! You oughtn't to be anybody's proprietor, Mr. Clennam. You're much too delicate."

"For the matter of that," returned Clennam, laughing, "I have not a large proprietary share in Cavalletto. His carving is his livelihood. He keeps the keys of the Factory, watches it every alternate night, and acts as a sort of housekeeper to it generally; but we have little work in the way of his ingenuity, though we give him what we have. No! I am rather his adviser than his proprietor. To call me his standing counsel and his banker would be nearer the fact. Speaking of being his banker, is it not curious, Pancks, that the ventures which run just now in so many people's heads should run even in little Cavalletto's?"

"Ventures?" retorted Pancks with a snort. "What ventures?"

"These Merdle enterprises."

"Oh? Investments," said Pancks. "Ay, ay! I didn't know you were speaking of investments."

His quick way of replying caused Clennam to look at him, with a doubt whether he meant more than he said. As it was accompanied, however, with a quickening of his pace and a corresponding increase in the laboring of his machinery, Arthur did not pursue the matter, and they soon arrived at his house.

A dinner of soup and a pigeon-pie, served on a little round table before the fire, and flavored with a bottle of good wine, oiled Mr. Pancks' works in a highly effective manner. So that when Clennam produced his Eastern pipe, and handed Mr. Pancks another Eastern pipe, the latter gentleman was perfectly comfortable.

They puffed for a while in silence, Mr. Pancks like a steam-vessel with wind, tide, calm water, and all other sea-going conditions in her favor. He was the first to speak, and he spoke thus:

"Yes. Investments is the word."

Clennam, with his former look, said "Ah!"

"I am going back to it, you see," said Pancks

"Yes. I see you are going back to it," returned Clennam, wondering why.

"Wasn't it a curious thing that they should run in little Altro's head? Eh?" said Pancks as he smoked. "Wasn't that how you put it?"

"That was what I said."

"Ay! But think of the whole Yard having got it. Think of their all meeting me with it, on my collecting days, here and there and every where. Whether they pay, or whether they don't pay. Merdle, Merdle, Merdle. Always Merdle."

"Very strange how these runs on an infatuation prevail," said Arthur.

"An't it?" returned Pancks. After smoking for a minute or so, more dryly than comported with his recent oiling, he added: "Because you see these people don't understand the subject."

"Not a bit," assented Clennam.

"Not a bit," cried Pancks. "Know nothing of figures. Know nothing of money questions. Never made a calculation. Never worked it, sir!"

"If they had—" Clennam was going on to say; when Mr. Pancks, without change of countenance produced a sound so far surpassing all his usual efforts, nasal or bronchial, that he stopped.

"If they had?" repeated Pancks, in an inquiring tone.

"I thought you—spoke," said Arthur, hesitating what name to give the interruption.

"Not at all," said Pancks. "Not yet. I may in a minute. If they had?"

"If they had," observed Clennam, who was a little at a loss how to take his friend, "why, I suppose they would have known better."

"How so, Mr. Clennam?" Pancks asked, quickly, and with an odd effect of having been from the commencement of the conversation loaded with the heavy charge he now fired off. "They're right, you know. They don't mean to be, but they're right."

"Right in sharing Cavalletto's inclination to speculate with Mr. Merdle?"

"Per-fectly, sir," said Pancks. "I've gone into it. I've made my calculations. I've worked it; they're safe and genuine." Relieved by having got to this, Mr. Pancks took as long a pull as his lungs would permit at his Eastern pipe, and looked sagaciously and steadily at Clennam while inhaling and exhaling too.

In those moments, Mr. Pancks began to give out the dangerous infection with which he was laden. It is the manner of communicating these diseases; it is the subtle way in which they go about.

"Do you mean, my good Pancks," asked Clennam, emphatically, "that you would put that thousand pounds of yours, let us say, for instance, out at this kind of interest?"

"Certainly," said Pancks. "Already done it, sir."

Mr. Pancks took another long inhalation, another long exhalation, another long sagacious look at Clennam.

"I tell you, Mr. Clennam, I've gone into it," said Pancks.

"He's a man of immense resources—enormous capital—government influence. They're the best schemes afloat. They're safe. They're certain."

"Well!" returned Clennam, looking first at him gravely, and then at the fire gravely. "You surprise me!"

"Bah!" Pancks retorted. "Don't say that, sir. It's what you ought to do yourself. Why don't you do as I do?"

Of whom Mr. Pancks had taken the prevalent disease, he could no more have told than if he had unconsciously taken a fever. Bred at first, as many physical diseases are, in the wickedness of men, and then disseminated in their ignorance, these epidemics, after a period, get communicated to many sufferers who are neither ignorant nor wicked. Mr. Pancks might, or might not, have caught the illness himself from a subject of this class; but, in this category he appeared before Clennam, and the infection he threw off was all the more virulent.

"And you have really invested," Clennam had already passed to that word, "your thousand pounds, Pancks?"

"To be sure, sir!" replied Pancks, boldly, with a puff of smoke. "And only wish it was ten."

Now, Clennam had two subjects lying heavy on his lonely mind that night; the one, his partner's long-deferred hope: the other, what he had seen and heard at his mother's. In the relief of having this companion, and of feeling that he could trust him, he passed on to both, and both brought him round again, with an increase and acceleration of force, to his point of departure.

It came about in the simplest manner. Quitting the investment subject, after an interval of silent looking at the fire through the smoke of his pipe, he told Pancks how and why he was occupied with the great national Department. "A hard case it has been, and a hard case it is on Doyce," he finished by saying, with all the honest feeling the topic roused in him.

"Hard indeed," Pancks acquiesced. "But you manage for him, Mr. Clennam?"

"How do you mean?"

"Manage the money part of the business?"

"Yes. As well as I can."

"Manage it better, sir," said Pancks. "Recompense him for his toils and disappointments. Give him the chances of the time. He'll never benefit himself in that way, patient and preoccupied workman. He looks to you, sir."

"I do my best, Pancks," returned Clennam, uneasily. "As to duly weighing and considering these new enterprises, of which I have had no experience, I doubt if I am fit for it. I am growing old."

"Growing old?" cried Pancks. "Ha, ha!"

There was something so indubitably genuine in the wonderful laugh, and series of snorts and puffs, engendered in Mr. Pancks's astonishment at, and utter rejection of the idea, that his being quite in earnest could not be questioned.

"Growing old?" cried Pancks. "Hear, hear, hear! Old? Hear him, hear him!"

The positive refusal expressed in Mr. Pancks's continued snorts, no less than in these exclamations, to entertain the sentiment for a single instant, drove Arthur away from it. Indeed, he was fearful of something happening to Mr. Pancks, in the violent conflict that took place between the breath he jerked out of himself and the smoke he jerked into himself. This abandonment of the second topic threw him on the third.

"Young, old, or middle-aged, Pancks," he said, when there was a favorable pause, "I am in a very anxious and uncertain state; a state that even leads me to doubt whether any thing now seeming to belong to me, may be really mine. Shall I tell you how this is? Shall I put a great trust in you?"

"You shall, sir," said Pancks, "if you believe me worthy of it."

"I do."

"You may!" Mr. Pancks's short and sharp rejoinder, confirmed by the sudden outstretching of his coaly hand, was most expressive and convincing. Arthur shook the hand warmly.

He then, softening the nature of his old apprehensions as much as was possible consistently with their being made intelligible, and never alluding to his mother by name, but speaking vaguely of a relation of his, confided to Mr. Pancks a broad outline of the misgivings he entertained, and of the interview he had witnessed. Mr. Pancks listened with such interest that, regardless of the charms of the Eastern pipe, he put it in the grate among the fire-irons, and occupied his hands during the whole recital in so erecting the loops and hooks of hair all over his head, that he looked, when it came to a conclusion, like a journeyman Hamlet in conversation with his father's spirit.

"Brings me back, sir," was his exclamation then, with a startling touch on Clennam's knee, "brings me back, sir, to the Investments! I don't say any thing of your making yourself poor, to repair a wrong you never committed. That's you. A man must be himself. But I say this. Fearing you may want money to save your own blood from exposure and disgrace—make as much as you can!"

Arthur shook his head, but looked at him thoughtfully too.

"Be as rich as you can, sir," Pancks adjured him, with a powerful concentration of all his energies on the advice. "Be as rich as you honestly can. It's your duty. Not for your sake, but for the sake of others. Take time by the forelock. Poor Mr. Doyce (who really is growing old) depends upon you. Your relative depends upon you. You don't know what depends upon you."

"Well, well, well!" returned Arthur. "Enough for to-night."

"One word more, Mr. Clennam," retorted Pancks, "and then enough for to-night. Why should you leave all the gains to the gluttons, knaves, and impostors? Why should you leave all the gains that are to be got to my proprietor and the like of him? Yet you're always doing it. When I say you, I mean such men as you. You know you are. Why, I see it every day of my life. I see nothing else. It's my business to see it. Therefore I say," urged Pancks, "Go in and win!"

"But what of Go in and lose?" said Arthur.

"Can't be done, sir," returned Pancks. "I have looked into it. Name up, everywhere—immense resources—enormous capital—great position—high connection—government influence. Can't be done!"

Gradually, after this closing exposition, Mr. Pancks subsided; allowed his hair to droop as much as it ever would droop on the utmost persuasion; reclaimed the pipe from the fire-irons, filled it anew, and smoked it out. They said little more; but were company to one another in silently pursuing the same subjects, and did not part until midnight. On taking his leave, Mr. Pancks, when he had shaken hands with Clennam, worked completely round him before he steamed out at the door. This Arthur received as an assurance that he might implicitly rely on Pancks, if he should ever come to need assistance; either in any of the matters of which they had spoken that night, or on any other subject that could in any way affect himself.

At intervals all next day, and even while his attention was fixed on other things, he thought of Mr. Pancks's investment of his thousand pounds, and of his having "looked into it." He thought of Mr. Pancks's being so sanguine in this matter, and of his not being usually of a sanguine character. He thought of the great National Department, and of the delight it would be to him to see Doyce better off. He thought of the darkly threatening place that went by the name of Home in his remembrance, and of the gathering shadows which made it yet more darkly threatening than of old. He observed anew that wherever he went, he saw, or heard, or touched, the celebrated name of Merdle: he found it difficult even to remain at his desk a couple of hours, without having it presented to one of his bodily senses through some agency or other. He began to think it was curious too that it should be everywhere, and that nobody but he should seem to have any mistrust of it. Though indeed he began to remember, when he got to this, even *he* did not mistrust it; he had only happened to keep aloof from it.

Such symptoms, when a disease of the kind is rife, are usually the signs of sickening.

CHAPTER L.

TAKING ADVICE.

When it became known to the Britons on the shore of the yellow Tiber, that their intelligent compatriot Mr. Sparkler was made one of the lords of their Circumlocution Office, they took it as a piece of news with which they had no nearer concern than with any other piece of news—any other Accident or Offense—in the English papers. Some laughed; some said, by way of complete excuse, that the post was virtually a sinecure, and any fool who could spell his name was good enough for it; some, and these were the more solemn political oracles, said that Decimus did wisely to strengthen himself, and that the sole constitutional purpose of all places within the gift of Decimus, was, that Decimus should strengthen himself. A few bilious Britons there were who would not subscribe to this article of faith; but their objection was purely theoretical. In a practical point of view, they listlessly abandoned the matter, as being the business of some other Britons unknown, somewhere or nowhere. In like manner, at home, great numbers of Britons maintained, for as long as four-and-twenty consecutive hours, that those invisible and nameless Britons "ought to take it up;" and that if they quietly acquiesced in it, they deserved it. But of what class the remiss Britons were composed, and where the unlucky creatures hid themselves, and why they hid themselves, and how it constantly happened that they neglected their interests, when so many other Britons were quite at a loss to account for their not looking after those interests, was not, either upon the shore of the yellow Tiber or the shore of the black Thames, made apparent to men.

Mrs. Merdle circulated the news, as she received congratulations on it, with a careless grace that displayed it to advantage, as the setting displays the jewel. Yes, she said, Edmund had taken the place. Mr. Merdle wished him to take it, and he had taken it. She hoped Edmund might like it, but really she didn't know. It would keep him in town a good deal, and he preferred the country. Still, it was not a disagreeable position—and it was a position. There was no denying that the thing was a compliment to Mr. Merdle, and was not a bad thing for Edmund, if he liked it. It was just as well that he should have something to do, and it was just as well that he should have something for doing it. Whether it would be more agreeable to Edmund than the army, remained to be seen.

Thus the bosom; accomplished in the art of seeming to make things of small account, and really enhancing them in the process. While Henry Gowan, whom Decimus had thrown away, went through the whole round of his acquaintance between the Gate of the People and the town of Albano, vowing, almost (but not quite) with tears in his eyes, that Sparkler was the sweetest-tempered, simplest-hearted, altogether most lovable jackass that ever grazed on the public common; and that only one circumstance could have delighted him (Gowan) more, than his (the beloved jackass's) getting this post, and that would have been his (Gowan's) getting it himself. He said, it was the very thing for Sparkler. There was nothing to do, and he would do it charmingly; thore was a handsome salary to draw, and he would draw it charmingly; it was a delightful, appropriate, capital appointment; and he almost forgave the donor his slight of himself, in his joy that the dear donkey for whom he had so great an affection was so admirably stabled. Nor did his benevolence stop here. He took pains, on all social occasions, to draw Mr. Sparkler out, and make him conspicuous before the company; and, although the considerate action always resulted in that young gentleman's making a dreary and forlorn mental spectacle of himself, the friendly intention was not to be doubted.

Unless, indeed, it chanced to be doubted by the object of Mr. Sparkler's affections. Miss Fanny was now in the difficult situation of being universally known in that light, and of not having dismissed Mr. Sparkler, however capriciously she used him. Hence, she was sufficiently identified with the gentleman to feel compromised by his being more than usually ridiculous; and hence, being by no means deficient in quickness, she sometimes came to his rescue against Gowan, and did him very good service. But, while doing this, she was ashamed of him, undetermined whether to get rid of him or more decidedly encourage him, distracted with apprehensions that she was every day becoming more and more immeshed in her uncertainties, and tortured by misgivings that Mrs. Merdle triumphed in her distress. With this tumult in her mind, it is no subject for surprise that Miss Fanny came home one night in a state of agitation from a concert and ball at Mr. Merdle's house, and, on her sister affectionately trying to soothe her, pushed that sister away from the toilet-table, at which she sat angrily trying to cry, and declared with a heaving bosom that she detested every body, and she wished she was dead.

"Dear Fanny, what is the matter? Tell me."

"Matter, you little Mole," said Fanny. "If you were not the blindest of the blind, you would have no occasion to ask me. The idea of daring to pretend to assert that you have eyes in your head, and yet ask me what's the matter!"

"Is it Mr. Sparkler, dear?"

"Mis-ter Spar-kler!" repeated Fanny, with unbounded scorn, as if he were not the last subject in the Solar system that could possibly be near her mind. "No, Miss Bat, it is not."

Immediately afterward, she became remorseful for having called her sister names; declaring with sobs that she knew she made herself hateful, but that every body drove her to it.

"I don't think you are well to-night," dear Fanny.

"Stuff and nonsense!" replied the young lady, turning angry again; "I am as well as you are. Perhaps I might say better, and yet make no boast of it."

Poor Little Dorrit, not seeing her way to the offering of any soothing words that would escape repudiation, deemed it best to remain quiet. At first, Fanny took this ill, too; protesting to her looking-glass, that of all the trying sisters a girl could have, she did think the most trying sister was a flat sister. That she knew she was at times a wretched temper; that she knew she made herself hateful; that when she made herself hateful, nothing would do her half the good of being told so; but that, being afflicted with a flat sister, she never *was* told so, and the consequence resulted that she was absolutely tempted and goaded into making herself disagreeable. Besides (she angrily told her looking-glass,) she didn't want to be forgiven. It was not a right example that she should be constantly stooping to be forgiven by a younger sister. And this was the Art of it—that she was always being placed in the position of being forgiven, whether she liked it or not. Finally, she burst into violent weeping, and, when her sister came and sat close at her side to comfort her, said, "Amy, you're an Angel!"

"But I tell you what, my Pet," said Fanny, when her sister's gentleness had calmed her, "it now comes to this; that things can not and shall not go on as they are at present going on, and that there must be an end of this, one way or other."

As the announcement was vague, though very peremptory, Little Dorrit returned, "Let us talk about it."

"Quite so, my dear," assented Fanny, as she dried her eyes. "Let us talk about it. I am rational again, now, and you shall advise me. *Will* you advise me, my sweet child?"

Even Amy smiled at the notion, but she said, "I will, Fanny, as well as I can."

"Thank you, dearest Amy," returned Fanny, kissing her. "You are my Anchor."

Having embraced her with great affection, Fanny took a bottle of sweet toilet water from the table, and called to her maid for a fine handkerchief. She then dismissed that attendant for the night, and went on to be advised; dabbing her eyes and forehead from time to time, to cool them.

"My love," Fanny began, "our characters and points of view are sufficiently different (kiss me again, my darling,) to make it very probable that I shall surprise you by what I am going to say. What I am going to say, my dear, is, that notwithstanding our property, we labor, socially speaking, under disadvantages. You don't quite understand what I mean, Amy?"

"I have no doubt I shall," said Amy, mildly, "after a few words more."

"Well, my dear, what I mean, is, that we are, after all, newcomers into fashionable life."

"I am sure, Fanny," Little Dorrit interposed in her zealous admiration, "no one need find that out in you."

"Well, my dear child, perhaps not," said Fanny, "though it's most kind and most affectionate in you, you precious girl, to say so." Here she dabbed her sister's forehead, and blew upon it a little. "But you are," resumed Fanny, "as is well known, the dearest little thing that ever was! To resume, my child. Pa is extremely gentlemanly and extremely well-informed, but he is, in some trifling respects, a little different from other gentlemen of his fortune; partly on account of what he has gone through, poor dear: partly, I fancy, on account of its often running in his mind that other people are thinking about that while he is talking to them. Uncle, my love, is altogether unpresentable. Though a dear creature, to whom I am tenderly attached, he is, socially speaking, shocking. Edward is frightfully expensive and dissipated. I don't mean that there is any thing ungenteel in that itself—far from it—but I do mean that he doesn't do it well, and that he doesn't, if I may so express myself, get the money's worth in the sort of dissipated reputation that attaches to him."

"Poor Edward," sighed Little Dorrit, with the whole family history in the sigh.

"Yes. And poor you and me too," returned Fanny, rather sharply. "Exactly so! Then, my dear, we have no mother, and we have a Mrs. General. And I tell you again, darling, that Mrs. General, if I may reverse a common proverb and adapt it to her, is a cat in gloves who *will* catch mice. That woman, I am quite sure and confident, will be our mother-in-law."

"I can hardly think, Fanny—" Fanny stopped her.

"Now, don't argue with me about it, Amy," said she, "because I know better." Feeling that she had been sharp again, she dabbed her sister's forehead again, and blew upon it again. "To resume once more, my dear. It then becomes a question with me (I am proud and spirited, Amy, as you very well know: too much so, I dare say) whether I shall make up my mind to take it upon myself to carry the family through."

"How?" asked her sister anxiously.

"I will not," said Fanny, without answering the question, "submit to be mother-in-lawed by Mrs. General; and I will not submit to be, in any respect whatever, either patronized or tormented by Mrs. Merdle."

Little Dorrit laid her hand upon the hand that held the bottle of sweet water, with a still more anxious look. Fanny, quite punishing her own forehead with the vehement dabs she now began to give it, fitfully went on.

"That he has, somehow or other, and how is of no consequence, attained a very good position, no one can deny. That it is a very good connection, no one can deny. And as to the question of clever or not clever, I doubt very much whether a clever husband would be suitable to me. I can not submit. I should not be able to defer to him enough."

"Oh, my dear, dear Fanny!" expostulated Little Dorrit, upon whom a kind of terror had been stealing as she perceived what her sister meant. "If you loved any one, all this feeling would change. If you loved any one, you would no more be yourself, but you would quite lose and forget yourself in your devotion to him. If you loved him, Fanny—" Fanny had stopped the dabbing hand, and was looking at her fixedly, and with a smile full of meaning.

"Oh, indeed!" cried Fanny. "Really? Bless me, how much some people know of some subjects! They say every one has a subject, and I certainly seem to have hit upon yours, Amy. There, you little thing, I was only in fun," dabbing her sister's forehead; "but, don't you be a silly puss, and don't you think flightily and eloquently about degenerate impossibilities. There! Now, I'll go back to myself."

"Dear Fanny, let me say first, that I would far rather we worked for a scanty living again, than I would see you rich and married to Mr. Sparkler."

"*Let* you say, my dear?" retorted Fanny. "Why, of course, I will *let* you say any thing. There's no constraint upon you, I hope. We are together to talk it over. And as to marrying Mr. Sparkler, I have not the least intention of doing so to-night my dear, or to-morrow morning either."

"But at some time?"

"At no time, for any thing I know at present," answered Fanny, with indifference. Then, suddenly changing her indifference into a burning restlessness, she added, "You talk about the clever men, you little thing! It's all very fine and easy to talk about the clever men; but where are they? *I* don't see them any where near *me!*"

"My dear Fanny, so short a time—"

"Short time or long time," interrupted Fanny, "I am impatient of our situation, I don't like our situation, and very little would induce me to change it. Other girls, differently reared and differently circumstanced altogether, might wonder at what I say or may do. Let them. They are driven by their lives and characters. I am driven by mine."

"Fanny, my dear Fanny, you know that you have qualities to make you the wife of one very superior to Mr. Sparkler."

"Amy, my dear Amy," retorted Fanny, parodying her words, "I know that I wish to have a more defined and distinct position, in which I can assert myself with greater effect against that insolent woman."

"Would you therefore—forgive my asking, Fanny—therefore marry her son?"

"Why, perhaps," said Fanny, with a triumphant smile. "There may be many less promising ways of arriving at an end than that, my dear. That piece of insolence may think, now, that it would be a great success to get her son off upon me, and shelve me. But, perhaps she little thinks how I would retort upon her if I married her son. I would oppose her in every thing, and compete with her. I would make it the business of my life."

Fanny set down the bottle when she came to this, and walked about the room; always stopping and standing still while she spoke.

"One thing I could certainly do, my child: I could make her older. And I would!"

This was followed by another walk.

"I would talk of her as an old woman. I would pretend to know—if I didn't, but I should from her son—all about her age. And she should hear me say, Amy: affectionately, quite dutifully and affectionately: how well she looked, considering her time of life. I could make her seem older, at once, by being myself so much younger. I may not be as handsome as she is; I am not a fair judge of that question, I suppose; but I know

I am handsome enough to be a thorn in her side. And I would be!"

"My dear sister, would you condemn yourself to an unhappy life for this?"

"It wouldn't be an unhappy life, Amy. It would be the life I am fitted for. Whether by disposition, or whether by circumstances, is no matter; I am better fitted for such a life than for almost any other."

There was something of a desolate tone in those words; but, with a short proud laugh, she took another walk, and after passing a great looking-glass came to another stop.

"Figure! Figure, Amy! Well. The woman has a good figure. I will give her her due, and not deny it. But, is it so far beyond all others that it is altogether unapproachable? Upon my word, I am not so sure of it. Give some much younger women the latitude as to dress that she has, being married; and we would see about that, my dear!"

Something in the thought that was agreeable and flattering, brought her back to her seat in a gayer temper. She took her sister's hands in hers, and clapped all four hands above her head as she looked in her sister's face, laughing:

"And the dancer, Amy, that she has quite forgotten—the dancer who bore no sort of resemblance to me, and of whom I never remind her, oh dear no!—should dance through her life, and dance in her way, to such a tune as would disturb her insolent placidity a little. Just a little, my dear Amy, just a little!"

Meeting an earnest and imploring look in Amy's face, she brought the four hands down, and laid only one on Amy's lips.

"Now, don't argue with me, child," she said, in a sterner way, "because it is of no use. I understand these subjects much better than you do. I have not nearly made up my mind, but it may be. Now we have talked this over comfortably, and may go to bed. You best and dearest little mouse, Good-Night!" With those words Fanny weighed her Anchor, and—having taken so much advice—left off being advised for that occasion.

Thenceforward, Amy observed Mr. Sparkler's treatment by his enslaver, with new reasons for attaching importance to all that passed between them. There were times when Fanny appeared quite unable to endure his mental feebleness, and when she became so sharply impatient of it that she would all but dismiss him for good. There were other times when she got on much better with him; when he amused her, and when her sense of superiority seemed to counterbalance that opposite side of the scale. If Mr. Sparkler had been other than the faithfulest and most submissive of swains, he was sufficiently hard pressed to have fled from the scene of his trials, and have set at least the whole distance from Rome to London between himself and his enchantress. But he had no greater will of his own than a boat has when it is towed by a steam-ship; and he followed his cruel mistress through rough and smooth, on equally strong compulsion.

Mrs. Merdle, during these passages, said little to Fanny, but said more about her. She was, as it were, forced to look at her, through her eye-glass, and in general conversation to allow commendations of her beauty to be wrung from her by its irresistible demands. The defiant character it assumed when Fanny heard these extollings (as it generally happened that she did), was not expressive of concessions to the impartial bosom; but the utmost revenge the bosom took was, to say audibly, "a spoilt beauty—but with that face and shape, who could wonder?"

It might have been about a month or six weeks after the night of the advice, when Little Dorrit began to think she detected some new understanding between Mr. Sparkler and Fanny. Mr. Sparkler, as if in adherence to some compact, scarcely ever spoke without first looking toward Fanny, for leave. That young lady was too discreet ever to look back again: but, if Mr. Sparkler had permission to speak, she remained silent; if he had not, she herself spoke. Moreover, it became plain whenever Henry Gowan attempted to perform the friendly office of drawing him out, that he was not to be drawn. And not only that, but Fanny would presently, without any pointed application in the world, chance to say something with such a sting in it, that Gowan would draw back as if he had put his hand into a bee-hive.

There was yet another circumstance which went a long way

to confirm Little Dorrit in her fears, though it was not a great circumstance in itself. Mr. Sparkler's demeanor toward herself changed. It became fraternal. Sometimes, when she was in the outer circle of assemblies—at their own residence, at Mrs. Merdle's, or elsewhere—she would find herself stealthily supported round the waist by Mr. Sparkler's arm. Mr. Sparkler never offered the slightest explanation of this attention; but merely smiled with an air of blundering, contented, good-natured proprietorship, which, in so heavy a gentleman, was ominously expressive.

Little Dorrit was at home one day, thinking abont Fanny with a heavy heart. They had a room at one end of their drawing-room suite, nearly all irregular bay-window, projecting over the street, and commanding all the picturesque life and variety of the Corso, both up and down. At three or four o'clock in the afternoon, English time, the view from this window was very bright and peculiar; and Little Dorrit used to sit and muse here, much as she had been used to while away the time in her balcony at Venice. Seated thus one day, she was softly touched on the shoulder, and Fanny said, "Well, Amy dear," and took her seat at her side. Their seat was a part of the window; when there was any thing in the way of a procession going on, they used to have bright draperies hung out at the window, and used to kneel or sit on this seat and look out at it, leaning on the brilliant color. But there was no procession that day, and Little Dorrit was rather surprised by Fanny's being at home at that hour, as she was generally out on horseback then.

"Well, Amy," said Fanny, "what are you thinking of, little one?"

"I was thinking of you, Fanny."

"No? What a coincidence! I declare here's some one else. You were not thinking of this some one else too; were you, Amy?"

Amy *had* been thinking of this some one else too; for, it was Mr. Sparkler. She did not say so, however, as she gave him her hand. Mr. Sparkler came and sat down on the other side of her, and she felt the fraternal railing come behind her, and apparently stretch on to include Fanny.

"Well, my little sister," said Fanny, with a sigh, "I suppose you know what this means?"

"She's as beautiful as she's doted on," stammered Mr. Sparkler—"and there's no nonsense about her—it's arranged"—

"You needn't explain, Edmund," said Fanny.

"No, my love," said Mr. Sparkler.

"In short, pet," proceeded Fanny, "on the whole, we are engaged. We must tell papa about it, either to-night or to-morrow, according to the opportunities. Then it's done, and very little more need be said."

"My dear Fanny," said Mr. Sparkler, with deference, "I should like to say a word to Amy."

"Well, well! Say it, for goodness' sake," returned the young lady.

"I am convinced, my dear Amy," said Mr. Sparkler, "that if ever there was a girl, next to your highly-endowed and beautiful sister, who had no nonsense about her—"

"We know all about that, Edmund," interposed Miss Fanny. "Never mind that. Pray go on to something else besides our having no nonsense about us.

"Yes, my love," said Mr. Sparkler. "And I assure you, Amy, that nothing can be a greater happiness to myself, myself—next to the happiness of being so highly honored with the choice of a glorious girl who hasn't an atom of—"

"Pray, Edmund, pray!" interrupted Fanny, with a slight pat of her pretty foot upon the floor.

"My love, you're quite right," said Mr. Sparkler, "and I know I have a habit of it. What I wished to declare was, that nothing can be a greater happiness to myself, myself—next to the happiness of being united to pre-eminently the most glorious of girls—than to have the happiness of cultivating the affectionate acquaintance of Amy. I may not myself," said Mr. Sparkler, manfully, "be up to the mark on some other subjects at a short notice, and I am aware that if you were to poll Society, the general opinion would be that I am not; but on the subject of Amy, I AM up to the mark!"

Mr. Sparkler kissed her, in witness thereof.

"A knife and fork and an apartment," proceeded Mr. Sparkler, growing, in comparison with his oratorical antecedents, quite diffuse, "will ever be at Amy's disposal My Governor, I am sure, will always be proud to entertain one whom I so much esteem. And regarding my mother," said Mr. Sparkler, "who is a remarkably fine woman, with—"

"Edmund, Edmund!" cried Miss Fanny, as before.

"With submission, my soul," pleaded Mr. Sparkler. "I know I have a habit of it, and I thank you very much, my adorable girl, for taking the trouble to correct it; but my mother is admitted on all sides to be a remarkably fine woman, and she really hasn't any—"

"That may be, or may not be," returned Fanny, "but pray don't mention it any more."

"I will not, my love," said Mr. Sparkler.

"Then in fact you have nothing more to say, Edmund; have you?" inquired Fanny.

"So far from it, my adorable girl," answered Mr. Sparkler, "I apologize for having said so much."

Mr. Sparkler perceived, by a kind of inspiration, that the question implied had he not better go? He therefore withdrew the fraternal railing, and neatly said that he would, with submission, take his leave. He did not go without being congratulated by Amy, as well as she could discharge that office in the flutter and distress of her spirits.

When he was gone, she said, "Oh, Fanny, Fanny!" and turned to her sister in the bright window, and fell upon her bosom and cried there. Fanny laughed at first; but soon laid her face against her sister's and cried too, loud and long. It was the last time Fanny ever showed that there was any hidden, suppressed, or conquered feeling in her on that matter. From that hour, the way she had chosen lay before her, and she trod it with her own imperious, self-supported step.

CHAPTER LI.

NO JUST CAUSE OR IMPEDIMENT WHY THESE TWO PERSONS SHOULD NOT BE JOINED TOGETHER.

Mr. Dorrit, on being informed by his elder daughter that she had accepted matrimonial overtures from Mr. Sparkler, to whom she had plighted her troth, received the communication at once with great dignity, and with a large display of parental pride; his dignity dilating with the widened prospect of advantageous ground from which to make acquaintances, and his parental pride being developed by Miss Fanny's ready sympathy with that great object of his existence. He gave her to understand that her noble ambition found harmonious echoes in his heart, and bestowed his blessing on her, as a child brimful of duty and good principle, self-devoted to the aggrandizement of the family name.

To Mr. Sparkler, when Miss Fanny permitted him to appear, Mr. Dorrit said he would not disguise that the alliance Mr. Sparkler did him the honor to propose was highly congenial to his feelings; both as being in unison with the spontaneous affections of his daughter Fanny, and as opening a family connection of a gratifying nature with Mr. Merdle, the master-spirit of the age. Mrs. Merdle, also, as a leading lady, rich in distinction, elegance, grace, and beauty, he mentioned in very laudatory terms. He felt it his duty to remark (he was sure a gentleman of Mr. Sparkler's fine sense would interpret him with all delicacy,) that he could not consider this proposal definitively determined on, until he should have had the privilege of holding some correspondence with Mr. Merdle; and of ascertaining it to be so far accordant with the views of that eminent gentleman, as that his (Mr. Dorrit's) daughter would be received on that footing which her station in life and her dowry and expectations warranted him in requiring that she should maintain in what he trusted he might be allowed, without the appearance of being mercenary, to call the Eye of the Great World. While saying this, which his character as a gentleman of some little station, and his character as a father, equally demanded of him, he would not be so diplomatic as to conceal that the proposal remained in hopeful abeyance, and under conditional acceptance, and that he thanked Mr. Sparkler for the compliment rendered to himself and to his family. He concluded with some further and more general observations on the—ha—character of an independent gentleman, and the—hum—character of a possibly too partial and admiring parent. To sum the whole up shortly, he received Mr. Sparkler's offer very much as he would have received three or four half-crowns from him in the days that were gone.

Mr. Sparkler, finding himself stunned by the words thus heaped upon his inoffensive head, made a brief though pertinent rejoinder; the same being neither more nor less than that he had long perceived Miss Fanny to have no nonsense about her, and that he had no doubt of its being all right with his Governor. At that point the object of his affections shut him up like a box with a spring lid, and sent him away.

Proceeding shortly afterward to pay his respects to the Bosom, Mr. Dorrit was received by it with great consideration. Mrs. Merdle had heard of this affair from Edmund. She had been surprised at first, because she had not thought Edmund a marrying man. Society had not thought Edmund a marrying man. Still, of course, she had seen, as a woman (we women did instinctively see these things, Mr. Dorrit!) that Edmund had been immensely captivated by Miss Dorrit, and she had openly said that Mr. Dorrit had much to answer for in bringing so charming a girl abroad to turn the heads of his countrymen.

"Have I the honor to conclude, madam," said Mr. Dorrit, "that the directions which Mr. Sparkler's affections have taken is—ha—approved of by you?"

"I assure you, Mr. Dorrit," returned the lady, "that, personally, I am charmed."

That was very gratifying to Mr. Dorrit.

"Personally," repeated Mrs. Merdle, "charmed."

This casual repetition of the word personally, moved Mr.

Dorrit to express his hope that Mr. Merdle's approval, too, would not be wanting.

"I can not," said Mrs. Merdle, "take upon myself to answer positively for Mr. Merdle; gentlemen, especially gentlemen who are what Society calls capitalists, having their own ideas of these matters. But I should think—merely giving an opinion, Mr. Dorrit—I should think Mr. Merdle would be, upon the whole—" here she held a review of herself before adding, at her leisure, "quite charmed."

At the mention of gentlemen whom Society called capitalists, Mr. Dorrit had coughed, as if some internal demur were breaking out of him. Mrs. Merdle had observed it, and went on to take up the cue.

"Though, indeed, Mr. Dorrit, it is scarcely necessary for me to make that remark, except in the mere openness of saying what is uppermost to one whom I so highly regard, and with whom I hope I may have the pleasure of being brought into still more agreeable relations. For, one can not but see the great probability of your considering such things from Mr. Merdle's own point of view, except indeed that circumstances have made it Mr. Merdle's accidental fortune or misfortune, to be engaged in business transactions, and that they, however vast, may a little cramp his horizon. I am a very child as to having any notion of business," said Mrs. Merdle; "but I am afraid, Mr. Dorrit, it may have that tendency."

This skillful see-saw of Mr. Dorrit and Mr. Merdle, so that each of them sent the other up, and each of them sent the other down, and neither had the advantage, acted as a sedative on Mr. Dorrit's cough. He remarked, with his utmost politeness, that he must beg to protest against its being supposed, even by Mrs. Merdle, the accomplished and graceful (to which compliment she bent herself,) that such enterprises as Mr. Merdle's, apart as they were from the puny undertakings of the rest of men, had any lower tendency than to enlarge and expand the genius in which they were conceived. "You are generosity itself," said Mrs. Merdle in return, smiling her best smile; "let us hope so. But I confess I am almost superstitious in my ideas about business."

Mr. Dorrit threw in another compliment here, to the effect

that business, like the time which was precious in it, was made for slaves; and that it was not for Mrs. Merdle, who ruled all hearts at her supreme pleasure, to have any thing to do with it. Mrs. Merdle laughed, and conveyed to Mr. Dorrit an idea that the Bosom flushed, which was one of her best effects.

"I say so much," she then explained, "merely because Mr. Merdle has always taken the greatest interest in Edmund, and has always expressed the strongest desire to advance his prospects. Edmund's public position I think you know. His private position rests wholly with Mr. Merdle. In my foolish incapacity for business, I assure you I know no more."

Mr. Dorrit again expressed, in his own way, the sentiment that business was below the ken of enslavers and enchantresses. He then mentioned his intention, as a gentleman and a parent, of writing to Mr. Merdle. Mrs. Merdle concurred with all her heart—or with all her art, which was exactly the same thing—and herself despatched a preparatory letter by the next post, to the eighth wonder of the world.

In his epistolary communication, as in his dialogues and discourses on the great question to which it related, Mr. Dorrit surrounded the subject with flourishes, as writing-masters embellish copy-books and ciphering-books; where the titles of the elementary rules of arithmetic diverge into swans, eagles, griffins, and other caligraphic recreations, and where the capital letters go out of their minds and bodies into ecstacies of pen and ink. Nevertheless, he did render the purport of his letter sufficiently clear to enable Mr. Merdle to make a decent pretense of having learned it from that source. Mr. Merdle replied to it accordingly. Mr. Dorrit replied to Mr. Merdle; Mr. Merdle replied to Mr. Dorrit; and it was soon announced that the corresponding powers had come to a satisfactory understanding.

Now, and not before, Miss Fanny burst upon the scene, completely arrayed for her new part. Now, and not before, she wholly absorbed Mr. Sparkler in her light, and shone for both, and twenty more. No longer feeling that want of a defined place and character which had caused her so much trouble, this fair ship began to stear steadily on a shaped course, and to swim with a weight and balance that developed her sailing qualities.

"The preliminaries being so satisfactorily arranged, I think I will now, my dear," said Mr. Dorrit, "announce—ha—formally, to Mrs. General—"

"Papa," returned Fanny, taking him up short, upon that name, "I don't see what Mrs. General has got to do with it."

"My dear," said Mr. Dorrit, "it will be an act of courtesy to—hum—a lady, well bred and refined—"

"Oh! I'm sick of Mrs. General's good breeding and refinement, papa," said Fanny. "I am tired of Mrs. General."

"Tired," repeated Mr. Dorrit, in reproachful astonishment, "of—ha—Mrs. General!"

"Quite disgusted with her, papa," said Fanny. "I really don't see what she has to do with my marriage. Let her keep to her own matrimonial projects—if she has any."

"Fanny," returned Mr. Dorrit, with a grave and weighty slowness upon him, contrasting strongly with his daughter's levity: "I beg the favor of your explaining—ha—what it is you mean."

"I mean, papa," said Fanny, "that if Mrs. General should happen to have any matrimonial projects of her own, I dare say they are quite enough to occupy her spare time. And that if she has not, so much the better; but still I don't wish to have the honor of making announcements to her."

"Permit me to ask you, Fanny," said Mr. Dorrit, "why not?"

"Because she can find my engagement out for herself, papa," retorted Fanny. "She is watchful enough, I dare say. I think I have seen her so. Let her find it out for herself. If she should not find it out for herself, she will know it when I am married. And I hope you will not consider me wanting in affection for you, papa, if I say it strikes me that will be quite time enough for Mrs. General."

"Fanny," returned Mr. Dorrit, "I am amazed, I am displeased, by this—hum—this capricious and unintelligible display of animosity toward—ha—Mrs. General."

"Do not, if you please, papa," urged Fanny, "call it animosity, because I assure you I do not consider Mrs. General worth my animosity."

At this Mr. Dorrit rose from his chair with a fixed look

of severe reproof, and remained standing in his dignity before his daughter. His daughter, turning the bracelet on her arm, and now looking at him, and now looking from him, said, "Very well, papa. I am truly sorry if you don't like it; but I can't help it. I am not a child, and I am not Amy, and I must speak."

"Fanny," gasped Mr. Dorrit, after a majestic silence, "if I request you to remain here, while I formally announce to Mrs. General, as an exemplary lady who is—hum—a trusted member of this family, the—ha—the change that is contemplated among us; if I—ha—not only request it, but—hum—insist upon it—"

"Oh, papa," Fanny broke in with pointed significance, "if you make so much of it as that, I have in duty nothing to do but comply. I hope I may have my thoughts upon the subject, however, for I really can not help it under the circumstances." So Fanny sat down with a meekness which, in the junction of extremes, became defiance; and her father either not deigning to answer, or not knowing what to answer, summoned Mr. Tinkler into his presence.

"Mrs. General."

Mr. Tinkler, unused to receive such short orders, in connection with the fair varnisher, paused. Mr. Dorrit, seeing the whole Marshalsea and its Testimonials in the pause, instantly flew at him with, "How dare you, sir? What do you mean?"

"I beg your pardon, sir," pleaded Mr. Tinkler, "I was wishful to know—"

"You wished to know nothing, sir," cried Mr. Dorrit, highly flushed. "Don't tell me you did. Ha. You didn't. You are guilty of mockery, sir."

"I assure you sir—" Mr. Tinkler began.

"Don't assure me!" said Mr. Dorrit. "I will not be assured by a domestic. You are guilty of mockery. You shall leave me—hum—the whole establishment shall leave me. What are you waiting for?"

"Only for my orders, sir."

"It's false," said Mr. Dorrit; "you have your orders. Ha—hum. My compliments to Mrs. General, and I beg the favor of her coming to me, if quite convenient, for a few minutes. Those are your orders."

In his execution of this mission, Mr. Tinkler perhaps expressed that Mr. Dorrit was in a raging fume. However that was, Mrs. General's skirts were very speedily heard outside coming along—one might have almost said bouncing along—with unusual expedition. Albeit, they settled down at the door and swept into the room with their customary coolness.

"Mrs. General," said Mr. Dorrit, "take a chair."

Mrs. General, with a graceful curve of acknowledgment, descended into the chair which Mr. Dorrit offered.

"Madam," pursued that gentleman, "as you have had the kindness to undertake the—hum—formation of my daughters, and as I am persuaded that nothing nearly affecting them can—ha—be indifferent to you—"

"Wholly impossible," said Mrs. General, in the calmest of ways.

"—I therefore wish to announce to you, madam, that my daughter now present—"

Mrs. General made a slight inclination of her head to Fanny, who made a very low inclination of her head to Mrs. General, and came loftily upright again.

"—That my daughter Fanny is—ha—contracted to be married to Mr. Sparkler, with whom you are acquainted. Hence, madam, you will be relieved of half your difficult charge—ha—difficult charge." Mr. Dorrit repeated it with his angry eye on Fanny. "But not, I hope, to the—hum—diminution of any other portion, direct or indirect, of the footing you have at present the kindness to occupy in my family."

"Mr. Dorrit," returned Mrs. General, with her gloved hands resting on one another in exemplary repose, "is ever considerate, and ever but too appreciative of my friendly services."

(Miss Fanny coughed, as much as to say, "You are right.")

"Miss Dorrit has no doubt exercised the soundest discretion of which the circumstances admitted, and I trust will allow me to offer her my sincere congratulations. When free from the trammels of passion," Mrs. General closed her eyes at the word, as if she could not utter it and see any body; "when occurring with the approbation of near relatives, and when cementing the proud structure of a family edifice, these are usually auspicious events. I trust Miss Dorrit will allow me to offer her my best congratulations."

Here Mrs. General stopped, and added internally, for the setting of her face, "Papa, potatos, poultry, prunes, and prism."

"Mr. Dorrit," she superadded, aloud, "is ever most obliging; and for the attention, and I will add distinction, of having this confidence imparted to me by himself and Miss Dorrit at this early time, I beg to offer the tribute of my thanks. My thanks and my congratulations are equally the meed of Mr. Dorrit and of Miss Dorrit."

"To me," observed Miss Fanny, "they are excessively gratifying—inexpressibly so. The relief of finding that you have no objection to make, Mrs. General, quite takes a load off my mind, I am sure. I hardly know what I should have done," said Fanny, "if you had interposed any objection, Mrs. General."

Mrs. General changed her gloves, as to the right glove being uppermost and the left undermost, with a Prunes and Prism smile.

"To preserve your aprobation, Mrs. General," said Fanny, returning the smile with one in which there was no trace of those ingredients, "will of course be the highest object of my married life; to lose it, would of course be perfect wretchedness. I am sure your great kindness will not object, and I hope papa will not object, to my correcting a small mistake you have made, however. The best of us are so liable to mistakes, that even you, Mrs. General, have fallen into a little error. The attention and distinction you have so impressively mentioned, Mrs. General, as attaching to this confidence, are, I have no doubt, of the most complimentary and gratifying description; but they don't at all proceed from me. The merit of having consulted you on the subject would have been so great in me, that I feel I must not lay claim to it when it really is not mine. It is wholly papa's. I am deeply obliged to you for your encouragement and patronage, but it was papa who asked for it. I have to thank you, Mrs. General, for relieving my breast of a great weight by so handsomely giving your consent to my engagement, but you have really nothing to thank me for. I hope you will always approve of my proceedings after I have left home, and that my sister also may long remain the favored object of your condescension, Mrs. General."

With this address, which was delivered in her politest manner, Fanny left the room with an elegant and cheerful air, to tear up stairs with a flushed face as soon as she was out of hearing, pounce in upon her sister, call her a little Dormouse, shake her for the better opening of her eyes, tell her what had passed below, and ask her what she thought about pa now?

Toward Mrs. Merdle, the young lady comported herself with great independence and self-possession; but not as yet with any more decided opening of hostilities. Occasionally they had a slight skirmish, as when Fanny considered herself patted on the back by that lady, or as when Mrs. Merdle looked particularly young and well; but Mrs. Merdle always soon terminated those passages of arms by sinking among her cushions with the gracefulest indifference, and finding her attention otherwise engaged. Society (for that mysterious creature sat upon the Seven Hills too) found Miss Fanny vastly improved by her engagement. She was much more accessible, much more free and engaging, much less exacting; insomuch that she now entertained a host of followers and admirers, to the bitter indignation of ladies with daughters to marry, who were to be regarded as having revolted from Society on the Miss Dorrit grievance, and erected a rebellious standard. Enjoying the flutter she caused, Miss Dorrit not only haughtily moved through it in her own proper person, but haughtily, even ostentatiously, led Mr. Sparkler through it too: seeming to say to them all, "If I think proper to march among you in triumphal procession, attended by this weak captive in bonds rather than a stronger one, that is my business. Enough that I choose to do it!" Mr. Sparkler, for his part, questioned nothing; but went whereever he was taken, did whatever he was told, felt that for his bride-elect to be distinguished was for him to distinguished on the easiest terms, and was truly grateful for being so openly acknowledged.

The winter passing on toward the spring while this condition of affairs prevailed, it became necessary for Mr. Sparkler to repair to England, and take his appointed part in the expression and direction of its genius, learning, commerce, spirit, and sense. The land of Shakspeare, Milton, Bacon, Newton, Watt, the land of a host of past and present abstract philosophers, natural philosophers, and subduers of Nature and Art in their myriad forms, called to Mr. Sparkler to come and take care of it, lest it should perish. Mr. Sparkler, unable to resist the agonized cry from the depths of his country's soul, declared that he must go.

It followed that the question was rendered pressing when, where, and how, Mr. Sparkler should be married to the foremost girl in all this world, with no nonsense about her. Its solution, after some little mystery and secrecy, Miss Fanny herself announced to her sister.

"Now, my child," said she, seeking her out one day, "I am going to tell you something. It is only this moment broached; and naturally I hurry to you the moment it *is* broached."

"Your marriage, Fanny?"

"My precious child," said Fanny, "don't anticipate me. Let me impart my confidence to you, you flurried little thing, in my own way. As to your guess, if I answered it literally, I should answer no. For really it is not my marriage that is in question, half as much as it is Edmund's."

Little Dorrit looked, and perhaps not altogether without cause, somewhat at a loss to understand this fine distinction.

"I am in no difficulty," exclaimed Fanny, "and in no hurry. I am not wanted at any public office, or to give any vote any where else. But Edmund is. And Edmund is deeply dejected at the idea of going away by himself, and, indeed, I don't like that he should be trusted by himself. For, if it's possible—and it generally is—to do a foolish thing, he is sure to do it."

As she concluded this impartial summary of the reliance that might be safely placed upon her future husband, she took off, with an air of business, the bonnet she wore, and dangled it by its strings upon the ground.

"It is far more Edmund's question, therefore, than mine. However, we need say no more about that. That is self-evident on the face of it. Well, my dearest Amy! The point arising, is he to go by himself, or is he not to go by himself, this other point arises, are we to be married here and shortly, or are we to be married at home months hence?"

"I see I am going to lose you, Fanny."

"What a little thing you are," cried Fanny, half tolerant and half impatient, "for anticipating one! Pray, my darling, hear me out. That woman," she spoke of Mrs. Merdle, of course, "remains here until after Easter; so, in the case of my being married here and going to London with Edmund, I should have the start of her. That is something. Further, Amy. That woman being out of the way, I don't know that I greatly object to Mr. Merdle's proposal to Pa that Edmund and I should take up our abode in that house—*you* know—where you once went with a dancer, my dear—until our own house can be chosen and fitted up. Further still, Amy. Papa having always intended to go to town himself, in the spring—you see, if Edmund and I were married here, we might go off to Florence, where Papa might join us, and we might all three travel home together. Mr. Merdle has entreated Pa to stay with him in that same mansion I have mentioned, and I suppose he will. But he is master of his own actions; and upon that point (which is not at all material), I can't speak positively."

The difference between papa's being master of his own actions and Mr. Sparkler's being nothing of the sort, was forcibly expressed by Fanny in her manner of stating the case. Not that her sister noticed it; for she was divided between regret at the coming separation, and a lingering wish that she had been included in the plans for visiting England.

"And these are the arrangements, Fanny, dear?"

"Arrangements!" repeated Fanny. "Now, really, child, you are a little trying. You know I particularly guarded myself against laying my words open to any such construction. What I said was, that certain questions present themselves; and these are the questions."

Little Dorrit's thoughtful eyes met hers, tenderly and quietly.

"Now, my own sweet girl," said Fanny, weighing her bonnet by the strings with considerable impatience, "it's no use staring. A little owl could stare. I look to you for advice, Amy. What do you advise me to do?"

"Do you think," asked Little Dorrit, persuasively, after a short hesitation, "do you think, Fanny, that if you were to put it off for a few months, it might be, considering all things, best?"

"No, little Tortoise," retorted Fanny, with exceeding sharpness. "I don't think any thing of the kind."

Here, she threw her bonnet from her altogether, and flounced into a chair. But, becoming affectionate almost immediately, she flounced out of it again, and kneeled down on the floor to take her sister, chair and all, in her arms.

"Don't suppose I am hasty or unkind, darling, because I really am not. But you are such a little oddity! You make one bite your head off, when one wants to be soothing beyond every thing. Didn't I tell you, you dearest baby, that Edmund can't be trusted by himself? And don't you know that he can't?"

"Yes, yes, Fanny. You said so, I know."

"And you know it, I know," retorted Fanny. "Well, my precious child! If he is not to be trusted by himself, it follows, I suppose, that I should go with him?"

"It—seems so, love," said Little Dorrit.

"Therefore, having heard the arrangements that are feasible to carry out that object, am I to understand, dearest Amy, that on the whole you advise me to make them?"

"It—seems so, love," said Little Dorrit again.

"Very well!" cried Fanny, with an air of resignation, "then I suppose it must be done! I came to you, my sweet, the moment I saw the doubt, and the necessity of deciding. I have now decided. So let it be!"

After yielding herself up, in this pattern manner, to sisterly advice and the force of circumstances, Fanny became quite benignant: as one who had laid her own inclinations at the feet of her dearest friend, and felt a glow of conscience in having made the sacrifice. "After all, my Amy," she said to her sister, "you are the best of small creatures, and full of good sense; and I don't know what I shall ever do without you!"

With which words she folded her in a closer embrace, and a really fond one.

"Not that I contemplate doing without you, Amy, by any means, for I hope we shall ever be next to inseparable. And now, my pet, I am going to give you a word of advice. When you are left alone here with Mrs. General—"

"I am to be left alone here with Mrs. General?" said Little Dorrit, quietly.

"Why, of course, my precious, till papa comes back! Unless you call Edward company, which he certainly is not, even when he is here, and still more certainly is not when he is away at Naples or in Sicily. I was going to say—but you are such a beloved little Marplot for putting one out—when you are left alone here with Mrs. General, Amy, don't you let her slide into any sort of artful understanding with you that she is looking after Pa, or that Pa is looking after her. She will, if she can. *I* know her sly manner of feeling her way with those gloves of hers. But don't you comprehend her on any account. And if Pa should tell you when he comes back, that he has it in contemplation to make Mrs. General your mamma (which is not the less likely because I am going away), my advice to you is, that you say at once, 'Papa, I beg to object most strongly. Fanny cautioned me about this, and she objected, and I object.' I don't mean to say that any objection from you, Amy, is likely to be of the smallest effect, or that I think you likely to make it with any degree of firmness. But there is a principle involved, a filial principle—and I implore you not to submit to be mother-in-lawed by Mrs. General, without asserting it in making every one about you as uncomfortable as possible. I don't expect you to stand by it—indeed, I know you won't, Pa being concerned—but I wish to rouse you to a sense of duty. As to any help from me, or as to any opposition that I can offer to such a match, you shall not be left in the lurch, my love. Whatever weight I may derive from my position as a married girl not wholly devoid of attractions—used, as that position always shall be, to oppose that woman—I will bring to bear, you may depend upon it, on the head and false hair (for I am confident it's not all real, ugly as it is, and unlikely as it appears that any one in their senses would go to the expense of buying it) of Mrs. General!"

Little Dorrit received this counsel without venturing to oppose it, but without giving Fanny any reason to believe that she intended to act upon it. Having now, as it were, formally wound up her single life and arranged her worldly affairs, Fanny proceeded with characteristic ardor, to prepare for the serious change in her condition.

The preparation consisted in the dispatch of her maid to Paris under the protection of the Courier, for the purchase of that outfit for a bride on which it would be extremely low, in the present narrative, to bestow an English name, but to which, (on a vulgar principle it observes of adhering to the language in which it professes to have been written) it declines to give a French one. The rich and beautiful wardrobe purchased by these agents, in the course of a few weeks made its way through the intervening country, bristling with custom-houses, garrisoned by an immense army of shabby mendicants in uniform, who incessantly repeated the Beggar's petition over it, as if every individual warrior among them was the ancient Belisarius : and of whom there were so many Legions, that unless the Courier had expended just one bushel and a half of silver money in relieving their distresses, they would have worn the wardrobe out before it got to Rome, by turning it over and over. Through all such dangers, however, it was triumphantly brought, inch by inch, and arrived at its journey's end in fine condition.

There it was exhibited to select companies of female viewers, in whose gentle bosoms it awakened implacable feelings. Concurrently, active preparations were made for the day on which some of its treasures were to be publicly displayed. Cards of breakfast-invitation were sent out to half the English in the city of Romulus; the other half made arrangements to be under arms, as criticising volunteers, at various outer points of the solemnity. The most high and illustrious English Signor Edgardo Dorrit came post through the deep mud and ruts (from forming a surface under the improving Neapolitan nobility) to grace the occasion. The best hotel, and all its culinary myrmidons, were set to work to prepare the feast. The drafts of Mr. Dorrit almost constituted a run on the Torlonia Bank. The British Consul hadn't had such a marriage in the whole of his Consularity.

The day came, and the She-Wolf in the Capitol might have snarled with envy to see how the Island Savages contrived these things now-a-days. The murderous-headed statues of the wicked Emperors of the Soldiery, whom sculptors had not been able to flatter out of their villainous hideousness, might have come off their pedestals to run away with the Bride. The choked old fountain, where erst the Gladiators washed, might have leaped into life again to honor the ceremony. The Temple of Vesta might have sprung up anew from its ruins, expressly to lend its countenance to the occasion. Might have done, but did not. Like sentient things—even like the lords and ladies of creation sometimes—might have done much, but did nothing. The celebration went off with admirable pomp: monks in black robes, white robes, and russet robes stopped to look after the carriages; wandering peasants, in fleeces of sheep, begged and piped under the house-windows; the English volunteers defiled; the day wore on to the hour of vespers; the festival wore away; the thousand churches rang their bells without any reference to it; and Saint Peter denied that he had had anything to do with it.

But, by that time the Bride was near the end of the first day's journey toward Florence. It was the peculiarity of these nuptials that they were all bride. Nobody noticed the Bridegroom. Nobody noticed the first Bridesmaid. Few could have seen Little Dorrit (who held that post) for the glare, even supposing many to have sought her. So, the Bride had mounted into her handsome chariot, incidentally accompanied by the Bridegroom; and after rolling for a few minutes smoothly over a fair pavement, had begun to jolt through a Slough of Despond, and through a long, long avenue of wrack and ruin. Other nuptial carriages are said to have gone the same road, before and since.

If Little Dorrit found herself left a little lonely and a little low that night, nothing would have done so much against her feeling of depression as the being able to sit at work by her father as in the old time, and help him to his supper and his rest. But that was not to be thought of now, when they sat in the state-equipage with Mrs. General on the coach-box. And as to supper! If Mr. Dorrit had wanted supper, there was an Italian cook and there was a Swiss confectioner, who must have put on caps as high as the Pope's Mitre, and have performed the mysteries of Alchemists in a copper-saucepaned laboratory below, before he could have got it.

He was sententious and didactic that night. If he had been simply loving, he would have done Little Dorrit more good; but she accepted him as he was—when had she not accepted him as he was!—and made the most and best of him. Mrs. General at length retired. Her retirement for the night was always her frostiest ceremony; as if she felt it necessary that the human imagination should be chilled into stone to prevent its following her. When she had gone through her rigid preliminaries, amounting to a sort of genteel platoon-exercise, she withdrew. Little Dorrit then put her arm round her father's neck to bid him good-night.

"Amy, my dear," said Mr. Dorrit, taking her by the hand, "this is the close of a day, that has—ha—greatly impressed and gratified me."

"A little tired you, dear, too?"

"No," said Mr. Dorrit, "no, I am not sensible of fatigue when it arises from an occasion so—hum—replete with gratification of the pnrest kind."

Little Dorrit was glad to find him in such heart, and smiled from her own heart.

"My dear," he continued. "This is an occasion—ha—teeming with a good example. With a good example, my favorite and attached child—hum—to you."

Little Dorrit, fluttered by his words, did not know what to say, though he stopped as if he expected her to say something.

"Amy," he resumed; "your dear sister, our Fanny, has contracted—ha hum—a marriage eminently calculated to extend the basis of our—ha—connection, and to—hum—consolidate our social relations. My love, I trust that the time is not far distant when some—ha—eligible partner may be found for you."

"Oh no! Let me stay with you. I beg and pray that I may stay with you! I want nothing but to stay and take care of you!"

She said it like one in sudden alarm.

"Nay, Amy, Amy," said Mr. Dorrit. "This is weak and foolish, weak and foolish. You have a—ha—responsibility imposed upon you by your position. It is to develop that position, and be—hum—worthy of that position. As to taking care of me, I can—ha—take care of myself. Or," he added, after a moment, "if I should need to be taken care of, I—hum—can, with the—ha—blessing of Providence, be taken care of. I—ha—hum—I can not, my dear child, think of engrossing, and—ha—as it were, sacrificing you."

Oh what a time of day at which to begin that profession of self-denial; at which to make it, with an air of taking credit for it; at which to believe it, if such a thing could be!

"Don't speak, Amy. I positively say I can not do it. I—ha—must not do it. My—hum—conscience would not allow it. I therefore, my love, take the opportunity afforded by this gratifying and impressive occasion of—ha—solemnly remarking, that it is now a cherished wish and purpose of mine to see you—ha—eligibly (I repeat eligibly) married.

"Oh no, dear! Pray!"

"Amy," said Mr. Dorrit, "I am well persuaded that if the topic were referred to any person of superior social knowledge, of superior delicacy and sense—let us say, for instance, to—ha—Mrs. General—that there would not be two opinions as to the—hum—affectionate character and propriety of my sentiments. But, as I know your loving and dutiful nature from—hum—from experience, I am quite satisfied that it is necessary to say no more. I have—hum—no husband to propose at present, my dear; I have not even one in view. I merely wish that we should—ha—understand each other. Hum. Good-night, my dear and sole remaining daughter. Good-night. God bless you!"

If the thought ever entered Little Dorrit's head that night that he could give her up lightly now, in his prosperity, and when he had it in his mind to replace her with a second wife, she drove it away. Faithful to him still, as in the worst times through which she had borne him single-handed, she drove the thought away; and entertained no harder reflection in her tearful unrest than that he now saw every thing through their wealth, and through the care he always had upon him that they should continue rich, and grow richer.

They sat in their equipage of state, with Mrs. General on

the box, for three weeks longer, and then he started for Florence to join Fanny. Little Dorrit would have been glad to bear him company so far, only for the sake of her own love, and then to have turned back alone, thinking of dear England. But though the Courier had gone on with the Bride, the Valet was next in the line; and the succession would not have come to her, as long as any one could be got for money.

Mrs. General took life easily—as easily, that is, as she could take any thing—when the Roman establishment remained in their sole occupation; and Little Dorrit would often ride out in a hired carriage that was left them, and alight alone and wander among the ruins of old Rome. The ruins of the vast old Amphitheatre, of the old Temples, of the old commemorative Arches, of the old trodden highways, of the old tombs, besides being what they were, to her were ruins of the old Marshalsea—ruins of her own old life—ruins of the faces and forms that of old peopled it—ruins of its loves, hopes, cares, and joys. Two ruined spheres of action and suffering were before the solitary girl, often sitting on some broken fragment; and in the lonely places, under the blue sky, she saw them both together.

Up, then, would come Mrs. General: taking all the color out of every thing, as Nature and Art had taken it out of herself; writing Prunes and Prism, in Mr. Eustace's text, wherever she could lay a hand; looking everywhere for Mr. Eustace and company, and seeing nothing else; scratching up the driest little bones of antiquity, and bolting them whole without any human visitings—like a Ghoul in gloves.

CHAPTER LII.

GETTING ON.

THE newly-married pair, on their arrival in Harley Street, Cavendish Square, London, were received by the Chief Butler. That great man was not interested in them, but on the whole endured them. People must continue to be married and given in marriage, or Chief Butlers would not be wanted. As nations are made to be taxed, so families are made to be butlered. The Chief Butler, no doubt, reflected that the course of nature required the wealthy population to be kept up, on his account.

He therefore condescended to look at the carriage from the hall-door without frowning at it, and said, in a very handsome way, to one of his men, "Thomas, help with the luggage." He even escorted the Bride up stairs into Mr. Merdle's presence; but this must be considered as an act of homage to the sex (of which he was an admirer, being notoriously captivated by the charms of a certain Duchess), and not as a committal of himself with the family.

Mr. Merdle was slinking about the hearth-rug, waiting to welcome Mrs. Sparkler. His hand seemed to retreat up his sleeve as he advanced to do so, and he gave her such a superfluity of coat-cuff that it was like being received by the popular conception of Guy Fawkes. When he put his lips to hers, besides, he took himself into custody by the wrists, and backed himself among the ottomans and chairs and tables, as if he were his own Police officer, saying to himself, "Now, none of that! Come! I've got you, you know, and you go quietly along with me!"

Mrs. Sparkler, installed in the rooms of state—the innermost sanctuary of down, silk, chintz, and fine linen—felt that so far her triumph was good, and her way made, step by step. On the day before her marriage, she had bestowed on Mrs. Merdle's maid, with an air of gracious indifference, in Mrs. Merdle's presence, a trifling little keepsake (bracelet, bonnet, and two dresses, all new), about four times as valuable as the present formerly made by Mrs. Merdle to her. She was now established in Mrs. Merdle's own rooms, to which some extra touches had been given to render them more worthy of her occupation. In her mind's eye, as she lounged there, surrounded by every luxurious accessory that wealth could obtain or invention devise, she saw the fair bosom that beat in unison with the exultation of her thoughts, competing with the Bosom that had been famous so long, outshining it, and deposing it. Happy? Fanny must have been happy. No more wishing one's self dead now.

The Courier had not approved of Mr. Dorrit's staying in the house of a friend, and had preferred to take him to a hotel in Brook Street, Grosvenor Square. Mr. Merdle ordered his carriage to be ready early in the morning, that he might wait upon Mr. Dorrit immediately after breakfast.

Bright the carriage looked, sleek the horses looked, gleaming the harness looked, luscious and lasting the liveries looked. A rich and responsible turn-out. An equipage for a Merdle. Early people looked after it as it rattled along the streets, and said, with awe in their breath, "There he goes!"

There he went, until Brook Street stopped him. Then, forth from its magnificent case came the jewel; not lustrous in itself, but quite the contrary.

Commotion in the office of the hotel. Merdle! The landlord, though a gentleman of a haughty spirit who had just driven a pair of thorough-bred horses into town, turned out to show him up stairs. The clerks and servants cut him off by back passages, and were found accidentally hovering in doorways and angles, that they might look upon him. Merdle! O ye sun, moon, and stars, the great man! The rich man, who had in a manner revised the New Testament, and already entered into the kingdom of Heaven. The man who could have any one he chose to dine with him, and who had made the money! As he went up the stairs, people were already posted on the lower stairs, that his shadow might fall upon them when he came down. So were the sick brought out and laid in the track of the Apostle—who had *not* got into the good society, and had *not* made the money.

Mr. Dorrit, dressing-gowned and newspapered, was at his breakfast. The Courier, with agitation in his voice, announced "Miss' Mairdale !" Mr. Dorrit's overwrought heart bounded as he leaped up.

"Mr. Merdle, this is—ha—indeed an honor. Permit me to express the—hum—sense, the high sense I entertain of this—ha hum—highly gratifying act of attention. I am well aware, sir, of the many demands upon your time, and its—ha—enormous value." Mr. Dorrit could not say enormous roundly enough for his own satisfaction. "That you should—ha—at this early hour, bestow any of your priceless time upon me, is —ha—a compliment that I acknowledge with the greatest esteem." Mr. Dorrit positively trembled in addressing the great man.

Mr. Merdle uttered, in his subdued, inward, hesitating voice, a few sounds that were to no purpose whatever, and finally said, "I am glad to see you, sir."

"You are very kind," said Mr. Dorrit. "Truly kind." By this time the visitor was seated, and was passing his great hand over his exhausted forehead. "You are well, I hope, Mr. Merdle ?"

"I am as well as I—yes, I am as well as I usually am," said Mr. Merdle.

"Your occupations must be immense."

"Tolerably so. But—Oh dear no, there's not much the matter with *me*," said Mr. Merdle, looking round the room.

"A little dyspeptic ?" Mr. Dorrit hinted.

"Very likely. But I—Oh, I am well enough," said Mr. Merdle.

There were black traces on his lips where they met, as if a little train of gunpowder had been fired there ; and he looked like a man who, if his natural temperament had been quicker, would have been very feverish that morning. This, and his heavy way of passing his hand over his forehead, had prompted Mr. Dorrit's solicitous inquiries.

"Mrs. Merdle," Mr. Dorrit insinuatingly pursued, "I left, as you will be prepared to hear, the—ha—observed of all observers, the—hum—admired of all admirers, the leading fascination and charm of Society in Rome. She was looking wonderfully well when I quitted it."

"Mrs. Merdle," said Mr. Merdle, "is generally considered a very attractive woman. And she is, no doubt. I am sensible of her being so."

"Who can be otherwise?" responded Mr. Dorrit.

Mr. Merdle turned his tongue in his closed mouth—it seemed rather a stiff and unmanageable tongue—moistened his lips, passed his hand over his forehead again, and looked all round the room again, principally under the chairs.

"But," he said, looking Mr. Dorrit in the face for the first time, and immediately afterward dropping his eyes to the buttons of Mr. Dorrit's waistcoat; "if we speak of attractions, your daughter ought to be the subject of our conversation. She is extremely beautiful. Both in face and figure she is quite uncommon. When the young people arrived last night, I was really surprised to see such charms."

Mr. Dorrit's gratification was such that he said—ha—he could not refrain from telling Mr. Merdle verbally, as he had already done by letter, what honor and happiness he felt in this union of their families. And he offered his hand. Mr. Merdle looked at the hand for a little while, took it on his for a moment as if his were a yellow salver or fish-slice, and then returned it to Mr. Dorrit.

"I thought I would drive round the first thing," said Mr. Merdle, "to offer my services, in case I can do any thing for you; and to say that I hope you will at least do me the honor of dining with me to-day, and every day when you are not better engaged, during your stay in town."

Mr. Dorrit was enraptured by these attentions.

"Do you stay long, sir?"

"I have not at present the intention," said Mr. Dorrit, "of—ha—exceeding a fortnight."

"That's a very short stay, after so long a journey," returned Mr. Merdle.

"Hum. Yes," said Mr. Dorrit. "But the truth is—ha—my dear Mr. Merdle, that I find a foreign life so well suited to my health and taste, that I—hum—have but two objects in my present visit to London. First, the—ha—the distinguished happiness and—ha—privilege which I now enjoy and appreciate; secondly, the arrangement—hum—the laying out, that is to say, in the best way of—ha hum—my money."

"Well, sir," said Mr. Merdle, after turning his tongue again, "if I can be of any use to you in that respect you may command me."

Mr. Dorrit's speech had had more hesitation in it than usual, as he approached the ticklish topic, for he was not perfectly clear how so exalted a potentate might take it. He had doubts whether reference to any individual capital, or fortune, might not seem a wretchedly retail affair to so wholesale a dealer. Greatly relieved by Mr. Merdle's affable offer of assistance, he caught at it directly, and heaped acknowledgments upon him.

"I scarcely—ha—dared," said Mr. Dorrit, "I assure you, to hope for so—hum—vast an advantage as your direct advice and assistance. Though of course I should, under any circumstances, like the—ha hum—rest of the civilized world, have followed in Mr. Merdle's train."

"You know we may almost say we are related, sir," said Mr. Merdle, curiously interested in the pattern of the carpet, "and, therefore, you may consider me at your service."

"Ha. Very handsome, indeed!" cried Mr. Dorrit. "Ha. Most handsome!"

"It would not," said Mr. Merdle, "be at the present moment easy for what I may call a mere outsider to come into any of the good things—of course I speak of my own good things—"

"Of course, of course!" cried Mr. Dorrit, in a tone implying that there were no other good things.

"—Unless at a high price. At what we are accustomed to term a very long figure."

Mr. Dorrit laughed in the buoyancy of his spirit. Ha, ha, ha! Long figure. Good. Ha. Very expressive to be sure!

"However," said Mr. Merdle, "I do generally retain in my own hands the power of exercising some preference—people in general would be pleased to call it favor—as a sort of compliment for my care and trouble."

"And public spirit and genius," Mr. Dorrit suggested.

Mr. Merdle, with a dry, swallowing action, seemed to dispose of those qualities like a bolus; then added, "As a sort of return for it. I will see, if you please, how I can exert this limited power (for people are jealous, and it is limited) to your advantage."

"You are very good," replied Mr. Dorrit. "You are *very* good."

"Of course," said Mr. Merdle, "there must be the strictest integrity and uprightness in these transactions; there must be the purest faith between man and man; there must be unimpeached and unimpeachable confidence, or business could not be carried on."

Mr. Dorrit hailed these generous sentiments with fervor.

"Therefore," said Mr. Merdle, "I can only give you a preference to a certain extent."

"I perceive. To a defined extent," observed Mr. Dorrit.

"Defined extent. And perfectly above board. As to my advice, however," said Mr. Merdle, "that is another matter. That, such as it is—"

Oh! Such as it was! (Mr. Dorrit could not bear the faintest appearance of its being depreciated, even by Mr. Merdle himself.)

"—That there is nothing in the bonds of spotless honor between myself and my fellow-man to prevent my parting with if I choose. And that," said Mr. Merdle, now deeply intent upon a dust-cart that was passing the windows, "shall be at your command whenever you think proper."

New acknowledgments from Mr. Dorrit. New passages of Mr. Merdle's hand over his forehead. Calm and silence. Contemplation of Mr. Dorrit's waistcoat-buttons by Mr. Merdle.

"My time being rather precious," said Mr. Merdle, suddenly getting up, as if he had been waiting in the interval for his legs, and they had just come, "I must be moving toward the City. Can I take you anywhere, sir? I shall be happy to set you down, or send you on. My carriage is at your disposal."

Mr. Dorrit bethought himself that he had business at his banker's. His banker's was in the City. That was fortunate. Mr. Merdle would take him into the City. But surely he might not detain Mr. Merdle while he assumed his coat? Yes he might, and must; Mr. Merdle insisted on it. So Mr. Dorrit, retiring into the next room, put himself under the hands of his valet, and in five minutes came back glorious.

Then, said Mr. Merdle, "Allow me, sir. Take my arm!" Then, leaning on Mr. Merdle's arm, did Mr. Dorrit descend the staircase, seeing the worshipers on the steps, and feeling that the light of Mr. Merdle shown by reflection in himself. Then, the carriage, and the ride into the City; and the people who looked at them; and the hats that flew off gray heads; and the general bowing and crouching before this wonderful mortal, the like of which prostration of spirit was not to be seen—no, by high Heaven, no! It may be worth thinking of by Fawners of all denominations—in Westminster Abbey and Saint Paul's Cathedral put together, on any Sunday in the year. It was a rapturous dream to Mr. Dorrit to find himself set aloft in this public car of triumph, making a magnificent progress to that befitting destination, the golden Street of the Lombards.

There, Mr. Merdle insisted on alighting and going his way a-foot, and leaving his poor equipage at Mr. Dorrit's disposition. So the dream increased in rapture when Mr. Dorrit came out of the bank alone, and people looked at *him* in default of Mr. Merdle, and when, with the ears of his mind, he heard the frequent exclamation as he rolled glibly along, "A wonderful man to be Mr. Merdle's friend!"

At dinner that day, although the occasion was not foreseen and provided for, a brilliant company of such as are not made of the dust of the earth, but of some superior article for the present unknown, shed their lustrous benediction upon Mr. Dorrit's daughter's marriage. And Mr. Dorrit's daughter that day began, in earnest, her competition with that woman not present; and began it so well, that Mr. Dorrit could all but have taken his affidavit, if required, that Mrs. Sparkler had all her life been lying at full length in the lap of luxury, and had never heard of such a rough word in the English tongue as Marshalsea.

Next day, and the day after, and every day, all graced by more dinner company, cards descended on Mr. Dorrit like theatrical snow. As the friend and relative by marriage of the illustrious Merdle, Bar, Bishop, Treasury, Chorus, Everybody, wanted to make or improve Mr. Dorrit's acquaintance. In Mr. Merdle's heaps of offices in the City, when Mr. Dorrit appeared at any of them on his business taking him Eastward (which it frequently did, for it throve amazingly), the name of Dorrit was always a passport to the great presence of Merdle. So the dream increased in rapture every hour, as Mr. Dorrit felt increasingly sensible that this connection had brought him forward indeed.

Only one thing sat otherwise than auriferously, and at the same time lightly, on Mr. Dorrit's mind. It was the Chief Butler. That stupendous character looked at him, in the course of his official looking at the dinners, in a manner that Mr. Dorrit considered questionable. He looked at him, as he passed through the hall and up the staircase, going to dinner, with a glazed fixedness that Mr. Dorrit did not like. Seated at table in the act of drinking, Mr. Dorrit still saw him through his wine-glass, regarding him with a cold and ghostly eye. It misgave him that the Chief Butler must have known a Collegian, and must have seen him in the College—perhaps had been presented to him. He looked as closely at the Chief Butler as such a man could be looked at, and yet he did not recall that he had ever seen him elsewhere. Ultimately he was inclined to think that there was no reverence in the man, no sentiment in the great creature. But, he was not relieved by that; for, let him think what he would, the Chief Butler had him in his supercilious eye, even when that eye was on the plate and other table-garniture, and he never let him out of it. To hint to him that this confinement in his eye was disagreeable, or to ask him what he meant, was an act too daring to venture upon; his severity with his employers and their visitors being terrific, and he never permitting himself to be approached with the slightest liberty.

CHAPTER LIII.

MISSING.

THE term of Mr. Dorrit's visit was within two days of being out, and he was about to dress for another inspection by the Chief Butler (whose victims were always dressed expressly for him), when one of the servants of the hotel presented himself, bearing a card. Mr. Dorrit, taking it, read:

"Mrs. Finching."

The servant waited in speechless deference.

"Man, man," said Mr. Dorrit, turning upon him with grievous indignation, "explain your motive in bringing me this ridiculous name. I am wholly unacquainted with it. Finching, sir?" said Mr. Dorrit, perhaps avenging himself on the Chief Butler by Substitute. "Ha! What do you mean by Finching?"

The man, man, seemed to mean Finching as much as any thing else, for he backed away from Mr. Dorrit's severe regard, as he replied, "A lady, sir."

"I know no such lady, sir," said Mr. Dorrit. "Take this card away. I know no Finching, of either sex."

"Ask your pardon, sir. The lady said she was aware she might be unknown by name. But she begged me to say, sir, that she had formerly the honor of being acquainted with Miss Dorrit. The lady said, sir, the youngest Miss Dorrit."

Mr. Dorrit knitted his brows, and rejoined, after a moment or two, "Inform Mrs. Finching, sir," emphasizing the name as if the innocent man were solely responsible for it, "that she can come up."

He had reflected, in his momentary pause, that unless she were admitted she might leave some message, or might say something below, having a disgraceful reference to that former state of existence. Hence the concession, and hence the appearance of Flora, piloted in by the man, man.

"I have not the pleasure," said Mr. Dorrit, standing, with the card in his hand, and with an air which imported that it would scarcely have been a first-class pleasure if he had had it, "of knowing either this name, or yourself, madam. Place a chair, sir."

The responsible man, with a start, obeyed, and went out on tiptoe. Flora, putting aside her vail with a bashful tremor upon her, proceeded to introduce herself. At the same time a singular combination of perfumes was diffused through the room, as if some brandy had been put by mistake in a lavender-water bottle, or as if some lavender-water had been put by mistake in a brandy bottle.

"I beg Mr. Dorrit to offer a thousand apologies and indeed they would be far too few for such an intrusion which I know must appear extremely bold in a lady and alone too but I thought it best upon the whole however difficult and even apparently improper though Mr. F.'s aunt would have willingly accompanied me and as a character of great force and spirit would probably have struck one possessed of such a knowledge of life as no doubt with so many changes must have been acquired, for Mr. F. himself said frequently that although well educated in the neighborhood of Blackheath at as high as eighty guineas which is a good deal for parents and the plate kept back too on going away but that is more a meanness than its value that he had learned more in his first year as a commercial traveler with a large commission on the sale of an article that nobody would hear of much less buy which preceded the wine trade a long time than in the whole six years in that academy conducted by a college Bachelor, though why a Bachelor more clever than a married man I do not see and never did but pray excuse me that is not the point."

Mr. Dorrit stood rooted to the carpet, a statue of mystification.

"I must openly admit that I have no pretensions," said Flora, "but having known the dear little thing which under altered circumstances appears a liberty but is not so intended and Goodness knows there was no favor in half a crown a day to such a needle as herself but quite the other way and as to any thing lowering in it far from it the laborer is worthy of his hire and

I am sure I only wish he got it oftener and more animal food and less rheumatism in the back and legs poor soul."

"Madam," said Mr. Dorrit, recovering his breath by a great effort, as the relict of the late Mr. Finching stopped to take hers; "madam," said Mr. Dorrit, very red in the face, "if I understand you to refer to—ha—to any thing in the antecedents of—hum—a daughter of mine, involving—ha hum—daily compensation, madam, I beg to observe that the—ha—fact, assuming it—ha—to *be* fact, never was within my knowledge. Hum. I should not have permitted it. Ha. Never! Never!"

"Unnecessary to pursue the subject," returned Flora, "and would not have mentioned it on any account except as supposing it a favorable and only letter of introduction but as to being fact no doubt whatever and you may set your mind at rest for the very dress I have on now can prove it and sweetly made though there is no denying that it would tell better on a better figure for my own is much too fat though how to bring it down I know not, pray excuse me I am roving off again."

Mr. Dorrit backed to his chair in a stony way, and seated himself, as Flora gave him a softening look and played with her parasol.

"The dear little thing," said Flora, "having gone off perfectly limp and white and cold in my own house or at least papa's for though not a freehold still a long lease at a peppercorn on the morning when Arthur—foolish habit of our youthful days and Mr. Clennam far more adapted to existing circumstances particularly addressing a stranger and that stranger a gentleman in an elevated station—communicated the glad tidings imparted by a person of the name of Pancks emboldens me."

At the mention of these two names, Mr. Dorrit frowned, stared, frowned again, hesitated with his fingers at his lips, as he had hesitated long ago, and said, "Do me the favor to—ha—state your pleasure, madam."

"Mr. Dorrit," said Flora, "you are very kind in giving me permission and highly natural it seems to me that you should be kind for though more stately I perceive a likeness filled out of course but a likeness still, the object of my intruding is my own without the slightest consultation with any human being and most decidedly not with Arthur—pray excuse me Doyce and Clennam I don't know what I am saying Mr. Clennam solus—for to put that individual linked by a golden chain to a purple time when all was ethereal out of any anxiety would be worth to me the ransom of a monarch not that I have the least idea how much that would come to but using it as the total of all I have in the world and more."

Mr. Dorrit, without greatly regarding the earnestness of these latter words, repeated, "State your pleasure, madam."

"It's not likely I well know," said Flora, "but it's possible and being possible when I had the gratification of reading in the papers that you had arrived from Italy and were going back I made up my mind to try it for you might come across him or hear something of him and if so what a blessing and relief to all!"

"Allow me to ask, madam," said Mr. Dorrit, with his ideas in wild confusion, "to whom—ha—TO WHOM," he repeated it with a raised voice in mere desperation, "you at present allude."

"To the foreigner from Italy who disappeared in the City as no doubt you have read in the papers equally with myself," said Flora, "not referring to private sources by the name of Pancks from which one gathers what dreadfully ill-natured things some people are wicked enough to whisper most likely judging others by themselves and what the uneasiness and indignation of Arthur—quite unable to overcome it Doyce and Clennam—can not fail to be."

It happened, fortunately for the elucidation of any intelligible result, that Mr. Dorrit had heard or read nothing about the matter. This caused Mrs. Finching, with many apologies for being in great practical difficulties as to finding the way to her pocket among the stripes of her dress, at length to produce a police handbill, setting forth that a foreign gentleman, of the name of Blandois, last from Venice, had unaccountably disappeared on such a night in such a part of the city of London; that he was known to have entered such a house at such an hour; that he was stated by the inmates of that house to have left it about so many minutes before midnight; and that he had never been beheld since. This, with exact particulars of time and locality, and with a good detailed description of the foreign gentleman who had so mysteriously vanished, Mr. Dorrit read at large.

"Blandois!" said Mr. Dorrit. "Venice! And this description! I know this gentleman. He has been in my house. He is intimately acquainted with a gentleman of good family (but in indifferent circumstances) of whom I am a—hum—patron."

"Then my humble and pressing entreaty is the more," said Flora, "that in traveling back you will have the kindness to look for this foreign gentleman along all the roads and up and down all the turnings and to make inquiries for him at all the hotels and orange trees and vineyards and volcanoes and places for he must be somewhere and why doesn't he come forward and say he's there and clear all parties up?"

"Pray, madam," said Mr. Dorrit, referring to the handbill again, "who is Clennam and Co.? Ha. I see the name mentioned here in connection with the occupation of the house which Monsieur Blandois was seen to enter: who is Clennam and Co.? Is it the individual of whom I had formerly—hum—some—ha—slight transitory knowledge, and to whom I believe you have referred? Is it—ha—that person?"

"It's a very different person indeed," replied Flora, "with no limbs and wheels instead and the grimmest of women though his mother."

"Clennam and Co. a—hum—a mother!" exclaimed Mr. Dorrit.

"And an old man besides," said Flora.

Mr. Dorrit looked as if he must immediately be driven out of his mind by this account. Neither was it rendered more favorable to sanity by Flora's dashing into a rapid analvsis of Mr. Flintwinch's cravat, and describing him, without the lightest boundary line of separation between his identity and Mrs. Clennam's, as a rusty screw in gaiters. Which compound of man and woman, no limbs, wheels, rusty screw, grimness, and gaiters, so completely stupefied Mr. Dorrit, that he was a spectacle to be pitied.

"But I would not detain you one moment longer," said Flora, upon whom his condition wrought its effect, though she was quite unconscious of having produced it, "if you would have the goodness to give me your promise as a gentleman that both in going back to Italy and in Italy too you would look for this Mr. Blandois high and low and if you found or heard of him make him come forward for the clearing of all parties."

By that time Mr. Dorrit had so far recovered from his bewilderment as to be able to say, in a tolerably connected manner, that he should consider that his duty. Flora was delighted with her success, and rose to take her leave.

"With a million thanks," said she, "and my address upon my card in case of any thing to be communicated personally, I will not send my love to the dear little thing for it might not be acceptable and indeed there is no dear little thing left in the transformation so why do it but both myself and Mr. F.'s Aunt ever wish her well and lay no claim to any favor on our side you may be sure of that but quite the other way for what she undertook to do she did and that is more than a great many of us do, not to say any thing of her doing it as well as it could be done and I myself am one of them for I have said ever since I began to recover the blow of Mr. F.'s death that I would learn the Organ of which I am extremely fond but of which I am ashamed to say I do not yet know a note, good-evening!"

When Mr. Dorrit, who attended her to the room-door, had had a little time to collect his senses, he found that the interview had summoned back discarded reminiscences which jarred with the Merdle dinner-table. He wrote and sent off a brief note excusing himself for that day, and ordered dinner presently in his own rooms at the hotel. He had another reason for this. His time in London was very nearly out, and was anticipated by engagements; his plans were made for returning; and he thought it behooved his importance to pursue some direct inquiry into the Blandois disappearance, and be in a condition to carry back to Mr. Henry Gowan the result of his own personal investigation. He therefore resolved that he would take advantage of that evening's freedom to go down to Clennam and Co.'s, easily to be found by the direction set forth in the handbill, and see the place, and ask a question or two there, himself.

Having dined as plainly as the establishment and the Courier would let him, and having taken a short sleep by the fire for his better recovery from Mrs. Finching, he set out in a hackney cabriolet alone. The deep bell of St. Paul's was striking nine as he passed under the shadow of Temple Bar, headless and forlorn in these degenerate days.

As he approached his destination through the by-streets and waterside-ways, that part of London seemed to him an uglier spot at such an hour than he had ever supposed it to be. Many long years had passed since he had seen it; he had never known much of it; and it wore a mysterious and dismal aspect in his eyes. So powerfully was his imagination impressed by it, that when his driver stopped, after having asked the way more than once, and said to the best of his belief this was the gateway they wanted, Mr. Dorrit stood hesitating, with the coach-door in his hand, half afraid of the dark look of the place.

Truly it looked as gloomy that night as even it had ever looked. Two of the handbills were posted on the entrance wall, one on either side, and as the lamp flickered in the night air, shadows passed over them, not unlike the shadows of fingers following the lines. A watch was evidently kept upon the place. As Mr. Dorrit paused, a man passed in from over the way, and another man passed out from some dark corner within; and both looked at him in passing, and both remained standing about.

As there was only only one house in the inclosure, there was no room for uncertainty, so he went up the steps of that house and knocked. There was a dim light in two windows on the first floor. The door gave back a dreary, vacant sound, as though the house were empty; but it was not, for a light was visible, and a step was audible, almost directly. They both came to the door, and a chain grated, and a woman with her apron thrown over her face and head stood in the aperture.

"Who is it?" said the woman.

Mr. Dorrit, much amazed by this appearance, replied that he was from Italy, and that he wished to ask a question relative to the missing person, whom he knew.

"Hi!" cried the woman, raising a cracked voice. "Jeremiah!"

Upon this, a dry old man appeared, whom Mr. Dorrit thought he identified by his gaiters, as the rusty screw. The woman was under apprehensions of the dry old man, for she whisked her apron away as he approached, and disclosed a pale, affrighted face. "Open the door, you fool," said the old man, "and let the gentleman in."

Mr. Dorrit, not without a glance over his shoulder toward his driver and the cabriolet, walked into the dim hall. "Now, sir," said Mr. Flintwinch, "you can ask any thing here you think proper; there are no secrets here, sir."

Before a reply could be made, a strong, stern voice, though a woman's, called from above, "Who is it?"

"Who is it?" returned Jeremiah. "More inquiries. A gentleman from Italy."

"Bring him up here!"

Mr. Flintwinch muttered, as if he deemed that unnecessary; but, turning to Mr. Dorrit, said, "Mrs. Clennam. She *will* do as she likes. I'll show you the way." He then preceded Mr. Dorrit up the blackened staircase; that gentleman, not unnaturally looking behind him on the road, saw the woman following, with her apron thrown over her head again in her former ghastly manner.

Mrs. Clennam had her books open on her little table. "Oh!" said she, abruptly, as she eyed her visitor with a steady look. "You are from Italy, sir, are you. Well?"

Mr. Dorrit was at a loss for any more distinct rejoinder at the moment than "Ha—well?"

"Where is this missing man? Have you come to give us information where he is? I hope you have?"

"So far from it, I—hum—have come to seek information."

"Unfortunately for us, there is none to be got here. Flintwinch, show the gentleman the hand-bill. Give him several to take away. Hold the light for him to read it."

Mr. Flintwinch did as he was directed, and Mr. Dorrit read it through, as if he had not previously seen it; glad enough of the opportunity of collecting his presence of mind, which the air of the house and of the people in it, had a little disturbed. While his eyes were on the paper, he felt that the eyes of Mr. Flintwinch and of Mrs. Clennam were on him. He found, when he looked up, that this sensation was not a fanciful one.

"Now you know as much," said Mrs. Clennam, "as we know, sir. Is Mr. Blandois a friend of yours?"

"No—hum—an acquaintance," answered Mr. Dorrit.

"You have no commission from him, perhaps?"

"I? Ha. Certainly not."

The searching look turned gradually to the floor, after taking Mr. Flintwinch's face in its way. Mr. Dorrit, discomfited by finding that he was the questioned instead of the questioner, applied himself to the reversal of that unexpected order of things.

"I am—ha—a gentleman of property, at present residing in Italy with my family, my servants, and—hum—my rather large establishment. Being in London for a short time on affairs connected with—ha—my estate, and hearing of this strange disappearance, I wished to make myself acquainted with the circumstances at first hand, because there is—ha, hum—an English gentleman in Italy whom I shall no doubt see on my return, who has been in habits of close and daily intimacy with Monsieur Blandois. Mr. Henry Gowan. You may know the name."

"Never heard of it."

Mrs. Clennam said it, and Mr. Flintwinch echoed it.

"Wishing to—ha—make the narrative coherent and consecutive to him," said Mr. Dorrit, "may I ask—say three questions?"

"Thirty, if you choose."

"Have you known Monsieur Blandois long?"

"Not a twelvemonth. Mr. Flintwinch, here, will refer to the books and tell you when, and by whom at Paris, he was introduced to us. If that," Mrs. Clennam added, "should be any satisfaction to you. It is poor satisfaction to us."

"Have you seen him often?"

"No. Twice. Once before, and—"

"That once," suggested Mr. Flintwinch.

"And that once."

"Pray, madam," said Mr. Dorrit, with a growing fancy upon him, as he recovered his importance, that he was yet in some superior way in the Commission of the Peace; "pray, madam, may I inquire, for the greater satisfaction of the gentleman whom I have the honor to—ha—retain, or protect, or let me say to—hum—know—to know— Was Monsieur Blandois here on business, on the night indicated on this printed sheet?"

"On what he called business," returned Mrs. Clennam.

"Is—ha—excuse me—is its nature to be communicated?"

"No."

It was evidently impracticable to pass the barrier of that reply.

"The question has been asked before," said Mrs. Clennam, "and the answer has been, No. We don't choose to publish our transactions, however unimportant, to all the town. We say, No."

"I mean, he took away no money with him, for example?" said Mr. Dorrit.

"He took away none of ours, sir, and got none here."

"I suppose," observed Mr. Dorrit, glancing from Mrs. Clennam to Mr. Flintwinch, and from Mr. Flintwinch to Mrs. Clennam, "you have no way of accounting to yourself for this mystery?"

"Why do you suppose so?" rejoined Mrs. Clennam.

Disconcerted by the cold and hard inquiry, Mr. Dorrit was unable to assign any reason for his supposing so.

"I account for it, sir," she pursued after an awkward silence on Mr. Dorrit's part, "by having no doubt that he is traveling somewhere, or hiding somewhere."

"Do you know—ha—why he should hide anywhere?"

"No."

It was exactly the same No as before, and put another barrier up.

"You asked me if I accounted for the disappearance to myself," Mrs. Clennam sternly reminded him, "not if I accounted for it to you. I do not pretend to account for it to you, sir. I understand it to be no more my business to do that, than it is yours to require that."

Mr. Dorrit answered with an apologetic bend of his head. As he stepped back, preparatory to saying he had no more to ask, he could not but observe how gloomily and fixedly she sat with her eyes fastened on the ground, and a certain air upon her of resolute waiting; also, how exactly the self-same expression was reflected in Mr. Flintwinch, standing at a little distance from her chair, with his eyes also on the ground, and his right hand softly rubbing his chin.

MISSING AND DREAMING.

At that moment, Mistress Affery (of course, the woman with the apron) dropped the candlestick she held, and cried out, "There! O good Lord! there it is again. Hark, Jeremiah! Now!"

If there were any sound at all, it was so slight that she must have fallen into a confirmed habit of listening for sounds; but Mr. Dorrit believed he did hear a something, like the falling of dry leaves. The woman's terror, for a very short space, seemed to touch the three; and they all listened.

Mr. Flintwinch was the first to stir. "Affery, my woman," said he, sidling at her, with his fist clenched, and his elbows quivering with impatience to shake her, "you are at your old tricks. You'll be walking in your sleep next, my woman, and playing the whole round of your distempered antics. You must have some physic. When I have shown this gentleman out I'll make you up such a comfortable dose, my woman; such a comfortable dose!"

It did not appear altogether comfortable in expectation to Mistress Affery; but Jeremiah, without further reference to his healing medicine, took another candle from Mrs. Clennam's table, and said, "Now, sir; shall I light you down?"

Mr. Dorrit professed himself obliged and went down. Mr. Flintwinch shut him out and chained him out, without a moment's loss of time. He was again passed by the two men, one going out and the other coming in; got into the vehicle he had left waiting, and was driven away.

Before he had gone far, the driver stopped to let him know that he had given his name, number, and address to the two men, on their joint requisition; and also the address at which he had taken Mr. Dorrit up, the hour at which he had been called from his stand, and the way by which he had come. This did not make the night's adventure run the less hotly in Mr. Dorrit's mind, either when he sat down by his fire again, or when he went to bed. All night he haunted the dismal house, saw the two people resolutely waiting, heard the woman with her apron over her face cry out about the noise, and found the body of the missing Blandois, now buried in a cellar, and now bricked up in a wall.

CHAPTER LIV.

A CASTLE IN THE AIR.

MANIFOLD are the cares of wealth and state. Mr. Dorrit's satisfaction in remembering that it had not been necessary for him to announce himself to Clennam and Co., or to make an allusion to his having ever had any knowledge of the intrusive person of that name, had been damped over night, while it was still fresh, by a debate that arose within him whether or no he should take the Marshalsea in his way back, and look at the old gate. He had decided not to do so; and had astonished the coachman by being very fierce with him for proposing to go over London Bridge and recross the river by Waterloo Bridge —a course which would have taken him almost within sight of his old quarters. Still, for all that, the question had raised a conflict in his breast; and, for some odd reason or no reason, he was vaguely dissatisfied. Even at the Merdle dinner-table next day, he was so out of sorts about it, that he continued at intervals to turn it over and over, in a manner frightfully inconsistent with the good society surrounding him. It made him hot to think what the Chief Butler's opinion of him would have been, if that illustrious personage could have plumbed with that heavy eye of his the stream of his meditations.

The farewell banquet was of a gorgeous nature, and wound up his visit in a most brilliant manner. Fanny combined with the attractions of her youth and beauty a certain weight of self-sustainment, as if she had been married twenty years. He felt that he could leave her with a quiet mind to tread the paths of distinction, and wished—but without abatement of patronage, and without prejudice to the retiring virtues of his favorite child—that he had such another daughter.

"My dear," he told her at parting, "our family looks to you to—ha—assert its dignity and—hum—maintain its importance. I know you will never disappoint it."

"No, papa," said Fanny, "you may rely upon that, I think. My best love to dearest Amy, and I will write to her very soon."

"Shall I convey any message to—ha—any body else?" asked Mr. Dorrit, in an insinuating manner.

"Papa," said Fanny, before whom Mrs. General instantly loomed, "no, I thank you. You are very kind, Pa, but I must beg to be excused. There is no other message to send, I thank you, dear papa, that it would be at all agreeable to you to take."

They parted in an outer drawing-room, where only Mr. Sparkler waited on his lady, and dutifully bided his time for shaking hands. When Mr. Sparkler was admitted to this closing audience, Mr. Merdle came creeping in with not much more appearance of arms in his sleeves than if he had been the twin brother of Miss Biffin, and insisted on escorting Mr. Dorrit down stairs. All Mr. Dorrit's protestations being in vain, he enjoyed the honor of being accompanied to the hall-door by this distinguished man, who (as Mr. Dorrit told him in shaking hands on the step) had really overwhelmed him with attentions and services, during this memorable visit. Thus they parted; Mr. Dorrit entering his carriage with a swelling breast, not at all sorry that his Courier, who had come to take leave in the lower regions, should have an opportunity of beholding the grandeur of his departure.

The aforesaid grandeur was yet full upon Mr. Dorrit when he alighted at his hotel. Helped out by the Courier and some half dozen of the hotel servants, he was passing through the hall with a serene magnificence, when lo! a sight presented itself that struck him dumb and motionless. John Chivery, in his best clothes, with his tall hat under his arm, his ivory-handled cane genteelly embarrassing his deportment, and a bundle of cigars in his hand!

"Now, young man," said the porter. "This is the gantleman. This young man has persisted in waiting, sir, saying you would be glad to see him."

Mr. Dorrit glared on the young man, choked, and said, in the mildest of tones, "Ah! Young John! It is Young John, I think; is it not?"

"Yes, sir," returned Young John.

"I—ha—thought it was Young John!" said Mr. Dorrit. "The young man may come up," turning to the attendants, as he passed on: "oh yes, he may come up. Let Young John follow, I will speak to him above."

Young John followed, smiling and much gratified. Mr. Dorrit's rooms were reached. Candles were lighted. The attendants withdrew.

"Now, sir," said Mr. Dorrit, turning round upon him and seizing him by the collar when they were safely alone. "What do you mean by this?"

The amazement and horror depicted in the unfortunate John's face—for he had rather expected to be embraced next—were of that powerfully expressive nature, that Mr. Dorrit withdrew his hand and merely glared at him.

"How dare you do this?" said Mr. Dorrit. "How do you presume to come here? How dare you insult me?"

"I insult you, sir?" cried Young John. "Oh!"

"Yes, sir," returned Mr. Dorrit. "Insult me. Your coming here is an affront, an impertinence, an audacity. You are not wanted here. Who sent you here? What—ha—the Devil do you do here?"

"I thought, sir," said Young John, with as pale and shocked a face as ever had been turned to Mr. Dorrit's in his life—even in his College life: "I thought, sir, you mightn't object to have the goodness to accept a bundle—"

"Damn your bundle, sir!" cried Mr. Dorrit, in irrepressible rage. "I—hum—don't smoke."

"I humbly beg your pardon, sir. You used to."

"Tell me that again," cried Mr. Dorrit, quite beside himself, "and I'll take the poker to you!"

John Chivery backed to the door

"Stop, sir!" cried Mr. Dorrit. "Stop! Sit down. Confound you, sit down!"

John Chivery dropped into the chair nearest the door, and Mr. Dorrit walked up and down the room; rapidly at first; then, more slowly. Once, he went to the window, and stood there with his forehead against the glass. All of a sudden, he turned and said:

RECEPTION OF AN OLD FRIEND.

"What else did you come for, sir?"

"Nothing else in the world, sir. Oh, dear me! Only to say, sir, that I hoped you was well, and only to ask if Miss Amy was well?"

"What's that to you, sir?" retorted Mr. Dorrit.

"It's nothing to me sir, by rights. I never thought of lessening the distance betwixt us, I am sure. I know it's a liberty, sir, but I never thought you'd have taken it ill. Upon my word and honor, sir," said Young John, with emotion, "in my poor way, I am too proud to have come, I assure you, if I had thought so."

Mr. Dorrit was ashamed. He went back to the window and leaned his forehead against the glass for some time. When he turned, he had his handkerchief in his hand, and he had been wiping his eyes with it, and he looked tired and ill.

"Young John, I am very sorry to have been hasty with you, but—ha—some remembrances are not happy remmbrances and—hum—you shouldn't have come."

"I feel that now, sir," returned John Chivery; "but I didn't before, and heaven knows I meant no harm, sir."

"No. No," said Mr. Dorrit. "I am—hum—sure of that. Ha. Give me your hand, Young John, give me your hand."

Young John gave it; but Mr. Dorrit had driven his heart out of it, and nothing could change his face now from its white, shocked look.

"There!" said Mr. Dorrit, slowly shaking hands with him. "Sit down again, Young John."

"Thank you, sir; but I'd rather stand."

Mr. Dorrit sat down instead. After painfully holding his head a little while, he turned it to his visitor, and said, with an effort to be easy:

"And how is your father, Young John? How—how—are they all, Young John?"

"Thank you, sir. They're all prety well, sir, They're not any ways complaining."

"Hum. You are in your—ha—old business, I see, John?" said Mr. Dorrit, with a glance at the offending bundle he had anathematized.

"Partly, sir. I am in my—" John hesitated a little, "father's business likewise."

"Oh, indeed!" said Mr. Dorrit. "Do you—ha hum—go upon the—ha—"

"Lock, sir? Yes, sir."

"Much to do, John?"

"Yes, sir; we're pretty heavy at present. I don't know how it is, but we generally *are* pretty heavy."

"At this time of the year, Young John?"

"Mostly at all times of the year, sir. I don't know the time that makes much difference to us. I wish you good-night, sir."

"Stay a moment John—ha—stay a moment. Hum. Leave me the cigars, John, I—ha—beg."

"Certainly, sir." John put them, with a trembling hand, on the table.

"Stay a moment, Young John; stay another moment. It would be a—ha—a gratification to me to send a little—hum—Testimonial, by such a trusty messenger, to be divided among—ha hum—them—*them*—according to their wants. Would you object to take it, John?"

"Not in any ways, sir. There's many of them, I'm sure, that would be the better for it."

"Thank you John. I—ha—I'll write it, John."

His hand shook, so that he was a long time writing it, and wrote it in a tremulous scrawl at last. It was a check for one hundred pounds. He folded it up, put it in Young John's hand, and pressed the hand in his.

"I hope you'll—ha—overlook—hum—what has passed, John."

"Don't speak of it, sir, on any accounts. I don't in any ways bear malice, I'm sure."

But nothing while John was there could change John's face to its natural color and expression, or restore John's natural manner.

"And John," said Mr. Dorrit, giving his hand a final pressure, and releasing it, "I hope we—ha—agree that we have spoken together in confidence; and that you will abstain, in going out, from saying any thing to any one that might—hum—suggest that—ha—once I—"

"Oh! I assure you, sir," returned John Chivery, "in my

poor humble way, sir, I am too proud and honorable to do it, sir."

Mr. Dorrit was not too proud and honorable to listen at the door, that he might ascertain for himself whether John really went straight out, or lingered to have any talk with any one. There was no doubt that he went direct out at the door, and away down the street with a quick step. After remaining alone for an hour, Mr. Dorrit rang for the Courier, who found him with his chair on the hearth-rug, sitting with his back toward him and his face to the fire. "You can take that bundle of cigars to smoke on the journey, if you like," said Mr. Dorrit, with a careless wave of his hand. "Ha—brought by—hum—little offering from—ha—son of old tenant of mine."

Next morning's sun saw Mr. Dorrit's equipage upon the Dover road, where every red-jacketed postillion was the sign of a cruel house, established for the unmerciful plundering of travelers. The whole business of the human race, between London and Dover, being spoliation, Mr. Dorrit was waylaid at Dartford, pillaged at Gravesend, rifled at Rochester, fleeced at Sittingbourne, and sacked at Canterbury. However, it being the Courier's business to get him out of the hands of the banditti, the Courier bought him off at every stage; and so the red-jackets went gleaming merrily along the spring landscape, rising and falling to a regular measure, between Mr. Dorrit in his snug corner, and the next chalky rise in the dusty highway.

Another day's sun saw him at Calais. And having now got the Channel between himself and John Chivery, he began to feel safe, and to find that the foreign air was lighter to breathe than the air of England.

On again by the heavy French roads for Paris. Having now quite recovered his equanimity, Mr. Dorrit, in his snug corner, fell to castle-building as he rode along. It was evident that he had a very large castle in hand. All day long he was running towers up, taking towers down, adding a wing here, putting on a battlement there, looking to the walls, strengthening the defenses, giving ornamental touches to the interior, making in all respects a superb castle of it. His preoccupied face so clearly denoted the pursuit in which he was engaged, that every cripple at the post-houses, not blind, who shoved his little battered tin box in at the carriage window for Charity in the name of Heaven, Charity in the name of our Lady, Charity in the name of all the Saints, knew as well what work he was at, as their countryman Le Brun could have known it himself, though he had made that English traveler the subject of a special physiognomical treatise.

Arrived at Paris, and resting there three days, Mr. Dorrit strolled much about the streets alone, looking in at the shop-windows, and particularly the jeweler's windows. Ultimately he went into the most famous jeweler's, and said he wanted to buy a little gift for a lady.

It was a charming little woman to whom he said it—a sprightly little woman, dressed in perfect taste, who came out of a green velvet bower to attend upon him, from posting up some dainty little books of account which one could hardly suppose to be ruled for the entry of any articles more commercial than kisses, at a dainty little shining desk which looked in itself like a sweetmeat.

For, example, then, said the little woman, what species of gift did Monsieur desire? A love-gift?

Mr. Dorrit smiled, and said, Eh, well! Perhaps. What did he know? It was always possible; the sex being so charming Would she show him some?

Most willingly, said the little woman. Flattered and enchanted to show him many. But pardon! To begin with, he would have the great goodness to observe that there were love-gifts and there were nuptial-gifts. For example, these ravishing ear-rings and this necklace so superb to correspond, were what one called a love-gift. These brooches and these rings, of a beauty so gracious and celestial, were what one called, with the permission of Monsieur, nuptial-gifts.

Perhaps it would be a good arrangement, Mr. Dorrit hinted, smiling, to purchase both, and to present the love-gift first, and to finish with the nuptial offering?

Ah Heaven! said the little woman, laying the tips of the fingers of her two little hands against each other, that would be generous indeed, that would be a special gallantry! And without doubt the lady so crushed with gifts would find them irresistible.

Mr. Dorrit was not sure of that. But, for example, the sprightly little woman was very sure of it, she said. So Mr. Dorrit bought a gift of each sort, and paid handsomely for it. As he strolled back to his hotel afterward, he carried his head high: having plainly got up his castle, now, to a much loftier altitude than the two square towers of Notre Dame.

Building away with all his might, but reserving the plans of his castle exclusively for his own eye, Mr. Dorrit posted away for Marseilles. Building on, building on, busily, busily, from morning to night. Falling asleep, and leaving great blocks of building materials dangling in the air; waking again, to resume work and get them into their places. What time the Courier in the rumble, smoking Young John's best cigars, left a little thread of thin light smoke behind—perhaps as *he* built a castle or two, with stray pieces of Mr. Dorrit's money.

Not a fortified town that they passed in all their journey was as strong, not a Cathedral summit was as high, as Mr. Dorrit's castle. Neither the Saone nor the Rhone sped with the swiftness of that peerless building; nor was the Mediterranean deeper than its foundations; nor were the distant landscapes on the Cornice road, nor the hills and bay of Genoa the Superb, more beautiful. Mr. Dorrit and his matchless castle were disembarked among the dirty white houses and dirtier felons of Civita Vecchia, and thence scrambled on to Rome as they could, through the filth that festered on the way

CHAPTER LV.

THE STORMING OF THE CASTLE IN THE AIR.

THE sun had gone down full four hours, and it was later than most travelers would like it to be for finding themselves outside the walls of Rome, when Mr. Dorrit's carriage, still on its last wearisome stage, rattled over the solitary Campagna. The savage herdsmen and the fierce-looking peasants, who had checkered the way while the light lasted, had all gone down with the sun, and left the wilderness blank. At some turns of the road, a pale flare on the horizon, like an exhalation from the ruin-sown land, showed that the city was yet far off; but this poor relief was rare and short-lived. The carriage dipped down again into a hollow of the black dry sea, and for a long time there was nothing visible save its petrified swell and the gloomy sky.

Mr. Dorrit, though he had his castle-building to engage his mind, could not be quite easy in that desolate place. He was far more curious, in every swerve of the carriage and every cry of the postillions, than he had been since he quitted London. The valet on the box evidently quaked. The Courier in the rumble was not altogether comfortable in his mind. As often as Mr. Dorrit let down the glass, and looked back at him (which was very often), he saw him smoking John Chivery out, it is true, but still generally standing up the while and looking about him, like a man who had his suspicions, and kept upon his guard. Then would Mr. Dorrit, pulling up the glass again, reflect that those postillions were cut-throat looking fellows, and that he would have done better to have slept at Civita Vecchia, and have started betimes in the morning. But, for all this, he worked at his castle in the intervals.

And now, fragments of ruinous inclosure, yawning window-gap and crazy wall, deserted houses, leaking wells, broken water-tanks, spectral cypress-trees, patches of tangled vine, and the changing of the track to a long, irregular, disordered lane, where every thing was crumbling away, from the unsightly buildings to the jolting road—now, these objects showed that they were nearing Rome. And now, a sudden twist and stoppage of the carriage inspired Mr. Dorrit with the mistrust that the brigand moment was come for twisting him into a ditch and robbing him; until, letting down the glass again and looking out, he perceived himself assailed by nothing worse than a funeral procession, which came mechanically chaunting by, with an indistinct show of dirty vestments, lurid torches, swinging censers, and a great cross borne before a priest. He was an ugly priest by torch-light; of a lowering aspect, with an overhanging brow; and as his eyes met those of Mr. Dorrit, looking bareheaded out of the carriage, his lips, moving as they chaunted, seemed to threaten that important traveler; likewise the action of his hand, which was in fact his manner of returning the traveler's salutation, seemed to come in aid of that menace. So thought Mr. Dorrit, made fanciful by the weariness of the building and traveling, as the priest drifted past him, and the procession straggled away, taking its dead along with it. Upon their so-different way went Mr. Dorrit's company too; and soon, with their coach-load of luxuries from the two great capitals of Europe, they were (like the Goths reversed) beating at the gates of Rome.

Mr. Dorrit was not expected by his own people that night. He had been; but they had given him up until to-morrow, not doubting that it was later than he would care, in those parts, to be out. Thus, when his equipage stopped at his own gate, no one but the porter appeared to receive him. Was Miss Dorrit from home? he asked. No. She was within. Good, said Mr. Dorrit to the assembling servants; let them keep where they were; let them help to unload the carriage; he would find Miss Dorrit for himself.

So he went up his grand staircase, slowly, and tired, and looked into various chambers which were empty, until he saw a light in a small ante-room. It was a curtained nook, like a tent, within two other rooms; and it looked warm, and bright in color, as he approached it through the dark avenue they made.

There was a draped door-way, but no door; and as he stopped here, looking in unseen, he felt a pang. Surely not like jealousy? For why like jealousy? There were only his daughter and his brother there: he, with his chair drawn to the hearth, enjoying the warmth of the evening wood-fire; she, seated at a little table, busied with some embroidery work. Allowing for the great difference in the still-life of the picture, the figures were much the same as of old; his brother being sufficiently like himself to represent himself, for a moment, in the composition. So had he sat many a night, over a coal-fire far away; so had she sat, devoted to him. Yet surely there was nothing to be jealous of in the old miserable poverty. Whence, then, the pang in his heart?

"Do you know, uncle, I think you are growing young again?"

Her uncle shook his head, and said, "Since when, my dear; since when?"

"I think," returned Little Dorrit, plying her needle, "that you have been growing younger for weeks past. So cheerful, uncle, and so ready and so interested!"

"My dear child—all you."

"All me, uncle!"

"Yes, yes. You have done me a world of good. You have been so considerate of me, and so tender with me, and so delicate in trying to hide your attentions from me, that, I—well, well, well! It's treasured up, my darling, treasured up."

"There is nothing in it but your own fresh fancy, uncle," said Little Dorrit, cheerfully.

"Well, well, well!" murmured the old man. "Thank God!"

She paused for an instant in her work to look at him, and her look revived that former pain in her father's breast; in his poor weak breast, so full of contradictions, vacillations, inconsistencies, the little peevish perplexities of this ignorant life, mists which the morning without a night only can clear away.

"I have been freer with you, you see, my dove," said the old man, "since we have been alone. I say, alone, for I don't count Mrs. General; I don't care for her; she has nothing to do with me. But I know Fanny was impatient of me. And I don't wonder at it, or complain of it, for I am sensible that I must be in the way, though I try to keep out of it as well as I can. I know I am not fit company for our company. My brother William," said the old man, admiringly, "is fit company for monarchs; but not so your uncle, my dear. Frederick Dorrit is no credit to William Dorrit, and he knows it quite well. Ah! Why, here's your father, Amy! My dear William, welcome back! My beloved brother, I am rejoiced to see you!"

(Turning his head in speaking, he had caught sight of him as he stood in the doorway.)

Little Dorrit, with a cry of pleasure, put her arms about her father's neck, and kissed him again and again. Her father was a little impatient, and a little querulous. "I am glad to find you at last, Amy," he said. "Ha! Really I am glad to find —hum—any one to receive me at last. I appear to have been —ha—so little expected, that, upon my word, I began—ha hum—to think it might be right to offer an apology for—ha—taking the liberty of coming back at all."

"It was so late, my dear William," said his brother, "that we had given you up for to-night."

"I am stronger than you, dear Frederick," returned his brother, with an elaboration of fraternity in which there was severity; "and I hope I can travel without detriment at—ha—any hour I choose."

"Surely, surely," returned the other, with a misgiving that he had given offense. "Surely, William."

"Thank you, Amy," pursued Mr. Dorrit, as she helped him to put off his wrappers, "I can do it without assistance. I—ha—need not trouble you, Amy. Could I have a morsel of bread and a glass of wine, or—hum—would it cause too much inconvenience?"

"Dear father, you shall have supper in a very few minutes."

"Thank you, my love," said Mr. Dorrit, with a reproachful frost upon him; "I—ha—am afraid I am causing inconvenience. Hum. Mrs. General pretty well?"

"Mrs. General complained of a headache, and of being fatigued; and so, when we gave you up, she went to bed, dear."

Perhaps Mr. Dorrit thought that Mrs. General had done well in being overcome by the disappointment of his not arriving.

At any rate, his face relaxed, and he said, with obvious satisfaction, "Extremely sorry to hear that Mrs. General is not well."

During this short dialogue, his daughter had been observant of him, with something more than her usual interest. It would seem as though he had a changed or worn appearance in her eyes, and he perceived and resented it; for he said, with renewed peevishness, when he had divested himself of his traveling cloak, and had come to the fire,

"Amy, what are you looking at? What do you see in me that causes you to—ha—concentrate your solicitude on me in that—hum—very particular manner?"

"I did not know it, father; I beg your pardon. It gladdens my eyes to see you again; that's all."

"Don't say that's all, because—ha—that's not all. You—hum—you think," said Mr. Dorrit, with an accusatory emphasis, "that I am not looking well."

"I thought you looked a little tired, love."

"Then you are mistaken," said Mr. Dorrit. "Ha, I am not tired. Ha, hum. I am very much fresher than I was when I went away."

He was so inclined to be angry that she said nothing more in her justification, but remained quietly beside him, embracing his arm. As he stood thus, with his brother on the other side, he fell into a heavy doze of not a minute's duration, and awoke with a start.

"Frederick," he said, turning on his brother, "I recommend you to go to bed immediately."

"No, William. I'll wait and see you sup."

"Frederick," he retorted, "I beg you to go to bed. I—ha—make it a personal request that you go to bed. You ought to have been in bed long ago. You are very feeble."

"Ha!" said the old man, who had no wish but to please him. "Well, well, well! I dare say I am."

"My dear Frederick," returned Mr. Dorrit, with an astonishing superiority to his brother's failing powers, "there can be no doubt of it. It is painful to me to see you so weak. Ha. It distresses me. Hum. I don't find you looking at all well. You are not fit for this sort of thing. You should be more careful, you should be very careful."

"Shall I go to bed?" asked Frederick.

"Dear Frederick," said Mr. Dorrit, "do, I adjure you! Good-night, brother. I hope you will be stronger to-morrow. I am not at all pleased with your looks. Good-night, dear fellow!" After dismissing his brother in this gracious way, he fell into a doze again, before the old man was well out of the room; and he would have stumbled forward upon the logs, but for his daughter's restraining hold.

"Your uncle wanders very much, Amy," he said, when he was thus roused. "He is less—ha—coherent, and his conversation is more—hum—broken, than I have—ha hum—ever known. Has he had any illness since I have been gone?"

"No, father."

"You—ha—see a great change in him, Amy?"

"I had not observed it, dear."

"Greatly broken," said Mr. Dorrit. "Greatly broken. My poor, affectionate, failing Frederick! Ha. Even taking into account what he was before, he is—hum—sadly broken."

His supper, which was brought to him there, and spread upon the little table where he had seen her working, diverted his attention. She sat at his side as in the days that were gone, for the first time since those days ended. They were alone, and she helped him to his meat and poured out his drink for him, as she had been used to do in the prison. All this happened now for the first time since their accession to wealth. She was afraid to look at him much, after the offense he had taken; but she noticed two occasions in the course of his meal when he all of a sudden looked at her, and looked about him, as if the association was so strong that he needed assurance from his sense of sight that they were not in the old prison-room. Both times he put his hand to his head as if he missed his old black cap—though it had been ignominiously given away in the Marshalsea, and had never got free to that hour, but still hovered about the yard on the head of his successor.

He took very little supper, but was a long time over it, and often reverted to his brother's declining state. Though he expressed the greatest pity for him, he was almost bitter upon him. He said that poor Frederick—ha hum—driveled. There was no other word to express it; driveled. Poor fellow! It was melancholy to reflect what Amy must have undergone from the excessive tediousness of his society—wandering and babbling on, poor dear estimable creature! wandering and babbling on—if it had not been for the relief she had had in Mrs. General. Extremely sorry, he then repeated with his former satisfaction, that that—ha—superior woman, was poorly.

Little Dorrit, in her watchful love, would have remembered the lightest thing he said or did that night, though she had had no subsequent reason to recall that night. She always remembered, that when he looked about him under the strong influence of the old association, he tried to keep it out of her mind, and perhaps out of his own too, by immediately expatiating on the great riches and great company that had encompassed him in his absence, and on the lofty position he and his family had to sustain. Nor did she fail to recall that there were two undercurrents, side by side, pervading all his discourse and all his manner; one, showing her how well he had got on without her, and how independent he was of her; the other, in a fitful and unintelligible way almost complaining of her, as if it had been possible that she had neglected him while he was away.

His telling her of the glorious state that Mr. Merdle kept, and of the Court that bowed before him, naturally brought him to Mrs. Merdle. So naturally indeed, that although there was an unusual want of sequence in the greater part of his remarks, he passed to her at once, and asked how she was.

"She is very well. She is going away next week."

"Home?" asked Mr. Dorrit.

"After a few weeks' stay upon the road."

"She will be a vast loss here," said Mr. Dorrit. "A vast—ha—acquisition at home. To Fanny, and to—hum—the rest of the—ha—great world."

Little Dorrit thought of the competition that was to be entered upon, and assented very softly.

"Mrs. Merdle is going to have a great farewell Assembly, dear, and a dinner before it. She has been expressing her anxiety that you should return in time. She has invited both you and me to her dinner."

"She is—ha—very kind. When is the day?"

"The day after to-morrow."

"Write round in the morning, and say that I have returned, and shall—hum—be delighted."

"May I walk with you up the stairs to your room, dear?"

"No!" he answered, looking angrily round; for he was moving away as if forgetful of leave-taking. "You may not, Amy. I want no help. I am your father, not your infirm uncle!" He checked himself, as abruptly as he had broken in to this reply, and said, "You have not kissed me, Amy. Good-night, my dear! We must marry—ah—we must marry *you*, now." With that he went, more slowly and more tired, up the staircase to his rooms, and, almost as soon as he got there, dismissed his valet. His next care was to look about him for his Paris purchases, and, after opening their cases and carefully surveying them, to put them away under lock and key. After that, what with dozing and what with castle-building, he lost himself for a long time, so that there was a touch of morning on the eastward rim of the desolate Campagna when he crept to bed.

Mrs. General sent up her compliments in good time next day, and hoped he had rested well after his fatiguing journey. He sent down his compliments, and begged to inform Mrs. General that he had rested very well indeed, and was in high condition. Nevertheless, he did not come forth from his own rooms until late in the afternoon; and, although he then caused himself to be magnificently arrayed for a drive with Mrs. General and his daughter, his appearance was scarcely up to his description of himself.

As the family had no visitors that day, its four members dined alone together. He conduated Mrs. General to the seat at his right hand, with immense ceremony; and Little Dorrit could not but notice, as she followed with her uncle, both that he was again elaborately dressed, and that his manner toward Mrs. General was very particular. The perfect formation of that accomplished lady's surface rendered it difficult to displace an atom of its genteel glaze, but Little Dorrit thought she descried a slight thaw of triumph in a corner of her frosty eye.

Notwithstanding what may be called in these pages the Pruney and Prismatic nature of the family banquet, Mr. Dorrit several times fell asleep while it was in progress. His fits of dozing were as sudden as they had been overnight, and were as short and profound. When the first of these slumberings seized him, Mrs. General looked almost amazed : but on each recurrence of the symptoms, she told her polite beads, Papa, Potatoes, Poultry, Prunes, and Prism ; and, by dint of going through that infallible performance very slowly, appeared to finish her rosary at about the same time as Mr. Dorrit started from his sleep.

He was again painfully aware of a somnolent tendency in Frederick (which had no existence out of his own imagination), and after dinner, when Frederick had withdrawn, privately apologized to Mrs. General for the poor man. "The most estimable and affectionate of brothers," he said, "but—ha hum —broken up altogether. Unhappily, declining fast."

"Mr. Frederick, sir," quoth Mrs. General, "is habitually absent and drooping, but let us hope it is not so bad as that."

Mr. Dorrit, however, was determined not to let him off. "Fast declining, madam. A wreck. A ruin. Mouldering away, before our eyes. Hum. Good Frederick!"

"You left Mrs. Sparkler quite well and happy, I trust?" said Mrs. General, after heaving a cool sigh for Frederick.

"Surrounded," replied Mr. Dorrit, "by—ha—all that can charm the taste, and—hum—elevate the mind. Happy, my dear madam, in a—hum—husband."

Mrs. General was a little fluttered ; seeming delicately to put the word away with her gloves, as if there were no knowing what it might lead to.

"Fanny," Mr. Dorrit continued, "Fanny, Mrs. General, has high qualities. Ha! Ambition—hum—purpose, consciousness of—ha—position, determination to support that position —ha hum—grace, beauty, and native nobility."

"No doubt," said Mrs. General, with a little extra stiffness.

"Combined with these qualities, madam," said Mr. Dorrit, "Fanny has—ha—manifested one blemish which has made me —hum—made me uneasy, and—ha—I must add, angry; but which, I trust, may now be considered at an end, even as to herself, and which is undoubtedly at an end as to—ha—others."

"To what, Mr. Dorrit," returned Mrs. General, with her

gloves again somewhat excited, "can you allude? I am at a loss to—"

"Do not say that, my dear madam," interrupted Mr. Dorrit.

Mrs. General's voice, as it died away, pronounced the words, "at a loss to imagine."

After which, Mr. Dorrit was seized with a doze for about a minute, out of which he sprang with spasmodic nimbleness.

"I refer, Mrs. General, to that—ha—strong spirit of opposition, or—hum—I might say—ha—jealousy in Fanny, which has occasionally risen against the—ha—sense I entertain of—hum—the claims of—ha—the lady with whom I have now the honor of communing."

"Mr. Dorrit," returned Mrs. General, "is ever but too obliging, ever but to appreciative. If there have been moments when I have imagined that Miss Dorrit has indeed resented the favorable opinion Mr. Dorrit has formed of my services, I have found, in that only too high opinion, my consolation and recompense."

"Opinions of your services, madam?" said Mr. Dorrit.

"Of," Mrs. General repeated, in an elegantly impressive manner, "my services."

"Of course your services alone, dear madam?" said Mr. Dorrit.

"I presume," retorted Mrs. General, in her former impressive manner, "of my services alone. For to what else," said Mrs. General, with a slightly interrogative action of her gloves, "could I impute—"

"To—ha—yourself, Mrs. General. Ha hum. To yourself and your merits," was Mr. Dorrit's rejoinder.

"Mr. Dorrit will pardon me," said Mrs. General, "if I remark that this is not a time or place for the pursuit of the present conversation. Mr. Dorrit will excuse me if I remind him that Miss Dorrit is in the adjoining room, and is visible to myself while I utter her name. Mr. Dorrit will forgive me if I observe that I am agitated, and that I find there are moments when weaknesses I suppose myself to have subdued return with redoubled power. Mr. Dorrit will allow me to withdraw."

"Hum. Perhaps we may resume this—ha—interesting conversation," said Mr. Dorrit, "at another time; unless it should be, what I hope it is not—hum—in any way disagreeable to—ha—Mrs. General."

"Mr. Dorrit," said Mrs. General, casting down her eyes as she rose with a bend, "must ever claim my homage and obedience."

Mrs. General than took herself off in a stately way, and not with that amount of trepidation upon her which might have been expected in a less remarkable woman. Mr. Dorrit, who had conducted his part of the dialogue with a certain majestic and admiring condescension—much as some people may be seen to conduct themselves in church, and to perform their part in the service—appeared, on the whole, very well satisfied with himself and with Mrs. General too. On the return of that lady to tea, she had touched herself up with a little powder and pomatum, and was not without moral enhancement, likewise; the latter showing itself in much sweet patronage of manner toward Miss Dorrit, and in an air of as tender interest in Mr. Dorrit as was consistent with rigid propriety. At the close of the evening, when she rose to retire, Mr. Dorrit took her by the hand, as if he were going to lead her out into the Piazza of the People to walk a minute by moonlight, and with great solemnity conducted her to the room door, where he raised her knuckles to his lips. Having parted from her with what may be conjectured to have been a rather bony kiss, of a cosmetic flavor, he gave his daughter his blessing, graciously. And having thus hinted that there was something remarkable in the wind, he again went to bed.

He remained in the seclusion of his own chanber next morning; but, early in the afternoon, sent down his best compliments to Mrs. General, by Mr. Tinkler, and begged she would accompany Miss Dorrit on an airing without him. His daughter was dressed for Mrs. Merdle's dinner before he appeared. He then presented himself, in a refulgent condition as to his attire, but looking indefinably shrunken and old. However, as he was plainly determined to be angry with her if she so much as asked him how he was, she only ventured to kiss his cheek, before accompanying him to Mrs. Merdle's with an anxious heart.

The distance that they had to go was very short, but he was at his building work again before the carriage had half traversed it. Mrs. Merdle received him with great distinction; the bosom was in admirable preservation, and on the best terms with itself; the dinner was very choice; and the company was very select.

It was principally English, saving that it comprised the usual French Count and the usual Italian Marchese—decorative social milestones, always to be found in certain places, and varying very little in appearance. The table was long, and the dinner was long; and Little Dorrit, overshadowed by a large pair of black whiskers and a large white cravat, lost sight of her father altogether, until a servant put a scrap of paper in her hand, with a whispered request from Mrs. Merdle that she would read it directly. Mrs. Merdle had written on it in pencil, "Pray come and speak to Mr. Dorrit. I doubt if he is well."

She was hurrying to him, unobserved, when he got up out of his chair, and leaning over the table, called to her, supposing her to be still in her place:

"Amy, Amy, my child!"

The action was so unusual, to say nothing of his strange eager appearance and strange eager voice, that it instantaneously caused a profound silence.

"Amy, my dear," he repeated. "Will you go and see if Bob is on the lock?"

She was at his side, and touching him, but he still perversely supposed her to be in her seat, and called out, still leaning over the table, "Amy, Amy. I don't feel quite myself. Ha. I don't know what's the matter with me. I particularly wish to see Bob. Ha. Of all the turnkeys, he's as much my friend as yours. See if Bob is in the lodge, and beg him to come to me."

All the guests were now in consternation, and everybody rose.

"Dear father, I am not there; I am here, by you."

"Oh! You are here, Amy! Good. Hum. Good. Ha. Call Bob. If he has been relieved, and is not on the lock, tell Mrs. Bangham to go and fetch him."

She was gently trying to get him away; but he resisted, and would not go.

"I tell you, child," he said, petulantly, "I can't be got up the narrow stairs without Bob. Ha. Send for Bob. Hum Send for Bob—best of all the turnkeys—send for Bob!"

He looked confusedly about him, and, becoming conscious of the number of faces by which he was surrounded, addressed them:

Ladies and gentlemen, the duty—ha—devolves upon me of—hum—welcoming you to the Marshalsea. Welcome to the Marshalsea! The space is—ha—limited—limited—the parade might be wider; but you will find it apparently grow larger after a time—a time, ladies and gentlemen—and the air is, all things considered, very good. It blows over the—ha—Surrey hills. Blows over the Surrey hills. This is the Snuggery. Hum. Supported by a small subscription of the—ha—Collegiate body. In return for which—hot water—general kitchen—and little domestic advantages. Those who are habituated to the—ha—Marshalsea, are pleased to call me its Father. I am accustomed to be complimented by strangers as the—ha—Father of the Marshalsea. Certainly, if years of residence may establish a claim to so—ha—honorable a title, I may accept the—hum—conferred distinction. My child, ladies and gentlemen. My daughter. Born here!"

She was not ashamed of it, or ashamed of him. She was pale and frightened; but she had no other care than to soothe him and get him away, for his own dear sake. She was between him and the wondering faces, turned round upon his breast with her own face raised to his. He held her clasped in his left arm, and between whiles her low voice was heard tenderly imploring him to go away with her.

"Born here," he repeated, shedding tears. "Bred here. Ladies and gentlemen, my daughter. Child of an unfortunate father, but—ha—always a gentleman. Poor, no doubt, but—hum—proud. Always proud. It has become a—hum—not infrequent custom for my—ha—personal admirers—personal admirers solely—to be pleased to express their desire to acknowledge my semi-official position here, by offering—ha—little tributes, which usually take the form of—ha—Testimonials—pecuniary Testimonials. In the acceptance of those—ha—voluntary recognitions of my humble endeavors to—hum—to uphold a Tone here—a Tone—I beg it to be understood that I

AN UNEXPECTED AFTER-DINNER SPEECH.

do not consider myself compromised. Ha. Not compromised. Ha. Not a beggar. No; I repudiate the title! At the same time far be it from me to—hum—to put upon the fine feelings by which my partial friends are actuated the slight of scrupling to admit that those offerings are—hum—highly acceptable. On the contrary, they are most acceptable. In my child's name, if not in my own, I make the admission in the fullest manner, at the same time reserving—ha—shall I say my personal dignity? Ladies and gentlemen, God bless you all!"

By this time, the exceeding mortification undergone by the Bosom had occasioned the withdrawal of the greater part of the company into other rooms. The few who had lingered thus long followed the rest, and Little Dorrit and her father were left to the servants and themselves. Dearest and most precious to her, he would come with her now, would he not? He replied to her fervid entreaties, that he would never be able to get up the narrow stairs without Bob, where was Bob, would nobody fetch Bob! Under pretense of looking for Bob, she got him out against the stream of gay company now pouring in for the evening assembly, and got him into a coach that had just set down its load, and got him home.

The broad stairs of his Roman palace were contracted in his failing sight to the narrow stairs of his London prison; and he would suffer no one but her to touch him, his brother excepted. They got him up to his room without help, and laid him down on his bed. And from that hour his poor maimed spirit, only remembering the place where it had broken its wings, canceled the dream through which it had since groped, and knew of nothing beyond the Marshalsea. When he heard footsteps in the street, he took them for the old weary tread in the yards. When the hour came for locking up, he supposed all strangers to be excluded for the night. When the time for opening came again, he was so anxious to see Bob, that they were fain to patch up a narrative how that Bob—many a year dead then, gentle turnkey—had taken cold, but hoped to be out to-morrow, or the next day, or the next at furthest.

He fell away into a weakness so extreme that he could not raise his hand. But he still protected his brother according to his long usage; and would say with some complacency, fifty times a day, when he saw him standing by his bed, "My good Frederick, sit down. You are very feeble indeed."

They tried him with Mrs. General, but he had not the faintest knowledge of her. Some injurious suspicion lodged itself in his brain, that she wanted to supplant Mrs. Bangham, and that she was given to drinking. He charged her with it in no measured terms; and was so urgent with his daughter to go round to the Marshal and entreat him to turn her out, that she was never reproduced after the first failure.

Saving that he once asked "If Tip had gone outside?" the remembrance of his two children not present seemed to have departed from him. But the child who had done so much for him, and had been so poorly repaid, was never out of his mind. Not that he spared her, or was fearful of her being spent by watching and fatigue; he was not more troubled on that score than he had usually been. No; he loved her in his old way. They were in the jail again, and she tended him, and he had constant need of her, and could not turn without her; and he even told her, sometimes, that he was content to have undergone a great deal for her sake. As to her, she bent over his bed with her quiet face against his, and would have laid down her own life to restore him.

When he had been sinking in this painless way for two or three days, she observed him to be troubled by the ticking of his watch—a pompous gold watch that made as great a to-do about its going, as if nothing else went but itself and Time. She suffered it to run down; but he was still uneasy, and showed that was not what he wanted. At length he roused himself to explain that he wanted money to be raised on this watch. He was quite pleased when she pretended to take it away for the purpose, and afterward had a relish for his little tastes of wine and jelly, that he had not had before.

He soon made it plain that this was so; for in another day or two he sent off his sleeve-buttons and finger-rings. He had an amazing satisfaction in intrusting her with these errands, and appeared to consider it equivalent to making the most methodical and provident arrangements. After his trinkets, or such of them as he had been able to see about him, were gone, his clothes engaged his attention; and it is as likely as not that he was kept alive for some days by the satisfaction of sending them, piece by piece, to an imaginary pawnbroker's.

Thus for ten days Little Dorrit bent over his pillow, laying her cheek against his. Sometimes she was so worn out that for a few minutes they would slumber together. Then she would awake; to recollect with fast-flowing silent tears what it was that touched her face, and to see, stealing over the cherished face upon the pillow, a deeper shadow than the shadow of the Marshalsea Wall.

Quietly, quietly, all the lines of the plan of the great Castle melted, one after another. Quietly, quietly, the ruled and cross-ruled countenance on which they were traced, became fair and blank. Quietly, quietly, the reflected marks of the prison bars and of the zig-zag iron on the wall-top, faded away. Quietly, quietly, the face subsided into a far younger likeness of her own than she had ever seen under the gray hair, and sank to rest.

At first her uncle was stark distracted. "Oh, my brother! Oh, William, William! You to go before me; you to go alone; you to go, and I to remain! You, so far superior, so distinguished, so noble; I, a poor useless creature, fit for nothing, and whom no one would have missed!"

It did her, for the time, the good of having him to think of, and to succor. "Uncle, dear uncle, spare yourself, spare me!"

The old man was not deaf to the last words. When he did begin to restrain himself, it was that he might spare her. He had no care for himself; but, with all the remaining power of the honest heart, stunned so long and now awaking to be broken, he honored and blessed her.

"O God," he cried, before they left the room, with his wrinkled hands clasped over her, "Thou seest this daughter of my dear dead brother! All that I have looked upon, with my half-blind and sinful eyes, Thou hast discerned clearly, brightly. Not a hair of her head shall be harmed before Thee. Thou wilt uphold her here, to her last hour. And I know Thou wilt reward her hereafter!"

They remained in a dim room near, until it was almost mid-night, quiet and sad together. At times his grief would seek relief in a burst like that in which it had found its earliest expression; but, besides that, his little strength would soon have been unequal to such strains, he never failed to recall her words, and to reproach himself and calm himself. The only utterance with which he indulged his sorrow, was the frequent exclamation that his brother was gone, alone; that they had been together in the outset of their lives, that they had fallen into misfortune together, that they had kept together through their many years of poverty, that they had remained together to that day; and that his brother was gone alone, alone!

They parted, heavy, and sorrowful. She would not consent to leave him any where but in his own room, and she saw him lie down in his clothes upon his bed, and covered him with her own hands. Then she sank upon her own bed, and fell into a deep sleep; the sleep of exhaustion and rest, though not of complete release from a pervading consciousness of affliction. Sleep, good Little Dorrit. Sleep through the night!

It was a moonlight night; but the moon rose late, being long past the full. When it was high in the peaceful firmament, it shone through half-closed lattice blinds into the solemn room where the stumblings and wanderings of a life had so lately ended. Two quiet figures were within the room; two figures, equally still and impassive, equally removed by an untraversable distance from the teeming earth and all that it contains, though soon to lie in it.

One figure reposed upon the bed. The other, kneeling on the floor, drooped over it; the arms easily and peacefully resting on the coverlet; the face bowed down, so that the lips touched the hand over which with its last breath it had bent. The two brothers were before their Father; far beyond the twilight judgments of this world; high above its mists and obscurities

THE NIGHT.

CHAPTER LVI.

INTRODUCES THE NEXT.

The passengers were landing from the packet on the pier at Calais. A low-lying place and a low-spirited place Calais was, with the tide ebbing out toward low water-mark. There had been no more water on the bar than had sufficed to float the packet in; and now the bar itself, with a shallow break of sea over it, looked like a lazy marine monster just risen to the surface, whose form was indistinctly shown as it lay asleep. The meagre light-house all in white, haunting the sea-board, as if it were the ghost of an edifice that had once had color and rotundity, dripped melancholy tears after its late buffeting by the waves. The long rows of gaunt black piles, slimy and wet and weather-worn, with funeral garlands of sea-weed twisted about them by the late tide, might have represented an unsightly marine cemetery. Every wave-dashed, storm-beaten object, was so low and so little, under the broad gray sky, in the noise of the wind and sea, and before the curling lines of surf, making at it ferociously, that the wonder was there was any Calais left, and that its low gates and low wall and low roofs and low ditches and low sand-hills and low ramparts and flat streets, had not yielded long ago to the undermining and besieging sea, like the fortifications children make on the sea-shore.

After slipping among oozy piles and planks, stumbling up wet steps, and encountering many salt difficulties, the passengers entered on their comfortless peregrination along the pier, where all the French vagabonds and English outlaws in the town (half the population) attended to prevent their recovery from bewilderment. After being minutely inspected by all the English, and claimed and reclaimed and counter-reclaimed as prizes by all the French, in a hand-to-hand scuffle three quarters of a mile long, they were at last free to enter the streets, and to make off in their various directions, hotly pursued.

Clennam, harassed by more anxieties than one, was among this devoted band. Having rescued the most defenseless of his compatriots from situations of great extremity, he now went his way alone, or as nearly alone as he could be, with a native gentleman in a suit of grease, and a cap of the same material, giving chase at a distance of some fifty yards, and continually calling after him, "Hi! Ice-say! You! Seer! Ice-say! Nice Oatel!"

Even this hospitable person, however, being left behind at last, Clennam pursued his way, unmolested. There was a tranquil air in the town after the turbulence of the Channel and the beach, and its dullness in that comparison was agreeable. He met new groups of his countrymen, who had all a straggling air of having at one time overblown themselves, like certain uncomfortable kinds of flowers, and of having become mere weeds. They had all an air, too, of lounging out a limited round, day after day, which strongly reminded him of the Marshalsea. But taking no further note of them than was sufficient to give birth to the reflection, he sought out a certain street and number, which he kept in his mind.

"So Pancks said," he murmured to himself, as he stopped before a dull house answering to the address. "I take his information to be correct, and his discovery, among Mr. Casby's loose papers, indisputable; but, without it, I should hardly have supposed this to be a likely place."

A dead sort of house, with a dead wall over the way and a dead gateway at the side, where a pendent bell-handle produced two dead tinkles, and a knocker produced a dead flat surface-tapping that seemed not to have depth enough in it to penetrate even the cracked door. However, the door jarred open on a dead sort of spring, and he closed it behind him as he entered a dull yard, soon brought to a close at the back by another dead wall, where an attempt had been made to train some creeping shrubs, which were dead; and to make a little fountain in a grotto, which was dry; and to decorate that with a little statue, which was gone.

The entry to the house was on the left, and it was garnished, as the outer gateway was, with two printed bills in French and English, announcing Furnished Apartments to let, with immediate possession. A strong, cheerful peasant woman, all stocking, petticoat, white cap, and ear-ring, stood here in a dark doorway, and said, with a pleasant show of teeth, "Ice-say! Seer! Who?"

Clennam, replying in French, said, the English lady; he wished to see the English lady. "Enter, then, and ascend, if you please," returned the peasant woman, in French likewise. He did both, and followed her up a dark, bare staircase to a back room on the first floor. Hence there was a gloomy view of the yard that was dull, and of the shrubs that were dead, and of the fountain that was dry, and of the pedestal of the statue that was gone.

"Monsieur Blandois," said Clennam.

"With pleasure, Monsieur."

Thereupon the woman withdrew, and left him to look at the room. It was the pattern of room always to be found in such a house. Cool, dull, and dark. Waxed floor very slippery. A room not large enough to skate in; not adapted to the easy pursuit of any other occupation. Red and white curtained windows, little straw mat, little round table, with a tumultuous assemblage of legs underneath, clumsy rush-bottomed chairs; two great red velvet arm-chairs, affording plenty of space to be uncomfortable in; bureau; chimney-glass in several pieces, pretending to be in one piece; pair of gaudy vases of very artificial flowers; between them a Greek warrior with his helmet off, sacrificing a clock to the genius of France.

After some pause, a door of communication with another room was opened, and a lady entered. She manifested great surprise on seeing Clennam, and her glance went round the room in search of some one else.

"Pardon me, Miss Wade. I am alone."

"It was not your name that was brought to me."

"No; I know that. Excuse me. I have already had experience that my name does not predispose you to an interview; and I ventured to mention the name of one I am in search of."

"Pray," she returned, motioning him to a chair so coldly, that he remained standing, "what name was it that you gave?"

"I mentioned the name of Blandois."

"Blandois?"

"A name you are acquainted with."

"It is strange," she said, frowning, "that you should still press an undesired interest in me and my acquaintances, in me and my affairs, Mr. Clennam. I don't know what you mean."

"Pardon me. You know the name?"

"What can you have to do with the name? What can I have to do with the name? What can you have to do with my knowing or not knowing any name? I know many names, and I have forgotten many more. This may be in the one class, or it may be in the other, or I may never have heard it. I am acquainted with no reason for examining myself, or for being examined about it."

"If you will allow me," said Clennam, "I will tell you my reason for pressing the subject. I admit that I do press it, and I must beg you to forgive me if I do so very earnestly. The reason is all mine. I do not insinuate that it is in any way yours."

"Well, sir," she returned, repeating, a little less haughtily than before, her former invitation to him to be seated; to which he now deferred, as she seated herself: "I am at least glad to know that this is not another bondswoman of some friend of yours, who is bereft of free choice, and whom I have spirited away. I will hear your reason, if you please."

"First, to identify the person of whom we speak," said Clennam, "let me observe that it is the person you met in London some time back. You will remember meeting him near the river—in the Adelphi?"

"You mix yourself most unaccountably with my business," she replied, looking full at him with stern displeasure. "How do you know that?"

"I entreat you not to take it ill. By mere accident."

"What accident?"

"Solely, the accident of coming upon you in the street and seeing the meeting."

"Do you speak of yourself, or of some one else?"

"Of myself. I saw it."

"To be sure, it was in the open street," she observed, after a few moments of less and less angry reflection. "Fifty people might have seen it. It would have signified nothing if they had."

"Nor do I make my having seen it of any moment, nor (otherwise than as an explanation of my coming here) do I connect my visit with it, or the favor that I have to ask."

"Oh! you have to ask a favor! It occurred to me," and the handsome face looked bitterly at him, "that your manner was softened, Mr. Clennam."

He was content to protest against this by a slight action without contesting it in words. He then referred to Blandois' disappearance, of which it was probable she had heard? No. However probable it was to him, she had heard of no such thing. Let him look round him (she said), and judge for himself what general intelligence was likely to reach the ears of a woman who had been shut up there while it was rife, devouring her own heart. When she had uttered this denial, which he believed to be true, she asked him what he meant by disappearance? That led to his narrating the circumstances in detail, and expressing something of his anxiety to discover what had really become of the man, and to repel the dark suspicions that clouded about his mother's house. She heard him with evident surprise, and with more marks of suppressed interest than he had before seen in her; still they did not overcome her distant, proud, and self-secluded manner. When he had finished, she said nothing but these words:

"You have not yet told me, sir, what I have to do with it, or what the favor is. Will you be so good as to come to that?"

"I assume," said Arthur, persevering in his endeavor to soften her scornful demeanor, "that being in communication—may I say, confidential communication?—with this person—"

"You may say, of course, whatever you like," she remarked; "but I do not subscribe to your assumptions, Mr. Clennam, or to any one's."

"—that being, at least, in personal communication with him," said Clennam, changing the form of his position, in the hope of making it unobjectionable, "you can tell me something of his antecedents, pursuits, habits, usual place of residence. Can give me some little clew by which to seek him out in the likeliest manner, and either produce him, or establish what has become of him. This is the favor I ask, and I ask it in a distress of mind for which I hope you will feel some consideration. If you should have any reason for imposing conditions upon me, I will respect it without asking what it is."

"You chanced to see me in the street with the man," she observed, after being, to his mortification, evidently more occupied with her own reflections on the matter than with his appeal. "Then you knew the man before?"

"Not before; afterward. I never saw him before, but I saw him again on this very night of his disappearance. In my mother's room, in fact. I left him there. You will read in this paper all that is known of him."

He handed her one of the printed bills, which she read with a steady and attentive face.

"This is more than *I* knew of him," she said, giving it back.

Clennam's looks expressed his heavy disappointment, perhaps his incredulity; for, she added in the same unsympathetic tone, "You don't believe it. Still, it is so. As to personal communication; it seems that there was personal communication between him and your mother. And yet you say you believe her declaration that she knows no more of him!"

A sufficiently expressive hint of suspicion was conveyed in these words, and in the smile by which they were accompanied, to bring the blood into Clennam's cheeks.

"Come, sir," she said, with a cruel pleasure in repeating the stab, "I will be as open with you as you can desire. I will confess that if I cared for my credit (which I do not), or had a good name to preserve (which I have not, for I am utterly indifferent to its being considered good or bad), I should regard myself as heavily compromised by having had any thing to do with this fellow. Yet he never passed in at my door—never sat in colloquy with me until midnight."

She took her revenge for her old grudge in thus turning his subject against him. Hers was not the nature to spare him, and she had no compunction.

"That he is a low, mercenary wretch; that I first saw him prowling about Italy (where I was, not long ago), and that I hired him there, as the suitable instrument of a purpose I happened to have, I have no objection to tell you. In short, it was worth my while, for my own pleasure—the gratification of a strong feeling—to pay a spy who would fetch and carry for money. I paid this creature. And I dare say that if I had wanted to make such a bargain, and if I could have paid him enough, and if he could have done it in the dark, free from all risk, he would have taken any life with as little scruple as he took my money. That, at least, is my opinion of him; and I see it is not very far removed from yours. Your mother's opinion of him, I am to assume (following your example of assuming this and that), was vastly different."

"My mother, let me remind you," said Clennam, "was first brought into communication with him in the unlucky course of business."

"It appears to have been an unlucky course of business that last brought her into communication with him," returned Miss Wade; "and business hours on that occasion were late."

"You imply," said Arthur, smarting under these cool-handed thrusts, of which he had deeply felt the force already, "that there was something—"

"Mr. Clennam," she composedly interrupted, "recollect that I have not spoken by implication about the man. He is, I say again, without disguise, a low, mercenary wretch. I suppose such a creature goes where there is occasion for him. If I had not had occasion for him, you would not have seen him and me together."

Wrung by her persistence in keeping that dark side of the case before him, of which there was a half-hidden shadow in his own breast, Clennam was silent.

"I have spoken of him as still living," she added, "but he may have been put out of the way for any thing I know. For any thing I care, also. I have no further occasion for him."

With a heavy sigh and a despondent air, Arthur Clennam slowly rose. She did not rise also, but said, having looked at him in the mean while with a fixed look of suspicion, and lips angrily compressed:

"He was the chosen associate of your dear friend, Mr. Gowan, was he not? Why don't you ask your dear friend to help you?"

The denial that he was a dear friend rose to Arthur's lips;

but he repressed it, remembering his old struggles and resolutions, and said:

"Further than that he has never seen Blandois since Blandois set out for England. Mr. Gowan knows nothing additional about him. He was a chance acquaintance, made abroad."

"A chance acquaintance made abroad!" she repeated. "Yes. Your dear friend has need to divert himself with all the acquaintances he can make, seeing what a wife he has. I hate his wife, sir."

The anger with which she said it, the more remarkable for being so much under her restraint, fixed Clennam's attention, and kept him on the spot. It flashed out of her fine dark eyes as they regarded him, quivered in her nostrils, and fired the very breath she exhaled; but her face was otherwise composed into a disdainful serenity, and her attitude was as calmly and haughtily graceful as if she had been in a mood of complete indifference.

"All I will say is, Miss Wade," he remarked, "that you can have received no provocation to a feeling in which I believe you have no sharer."

"You may ask your dear friend, if you choose," she returned, "for his opinion upon that subject."

"I am scarcely on those intimate terms with my dear friend," said Arthur, in spite of his resolutions, "that would render my approaching the subject very probable, Miss Wade."

"I hate him," she returned, "worse than his wife, because I was once dupe enough, and false enough to myself, almost to love him. You have seen me, sir, only on commonplace occasions, when I dare say you have thought me a commonplace woman, a little more self-willed than the generality. You don't know what I mean by hating, if you know me no better than that; you can't know, without knowing with what care I have studied myself, and people about me. For this reason I have for some time inclined to tell you what my life has been—not to propitiate your opinion, for I set no value on it; but that you may comprehend, when you think of your dear friend and his dear wife, what I mean by hating. Shall I give you a paper I have written and put by for your perusal, or shall I hold my hand?"

Arthur begged her to give it to him. She went to the bureau, unlocked it, and took from an inner drawer a few folded sheets of paper. Without any conciliation of him, scarcely addressing him, rather speaking as if she were speaking to her own looking-glass for the justification of her own stubbornness, she said, as she gave them to him:

"Now you may know what I mean by hating! Enough of that. Sir, whether you find me temporarily and cheaply lodging in an empty London house or in a Calais apartment, you find Harriet with me. You may like to see her before you leave. Harriet, come in!" She called Harriet again. The second call produced Harriet, once Tattycoram.

"Here is Mr. Clennam," said Miss Wade; "not come for you; he has given you up. I suppose you have, by this time?"

"Having no authority or influence—yes," assented Clennam.

"Not come in search of you, you see; but still seeking some one. He wants to find out that Blandois man."

"With whom I saw you in the Strand in London," hinted Arthur.

"If you know any thing of him, Harriet, except that he came from Venice—which we all know—tell it to Mr. Clennam freely."

"I know nothing more about him," said the girl.

"Are you satisfied?" Miss Wade inquired of Arthur.

He had no reason to disbelieve them; the girl's manner being so natural as to be almost convincing, if he had had any previous doubts. He replied, "I must seek for intelligence elsewhere."

He was not going in the same breath; but he had risen before the girl entered, and she evidently thought he was. She looked quickly at him, and said,

"Are they well, sir?"

"Who?"

She stopped herself in saying what would have been "all of them;" glanced at Miss Wade; and said, "Mr. and Mrs. Meagles."

"They were, when I last heard of them. They are not at home. By-the-way, let me ask you. Is it true that you were seen there?"

"Where? Where does any one say I was seen?" returned the girl, sullenly casting down her eyes.

"Looking in at the garden gate of the cottage?"

"No," said Miss Wade. "She has never been near it."

"You are wrong, then," said the girl. "I went down there, the last time we were in London. I went one afternoon when you left me alone. And I did look in."

"You poor-spirited girl," returned Miss Wade with infinite contempt; "does all our companionship, do all our conversations, do all your old complainings, tell for so little as that?"

"There was no harm in looking in at the gate for an instant," said the girl. "I saw by the windows that the family were not there."

"Why should you go near the place?"

"Because I wanted to see it. Because I felt that I should like to look at it again."

As each of the two handsome faces looked at the other, Clennam felt how each of the two natures must be constantly tearing the other to pieces.

"Oh!" said Miss Wade, coldly subduing and removing her glance; "if you had any desire to see the place where you led the life from which I rescued you because you had found out what it was, that is another thing. But is that your truth to me? Is that your fidelity to me? Is that the common cause I make with you? You are not worth the confidence I have placed in you. You are not worth the favor I have shown you. You are no higher than a spaniel, and had better go back to the people who did worse than whip you."

"If you speak so of them with any one else by to hear, you'll provoke me to take their part," said the girl.

"Go back to them," Miss Wade retorted. "Go back to them."

"You know very well," retorted Harriet in her turn, "that I won't go back to them. You know very well that I have thrown them off, and never can, never shall, never will, go back to them. Let them alone, then, Miss Wade."

"You prefer their plenty to your less fat living here," she rejoined. "You exalt them and slight me. What else should I have expected? I ought to have known it."

"It's not so," said the girl, flushing high, "and you don't

say what you mean. I know what you mean. You are reproaching me, under-handed, with having nobody but you to look to. And because I have nobody but you to look to, you think you are to make me do, or not do, every thing you please, and are to put any affront upon me. You are as bad as they were, every bit. But I will not be quite tamed and made submissive. I will say again that I went to look at the house, because I had often thought that I should like to see it once more. I will ask again how they are, because I once liked them, and at times thought they were kind to me."

Hereupon Clennam said that he was sure they would still receive her kindly, if she should ever desire to return.

"Never!" said the girl, passionately. "I shall never do that. Nobody knows that better than Miss Wade, though she taunts me because she has made me her dependent. And I know I am so; and I know she is overjoyed when she can bring it to my mind."

"A good pretense!" said Miss Wade, with no less anger, haughtiness, and bitterness; "but too threadbare to cover what I plainly see in this. My poverty will not bear competition with their money. Better go back at once, better go back at once, and have done with it!"

Arthur Clennan looked at them, standing a little distance asunder in the dull confined room, each proudly cherishing her own anger; each, with a fixed determination, torturing her own breast, and torturing the other's. He said a word or two of leave-taking; but Miss Wade barely inclined her head, and Harriet, with the assumed humiliation of an abject dependent and serf (but not without defiance for all that), made as if she were too low to notice or to be noticed.

He came down the dark winding stairs into the yard, with an increased sense upon him of the gloom of the wall that was dead, and of the shrubs that were dead, and of the fountain that was dry, and of the statue that was gone. Pondering much on what he had seen and heard in that house, as well as on the failure of all his efforts to trace the suspicious character who was lost, he returned to London and to England by the packet that had taken him over. On the way he unfolded the sheets of paper, and read in them what is repeated in the next chapter.

CHAPTER LVII.

THE HISTORY OF A SELF-TORMENTOR.

I HAVE the misfortune of not being a fool. From a very early age I have detected what those about me thought they hid from me. If I could have been habitually imposed upon, instead of habitually discerning the truth, I might have lived as smoothly as most fools do.

My childhood was passed with a grandmother; that is to say, with a lady who represented that relative to me, and who took that title on herself. She had no claim to it, but I—being to that extent a little fool—had no suspicion of her. She had some children of her own family in her house, and some children of other people. All girls; ten in number, including me. We all lived together, and were educated together.

I must have been about twelve years old when I began to see how determinedly those girls patronized me. I was told I was an orphan. There was no other orphan among us; and I perceived (here was the first disadvantage of not being a fool) that they conciliated me in an insolent pity, and in a sense of superiority. I did not set this down as a discovery, rashly. I tried them often. I could hardly make them quarrel with me. When I succeeded with any of them, they were sure to come, after an hour or two, and begin a reconciliation. I tried them over and over again, and I never knew them wait for me to begin. They were always forgiving me, in their vanity and condescension. Little images of grown people!

One of them was my chosen friend. I loved that stupid mite in a passionate way, that she could no more deserve, than I can remember without feeling ashamed of, though I was but a child. She had what they called an amiable temper, an affectionate temper. She could distribute, and did distribute, pretty looks and smiles to every one among them. I believe there was not a soul in the place, except myself, who knew that she did it purposely to wound and gall me!

Nevertheless, I so loved that unworthy girl, that my life was made stormy by my fondness for her. I was constantly lectured and disgraced for what was called "trying her;" in other words, charging her with her little perfidy, and throwing her into tears by showing her that I read her heart. However, I loved her faithfully; and one time I went home with her for the holidays.

She was worse at home than she had been at school. She had a crowd of cousins and acquaintances, and we had dances at her house, and went out to dances at other houses; and, both at home and out, she tormented my love beyond endurance. Her plan was to make them all fond of her, and so drive me wild with jealousy; to be familiar and endearing with them all, and so make me mad with envying them. When we were left alone in our bed-room at night, I would reproach her with my perfect knowledge of her baseness; and then she would cry and cry, and say I was cruel, and then I would hold her in my arms till morning, loving her as much as ever, and often feeling as if rather than suffer so, I could so hold her in my arms, and plunge to the bottom of a river—where I would still hold her after we were both dead.

It came to an end, and I was relieved. In the family there was an aunt, who was not fond of me. I doubt if any of the family liked me much; but I never wanted them to like me, being altogether bound up in the one girl. The aunt was a young woman, and she had a serious way with her eyes of watching me. She was an audacious woman, and openly looked compassionately at me. After one of the nights that I have spoken of, I came down into a green-house before breakfast. Charlotte (the name of my false young friend) had gone down before me, and I heard this aunt speaking to her about me as I entered. I stopped where I was, among the leaves, and listened.

The aunt said, "Charlotte, Miss Wade is wearing you to death, and this must not continue." I repeat the very words I heard.

Now what did she answer? Did she say, "It is I who am

wearing her to death—I who am keeping her on a rack, and am the executioner; yet she tells me every night that she loves me devotedly, though she knows what I make her undergo?" No! my first memorable experience was true to what I knew her to be, and to all my experience. She began sobbing and weeping (to secure the aunt's sympathy to herself), and said, "Dear aunt, she has an unhappy temper; other girls at school besides I try hard to make it better; we all try hard."

Upon that the aunt fondled her, as if she had said something noble, instead of despicable and false, and kept up the infamous pretense by replying, "But there are reasonable limits, my dear love, to every thing; and I see that this poor, miserable girl causes you more constant and useless distress than even so good an effort justifies."

The poor, miserable girl came out of her concealment, as you may be prepared to hear, and said, "Send me home." I never said another word to either of them, or to any of them, but "Send me home, or I will walk home alone, night and day!"

When I got home, I told my supposed grandmother that unless I was sent away to finish my education somewhere else, before that girl came back, or before any one of them came back, I would burn my sight away, by throwing myself into the fire, rather than I would endure to look at their plotting faces.

I went among young women next, and I found them no better. Fair words and false pretenses; but I penetrated below those assertions of themselves and depreciations of me, and they were no better. Before I left them, I learned that I had no grandmother and no recognized relation. I carried the light of that information both into my past and into my future. It showed me many new occasions on which people triumphed over me, when they made a pretense of treating me with consideration or doing me a service.

A man of business had a small property in trust for me. I was to be a governess. I became a governess, and went into the family of a poor nobleman, where there were two daughters—little children, but the parents wished them to grow up, if possible, under one instructress. The mother was young and pretty. From the first, she made a show of behaving to me with great delicacy. I kept my resentment to myself; but I knew very well that it was her way of petting the knowledge that she was my mistress, and might have behaved differently to her servant if it had been her fancy.

I say I did not resent it, nor did I; but I showed her, by not gratifying her, that I understood her. When she pressed me to take wine, I took water. If there happened to be any thing choice at table, she always sent it to me; but I always declined it, and ate of the rejected dishes. These disappointments of her patronage were a sharp retort, and made me feel independent.

I liked the children. They were timid, but, on the whole, disposed to attach themselves to me. There was a nurse, however, in the house, a rosy-faced young woman, always making an obtrusive pretense of being gay and good-humored, who had nursed them both, and who had secured their affections before I saw them. I could almost have settled down to my fate but for this woman. Her artful devices for keeping herself before the children in constant competition with me might have blinded many in my place; but I saw through them from the first. On the pretext of arranging my rooms and waiting on me and taking care of my wardrobe (all of which she did busily,) she was never absent. The most crafty of her many subtleties was her feint of seeking to make the children fonder of me. She would lead them to me, and coax them to me. "Come to good Miss Wade, come to dear Miss Wade, come to pretty Miss Wade. She loves you very much. Miss Wade is a clever lady, who has read heaps of books, and can tell you far better and more interesting stories than I know. Come and hear Miss Wade!" How could I engage their attention, when my heart was burning against these insolent designs? How could I wonder, when I saw their innocent faces shrinking away, and their arms twining round her neck instead of mine? Then she would look up at me, shaking their curls from her face, and say, "They'll come round, soon, Miss Wade; they're very simple and loving, ma'am; don't be at all cast down about it, ma'am"—exulting over me!

There was another thing the woman did. At times, when

she saw that she had safely plunged me into a black despondent brooding by these means, she would call the attention of the children to it, and would show them the difference between herself and me. "Hush! Poor Miss Wade is not well. Don't make a noise, my dears, her head aches. Come and comfort her. Come and ask her if she is better; come and ask her to lie down. I hope you have nothing on your mind, ma'am. Don't take on, ma'am, and be sorry!"

It became intolerable. Her ladyship my mistress coming in one day when I was alone, and at the height of feeling that I could support it no longer, I told her I must go. I could not bear the presence of that woman Dawes.

"Miss Wade! Poor Dawes is devoted to you; would do any thing for you!"

I knew beforehand she would say so; I was quite prepared for it; I only answered it was not for me to contradict my mistress; I must go.

"I hope, Miss Wade," she returned, instantly assuming the tone of superiority she had always so thinly concealed, "that nothing I have ever said or done since we have been together has justified your use of that disagreeable word, Mistress. It must have been wholly inadvertent on my part. Pray tell me what it is."

I replied that I had no complaint to make, either of my mistress, or to my mistress; but I must go.

She hesitated a moment, and then sat down beside me, and laid her hand on mine. As if that honor would obliterate any remembrance!

"Miss Wade, I fear you are unhappy, through causes over which I have no influence."

I smiled, thinking of the experience the word awakened, and said, "I have an unhappy temper, I suppose."

"I did not say that."

"It is an easy way of accounting for any thing," said I.

"It may be; but I did not say so. What I wish to approach is something very different. My husband and I have exchanged some remarks upon the subject, when we have observed with pain that you have not been easy with us."

"Easy? Oh! You are such great people, my lady," said I.

"I am unfortunate in using a word which may convey a meaning—and evidently does—quite opposite to my intention." (She had not expected my reply, and it shamed her.) "I only mean, not happy with us. It is a difficult topic to enter on; but, from one young woman to another, perhaps—in short, we have been apprehensive that you may allow some family circumstances of which no one can be more innocent than yourself, to prey upon your spirits. If so, let us entreat you not to make them a cause of grief. My husband himself, as is well known, formerly had a very dear sister, who was not in law his sister, but who was universally beloved and respected—"

I saw directly that they had taken me in for the sake of the dead woman, whoever she was, and to have that boast of me and advantage of me; I saw, in the nurse's knowledge of it, an encouragement to goad me as she had done; and I saw, in the children's shrinking away, a vague impression that I was not like other people. I left that house that night.

After one or two short and very similar experiences, which are not to the present purpose, I entered another family where I had but one pupil: a girl of fifteen, who was the only daughter. The parents here were elderly people: people of station, and rich. A nephew whom they had brought up, was a frequent visitor at the house, among many other visitors; and he began to pay me attention. I was resolute in repulsing him; for I had determined, when I went there, that no one should pity me or condescend to me. But he wrote me a letter. It led to our being engaged.

He was a year younger than I, and young-looking even when that allowance was made. He was on absence from India, where he had a post that was soon to grow into a very good one. In six months we were to be married, and were to go to India. I was to stay in the house, and was to be married from the house. Nobody objected to any part of the plan.

I can not avoid saying he admired me; but if I could, I would. Vanity has nothing to do with the declaration, for his admiration worried me. He took no pains to hide it; and caused me to feel among the rich people as if he had bought me for my looks, and made a show of his purchase to justify himself. They appraised me in their own minds, I saw, and were curiou to ascertain what my full value was. I resolved that they should not know. I was immovable and silent before them, and would have suffered any one of them to kill me, sooner then I would have laid myself out to bespeak their approval.

He told me I did not do myself justice. I told him I did, and it was because I did and meant to do so to the last, that I would not stoop to propitiate any of them. He was concerned and even shocked when I added that I wished he would not parade his attachment before them ; but he said he would sacrifice even the honest impulses of his affection to my peace.

Under that pretense, he began to retort upon me. By the hour together he would keep at a distance from me, talking to any one rather than to me. I have sat alone and unnoticed half an evening, while he conversed with his young cousin, my pupil. I have seen all the while, in people's eyes, that they thought the two looked nearer on an equality than he and I. I have sat, divining their thoughts, until I have felt that his young appearance made me ridiculous, and have raged against myself for ever loving him.

For I did love him once. Undeserving as he was, and little as he thought of all these agonies that it cost me—agonies which should have made him wholly and gratefully mine to his life's end—I loved him. I bore with his cousin's praising him to my face, and with her pretending to think that it pleased me, but full well knowing it rankled in my breast—for his sake. While I have sat in his presence recalling all my slights and wrongs, and deliberating whether I should not fly from the house at once and never see him again—I have loved him.

His aunt (my mistress, you will please to remember) deliberately, willfully, added to my trials and vexations. It was her delight to expatiate on the style in which we were to live in India, and on the establishment we should keep, and the company we should entertain, when he got his advancement. My pride rose against this barefaced way of pointing out the contrast my married life was to present to my then dependent and inferior position. I suppressed my indignation ; but I showed her that her intention was not lost upon me, and I repaid her annoyances by affecting humility. What she described would surely be a great deal too much honor for me, I would tell her. I was afraid I might not be able to support so great a change. Think of a mere governess, her daughter's governess, coming to that high distinction! It made her uneasy, and made them all uneasy, when I answered in this way. They knew that I fully understood her.

It was at the time when my troubles were at their highest, and when I was most incensed against my lover for his ingratitude in caring as little as he did for the innumerable distresses and mortifications I underwent on his account, that your dear friend, Mr. Gowan, appeared at the house. He had been intimate there for a long time, but had been abroad. He understood the state of things at a glance, and he understood me.

He was the first person I had ever seen in my life who had understood me. He was not in the house three times before I knew that he accompanied every movement of my mind. In his cold easy way with all of them, and with me, and with the whole subject, I saw it clearly. In his light protestations of admiration of my future husband, in his enthusiasm regarding our engagement and our prospects, in his hopeful congratulations on our future wealth and his despondent references to his own poverty—all equally hollow, and jesting, and full of mockery—I saw it clearly. He made me feel more and more resentful, and more and more contemptible, by always presenting to me every thing that surrounded me, with some new hateful light upon it, while he pretended to exhibit it in its best aspect for my admiration and his own. He was like the dressed-up Death in the Dutch series; whatever figure he took upon his arm, whether it was youth or age, beauty or ugliness, whether he danced with it, sang with it, played with it, or prayed with it, he made it ghastly.

You will understand, then, that when your dear friend complimented me, he really condoled with me; that when he soothed me under my vexations, he laid bare every smarting wound I had; that when he declared my "faithful swain" to be "the most loving young fellow in the world, with the tenderest heart that ever beat," he touched my old misgiving that I was made ridiculous. These were not great services, you may say. They were acceptable to me, because they echoed my own mind, and confirmed my own knowledge. I soon began to like the society of your dear friend better than any other.

When I perceived (which I did, almost as soon) that jealousy was growing out of this, I liked his society still better. Had I not been subjected to jealousy, and were the endurances to be all mine? No. Let him know what it was! I was delighted that he should know it; I was delighted that he should feel keenly, and I hoped he did. More than that. He was tame in comparison with Mr. Gowan, who knew how to address me on equal terms, and how to anatomize the wretched people around us.

This went on, until the aunt, my mistress, took it upon herself to speak to me. It was scarcely worth alluding to; she knew I meant nothing; but she suggested from herself, knowing it was only necessary to suggest, that it might be better, if I were a little less companionable with Mr. Gowan.

I asked her how she could answer for what I meant? She could always answer, she replied, for my meaning nothing wrong. I thanked her, but said I would prefer to answer for myself, and to myself. Her other servants would probably be grateful for good characters, but I wanted none. Other conversation followed, and indueed me to ask her how she knew that it was only necessary for her to make a suggestion to me to have it obeyed? Did she presume on my birth, or on my hire? I was not bought, body and soul. She seemed to think that her distinguished nephew had gone into a slave-market and purchased a wife.

It would probably have come, sooner or later, to the end to which it did come, but she brought it to its issue at once. She told me, with assumed commiseration, that I had an unhappy temper. On this repetition of the old wicked injury, I withheld no longer, but exposed to her all I had known of her and seen in her, and all I had undergone within myself since I had occupied the despicable position of being engaged to her nephew. I told her that Mr. Gowan was the only relief I had in my degradation; that I had borne it too long, and that I shook it off too late; but that I would see none of them more. And I never did.

Your dear friend followed me to my retreat, and was very droll on the severance of the connection; though he was sorry, too, for the excellent people (in their way the best he had ever met), and deplored the necessity of breaking mere house-flies on the wheel. He protested before long, and far more truly than I then supposed, that he was not worth acceptance by a woman of such endowments, and such power of character; but—well, well!—

Your dear friend amused me and amused himself as long as it suited his inclinations; and then reminded me that we were both people of the world, that we both understood mankind, that we both knew there was no such thing as romance, that we were both prepared for going different ways to seek our fortunes like people of sense, and that we both foresaw that whenever we encountered one another again we should meet as the best friends on earth. So he said, and I did not contradict him.

It was not very long before I found that he was courting his present wife, and that she had been taken away to be out of his reach. I hated her then, quite as much as I hate her now; and naturally, therefore, could desire nothing better than that she should marry him. But I was restlessly curious to look at her—so curious that I felt it to be one of the few sources of entertainment left to me. I traveled a little; traveled until I found myself in her society, and in yours. Your dear friend, I think, was not known to you then, and had not given you those signal marks of his friendship which he afterward bestowed upon you.

In that company I found a girl, in some circumstances of whose position there was a singular likeness to my own, and in whose character I was interested and pleased to see much of the rising against swolen patronage and selfishness, calling themselves kindness, protection, benevolence, and other fine names, which I have described as inherent in my nature. I often heard it said, too, that she had "an unhappy temper." Well understanding what was meant by the convenient phrase, and wanting a companion with a knowledge of what I knew, I thought I would try to release the girl from her bondage and sense of injustice. I have no occasion to tell you that I succeeded.

We have been together ever since, sharing my small means.

CHAPTER LVIII.

WHO PASSES BY THIS ROAD SO LATE?

ARTHUR CLENNAM had made his unavailing expedition to Calais, in the midst of a great pressure of business. A certain barbaric Power with valuable possessions on the map of the world, had occasion for the services of one or two engineers, quick in invention and determined in execution: practical men, who could make the men and means their ingenuity perceived to be wanted out of the best materials they could find at hand; and who were as bold and fertile in the adaptation of such materials to their purpose as in the conception of their purpose itself. This Power, being a barbaric one, had no idea of stowing away a great national object in a Circumlocution Office, as strong wine is hidden from the light in a cellar until its fire and youth are gone, and the laborers who worked in the vineyard and pressed the grapes are dust. With characteristic ignorance, it acted on the most decided and energetic notions of How to do it; and never showed the least respect for, or gave any quarter to, the great political science How not to do it. Indeed, it had a barbarous way of striking the latter art and mystery dead, in the person of any enlightened subject who practiced it.

Accordingly, the men who were wanted were sought out and found; which was in itself a most uncivilized and irregular way of proceeding. Being found, they were treated with great confidence and honor (which again showed dense political ignorance), and were invited to come at once and do what they had to do. In short, they were regarded as men who meant to do it, engaging with other men who meant it to be done.

Daniel Doyce was one of those chosen. There was no foreseeing at that time whether he would be absent months, or years. The preparations for his departure, and the conscientious arrangement for him of all the details and results of their joint business, had necessitated labor within a short compass of time, which had occupied Clennam day and night. He had slipped across the water in his first leisure, and had slipped as quickly back again for his farewell interview with Doyce.

Him Arthur now showed, with pains and care, the state of their gains and losses, responsibilities and prospects. Daniel went through it all in his patient manner, and admired it all exceedingly. He audited the accounts as if they were a far more ingenious piece of mechanism than he had ever constructed, and afterward stood looking at them, weighing his hat over his head by the brims, as if he were absorbed in the contemplation of some wonderful engine.

"It's all beautiful, Clennam, in its regularity and order. Nothing can be plainer. Nothing can be better."

"I am glad you approve, Doyce. Now, as to the management of our capital while you are away, and as to the conversion of so much of it as the business may not need from time to time—" His partner stopped him.

"As to that, and as to every thing else of that kind, all rests with you. You will continue in all such matters to act for both of us, as you have done hitherto, and to lighten my mind of a load it is much relieved from."

"Though, as I often tell you," returned Clennam, "you unreasonably depreciate your business qualities."

"Perhaps so," said Doyce, smiling. "And perhaps not. Anyhow, I have a calling that I have studied more than such matters, and that I am better fitted for. I have perfect confidence in my partner, and I am satisfied that he will do what is best. If I have a prejudice connected with money and money-figures," continued Doyce, laying that plastic workman's thumb of his on the lappel of his partner's coat, "it is against speculating. I don't think I have any other. I dare say I entertain that prejudice only because I have never given my mind fully to the subject."

"But you shouldn't call it prejudice," said Clennam. "My dear Doyce, it is the soundest sense."

"I am glad you think so," returned Doyce, with his gray eye looking kind and bright.

"It so happens," said Clennam, "that just now, not half an

hour before you came down, I was saying the same thing to Pancks, who looked in here. We both agreed, that to travel out of safe investments is one of the most dangerous, as it is one of the most common, of those follies which often deserve the name of vices."

"Pancks!" said Doyce, tilting up his hat at the back, and nodding with an air of confidence. "Ay, ay, ay! That's a cautious fellow!"

"He is a very cautious fellow indeed," returned Arthur. "Quite a specimen of caution."

They both appeared to derive a larger amount of satisfaction from the cautious character of Mr. Pancks than was quite intelligible, judged by the surface of their conversation.

"And now," said Daniel, looking at his watch, "as time and tide wait for no one, my trusty partner, and as I am ready for starting, bag and baggage, at the gate below, let me say a last word. I want you to grant a request of mine."

"Any request you can make—except," Clennam was quick with his exception, for his partner's face was quick in suggesting it, "except that I will abandon your invention."

"That's the request, and you know it is," said Doyce.

"I say, No, then. I say positively, No. Now, that I have begun, I will have some definite reason, some responsible statement, something in the nature of a real answer, from those people."

"You will not," returned Doyce, shaking his head. "Take my word for it, you never will."

"At least, I'll try," said Clennam. "It will do me no harm to try."

"I am not certain of that," rejoined Doyce, laying his hand persuasively on his shoulder. "It has done me harm, my friend. It has aged me, tired me, vexed me, disappointed me. It does no man any good to have his patience worn out, and to think himself ill-used. I fancy, even already, that useless attendance on delays and evasions has made you something less elastic than you used to be."

"Private anxieties may have done that for the moment," said Clennam, "but not official harrying. Not yet. I am not hurt yet."

"Then you won't grant my request?"

"Decidedly, No," said Clennam. "I should be ashamed if I submitted to be so soon driven out of the field, where a much older and a much more sensitively interested man contended with fortitude so long."

As there was no moving him, Daniel Doyce returned the grasp of his hand, and, casting a farewell look round the counting-house, went down stairs with him. Doyce was to go to Southampton to join the small staff of his fellow-travelers; and a coach was at the gate, well furnished and packed, and ready to take him there. The workmen were at the gate to see him off, and were mightily proud of him. "Good luck to you, Mr. Doyce!" said one of the number. "Wherever you go they'll find as they've got a man among 'em, a man as knows his tools and his tools knows, a man as is willing and a man as is able, and if that's not a man, where is a man?" This oration from a gruff volunteer in the background, not previously suspected of any powers in that way, was received with three loud cheers; and the speaker became a distinguished character forever afterward. In the midst of the three loud cheers, Daniel gave them all a hearty "Good-by, men!" and the coach disappeared from sight, as if the concussion of the air had blown it out of Bleeding Heart Yard.

Mr. Baptist, as a grateful little fellow in a position of trust, was among the workmen, and had done as much toward the cheering as a mere foreigner could. In truth, no men on earth can cheer like Englishmen, who do so rally one another's blood and spirit when they cheer in earnest, that the stir is like the rush of their whole history, with all its standards waving at once, from Saxon Alfred's downward. Mr. Baptist had been in a manner whirled away before the onset, and was taking his breath in quite a scared condition when Clennam beckoned him to follow up stairs, and return the books and papers to their places.

In the lull consequent on the departure—in that first vacuity which ensues on every separation, foreshadowing the great separation that is always overhanging all mankind—Arthur stood at his desk, looking dreamily out at a gleam of sun. But his liberated attention soon reverted to the theme that was foremost in his thoughts, and began, for the hundredth time, to dwell upon every circumstance that had impressed itself upon his mind, on the mysterious night when he had seen the man at his mother's. Again the man jostled him in the crooked street, again he followed the man and lost him, again he came upon the man in the court-yard looking at the house, again he followed the man and stood beside him on the door-steps.

"Who passes by this road so late?
Compagnon de la Majolaine;
Who passes by this road so late?
Always gay!"

It was not the first time, by many, that he had recalled the song of the child's game, of which the fellow had hummed this verse while they stood side by side; but he was so unconscious of having repeated it audibly, that he started to hear the next verse,

"Of all the king's knights 'tis the flower,
Compagnon de la Majolaine;
Of all the king's knights 'tis the flower,
Always gay!"

Cavalletto had deferentially suggested the words and tune, supposing him to have stopped short for want of more.

"Ah! You know the song, Cavalletto?"

"By Bacchus, yes, sir! They all know it in France. I have heard it many times sung by the little children. The last time when it I have heard," said Mr. Baptist, formerly Cavalletto, who usually went back to his native construction of sentences when his memory went near home, "is from a sweet little voice. A little voice, very pretty, very innocent. Altro!"

"The last time *I* heard it," returned Arthur, "was in a voice quite the reverse of pretty, and quite the reverse of innocent." He said it more to himself than to his companion, and added, to himself, repeating the man's next words. "Death of my life, sir, it's my character to be impatient!"

"EH!" cried Cavalletto, astounded, and with all his color gone in a moment.

"What is the matter?"

"Sir! You know where I have heard that song the last time?"

With his rapid native action, his hands made the outline of a high hook nose, pushed his eyes near together, dishevelled his hair, puffed out his upper lip to represent a thick mustache, and threw the heavy end of an ideal cloak over his shoulder. While doing this, with a swiftness incredible to one who has not watched an Italian peasant, he indicated a very remarkable and sinister smile. The whole change passed over him like a flash of light, and he stood in the same instant, pale and astonished, before his patron.

"In the name of Fate and wonder," said Clennam, "what do you mean? Do you know a man by the name of Blandois?"

"No!" said Mr. Baptist, shaking his head.

"You have just now described a man who was by, when you heard that song; have you not!"

"Yes!" said Mr. Baptist, nodding fifty times.

"And was he not called Blandois?"

"No!" said Mr. Baptist. "Altro, Altro, Altro, Altro!" He could not reject the name sufficiently, with his head and his right forefinger going at once.

"Stay!" cried Clennam, spreading out the handbill on his desk. "Was this the man? You can understand what I read aloud?"

"Altogether. Perfectly."

"But look at it, too. Come here and look over me, while I read."

Mr. Baptist approached, followed every word with his quick eyes, saw and heard it all out with the greatest impatience, then clapped his two hands flat upon the bill as if he had fiercely caught some noxious creature, and cried, looking eagerly at Clennam, "It is the man! Behold him!"

"This is of far greater moment to me," said Clennam, in agitation, "than you can imagine. Tell me where you knew the man."

Mr. Baptist, releasing the paper very slowly, and with great discomfiture, and drawing himself back two or three paces, and making as though he dusted his hands, returned, very much against his will:

"At Marsiglia—Marseilles."

What was he ?"

A prisoner, and—Altro ! I believe yes !—an," Mr. Baptist crept closer again to whisper it, "Assassin !"

Clennam fell back as if the word had struck him a blow : so terrible did it make his mother's communication with the man appear. Cavalletto dropped on one knee, and implored him, with a redundancy of gesticulation, to hear what had brought himself into such foul company.

He told with perfect truth how it had come of a little contraband trading, and how he had in time been released from prison, and how he had gone away from those antecedents. How, at the house of entertainment called the Break of Day at Chalons on the Saone, he had been awakened in his bed at night, by the same assassin, then assuming the name of Lagnier, though his name had formerly been Rigaud; how the assassin had proposed that they should join their fortunes together; how he held the assassin in such dread and aversion that he had fled from him at daylight; and how he had ever since been haunted by the fear of seeing the assassin again and being claimed by him as an acquaintance. When he had related this, with an emphasis and poise on the word peculiarly belonging to his own language, and which did not serve to render it less terrible to Clennam, he suddenly sprang to his feet, pounced upon the bill again, and with a vehemence that would have been absolute madness in any man of Northern origin, cried, "Behold the same assassin ! Here he is !"

In his passionate raptures, he at first forgot the fact that he had lately seen the assassin in London. On his remembering it, it suggested hope to Clennam that the recognition might be of later date than the night of the visit at his mother's; but Cavalletto was too exact and clear about time and place, to leave any opening for doubt that it had preceded that occasion.

"Listen," said Arthur, very seriously. "This man, as we have read here, has wholly disappeared."

"Of it I am well content !" said Cavalletto, raising his eyes, piously. "A thousand thanks to Heaven ! Accursed assassin !"

"Not so," returned Clennam; "for, until something more is heard of him, I can never know an hour's peace."

"Hold, Benefactor; that is quite another thing. A million of excuses!"

"Now, Cavalletto," said Clennam, gently turning him by the arm, so that they looked into each other's eyes. "I am certain that for the little I have been able to do for you, you are the most sincerely grateful of men."

"I swear it!" cried the other.

"I know it! If you can find this man, or discover what has become of him, or gain any later intelligence whatever of him, you would render me a service above any other service I could receive in the world, and would make me (with far greater reason) as grateful to you as you are to me."

"I know not where to look," cried the little man, kissing Arthur's hand in a transport. "I know not where to begin. I know not where to go. But, courage! Enough! It matters not! I go, in this instant of time!"

"Not a word to any one but me, Cavalletto."

"Al-tro!" cried Cavalletto; and was gone with great speed.

CHAPTER LIX.

MISTRESS AFFERY MAKES A CONDITIONAL PROMISE RESPECTING HER DREAMS.

Left alone in his counting-house, with the expressive looks and gestures of Mr. Baptist, otherwise Giovanni Baptista Cavalletto, vividly before him, and his emphatic words still sounding in his ears, Clennam entered on a day of misery. It was in vain that he tried to control his attention by directing it to any business occupation or train of thought; it rode at anchor by the one haunting topic, and would hold to no other idea. Let him with his utmost resolution set what task he would to his mind, his mind refused it, and only forced the theme of distress upon him with a strength proportionate to that of the endeavor. In every light, in every shadow, in many variations of form, each separately attended by its own train of consequences, the one painful subject mastered him. As though a criminal should be chained in a stationary boat on a deep, clear river, condemned, whatever countless leagues of water flowed past him, always to see the body of the fellow-creature he had drowned lying at the bottom; immovable and unchangeable, except as the eddies made it broad or long, now expanding, now contracting its fearful lineaments; so Arthur, below the shifting current of transparent thoughts and fancies, which were gone and succeeded by others as soon as come, saw, steady and dark, and not to be stirred from its place, this thing that he endeavored with all his might to rid himself of, and that he could not fly from.

The assurance he now had, that Blandois, whatever his right name, was one of the worst of characters, greatly augmented the weight of his anxieties. Though the disappearance should be accounted for to-morrow, the fact that his mother had been in communication with such a man, would remain unalterable. That the communication had been of a secret kind, and that she had been submissive to him and afraid of him, he hoped might be known to no one beyond himself; yet, knowing it, how could he separate it from his old vague fears, and how believe that there was nothing evil in such relations?

Her resolution not to enter on the question with him, and his knowledge of her indomitable character, enhanced his oppressive sense of helplessness. It was like the torture of a dream to believe that shame and exposure were impending over her and his father's memory, and to be shut out, as by a brazen wall, from the possibility of coming to their aid. The purpose he had brought home to his native country, and the object he had ever since kept in view, were, with her greatest determination, defeated by his mother herself, at the time of all others when he feared that they pressed most. His advice, energy, activity, money, credit, all his resources whatsoever, were all made useless. If she had been possessed of the old fabled influence, and had turned those who looked upon her into stone, she could not have rendered him more completely powerless (so it seemed to him in his distress of mind) than she did when she turned her unyielding face to his in her gloomy room.

But the light of that day's discovery, shining on these considerations, roused him to take a more decided course of action. Confident in the rectitude of his purpose, and impelled by a sense of overhanging danger closing in around him, he resolved, if his mother would still admit of no approach, to make a desperate appeal to Mistress Affery. If she could be brought to become communicative, and to do what lay in her to break the spell of secrecy that enshrouded the house, he might shake off the paralysis of which every hour that passed over his head made him more acutely sensible. With Cavalletto certainly at work for him, and Affery won over to be as ardent, though less intelligent, he might yet save his mother (and with her his name) from a great calamity. This was the result of his day's misery, and this was the decision he put in practice when the day closed in.

His first disappointment, on arriving at the house, was to find the door open, and Mr. Flintwinch smoking a pipe on the steps. If circumstances had been commonly favorable, Mistress Affery would have opened the door to his knock. Circumstances being uncommonly unfavorable, the door stood open, and Mr. Flintwinch was smoking his pipe on the steps.

"Good-evening," said Arthur.

"Good-evening," said Mr. Flintwinch.

The smoke came very crookedly out of Mr. Flintwinch's mouth, as if it circulated through the whole of his wry figure and came back by his wry throat, before coming forth to mingle with the smoke from the crooked chimneys, and the mists from the crooked river.

"Have you any news?" said Arthur.

"We have no news," said Jeremiah.

"I mean of the foreign man," Arthur explained.

"*I* mean of the foreign man," said Jeremiah.

He looked so grim, as he stood askew, with the knot of his cravat under his ear, that the thought passed into Clennam's mind, and not for the first time by many, could Mr. Flintwinch, for a purpose of his own, have got rid of Blandois? Could it have been his secret and his safety, that were at issue? He was small and bent, and perhaps not actively strong; yet he was as tough as an old yew tree, and as crafty and cruel as an old jackdaw. Such a man coming behind a much younger and more vigorous man, and having the will to put an end to him and no relenting, might do it pretty surely in that solitary place at a late hour.

While in the morbid condition of his thoughts these thoughts drifted over the main one that was always in Clennam's mind, Mr. Flintwinch, regarding the opposite house over the gateway with his neck twisted and one eye shut up, stood smoking with a vicious expression upon him, more as if he was trying to bite off the stem of his pipe, than as if he were enjoying it. Yet he was enjoying it, in his way.

"You'll be able to take my likeness the next time you call, Arthur, I should think," said Mr. Flintwinch dryly, as he stooped to knock the ashes out.

Rather conscious and confused, Arthur asked his pardon, if he had stared at him unpolitely. "But my mind runs so much upon this matter," he said, "that I lose myself."

"Hah! Yet I don't see," returned Mr. Flintwinch, quite at his leisure, "why it should trouble *you*, Arthur."

"No?"

"No," said Mr. Flintwinch, very shortly and decidedly, much as if he were of the canine race, and snapped at Arthur's hand.

"Is it nothing to me to see those placards about? Is it nothing to me to see my mother's name and residence hawked up and down in such an association?"

"I don't see," returned Mr. Flintwinch, scraping his horny cheek, "that it need signify much to you. But I'll tell you what I do see, Arthur," glancing up at the windows; "I see the light of fire and candle in your mother's room!"

"And what has that to do with it?"

"Why, sir, I read by it," said Mr. Flintwinch, screwing himself at him, "that if it's advisable (as the proverb says it is) to let sleeping dogs lie, it's just as advisable, perhaps, to let missing dogs lie. Let 'em be. They generally turn up soon enough."

Mr. Flintwinch turned short round when he had made this remark, and went into the dark hall. Clennam stood there, following him with his eyes, as he dipped for a light in the phosphorus-box in the little room at the side, got one after three or four dips, and lighted the dim lamp against the wall. All the while Clennam was pursuing the probabilities—rather as if they were being shown to him by an invisible hand, than as if he himself were conjuring them up—of Mr. Flintwinch's ways and means of doing that darker deed, and removing its traces by any of the black avenues of shadow that lay around them.

"Now, sir," said the testy Jeremiah; "will it be agreeable to walk up stairs?"

"My mother is alone, I suppose?"

"Not alone," said Mr. Flintwinch. "Mr. Casby and his daughter are with her. They came in while I was smoking, and I staid behind to have my smoke out."

This was the second disappointment. Arthur made no remark upon it, however, and repaired to his mother's room, where Mr. Casby and Flora had been taking tea, anchovy paste, and hot buttered toast. The relics of those delicacies were not yet removed, either from the table or from the scorched countenance of Affery, who, with the kitchen toasting-fork still in her hand, looked like a sort of allegorical personage, except that she had a considerable advantage over the general run of such personages, in point of significant emblematical purpose.

Flora had laid her bonnet and shawl upon the bed, with a care indicative of an intention to stay some time. Mr. Casby, too, was beaming near the hob, with his benevolent knobs shining as if the warm butter of the toast were exuding through the patriarchal skull, and with his face as ruddy as if the coloring matter of the anchovy paste were mantling in the patriarchal visage. Seeing this, as he exchanged the usual salutations, Clennam decided to speak to his mother without postponement.

It had long been customary, as she never changed her room, for those who had any thing to say to her apart, to wheel her to her desk; where she sat, usually with the back of her chair turned toward the rest of the room, and the person who talked with her seated in a corner, on a stool which was always set in that place for that purpose. Except that it was long since the mother and son had spoken together without the intervention of a third person, it was an ordinary matter of course within the experience of visitors, for Mrs. Clennam to be asked, without a word of apology for the interruption, if she could be spoken with on a matter of business, and, on her replying in tho affirmative, to be wheeled into the position described.

Therefore, when Arthur now made such an apology, and such a request, and moved her to her desk, and seated himself on the stool, Mrs. Finching merely began to talk louder and faster, as a delicate hint that she could overhear nothing, and Mr. Casby stroked his long white locks with sleepy calmness.

"Mother, I have heard something to-day which I feel persuaded you don't know, and which I think you should know, of the antecedents of that man I saw here."

"I know nothing of the antecedents of the man you saw here, Arthur."

She spoke aloud. He had lowered his own voice to a whisper; but she rejected that advance toward confidence as she rejected every other, and spoke in her usual key and in her usual stern voice.

"I have received it on no circuitous information; it has come to me direct."

She asked him, exactly as before, if he were there to tell her what it was?

"I thought it right that you should know it."

"And what is it?"

"He has been a prisoner in a French jail."

She answered with confidence, "I should think that very likely."

"But in a jail for criminals, mother. On an accusation of murder."

She started at the word, and her looks expressed her natural horror Yet she still spoke aloud when she demanded

"Who told you so?"

"A man who was his fellow-prisoner."

"That man's antecedents, I suppose, were not known to you before he told you?"

"No."

"Though the man himself was?"

"Yes."

"My case, and Flintwinch's, in respect of this other man! I dare say the resemblance is not so exact though, as that your informant became known to you through a letter from a correspondent, with whom he had deposited money? How does that part of the parallel case stand?"

Arthur had no choice but to say that his informant had not become known to him through the agency of any such credentials or indeed of any credentials at all. Mr. Clennam's attentive frown expanded by degrees into a severe look of triumph, and she retorted with emphasis, "Take care how you judge others. I say to you, Arthur, for your good, take care how you judge!"

Her emphasis had been derived from her eyes quite as much as from the stress she laid upon her words. She continued to look at him, and if, when he entered the house, he had had any latent hope of prevailing in the least with her, she now looked it out of his heart.

"Mother, shall I do nothing to assist you?"

"Nothing."

"Will you intrust me with no confidence, no charge, no explanation? Will you take no counsel with me? Will you not let me come near you?"

"How can you ask me? You separated yourself from my affairs. It was not my act; it was yours. How can you consistently ask me such a question? You know that you left me to Flintwinch, and that he occupies your place."

Glancing at Jeremiah, Clennam saw in his very gaiters that his attention was closely directed to them, though he stood leaning against the wall scraping his jaw, and pretending to listen to Flora, as she held forth in a most distracting manner on a chaos of subjects, in which mackerel, and Mr. F.'s Aunt in a swing, had become entangled with cockchafers and the wine trade.

"A prisoner, in a French jail, on an accusation of murder," repeated Mrs. Clennam, steadily going over what her son had said. "That is all you know of him from a fellow-prisoner?"

"In substance, all."

"And was the fellow-prisoner his accomplice, and a murderer, too? But, of course, he gives a better account of himself; it is needless to ask. This will supply the rest of them here with something new to talk about and think about. Casby, Arthur tells me—"

"Stay, mother! Stay, stay!" He interrupted her, hastily, for it had not entered his imagination that she would openly proclaim what he had told her.

"What now?" she said, with displeasure. "What more?"

"I beg you to excuse me, Mr. Casby—and you, too, Mrs. Finching—for one other moment, with my mother—"

He had laid his hand upon her chair, or she would otherwise have wheeled it round with the touch of her foot upon the ground. They were still face to face. She looked full at him as he ran over the possibilities of some result he had not intended and could not foresee being influenced by Cavalletto's disclosure becoming a matter of notoriety, and hurriedly arrived at the conclusion that it had best not be talked about; though perhaps he was guided by no more distinct reason than that he had taken it for granted that his mother would reserve it to herself and her partner.

"What now?" she said again, impatiently. "What is it?"

"I did not mean, mother, that you should repeat what I have communicated. I think you had better not repeat it."

"Do you make that a condition with me?"

"Well! Yes."

"Observe, then! It is you who make this a secret," said she, holding up her forefinger, "and not I. It is you, Arthur, who bring here doubts and suspicions and entreaties for explanation, and it is you, Arthur, who bring secrets here. What is it to me, do you think, where the man has been, or what he has been? What can it be to me? The whole world may know it, if they care to know it; it is nothing to me. Now, let me go."

He yielded to her imperious but elated look, and turned her chair back to the place from which he had wheeled it. In doing so he saw elation in the face of Mr. Flintwinch, which most assuredly was not inspired by Flora. This turning of his intelligence, and his whole attempt and design against himself, did even more than his mother's fixedness and firmness to convince him that his utmost efforts with her were idle. Nothing remained but the appeal to his old friend Mistress Affery.

But, even to get to the very doubtful and preliminary stage of making the appeal, seemed one of the least promising of human undertakings. She was so completely under the thrall of the two clever ones, was so systematically kept in sight by one or other of them, and was so afraid to go about the house besides, that every opportunity of speaking to her alone appeared to be forestalled. Over and above that, Mistress Affery by some means (it was not very difficult to guess, through the sharp arguments of her liege lord) had acquired such a lively conviction of the hazard of saying any thing under any circumstances, that she had remained all this time in a corner guarding herself from approach with that symbolical instrument of hers; so that, when a word or two had been addressed to her by Flora, or even by the bottle-green patriarch himself, she had warded off conversation with the toasting-fork, like a dumb woman.

After several abortive attempts to get Affery to look at him while she cleared the table and washed the tea-service, Arthur thought of an expedient which Flora might originate; to whom he therefore whispered, "Could you say you would like to go through the house?"

Now poor Flora, being always in fluctuating expectation of the time when Clennam would renew his boyhood, and be madly in love with her again, received the whisper with the utmost delight, not only as rendered precious by its mysterious character, but as preparing the way for a tender interview in which he would declare the state of his affections. She immediately began to work out the hint.

"Ah dear me the poor old room," said Flora, glancing round, "looks just as ever Mrs. Clennam I am touched to see except for being smokier which was to be expected with time and which we must all expect and reconcile ourselves to being whether we like it or not as I am sure I have had to do myself if not exactly smokier dreadfully stouter which is the same or worse, to think of the days when papa used to bring me here the least of girls a perfect mass of chillblains to be stuck upon a chair with my feet upon the rails and stare at Arthur—pray excuse me, Mr. Clennam—the least of boys in the frightfullest of frills and jackets ere yet Mr. F. appeared a misty shadow on the horizon paying attentions like the well-known spectre of some place in Germany beginning with a B is a moral lesson inculcating that all the paths in life are similar to the paths down in the North of England where they get the coals and make the iron and things graveled with ashes!"

Having paid the tribute of a sigh to the instability of human existence, Flora hurried on with her purpose.

"Not that at any time," she proceeded, "its worst enemy could have said it was a cheerful house for that it was never made to be but always highly impressive, fond memory recalls an occasion in youth ere yet the judgment was mature when Arthur—confirmed habit, Mr. Clennam—took me down into an unused kitchen eminent for mouldiness and proposed to secrete me there for life and feed me on what he could hide from his meals when he was not at home for the holidays and on dry bread in disgrace which at that halcyon period too frequently occurred, dear me would it be inconvenient or asking too much to beg to be permitted to revive those scenes and walk through the house?"

Mrs. Clennam who responded with a constrained grace to Mrs. Finching's good nature in being there at all, though her visit, (before Arthur's unexpected arrival) was, undoubtedly, an act of pure good nature and no self gratification, intimated that all the house was open to her. Flora rose, and looked to Arthur for his escort. "Certainly," said he, aloud; "and Affery will light us, I dare say."

Affery was excusing herself with "Don't ask nothing of me, Arthur!" when Mr. Flintwinch stopped her with "Why not? Affery, what's the matter with you, woman? Why not, jade?" Thus expostulated with, she came unwillingly out of her corner, resigned the toasting-fork into one of her husband's hands, and took the candlestick he offered from the other.

"Go before, you fool!" said Jeremiah. "Are you going up or down, Mrs. Finching?"

Flora answered, "Down."

"Then go before, and down, you Affery," said Jeremiah. "And do it properly, or I'll come rolling down the banisters, and tumbling over you!"

Affery headed the exploring party; Jeremiah closed it. He evidently had no intention of leaving them. Clennam looked back and saw him following, three stairs behind, in the coolest and most methodical manner. He exclaimed in a low voice, "Is there no getting rid of him!" Flora kindly reassured his mind by replying, promptly, "Though not exactly proper Arthur and a thing I couldn't think of before a younger man and a stranger still I don't mind him if you so particularly wish it and provided you'll have the goodness not to take me too tight!"

Wanting the heart to explain that this was not at all what he meant, Arthur extended his supporting arm round Flora's figure. "Oh my gracious me," said she, "you are very obedient indeed really and it's extremely honorable and gentlemanly in you I am sure but still at the same time if you would like to be a little tighter than that I shouldn't consider it intruding."

In this preposterous attitude, unspeakably at variance with his anxious mind, Clennam descended to the basement of the house, finding that wherever it became darker than elsewhere, Flora became heavier, and that when the house was lightest, she was too. Returning from the dismal kitchen regions, which were as dreary as they could be, Mistress Affery passed with the light into his father's old room, and then into the old dining-room, always passing on before like a phantom that was not to be overtaken, and neither turning nor replying when he whispered, "Affery! I want to speak to you!"

In the dining-room a sentimental desire came over Flora to look into the dragon closet which had so often swallowed Arthur in the days of his boyhood—not impossibly because, as a very dark closet, it was a likely place to be heavy in. Arthur, fast subsiding into despair, had opened it, when a knock was heard at the outer door.

Mistress Affery, with a suppressed cry, threw her apron over her head.

"What? You want another dose!" said Mr. Flintwinch. "You shall have it, my woman—you shall have a good one! Oh! You shall have a sneezer—you shall have a teazer!"

"In the mean time, is anybody going to the door?" said Arthur.

"In the mean time, I am going to the door, sir," replied the old man, so savagely as to render it pretty clear that in a choice of difficulties he felt he must go, though he would have preferred not to go. "Stay here the while, all. Affery, woman, move an inch, or speak one word in your foolishness, and I'll treble your dose!"

The moment he was gone, Arthur released Mrs. Finching with some difficulty, by reason of that lady's misunderstanding his intentions, and making her arrangements with a view to tightening instead of slackening.

"Affery, speak to me now!"

"Don't touch me, Arthur!" she cried, shrinking from him. "Don't come near me. He'll see you. Jeremiah will. Don't!"

"He can't see me," returned Arthur, suiting the action to the word, "if I blow the candle out."

"He'll hear you," cried Affery.

"He can't hear me," returned Arthur, suiting the action to the word again, "if I draw you into this black closet, and speak here. Why do you hide your face?"

"Because I am afraid of seeing something."

"You can't be afraid of seeing any thing in this darkness, Affery."

"Yes, I am. Much more than if it was light."

"What are you afraid of, and why?"

FLORA'S TOUR OF INSPECTION.

"I don't know what; but I do know why."

"Tell me why, then?"

"Because the house is full of mysteries and secrets; because it's full of whisperings and counselings; because it's full of noises. There never was such a house for noises. I shall die of 'em, if Jeremiah don't strangle me first, as I expect he will."

"I have never heard any noises here worth speaking of."

"Ah! But you would, though, if you lived in the house, and was obliged to go about it as I am," said Affery; "and you'd feel that they was so well worth speaking of that you'd feel you was choking through not being allowed to speak of 'em. Here's Jeremiah! You'll get me killed."

"My good Affery, I solemnly declare to you that I can see the light of the open door on the pavement of the hall, and so could you if you would uncover your face and look."

"I durstn't do it," said Affery, "I durstn't never, Arthur. I'm always blindfolded when Jeremiah ain't a-looking, and sometimes even when he is."

"He can not shut the door without my seeing him," said Arthur. "You are as safe with me as if he was fifty miles away."

("I wish he was!" cried Affery.)

"Affery, I want to know what is amiss here; I want some light thrown for me on the secrets of this house."

"I tell you, Arthur," she interrupted, "noises is the secrets, rustlings and stealings about, tremblings and throbbings, treads overhead and treads underneath."

"But those are not all the secrets."

"I don't know," said Affery. "Don't ask me no more. Your old sweetheart ain't far off, and she's a blabber."

His old sweetheart being, in fact, so near at hand that she was then reclining against him in a flutter, at a very substantial angle of forty-five degrees, here interposed to assure Mistress Affery, with greater earnestness than directness of asseveration, that whatever she heard should go no further, but should be kept inviolate, "if on no other account on Arthur's—sensible of intruding in being too familiar, Doyce and Clennam's."

"I make my imploring appeal to you, Affery, to you, one of

the few agreeable early remembrances I have, for my mother's sake, for your husband's sake, for my own, for all our sakes. I am sure you can tell me something connected with the coming here of this man if you will."

"Why, then I'll tell you, Arthur," returned Affery—"Jeremiah's a-coming!"

"No, indeed he is not. The door is open, and he is standing outside, talking."

"I'll tell you, then," said Affery, after listening, "that the first time he ever come he heard the noises his own self. 'What the Devil's that?' he said to me. 'I don't know what it is,' I says to him, catching hold of him, 'but I have heard it over and over again.' While I says it, he stands a-looking at me, all of a shake, he do."

"Has he been here often?"

"Only that night and the last night."

"What did you see of him on the last night, after I was gone?"

"Them two clever ones had him all to themselves. Jeremiah come a-dancing at me sideways, after I had let you out (he always comes a-dancing at me sideways when he's going to hurt me), and he said to me, 'Now, Affery,' he said, 'I am a-coming ahind you, my woman, and a-going to run you up.' So he took and squeezed the back of my neck in his hand till it made me open my mouth, and then he pushed me before him to bed, squeezing all the way. That's what he calls running me up, he do. Oh, he's a wicked one!"

"And did you hear or see no more, Affery?"

"Don't I tell you I was sent to bed, Arthur? Here he is!"

"I assure you he is still at the door. Those whisperings and counselings, Affery, that you have spoken of. What are they?"

"How should I know! Don't ask me nothing about 'em, Arthur. Get away!"

"But, my dear Affery, unless I can gain some insight into this hidden business, in spite of your husband and in spite of my mother, ruin will come of it."

"Don't ask me nothing," repeated Affery. "I have been in a dream forever so long. Get away, get away!"

"You said that before," returned Arthur. "You used the same words that night, at the door, when I asked you what was going on here. What do you mean by being in a dream?"

"I an't a-going to tell you. Get away! I shouldn't tell you if you was by yourself, much less with your old sweetheart here."

It was equally vain for Arthur to entreat, and for Flora to protest. Affery, who had been trembling and struggling the whole time, turned a deaf ear to all adjuration, and was bent on forcing herself out of the closet.

"I'd sooner scream to Jeremiah than say another word!" she said. "I'll call out to him, Arthur, if you don't give over speaking to me. Now's the very last word I'll say afore I call to him. If ever you begin to get the better of them two clever ones your own self (which you ought to it, as I told you when you first come home, for you haven't been a-living here long years, to be made afeard of your life as I have,) then do you get the better of 'em afore my face, and then do you say to me, Affery, tell your dreams! Maybe, then I'll tell 'em!"

The shutting of the door stopped Arthur from replying They glided into the places where Jeremiah had left them, and Clennam, stepping forward as that old gentleman returned, informed him that he had accidentally extinguished the candle. Mr. Flintwinch looked on as he relighted it at the lamp in the hall, and preserved a profound taciturnity respecting the person who had been holding him in conversation. Perhaps his irascibility demanded compensation for some tediousness that the visitor had expended on him; but, however that was, he took such umbrage at seeing his wife with her apron over her head, that he charged at her, and taking her vailed nose between his thumb and finger, appeared to throw the whole screw-power of his person into the wring he gave it.

Flora, now permanently heavy, did not release Clennam from the survey of the house until it had extended even to his old garret bedchamber. His thoughts were otherwise occupied than with the tour of inspection. Yet he took particular notice at the time, as he afterward had occasion to remember, that the airless smell of the place was very oppressive, that it was very dusty, and that there was some resistance to the opening of a room door, which occasioned Affery to cry out that somebody was hiding inside, and to continue to believe so, though somebody was sought and not discovered. When they at last returned to his mother's room they found her shading her face with her muffled hand, and talking in a low voice to the Patriarch as he stood before the fire; whose blue eyes, polished head, and silken locks, turning toward them as they came in, imparted an inestimable value and inexhaustible love of his species to his remark:

"So you have been seeing the premises, seeing the premises—premises—seeing the premises."

It was not in itself a jewel of benevolence or wisdom, yet he made it an exemplar of both that one would have liked to have a copy of.

CHAPTER LX.

THE EVENING OF A LONG DAY.

THAT illustrious man and great national ornament, Mr. Merdle, continued his shining course. It began to be widely understood that one who had done society the admirable service of making so much money out of it, could not suffice to remain a commoner. A baronetcy was spoken of with confidence; a peerage was frequently mentioned. Rumor had it that Mr. Merdle had set his golden face against a baronetcy; that he had plainly intimated to Lord Decimus that a baronetcy was not enough for him; that he had said, "No: a Peerage, or plain Merdle." This was reported to have plunged Lord Decimus as nigh to his noble chin in a slough of doubts as could be the case with so lofty a personage. For the Barnacles, as a group of themselves in creation, had an idea that such distinctions belonged to them; and that when a soldier, sailor, or lawyer, became ennobled, they let him in, as it were, by an act of condescension, at the family door, and immediately shut it again. Not only (said Rumor) had the troubled Decimus his own hereditary part in the impression, but he also knew of several Barnacle claims already on the file, which came into collision with that of the master spirit. Right or wrong, Rumor was very busy; and Lord Decimus, while he was, or was supposed to be, in stately excogitation of the difficulty, lent her some countenance, by taking, on several public occasions, one of those elephantine trots of his through a wilderness of overgrown sentences, waving Mr. Merdle about on his trunk as Gigantic Enterprise, the Wealth of England, Elasticity, Credit, Capital, Prosperity, and all manner of blessings.

So quietly did the mowing of the old scythe go on, that fully three months had passed unnoticed since two English brothers had been laid in one tomb in the strangers' cemetery at Rome. Mr. and Mrs. Sparkler were established in their own house—

a little mansion, rather of the Tite Barnacle class—quite a triumph of inconvenience, with a perpetual smell in it of the day before yesterday's soup and coach-horses, but extremely dear, as being exactly in the centre of the habitable globe. In this enviable abode (and envied it really was by many people) Mrs. Sparkler had intended to proceed at once to the demolition of the Bosom, when active hostilities had been suspended by the arrival of the Courier with his tidings of death. Mrs. Sparkler, who was not unfeeling, had received them with a violent burst of grief which had lasted twelve hours; after which she had arisen to see about her mourning, and to take every precaution that could insure its being as becoming as Mrs. Merdle's. A gloom was then cast over more than one distinguished family (according to the politest sources of intelligence,) and the Courier went back again.

Mr. and Mrs. Sparkler had been dining a one with their gloom cast over them, and Mrs. Sparkler reclined on a drawing-room sofa. It was a hot summer Sunday evening. The residence in the centre of the habitable globe, at all times stuffed and close as if it had an unenviable cold in its head, was that evening particularly stifling. The bells of the churches had done their worst in the way of clanging and twanging among the jarring echoes of the streets, and the lighted windows of the churches had ceased to be yellow in the gray dusk, and had died out opaque black. Mrs. Sparkler, lying on her sofa looking through an open window at the opposite side of a narrow street, over boxes of mignonette and flowers, was tired of the view. Mrs. Sparkler, looking at another window, where her husband stood in the balcony, was tired of the view. Mrs. Sparkler, looking at herself in her mourning, was even tired of that view; though, naturally, not so tired of that as of the other two.

"It's like lying in a well," said Mrs. Sparkler, changing her position, fretfully. "Dear me, Edmund, if you have any thing to say, why don't you say it?"

Mr. Sparkler might have replied with ingenuousness, "My life, I have nothing to say." But as the repartee did not occur to him, he contented himself with coming in from the balcony and standing at the side of his wife's couch.

"Good gracious, Edmund!" said Mrs. Sparkler, more fretfully still; "you are absolutely putting mignonette up your nose! Pray don't!"

Mr. Sparkler, in absence of mind—perhaps a more literal absence of mind than is usually understood by the phrase—had so smelt at a sprig in his hand as to be on the verge of the offense in question. He smiled, said, "I ask your pardon, my dear," threw it out of window, and came back again.

"You make my head ache by remaining in that position, Edmund," said Mrs. Sparkler, raising her eyes to him, after another minute; "you look so aggravatingly large by this light. Do sit down."

"Certainly, my dear," said Mr. Sparkler, and took a chair on the same spot.

"If I didn't know this was the end of July," said Fanny, yawning in a dreamy manner, "I should have felt certain it was the longest day. I never did experience such a day."

"Is this your fan, my love?" asked Mr. Sparkler, picking up one, and presenting it.

"Edmund," returned his wife more wearily yet, "don't ask weak questions, I entreat you not. Whose can it be but mine?"

"Yes, I thought it was yours," said Mr. Sparkler.

"Then you shouldn't ask," retorted Fanny. After a little while she turned on her sofa and exclaimed, "Dear me, dear me, there never was such a long day as this!" After another little while she got up slowly, walked about, and came back again.

"My dear," said Mr. Sparkler, flashing with an original conception, "I think you must have got the fidgets."

"Oh! Fidgets!" repeated Mrs. Sparkler. "Don't!"

"My adorable girl," urged Mr. Sparkler, "try your aromatic vinegar. I have often seen my mother try it, and it seemingly refreshed her. And she is, as I belive you are aware, a remarkably fine woman with no non—"

"Good Gracious!" exclaimed Fanny, starting up again, "it's beyond all patience! This is the most wearisome day that ever did dawn npon the world, I am certain!"

"Mr. Sparkler looked meekly after her as she lounged about

the room, and he appeared to be a little frightened. When she had tossed a few trifles about, and had looked down into the darkening street out of all the three windows, she returned to her sofa, and threw herself among its pillows.

"Now, Edmund, come here! Come a little nearer, because I want to be able to touch you with my fan, that I may impress you very much with what I am going to say. That will do. Quite close enough. Oh, you *do* look so big!"

Mr. Sparkler apologized for the circumstance, pleaded that he couldn't help it, and said that "our fellows," without more particularly indicating whose fellows, used to call him by the name of Quinbus Flartrin, Junior, or the Young Man Mountain.

"You ought to have told me so before," said Fanny.

"My dear," returned Mr. Sparkler, rather gratified, "I didn't know it would interest you, or I would have made a point of telling you."

"There! For goodness' sake, don't talk," said Fanny; "I want to talk myself. Edmund, we really must not be alone any more. I must take such precautions as will prevent my being ever again reduced to the state of dreadful depression in which I am this evening."

"My dear," answered Mr. Sparkler; "being, as you are well known to be, a remarkably fine woman, with no—"

"Oh, good GRACIOUS!" cried Fanny.

Mr. Sparkler was so discomposed by the energy of this exclamation, accompanied with a flouncing up from the sofa and a flouncing down again, that a minute or two elapsed before he felt himself equal to saying, in explanation:

"I mean, my dear, that every body knows you are calculated to shine in society."

"Calculated to shine in society," retorted Fanny, with great irritability and impatience; "yes, indeed! And then what happens? I no sooner recover, in a visiting point of view, the shock of poor dear papa's death, and my poor uncle's—though I do not disguise from myself that the last was a happy release; for, if you are not presentable, you had much better die—"

"You are not referring to me, my love, I hope?" Mr. Sparkler humbly interrupted.

"Edmund, Edmund, you would wear out a Saint. Am I not expressly speaking of my poor uncle?"

"You looked with so much expression at myself, my dear girl," said Mr. Sparkler, "that I felt a little uncomfortable. Thank you, my love."

"Now you have put me out," observed Fanny, with a toss of her fan, "and I had better go to bed."

"Don't do that, my love," urged Mr. Sparkler. "Take time."

Fanny took a good deal of time; lying back with her eyes shut, and her eyebrows raised with a hopeless expression, as if she had utterly given up all terrestrial affairs. At length, without the slightest notice, she opened her eyes again, and recommenced in a short, sharp manner.

"What happens, then, I ask? What happens? Why, I find myself, at the very period when I might shine most in society, and should most like, for very momentous reasons, to shine in society—I find myself to a certain extent disqualified for going into society. It's too bad, really!"

"My dear," said Mr. Sparkler, "I don't think it need keep you at home."

"Edmund, you ridiculous creature," returned Fanny, with great indignation; "do you suppose that a woman in the bloom of youth, and not wholly devoid of personal attractions, can put herself, at such a time, in competition as to figure with a woman in every other way her inferior? If you do suppose such a thing, your folly is boundless."

Mr. Sparkler submitted that he had thought "it might be got over."

"Got over!" repeated Fanny, with immeasurable scorn.

"For a time," Mr. Sparkler submitted.

Honoring the last feeble suggestion with no notice, Mrs. Sparkler declared with bitterness that it really was too bad, and that positively it was enough to make one wish one was dead!

"However," she said, when she had in some measure recovered from her sense of personal ill-usage, "provoking as it is, and cruel as it seems, I suppose it must be submitted to."

"Especially as it was to be expected," said Mr. Sparkler.

"Edmund," returned his wife, "if you have nothing more

becoming to do than to attempt to insult the woman who has honored you with her hand, when she finds herself in adversity, I think *you* had better go to bed."

Mr. Sparkler was much afflicted by the charge, and offered a most tender and earnest apology. His apology was accepted, but Mrs. Sparkler requested him to go round to the other side of the sofa and sit in the window-curtain, to tone himself down.

"Now, Edmund," she said, stretching out her fan, and touching him with it at arm's length, "what I was going to say to you when you began as usual to prose and worry, is, that I shall guard against our being alone any more, and that when circumstances prevent my going out to my own satisfaction, I must arrange to have some people or other always here; for I really can not and will not have another such day as this has been."

Mr. Sparkler's sentiments as to the plan were, in brief, that it had no nonsense about it. He added, "And besides, you know it's likely that you'll soon have your sister—"

"Dearest Amy, yes!" cried Mrs. Sparkler, with a sigh of affection. "Darling little thing! Not, however, that Amy would do here alone."

Mr. Sparkler was going to say "No?" interrogatively. But he saw his danger, and said it assentingly. "No. Oh dear no; she wouldn't do here alone."

"No, Edmund. For, not only are the virtues of the precious child of that still character that they require a contrast—require life and movement around them, to bring them out in their right colors and make one love them of all things—but she will require to be roused, on more accounts than one."

"That's it!" said Mr. Sparkler. "Roused."

"Pray don't, Edmund. Your habit of interrupting without having the least thing in the world to say, distracts one. You must be broken of it. Speaking of Amy; my poor little pet was devotedly attached to poor papa, and no doubt will have lamented his loss exceedingly, and grieved very much. I have done so myself. I have felt it dreadfully. But Amy will no doubt have felt it even more, from having been on the spot the whole time, and having been with poor dear papa at the last: which I unhappily was not."

Here Fanny stopped to weep, and to say, "Dear, dear, beloved papa! How truly gentlemanly he was! What a contrast to poor uncle!"

"From the effects of that trying time," she pursued, "my good little Mouse will have to be roused. Also, from the effects of this long attendance upon Edward in his illness; an attendance which is not yet over, which may even go on for some time longer, and which in the meanwhile unsettles us all, by keeping poor dear papa's affairs from being wound up. Fortunately, however, the papers with his agents here, being all sealed up and locked up, as he left them when he providentially came to England, the affairs are in that state of order that they can wait until Tip—our childish name for my brother Edward—recovers his health in Sicily, sufficiently to come over, and administer, or execute, or whatever it is."

"He couldn't have a better nurse to bring him round," Mr. Sparkler made bold to opine.

"For a wonder, I can agree with you," returned his wife, languidly turning her eyelids a little in his direction (she held forth, in general, as if to the drawing-room furniture), "and can adopt your words. He couldn't have a better nurse to bring him round. There are times when my dear child is a little wearing to an active mind; but, as a nurse, she is Perfection. Best of Amys!"

Mr. Sparkler, growing rash on his late success, observed that Edward had had, biggodd, a long bout of it, my dear girl.

"If Bout, Edmund," returned Mrs. Sparkler, "is the slang term for indisposition, he has. If it is not, I am unable to give an opinion on the barbarous language you address to Edward's sister. That he contracted Malaria Fever somewhere: either by traveling day and night to Rome, where, after all, he arrived too late to see poor dear papa before his death: or under some other unwholesome circumstances: is indubitable, if that is what you mean. Likewise, that his extremely careless life has made him a very bad subject for it indeed."

Mr. Sparkler considered it a parallel case to that of some of our fellows in the West Indies with Yellow Jack. Mrs. Sparkler closed her eyes again, and refused to have any consciousness of our fellows, of the West Indies, or of Yellow Jack.

"So, Amy," she pursued when she reopened her eyelids,

"will require to be roused from the effects of many tedious and anxious weeks. And lastly, she will require to be roused from a low tendency which I know very well to be at the bottom of her heart. Don't ask me what it is, Edmund, because I must decline to tell you."

"I am not going to, my dear," said Mr. Sparkler.

"I shall thus have much improvement to effect in my sweet child," Mrs. Sparkler continued, "and can not have her near me too soon. Amiable and dear little Twoshoes! As to the settlement of poor papa's affairs, my interest in that is not very selfish. Papa behaved very generously to me when I was married, and I have little or nothing to expect. Provided he has made no will that can come into force, leaving a legacy to Mrs. General, I am contented. Dear papa, poor papa!"

She wept again, but Mrs. General was the best of restoratives. The name soon stimulated her to dry her eyes and say:

"It is a highly encouraging circumstance in Edward's illness, I am thankful to think, and gives one the greatest confidence in his sense not being impaired, or his proper spirit weakened—down to the time of poor dear papa's death at least—that he paid off Mrs. General instantly, and sent her out of the house. I applaud him for it. I could forgive him a great deal, for doing with such promptitude so exactly what I would have done myself!"

Mrs. Sparkler was in the full glow of her gratification, when a double knock was heard at the door. A very odd knock. Low, as if to avoid making a noise and attracting attention. Long, as if the person knocking were pre-occupied in mind, and forgot to leave off.

"Halloa!" said Mr. Sparkler. "Who's this!"

"Not Amy and Edward, without notice and without a carriage!" said Mrs. Sparkler. "Look out."

The room was dark, but the street was lighter, because of its lamps. Mr. Sparkler's head peeping over the balcony looked so very bulky and heavy that it seemed on the point of over-balancing him and flattening the unknown below.

"It's one fellow," said Mr. Sparkler. "I can't see who—stop though!"

On this second thought he went out into the balcony again

and had another look. He came back as the door was opened, and announced that he believed he had identified "his governor's tile" He was not mistaken, for his governor, tile in hand, was introduced immediately afterward.

"Candles!" said Mrs. Sparkler, with a word of excuse for the darkness.

"It's light enough for me," said Mr. Merdle.

When the candles were brought in, Mr. Merdle was standing behind the door, picking his lips. "I thought I'd give you a call," said he, "I am rather particularly occupied just now; and as I happened to be out for a stroll, I thought I'd give you a call."

As he was in dinner dress, Fanny asked him where he had been dining?

"Well," said Mr. Merdle, "I haven't been dining any where, particularly."

"Of course, you have dined?" said Fanny.

"Why—no, I haven't dined," said Mr. Merdle.

He passed his hand over his yellow forehead, and considered, as if he were not sure about it. Some thing to eat, was proposed. "No, thank you," said Mr. Merdle, "I don't feel inclined for it. I was to have dined out along with Mrs. Merdle. But as I didn't feel inclined for dinner, I let Mrs. Merdle go by herself, just as we were getting into the carriage, and thought I'd take a stroll instead."

Would he have tea or coffee? "No, thank you," said Mr. Merdle. "I looked in at the Club, and got a bottle of wine."

At this period of his visit, Mr. Merdle took the chair which Edmund Sparkler had offered him, and which he had hitherto been pushing slowly before him by the back, like a dull man with a pair of skates on for the first time, who could not make up his mind to start. He now put his hat upon another chair beside him, and looking down into it as if it were some twenty feet deep, said again, "You see, I thought I'd give you a call."

"Flattering to us," said Fanny, "for you are not a calling man."

"N—no," returned Mr. Merdle, who was by this time taking

himself into custody under both coat-sleeves. "No, I am not in general a calling man."

"You have too much to do, for that," said Fanny. "Having so much to do, Mr. Merdle, loss of appetite is a serious thing with you, and you must have it seen to. You must not be ill."

"Oh! I am very well," replied Mr. Merdle, after deliberating about it. "I am as well as I usually am. I am well enough. I am as well as I want to be."

The master-mind of the age, true to its characteristic of being at all times a mind that had as little as possible to say for itself, and a great difficulty in saying it, became mute again. Mrs. Sparkler, of whom it may be remarked by poetical adoption, that nothing lived in the drawing-room 'twixt her and silence, began to wonder how long the master-mind meant to stay

"I was speaking of poor papa when you came in, sir."

"Aye, indeed? Quite a coincidence," said Mr. Merdle.

Fanny did not see that; but felt it incumbent on her to continue talking "I was saying," she therefore pursued, "that my brother's illness had occasioned a delay in examining and arranging papa's property."

"Yes," said Mr. Merdle; "yes, there has been a delay."

"Not that it is of consequence," said Fanny.

"Not," assented Mr. Merdle, after having examined the cornice of all that part of the room which was within his range; "not that it is of any consequence."

"My only anxiety is," said Fanny, "that Mrs. General should not get any thing."

"*She* won't get any thing," said Mr. Merdle.

Fanny was delighted to hear him express the opinion. Mr. Merdle, after taking another gaze into the depths of his hat, as if he thought he saw something at the bottom, rubbed his hair, and slowly appended to his last remark the confirmatory words, "Oh dear no. No. Not she. Not likely."

As the topic seemed exhausted, and Mr. Merdle too, Fanny inquired if he were going to take up Mrs. Merdle and the carriage in his way home?

"No," he answered; "I shall go by the shortest way and leave Mrs. Merdle to—" here he looked all over the palms of

MR. MERDLE A BORROWER.

both his hands, as if he were telling his own fortune—"to take care of herself. I dare say she'll manage to do it."

"Probably," said Fanny.

There was then a long silence; during which, Mrs. Sparkler, lying back on her sofa again, shut her eyes and raised her eyebrows in her former retirement from mundane affairs.

"But, however," said Mr. Merdle, suddenly, "I am equally detaining you and myself. I thought I'd give you a call."

"Charmed, I am sure," said Fanny.

"So I am off," added Mr. Merdle, getting up. "Could you lend me a penknife?"

It was an odd thing, Fanny smilingly observed, for her who could seldom prevail upon herself even to write a letter, to lend to a man of such vast business as Mr. Merdle. "Isn't it?" Mr. Merdle acquiesced; "but I shall want one to-night; and I know you have got several little wedding keepsakes about, with scissors and tweezers, and such things in them. You shall have it back to-morrow."

"Edmund," said Mrs. Sparkler, "open (now very carefully, if you please) the mother-of-pearl box on my little table there, and give Mr. Merdle the mother-of-pearl penknife."

"Thank you," said Mr. Merdle; "but if you have got one with a darker handle, I should prefer one with a darker handle."

"Tortoise-shell?"

"Thank you," said Mr. Merdle; "yes. I should prefer tortoise-shell."

Edmund accordingly received instructions to open the tortoise-shell box, and give Mr. Merdle the tortoise-shell knife. On his doing so, his wife said to the master-spirit, graciously:

"I will forgive you if you ink it."

"I won't ink it," said Mr. Merdle.

The illustrious visitor then put out his coatcuff, and for a moment entombed Mrs. Sparkler's hand: wrist, bracelet, and all. Where his own hand shrunk to was not made manifest, but it was as remote from Mrs. Sparkler's sense of touch as if he had been a highly meritorious Chelsea Veteran or Greenwich Pensioner.

Thoroughly convinced, as he went out of the room, that it

was the longest day that ever did come to an end at last, and that there never was a woman, not wholly devoid of personal attractions, so worn out by idiotic and lumpish people, Fanny passed into the balcony for a breath of air. Waters of vexation filled her eyes; and they had the effect of making the famous Mr. Merdle, in going down the street, appear to leap, and waltz, and gyrate, as if he were possessed by devils.

CHAPTER LXI.

THE CHIEF BUTLER RESIGNS THE SEALS OF OFFICE.

THE dinner-party was at the great Physician's. Bar was there, and in full force. Ferdinand Barnacle was there, and in his most engaging state. Few ways of life were hidden from Physician, and he was oftener in its darkest places than even Bishop himself. There were brilliant ladies about London who perfectly doted on him, my dear, as the most charming creature and the most delightful person, who would have been horrified to find themselves so close to him if they could have known on what sights those thoughtful eyes of his had rested within an hour or two, and near to whose beds and under what roofs his composed figure had stood. But Physician was a quiet man, who performed neither on his own trumpet, nor on the trumpets of other people. Many wonderful things did he see and hear, and much irreconcilable moral contradiction did he pass his life among; yet his equality of compassion was no more disturbed than the Divine Master's of all healing was. He went, like the rain, among the just and unjust, doing all the good he could, and neither proclaiming it in the synagogues nor at the corners of streets.

As no man of large experience of humanity, however quietly carried it may be, can fail to be invested with an interest peculiar to the possession of such knowledge, Physician was an attractive man. Even the daintier gentlemen and ladies who had no idea of his secret, and who would have been startled out of more wits than they had, by the monstrous impropriety of his proposing to them "Come and see what I see!" confessed his attraction. Where he was, something real was. And half a grain of reality, like the smallest portion of some other scarce natural production, will flavor an enormous quantity of diluent.

It came to pass, therefore, that Physician's little dinners always presented people in their least conventional lights. The guests said to themselves, whether they were conscious of it or no, "Here is a man who really has an acquaintance with us as we are, who is admitted to some of us every day with our wigs and paint off, who hears the wanderings of our minds, and sees the undisguised expression of our faces, when both are past our control—we may as well make an approach to reality with him, for the man has got the better of us and is too strong for us." Therefore Physician's guests came out so surprisingly at his round table that they were almost natural.

Bar's knowledge of that agglomeration of jurymen which is called humanity, was as sharp as a razor; yet a razor is not a convenient instrument except for close-shaving, and Physician's plain, bright scalpel, though far less keen, was adaptable to far wider purposes. Bar knew all about the gullibility and knavery of people, but Physician could have given him a better insight into their tendernesses and affections, in one week of his rounds, than Westminster Hall and all the circuits put together in threescore years and ten. Bar always had a suspicion of this, and perhaps was glad to encourage it (for if the world were really a great Law Court one would think that the last day of Term could not too soon arrive), and so he liked and respected Physician quite as much as any other kind of man did.

Mr. Merdle's default left a Banquo's chair at the table; but if he had been there, he would have merely made the difference of Banquo in it, and consequently he was not much missed. Bar, who picked up all sorts of odds and ends about Westminster Hall, much as a raven would have done if he had passed as much of his time there, had been picking up a good many straws lately, and tossing them about to see which way the Merdle wind blew. He now had a little talk on the subject with Mrs. Merdle herself; sliding up to that lady, of course, with the double eye-glass and the jury droop.

"A certain bird," said Bar—and he looked as if it could be no other bird than a magpie—"has been whispering among us lawyers lately, that there is to be an addition to the titled personages of this realm."

"Really?" said Mrs. Merdle.

"Yes," said Bar. "Has not the bird been whispering in very different ears from ours—in lovely ears?" He drooped, and looked expressively at Mrs. Merdle's nearest ear-ring.

"Do you mean mine?" asked Mrs. Merdle.

"When I say, lovely," said Bar, drooping again, "I always mean you."

"You never mean any thing, I think," returned Mrs. Merdle (not displeased).

"Oh, cruelly unjust!" said Bar. "But the bird?"

"I am the last person in the world to hear news," observed Mrs. Merdle, carelessly arranging her stronghold. "Who is it?"

"What an admirable witness you would make!" said Bar. "No jury (unless we could impannel one of blind men) could resist you, if you were ever so bad a one; but you would be such a good one!"

"Why, you ridiculous man?" asked Mrs. Merdle, laughing.

Bar waved his double eye-glass three or four times, between himself and the Bosom, as a rallying answer, and inquired, in his most insinuating accents:

"What am I to call the most elegant, accomplished, and charming of women, a few weeks, or it may be a few days, hence?"

"Didn't your bird tell you what to call her?" answered Mrs. Merdle. "Do ask it to-morrow, and tell me the next time you see me what it says!"

This led to further passages of similar pleasantry between the two; but Bar, with all his sharpness, got nothing out of them. Physician, on the other hand, taking Mrs. Merdle down to her carriage, and attending on her as she put on her cloak, inquired into the symptoms with his usual calm directness.

"May I ask," he said, "is this true about Merdle?"

"My dear doctor," she returned, "you ask me the very question that I was half disposed to ask you."

"To ask me! Why me?"

"Upon my honor, I think Mr. Merdle reposes greater confidence in you than in any one."

"On the contrary, he tells me absolutely nothing, even professionally. You have heard the talk, of course?"

"Of course I have. But you know what Mr. Merdle is; you know how taciturn and reserved he is. I assure you I have no idea what foundation for it there may be. I should like it to be true; why should I deny that to you? You would know better, if I did!"

"Just so," said Physician.

"But whether it is all true, or partly true, or entirely false, I am wholly unable to say. It is a most provoking situation, a most absurd situation; but you know Mr. Merdle, and are not surprised."

Physician was not at all surprised, handed her into her carriage, and bade her Good-night. He stood for a moment at his own hall-door, looking sedately at the elegant equipage as it rattled away. On his return up stairs, the rest of the guests soon dispersed, and he was left alone. Being a great reader of all kinds of literature (and never at all apologetic for that weakness) he sat down comfortably to read.

The clock upon his study table pointed to a few minutes short of twelve when his attention was called to it by a ringing at the door bell. A man of plain habits, he had sent his servants to bed, and must needs go down to open the door. He went down, and at the door found a man without hat or coat, whose shirt sleeves were rolled up tight to his shoulders. For a moment he thought the man had been fighting; the rather, as he was much agitated and out of breath. A second look, however, showed him that the man was particularly clean, and not otherwise disordered in his dress than as it answered this description.

"I come from the warm baths, sir, round in the neighboring street."

"And what is the matter at the warm baths?"

"Would you please to come directly, sir. We found that lying on the table."

He put into the physician's hand a scrap of paper. Physician looked at it, and read his own name and address written in pencil; nothing more. He looked closer at the writing, looked at the man, took his hat from its peg, put the key of his door in his pocket, and they hurried away together.

When they came to the warm baths, all the other people belonging to that establishment were looking out for them at the door, and running up and down the passages. "Request everybody else to keep back, if you please," said the physician aloud to the master, "and do you take me straight to the place, my friend."

The messenger hurried before him, past a number of little rooms, and turning into one at the end of a long narrow passage, looked round the door. Physician was close upon him, and looked round the door too.

There was a bath in that corner, from which the water had been hastily drained off. Lying in it, as in a grave or sarcophagus, with a hurried drapery of sheet and blanket thrown across it, was the body of a heavily-made man, with an obtuse head, and coarse, common features. A skylight had been opened to release the steam with which the room had been filled; but it hung, condensed into water-drops, heavily upon the walls, and heavily upon the face and figure in the bath. The room was still hot, and the marble of the bath still warm; but the face and figure were clammy to the touch. The white marble at the bottom of the bath, was veined with a dreadful red. On the ledge at the side were an empty laudanum bottle and a tortoise-shell-handled penknife—soiled, but not with ink.

"Separation of the jugular vein—death rapid—been dead at least half an hour." This echo of the physician's words ran through the passages and little rooms, and through the house, while he was yet straightening himself from having bent down to reach to the bottom of the bath, and was yet dabbling his hands in water; redly veining it like the marble before it turned to one tint.

He turned his eyes to the dress upon the sofa, and to the watch, money, and pocket-book upon the table. A folded note, half buckled up in the pocket-book, and half protruding from it, caught his observant glance. He looked at it, touched it, pulled it a little further out from among the leaves, said quietly, "This is addressed to me," and opened and read it.

There were no directions for him to give. The people of the house knew what to do; the proper authorities were soon brought; and they took an equable business-like possession of the deceased and of what had been his property, with no greater disturbance of manner or countenance than usually attends the winding up of a clock. Physician was glad to walk out into the free night air—was even glad, in spite of his great experience, to sit down upon a door-step for a little while, being sick and faint.

Bar was a near neighbor of his, and, when he came to the house, he saw a light in the room where he knew his friend often sat late, getting up his work. As the light was never there when Bar was not, it gave him assurance that Bar was not yet in bed. In fact, this busy bee had a verdict to get to-morrow, against evidence, and was improving the shining hours in setting snares for the gentlemen of the jury.

Physician's knock astonished Bar; but as he immediately suspected that somebody had come to tell him that somebody else was robbing him, or otherwise trying to get the better of him, he came down promptly and softly. He had been clearing his head with a lotion of cold water as a good preparative to finding hot water for the heads of the jury, and had been reading with the neck of his shirt thrown wide open, that he might the more freely choke the opposite witnesses. In consequence, he came down looking rather wild. Seeing Physician, the least expected of men, he looked wilder and said, "What's the matter?"

"You asked me once what Merdle's complaint, was."

"Extraordinary answer! I remember that I did."

"I told you I had not found it out."

"Yes. I know you did."

"I have found it out."

"My God!" said Bar, starting back, and putting his hand upon the other's breast. "And so have I! I see it in your face."

They went into the nearest room, where Physician gave him the letter to read. He read it through half a dozen times. There was not much in it as to quantity, but it made a great demand on his close and continuous attention. He could not sufficiently give utterance to his regret that he had not himself found a clew to this. The smallest clew, he said, would have made him master of the case. And what a case it would have been to have got to the botttom of!

Physician had engaged to break the intelligence in Harley

Street, Bar could not at once return to his inveiglements of the most enlightened and remarkable jury he had ever seen in that box; with whom, he could tell his learned friend, no shallow sophistry would go down, and no unhappily abused professional tact and skill prevail (this was the way he meant to begin with them); so he said he would go too, and would loiter to and fro near the house, while his friend was inside. They walked there, the better to recover self-possession in the air; and the first cold dawn of day was fluttering the night when Physician knocked at the door. A footman of rainbow hues, in the public eye, was sitting up for his master—that is to say, was fast asleep in the kitchen; over a couple of candles and a newspaper, demonstrating the great accumulation of mathematical odds against the probabilities of a house being set on fire by accident. When this serving man was roused, Physician had still to await the rousing of the Chief Butler. At last that noble creature came into the dining-room in a flannel gown and list shoes; but with his cravat on, and a Chief Butler still. It was morning now; Physician had opened the shutters of one window while waiting, that he might see the light.

"Mrs. Merdle's maid must be called and told to get Mrs. Merdle up, and prepare her as gently as she can, to see me. I have dreadful news to break to her."

Thus Physician to the Chief Butler. The latter, who had a candle in his hand, called his man to take it away. Then he approached the window with dignity; looking on at Physician's news exactly as he had looked on at the dinners in that very room.

"Mr. Merdle is dead."

"I should wish," said the Chief Butler, "to give a month's notice."

"Mr. Merdle has destroyed himself."

"Sir," said the Chief Butler, "that is very unpleasant to the feelings of one in my position, as calculated to awaken prejudice; and I should wish to leave immediate."

"If you are not shocked, are you not surprised, man!" demanded the Physician warmly.

The Chief Butler, erect and calm, replied in these memorable words. "Mr. Merdle never was the gentleman, and no ungentlemanly act on Merdle's part would surprise me. Is there any body else I can send to you, sir, or any other directions I can give before I leave, respecting what you would wish to be done?"

When Physician, after discharging himself of his trust up stairs, rejoined Bar in the street, he said no more of his interview with Mrs. Merdle than that he had not yet told her all, but that what he had told her she had borne pretty well. Bar had devoted his leisure in the street to the construction of a most ingenious man-trap for catching the whole of his Jury at a blow; having got that matter settled in his mind, it was lucid on the late catastrophe, and they walked home slowly, discussing it in every bearing as they went. Before parting at Physician's door, they both looked up at the sunny morning sky, into which the smoke of a few early fires and the breath and voices of a few early stirrers were peacefully rising, and then looked round upon the immense city, and said, "If all those hundreds and thousands of beggared people who were yet asleep, could only know, as they two spoke, the ruin that impended over them, what a fearful cry against one miserable soul would go up to Heaven!"

The report that the great man was dead got about with astonishing rapidity. At first, he was dead of all the diseases that ever were known, and of several bran-new maladies invented with the speed of light to meet the demand of the occasion. He had concealed a dropsy from infancy, he had inherited a large estate of water on the chest from his grandfather, he had had an operation performed upon him every morning of his life for eighteen years, he had been subject to the explosion of important veins in his body after the manner of fire-works, he had had something the matter with his lungs, he had had something the matter with his heart, he had had something the matter with his brain. Five hundred people who sat down to breakfast entirely uninformed on the whole subject, believed before they had done breakfast that they privately and personally knew Physician to have said to Mr. Merdle, "You must expect to go out, some day, like the snuff of a candle," and that they knew Mr. Merdle to have said to Physician, "A man can die but once." By about eleven o'clock in the forenoon, something the matter with the brain, became the favorite; and by twelve the something had been distinctly ascertained to be "Pressure."

Pressure was so entirely satisfactory to the public mind, and seemed to make every body so comfortable, that it might have lasted all day but for Bar's having taken the real state of the case into Court at half-past nine. This led to its beginning to be currently whispered all over London by about one, that Mr. Merdle had killed himself. Pressure, however, so far from being overthrown by this discovery, became a greater favorite than ever. There was a general moralizing upon Pressure in every street. All the people who had tried to make money and had not been able to do it, said, There you were! You no sooner began to devote yourself to the pursuit of wealth than you got Pressure. The idle people improved the occasion in a similar manner. See, said they, what you have brought yourself to by work, work, work! You persisted in working, you overdid it, Pressure came, and you were done for! This consideration was very potent in many quarters, but nowhere more so than among the young clerks and partners who had never been in the slightest danger of overdoing it. These one and all declared, quite piously, that they hoped they would never forget the warning as long as they lived, and that their conduct would be so regulated as to keep off Pressure, and preserve them, a comfort to their friends, for many years.

But, at about the time of High 'Change, Pressure began to wane, and appalling whispers to circulate, east, west, north and south. At first they were faint, and went no further than a doubt whether Mr. Merdle's wealth would be found to be as vast as had been supposed; whether there might not be a temporary difficulty in "realizing" it; whether there might not even be a temporary suspension (say a month or so) on the part of the wonderful Bank. As the whispers became louder, which they did from that time every minute, they became more threatening. He had sprung from nothing, by no natural growth or process that any one could account for; he had been, after all, a low, ignorant fellow; he had been a down-looking man, and no one had ever been able to catch his eye; he had been taken up in quite an unaccountable manner, he had never had any money of his own, his ventures had been utterly reckless, and his expenditure had been enormous. In steady progression, as the day declined, the talk rose in sound and purpose like a rising sea. He had left a letter at the Baths addressed to his physician, and his physician had got the letter, and the letter would be produced at the Inquest on the morrow, and it would fall like a thunderbolt upon the multitude he had deluded. Numbers of men in every profession and trade would be blighted by his insolvency; old people who had been in easy circumstances all their lives would have no place of repentance for their trust in him but the workhouse, legions of women and children would have their whole future desolated by the hand of this mighty scoundrel. Every partaker of his magnificent feasts would be seen to have been a sharer in the plunder of innumerable homes; every servile worshiper of riches who had helped to set him upon his pedestal, would have done better to worship the Devil point-blank. So, the talk lashed louder and higher by confirmation on confirmation, and by edition after edition of the evening papers, swelled into such a roar when night came, as might have brought one to believe that a solitary watcher on the gallery above the Dome of Saint Paul's would have perceived the night air to be laden with a heavy muttering of the name of Merdle, coupled with every variety of execration.

For the late Mr. Merdle's complaint was, simply, Forgery and Robbery. He, the uncouth object of such wide-spread adulation, the sitter at great men's feasts, the roc's egg of great ladies' assemblies, the subduer of exclusiveness, the leveler of pride, the patron of patrons, the bargain-driver with a minister for Lordships of the Circumlocution Office, the recipient of more acknowledgment within some twenty years, at most, than had been bestowed in any land upon all the principal public benefactors, and upon all the leaders of all the Arts and Sciences, with their works to testify for them, during two centuries at least—he, the shining wonder, the next constellation to be followed by the wise men bringing gifts, until it stopped over certain carrion in a bath and disappeared, was simply the greatest Forger and the greatest Thief that ever cheated the gallows.

CHAPTER LXII.

REAPING THE WHIRLWIND.

WITH a precursory sound of huried breath and hurried feet, Mr. Pancks rushed into Arthur Clennam's Counting-house. The Inquest was over, the letter was public, the Bank was broken, the other model structures of straw had taken fire and were turned to smoke. The admired piratical ship had blown up in the midst of a vast fleet of ships of all rates, and boats of all sizes; and on the deep was nothing but ruin; nothing but burning hulls, bursting magazines, great guns self-exploded, tearing fiends and neighbors to pieces, drowning men clinging to unseaworthy spars and going down every minute, spent swimmers, floating dead, and sharks.

The usual diligence and order of the Counting-house at the works were overthrown with so much more. Unopened letters and unsorted papers lay strewn about the desk. In the midst of these tokens of prostrated energy and dismissed hope, the master of the Counting-house stood idle in his usual place, with his arms crossed on the desk, and his head bowed down upon them.

Mr. Pancks rushed in and saw him, and stood still. In another minute, Mr. Pancks's arms were on the desk, and Mr. Pancks's head was bowed upon them, and for some time they remained in these attitudes, idle and silent, with the width of the little room between them.

Mr. Pancks was the first to lift up his head and speak.

"I persuaded you to it, Mr. Clennam. I know it. Say what you will. You can't say more to me than I say to myself. You can't say more than I deserve."

"Oh, Pancks, Pancks!" returned Clennam, "don't speak of deserving. What do I, myself, deserve?"

"Better luck," said Pancks.

"I," pursued Clennam, without attending to him, "who have

ruined my partner! Pancks, Pancks, I have ruined Doyce! The honest, self-helpful, indefatigable old man, who has worked his way all through his life; the man who has contended against so much disappointment, and who has brought out of it such a good and trusting nature; the man I have felt so much for and hoped (and meant) to be so true and useful to; I have ruined him—brought him to shame and disgrace—ruined him, ruined him!"

The agony into which the reflection wrought his mind was so distressing to see, that Mr. Pancks took hold of himself by the hair of his head, and tore it in desperation at the spectacle.

"Reproach me!" cried Pancks. "Reproach me, sir, or I'll do myself an injury. Say, You fool, you villain. Say, Ass, how could you do it; Beast, what did you mean by it! Catch hold of me somewhere! Say something abusive to me!" All the time Mr. Pancks was tearing at his tough hair in a most pitiless and cruel manner.

"If you had never yielded to this fatal mania, Pancks," said Clennam, more in commiseration than retaliation, "it would have been how much better for you, and how much better for me!"

"At me again, sir!" cried Pancks, grinding his teeth in remorse. "At me again!"

"If you had never gone into those accursed calculations, and brought out your results with such abominable clearness," groaned Clennam, "it would have been how much better for you, Pancks, and how much better for me!"

"At me again, sir!" exclaimed Pancks, loosening his hold of his hair; "at me again, and again!"

Clennam, however, finding him already beginning to be pacified, had said all he wanted to say, and more. He wrung his hand, only adding, "Blind leaders of the blind, Pancks! Blind leaders of the blind! But Doyce, Doyce, Doyce; my injured partner!" That brought his head down on the desk again.

Their former attitudes and their former silence were once more first encroached upon by Pancks.

"Not been to bed, sir, since it began to get about. Been

high and low, on the chance of finding some hope of saving cinders from the fire. All is vain. All gone. All vanished."

"I know it," returned Clennam, "too well."

Mr. Pancks filled up a pause with a groan that came out of the very depths of his soul.

"Only yesterday, Pancks," said Arthur; "only yesterday, Monday, I had the fixed intention of selling, realizing, and making an end of it."

"I can't say as much for myself, sir," returned Pancks. "Though it's wonderful how many people I've heard of who were going to realize yesterday, of all days in the three hundred and sixty-five, if it hadn't been too late!"

His steam-like breathings, usually droll in their effect, were more tragic than so many groans, while, from head to foot, he was in that begrimed, besmeared, neglected state that he might have been an authentic portrait of Misfortune, which could scarcely be discerned through its want of cleaning.

"Mr. Clennam, had you laid out—every thing?" He got over the break before the last word, and also brought out the last word itself with great difficulty.

"Every thing."

Mr. Pancks took hold of his tough hair again, and gave it such a wrench that he pulled out several prongs of it. After looking at these with an eye of wild hatred, he put them in his pocket.

"My course," said Clennam, brushing away some tears that had been silently dropping down his face, "must be taken at once. What wretched amends I can make must be made. I must clear my unfortunate partner's reputation. I must retain nothing for myself. I must resign to our creditors the power of management I have so much abused: and I must work out as much of my fault—or crime—as is susceptible of being worked out, in the rest of my days."

"Is it impossible, sir, to tide over the present?"

"Out of the question. Nothing can be tided over now, Pancks. The sooner the business can pass out of my hands the better for it. There are engagements to be met, this week, which would of themselves bring the catastrophe, even if I would postpone it for a day, by going on for that space, secretly knowing what I know. All last night I thought of what I would do; what remains, is to do it."

"Not entirely of yourself?" said Pancks, whose face was as damp as if his steam were turning into water as fast as he dismally blew it off. "Have some legal help."

"Perhaps I had better."

"Have Rugg."

"There is not much to do. He will do it as well as another."

"Shall I fetch Rugg, Mr. Clennam?"

"If you could spare the time. I should be much obliged to you."

Mr. Pancks put on his hat that moment, and steamed away to Pentonville. While he was gone, Arthur never raised his head from the desk, but remained in that one position; repentant, self-accused, and convicted.

Mr. Pancks brought his friend and professional adviser, Mr. Rugg, back with him. Mr. Rugg had had such ample experience on the road of Mr. Pancks's being at that present in an impracticable state of mind, that he opened his professional mediation by requesting that gentleman to take himself out of the way. Mr. Pancks, crushed and submissive, obeyed.

"He is not unlike what my daughter was, sir, when we began the Breach of Promise action of Rugg and Dawkins, in which she was Plaintiff," said Mr. Rugg. "He takes too strong and direct an interest in the case. His feelings are worked upon. There is no getting on in our profession with feelings, sir."

As he pulled off his gloves and put them in his hat, he saw, in a side glance or two, that a great change had come over his client.

"I am sorry to perceive, sir," said Mr. Rugg, "that you have been allowing your own feelings to be worked upon. Now, pray don't, pray don't. These losses are much to be deplored, sir, but we must look 'em in the face."

"If the money I have sacrificed had been all my own, Mr. Rugg," said Mr. Clennam, "I should have cared far less."

"Indeed, sir?" said Mr. Rugg, with a cheerful air. "You surprise me. That's singular, sir. I have generally found in my experience that it's their own money people are most particular about. I have seen people get rid of a good deal of other people's money, and bear it very well—very well indeed."

With these comforting remarks, Mr. Rugg seated himself on an office-stool at the desk, and proceeded to business.

"Now, Mr. Clennam, by your leave, let us go into the matter. Let us see the state of the case. The question is simple. The question is the usual plain straightforward common-sense question. What can we do for ourself? What can we do for ourself?"

"That is not the question with me, Mr. Rugg," said Arthur. "You mistake it in the beginning. It is, what can I do for my partner—how can I best make reparation to him?"

"I am afraid, sir, do you know," argued Mr. Rugg, persuasively, "that you are still allowing your feelings to be worked upon? I don't like the term 'reparation,' sir, except as a lever in the hands of counsel. Will you excuse my saying that I feel it my duty to offer you the caution that you really must not allow your feelings to be worked upon?"

"Mr. Rugg," said Clennam, nerving himself to go through with what he had resolved upon, and surprising that gentleman by appearing, in his despondency, to have a settled determination of purpose, "you give me the impression that you will not be much disposed to adopt the course I have made up my mind to take. If your disapproval of it should render you unwilling to discharge such business as it necessitates, I am sorry for it, and must seek other aid. But I will represent to you at once, that to argue against it with me is useless."

"Very good, sir," answered Mr. Rugg, shrugging his shoulders. "Very good, sir. Since the business is to be done by some hands, let it be done by mine. Such was my principle in the case of Rugg and Dawkins. Such is my principle in most cases."

Clennam then proceeded to state to Mr. Rugg his fixed resolution. He told Mr. Rugg that his partner was a man of rare simplicity and integrity, and that in all he meant to do he was guided above all things by a knowledge of his partner's character, and a respect for his feelings. He explained that his partner was then absent on an enterprise of great importance, and that it particularly behooved himself publicly to accept the blame of what he had rashly done, and publicly to exonerate his partner from all participation in the responsibility of it, lest the successful conduct of that enterprise should be endangered by the slightest suspicion wrongfully attaching to his partner's honor and credit in another country. He told Mr. Rugg that to clear his partner morally, to the fullest extent, and publicly and unreservedly to declare that he, Arthur Clennam, of that Firm, had of his own sole act, and even expressly against his partner's caution, embarked its resources in the swindles that had lately perished, was the only real atonement within his power, was a better atonement to the particular man than it would be to very many men, and was therefore the atonement he had first to make. With this view, his intention was to print a declaration to the foregoing effect, which he had already drawn up, and besides circulating it among all who had dealings with the House, to advertise it in the public papers. Concurrently with this measure (the description of which cost Mr. Rugg innumerable wry faces and great uneasiness in his limbs), he would address a letter to all the creditors, exonerating his partner in a solemn manner, informing them of the stoppage of the House until their pleasure could be known and his partner communicated with, and humbly submitting himself to their direction. If, through their consideration for his partner's innocence, the affairs could ever be got into such train as that the business could be profitably resumed, and its present downfall overcome, then his own share in it would revert to his partner, as the only reparation he could make to him in money value for the distress and loss he had unhappily brought upon him, and he himself, at as small a salary as he could live upon, would ask to be allowed to serve it as a faithful clerk.

Though Mr. Rugg saw plainly that there was no preventing this from being done, still the wryness of his face and the uneasiness of his limbs so sorely required the propitiation of a Protest, that he made one. "I offer no objection, sir," said he, "I argue no point with you. I will carry out your views, sir; but under protest." Mr. Rugg then stated, not without prolixity, the heads of his protest. These were, in effect, Because the whole town, or he might say the whole country, was in the first madness of the late discovery, and the resentment against the unfortunate victims would be very strong; those who had not been deluded being certain to wax exceedingly wroth with them for not having been as wise as they were; and those who had been deluded being certain to find excuses and reasons for themselves, of which they were equally certain to see that other sufferers were wholly devoid; not to mention the great probability of every individual sufferer persuading himself, to his violent indignation, that but for the example of all the other sufferers he never would have put himself in the way of suffering. Because such a declaration as Clennam's, made at such a time, would certainly draw down upon him a storm of animosity, rendering it impossible to calculate on forbearance in the creditors, or even on unanimity among them, and exposing him a solitary target to a straggling cross-fire, which might bring him down from half a dozen quarters at once.

To all this Clennam merely replied that, granting the whole protest, nothing in it lessened the force, or could lessen the force, of the voluntary and public exoneration of his partner. He therefore, once for all, requested Mr. Rugg's immediate aid in getting the business dispatched. Upon that, Mr. Rugg fell to work; and Arthur, retaining no property to himself but his clothes and books, and a little loose money, placed his small private banker's account with the papers of the business.

The disclosure was made, and the storm raged fiercely. Thousands of people were wildly staring about for somebody alive to heap reproaches on; and this notable case, courting publicity, set the living somebody so much wanted on a scaffold. When people who had nothing to do with the case were so sensible of its flagrancy, people who lost money by it could scarcely be expected to deal mildly with it. Letters of reproach and invective showered in from the creditors; and Mr. Rugg, who sat upon the high stool every day and read them all, informed his client, within a week, that he feared there were writs out.

"I must take the consequences of what I have done," said Clennam. "The writs will find me here."

On the very next morning, as he was turning into Bleeding-Heart Yard by Mrs. Plornish's corner, Mrs. Plornish stood at the door waiting for him, and mysteriously besought him to step into Happy Cottage. There he found Mr. Rugg.

"I thought I'd wait for you here. I wouldn't go on to the Counting-house this morning if I was you, sir."

"Why not, Mr. Rugg?"

"There are as many as five out, to my knowledge."

"It can not be too soon over," said Clennam. "Let them take me, for Heaven's sake."

"Yes, but," said Mr. Rugg, getting between him and the door, "hear reason, hear reason. They'll take you soon enough, Mr. Clennnan, I don't doubt; but, hear reason. It almost always happens in these cases that some insignificant matter pushes itself in front and makes much of itself. Now, I find there's a little one out—a mere Palace Court jurisdiction—and I have reason to believe that a caption may be made upon that. I wouldn't be taken upon that."

"Why not?" asked Clennam.

"I'd be taken on a full-grown one, sir," said Mr. Rugg. "It's as well to keep up appearances. As your professional adviser, I should prefer your being taken on a writ from one of the superior courts, if you have no objection to do me that favor. It looks better."

"Mr. Rugg," said Arthur, in his dejection, "my only wish is, that it should be over. I will go on, and take my chance."

"Another word of reason, sir!" cried Mr. Rugg. "Now, this *is* reason. The other may be taste; but this is reason. If you should be taken on the little one, sir, you would go to the Marshalsea. Now, you know what the Marshalsea is. Very close. Excessively confined. Whereas in the King's Bench—" Mr. Rugg waved his right hand freely, as expressing abundance of space.

"I would rather," said Clennam, "be taken to the Marshalsea than to any other prison."

"Do you say so indeed, sir?" returned Mr. Rugg. "Then this is taste, too, and we may be walking."

He was a little offended at first, thongh he soon overlooked it. They walked through the Yard to the other end. The Bleeding Hearts were more interested in Arthur since his reverses than formerly: now regarding him as one who was true to the place and had taken up his freedom. Many of them came out to look after him, and to observe to one another with great unctuousness that he was "pulled down by it." Mrs. Plorish and her father stood at the top of the steps at their own end, much depressed and shaking their heads.

There was nobody visible in waiting when Arthur and Mr. Rugg arrived at the Counting-house. But an elderly member of the Jewish persuasion preserved in rum followed them close, and looked in at the glass before Mr. Rugg had opened one of the day's letters. "Oh!" said Mr. Rugg, looking up. "How do you do? Step in.—Mr. Clennam, I think this is the gentleman I was mentioning."

The gentleman explained the object of his visit to be "a trifling madder o' bithznithz," and executed his legal function.

"Shall I accompany you, sir?" said Mr. Rugg politely, rubbing his hands.

"I would rather go alone, thank you," Clennam answered. "Be so good as send me my clothes." Mr. Rugg, in a light airy way, replied in the affirmative, and shook hands with him. He and his attendant then went down stairs, got into the first conveyance they found, and drove to the old gates.

"Where I little thought, God forgive me," said Clennam to himself, "that I should ever enter thus!"

Mr. Chivery was on the Lock, and Young John was in the Lodge; either newly released from it, or waiting to take his own spell of duty. Both were more astonished on seeing who the new prisoner was than one might have thought turnkeys would have been. The elder Mr. Chivery shook hands with him in a shamefaced kind of way, and said, "I don't call to mind, sir, as I was ever less glad to see you." The younger Mr. Chivery, more distant, did not shake hands with him at all; he stood looking at him in a state of indecision so observable that it even came within the observation of Clennam with his heavy eyes and heavy heart. Presently afterward, Young John disappeared into the jail.

As Clennam knew enough of the place to know that he was required to remain in the Lodge a certain time, he took a seat in a corner, and feigned to be occupied with the persual of letters from his pocket. They did not so engross his attention, however, but that he saw with gratitude how the elderly Mr. Chivery kept the Lodge clear of prisoners; how he signed to some, with his keys, not to come in, and how he nudged others with his elbow to go out, and how he made his misery as easy to him as he could.

He was sitting with his eyes fixed on the floor, recalling the past, brooding over the present, and not attending to either, when he felt himself touched upon the shoulder. It was by Young John; and he said, "You can come now."

He got up and followed Young John. When they had gone a step or two within the inner iron gate, Young John said to him:

"You want a room. I have got you one."

"I thank you heartily."

Young John turned about again, and took him in at the old door-way, up the old stair-case, into the old room. Arthur stretched out his hand. Young John looked at it, looked at him—sternly, and yet with his tears in his eyes—swelled, choked, and said:

"I don't know as I can. No, I find I can't. But I thought you'd like the room, and here it is for you."

Surprise at this behavior yielded when he was gone (he went away) directly to the feelings which the empty room awakened in Clennam's wounded breast, and to the crowding associations with the one good and gentle creature who had sanctified it. Her absence in his altered fortunes made it, and him in it, so very desolate and so much in need of such a spirit of love and truth, that he turned his face against the wall to weep, and sobbed out, as his heart relieved itself, "Oh, my Little Dorritt!"

CHAPTER LXIII.

THE PUPIL OF THE MARSHALSEA.

THE day was sunny, and the Marshalsea, with the hot noon striking upon it, was unwontedly quiet. Arthur Clennam dropped into a solitary arm-chair, itself as faded as any debtor in the jail, and yielded himself to his thoughts.

In the unnatural peace of having gone through the dreaded arrest, and got there—the first change of feeling which the prison most commonly induced, and from which dangerous resting-place so many men had slipped down to the depths of degradation and disgrace, by so many ways—he could think of some passages in his life, almost as if he were removed from them into another state of existence. Taking into account where he was, the interest that had first brought him there when he had been free to keep away, and the gentle presence that was equally inseparable from the walls and bars about him, and from the impalpable remembrances of his later life which no walls nor bars could imprison, it was not remarkable that every thing his memory turned upon should bring him round again to Little Dorrit. Yet it was remarkable to him, not because of the fact itself, but because of the reminder it brought with it, how much that dear little creature had influenced his better resolutions.

None of us clearly know to whom or to what we are indebted in this wise, until some marked stoppage in the whirling wheel of life brings the right perception with it. It comes with sickness, it comes with sorrow, it comes with the loss of the dearly loved, it is one of the most frequent uses of adversity. It came to Clennam in his adversity, strongly and tenderly. "When I first gathered myself together," he thought, "and set something like purpose before my jaded eyes, whom had I before me, toiling on, for a good object's sake, without encouragement, without notice, against ignoble obstacles, that would have turned an army of received heroes and heroines? One weak girl! When

I tried to conquer my misplaced love, and to be generous to the man who was more fortunate than I, though he should never know it or repay me with a gracious word, in whom had I watched patience, self-denial, self-subdual, charitable construction, the noblest generosity of the affections? In the same pure girl! If I, a man, with a man's advantages and means and energies, had slighted the whisper in my heart that, if my father had erred, it was my first duty to conceal the fault and to repair it, what youthful figure with tender feet going almost bare on the damp ground, with spare hands ever working, with its slight shape but half protected from the sharp weather, would have stood before me to put me to shame? My Little Dorrit's." Thus always, as he sat alone in the faded chair, thinking. Always, Little Dorrit. Until it seemed to him as if he met the reward of having wandered away from her, and suffered any thing to pass between him and his remembrance of her virtues.

His door was opened, and the head of the elder Chivery was put in a very little way, without being turned toward him.

"I am off the Lock, Mr. Clennam, and going out. Can I do any thing for you?"

"Many thanks. Nothing."

"You'll excuse me opening the door," said Mr. Chivery; "but I couldn't make you hear."

"Did you knock?"

"Half a dozen times."

Rousing himself, Clennam observed that the prison had awakened from its noontide doze, that the inmates were loitering about the shady yard, and that it was late in the afternoon. He had been thinking for hours.

"Your things is come," said Mr. Chivery, "and my son is going to carry 'em up. I should have sent 'em up, but for his wishing to carry 'em himself. Indeed he would have 'em himself, and so I couldn't send 'em up. Mr. Clennan, could I say a word to you?"

"Pray come in," said Arthur; for Mr. Chivery's head was still put in at the door a very little way, and Mr. Chivery had but one ear upon him, instead of both eyes. This was native delicacy in Mr. Chivery—true politeness; though his exterior had very much of a turnkey about it, and not the least of a gentleman.

"Thank you, sir," said Mr. Chivery, without advancing; "it's no odds me coming in. Mr. Clennam, don't you take no notice of my son (if you'll be so good), in case you find him cut up anyways difficult. My son has a art, and my son's art is in the right place. Me and his mother knows where to find it, and we find it sitiwated correct."

With this incomprehensible speech, Mr. Chivery took his ear away, and shut the door. He might have been gone ten minutes, when his son succeeded him.

"Here's your portmanteau," he said to Arthur, putting it carefully down.

"It's very kind of you. I am ashamed that you should have the trouble."

He was gone before it came to that, but soon returned, saying, exactly as before, "Here's your black box;" which he also put down with care.

"I am very sensible of this attention to a prisoner. I hope we may shake hands now, Mr. John."

Young John, however, drew back, turning his right wrist in a socket made of his left thumb and middle finger, and said, as he had said at first, "I don't know as I can. No; I find I can't!" He then stood regarding the prisoner sternly, though with a swelling humor in his eyes that looked like water.

"Why are you angry with me," said Clennam, "and yet so ready to do me these kind services? There must be some mistake between us. If I have done any thing to occasion it, I am sorry."

"No mistake, sir," returned John, turning the wrist backward and forward in the socket, for which it was rather tight. "No mistake, sir, in the feelings with which my eyes behold you at the present moment! If I was at all fairly equal to your weight, Mr. Clennam—which I am not; and if you weren't under a cloud—which you are; and if it wasn't against all rules of the Marshalsea—which it is; those feelings are such, that they would stimulate me, more to having it out with you in a round on the present spot, than to any thing else I could name."

Arthur looked at him for a moment in some wonder, and some little anger. "Well, well!" he said. "A mistake, a mistake!" Turning away, he sat down, with a heavy sigh, in in the faded chair again.

Young John followed him with his eyes, and, after a short pause, cried out, "I beg your pardon!"

"Freely granted," said Clennam, waving his hand, without raising his sunken head. "Say no more. I am not worth it."

"This furniture, sir," said Young John, in a voice of mild and soft explanation, "belongs to me. I am in the habit of letting it out to parties without furniture, that have the room. It ain't much, but it's at your service. Free, I mean. I could not think of letting you have it on any other terms. You're welcome to it for nothing, sir."

Arthur raised his head again to thank him, and to say he could not accept the favor. John was still turning his wrist, and still contending with himself in his former divided manner.

"What is the matter between us?" said Arthur.

"I decline to name it, sir," returned Young John, suddenly turning loud and sharp. "Nothing's the matter."

Arthur looked at him again, in vain, for any explanation of his behavior. After a while, Arthur turned away his head again. Young John said, presently afterward, with the utmost mildness:

"The little round table, sir, that's nigh your elbow, was—you know whose—I needn't mention him—he died a great gentleman. I bought it of an individual that he gave it to, and that lived here after him. But the individual wasn't any ways equal to him. Most individuals would find it hard to come up to his level."

Arthur drew the little table nearer, rested his arm upon it, and kept it there.

"Perhaps you may not be aware, sir," said Young John, "that I intruded upon him when he was over here in London. On the whole he was of opinion that it *was* an intrusion, though he was so good as to ask me to sit down and to inquire after father and all other friends. Leastways humblest acquaintances. He looked, to me, a good deal changed, and I said so when I came back. I asked him if Miss Amy was well—"

"And she was?"

"I should have thought you would have known without putting the question to such as me," returned Young John, after appearing to take a large invisible pill. "Since you do put the question, I am sorry I can't answer it. But the fact is, he looked upon the inquiry as a liberty, and said, 'What was that to me?' It was then I became quite aware I was intruding; of which I had been fearful before. However, he spoke very handsome afterward; very handsome."

They were both silent for several minutes; except that Young John remarked, at about the middle of the pause, "He both spoke and acted very handsome."

It was again Young John who broke the silence by inquiring;

"If it's not a liberty, how long may it be your intentions, sir, to go without eating and drinking?"

"I have not felt the want of any thing yet," returned Clennam. "I have no appetite just now."

"The more reason why you should take some support, sir," urged Young John. "If you find yourself going on sitting here for hours and hours partaking of no refreshment, because you have no appetite, why then you should and must partake of refreshment without an appetite. I'm going to have tea in my own apartment. If it's not a liberty, please to come and take a cup. Or I can bring a tray here in two minutes."

Feeling that Young John would impose that trouble on himself if he refused, and also feeling anxious to show that he bore in mind both the elder Mr. Chivery's entreaty, and the younger Mr. Chivery's apology, Arthur rose and expressed his willingness to take a cup of tea in Mr. John's apartment. Young John locked his door for him as they went out, slid the key into his pocket with great dexterity, and led the way to his own residence.

It was at the top of the house nearest to the gateway. It was the room to which Clennam had hurried, on the day when the enriched family had left the prison forever, and where he had lifted her up insensible from the floor. He foresaw where they were going, as soon as their feet touched the staircase. The room was so far changed that it was papered now, and had been repainted, and was far more comfortably furnished;

but he could recall it just as he had seen it in that single glance, when he raised her from the ground and carried her down to the carriage.

Young John looked hard at him, biting his fingers.

"I see you recollect the room, Mr. Clennam?"

"I recollect it well, Heaven bless her!"

Oblivious of the tea, Young John continued to bite his fingers and to look at his visitor, as long as his visitor continued to glance about the room. Finally, he made a start at the tea-pot, gustily rattled a quantity of tea into it from a canister, and set off for the common kitchen to fill it with hot water.

The room was so eloquent to Clennam, in the changed circumstances of his return to the miserable Marshalsea—it spoke to him so mournfully of her, and of his loss of her—that it would have gone hard with him to resist it, even though he had not been alone. Alone, he did not try. He laid his hand on the insensible wall as tenderly as if it had been herself that he touched, and pronounced her name in a low voice. He stood at the window, looking over the prison-parapet with its grim spiked border, and from his soul he breathed a benediction through the summer haze toward the distant land where she was rich and prosperous.

Young John was some time absent, and, when he came back, showed that he had been outside by bringing with him fresh butter in a cabbage-leaf, some thin slices of boiled ham in another cabbage-leaf, and a little basket of water-cresses and salad herbs. When these were arranged upon the table to his satisfaction they sat down to tea.

Clennam tried to do honor to the meal, but unavailingly. The ham sickened him, the bread seemed to turn to sand in his mouth. He could force nothing upon himself but a cup of tea.

"Try a little something green," said Young John, handing him the basket.

He took a sprig or so of water-cress, and tried again; but the bread turned to a heavier sand than before, and the ham (though it was good enough of itself) seemed to blow a faint simoon of ham through the whole Marshalsea.

AT MR. JOHN CHIVERY'S TEA TAB E

"Try a little more something green, sir," said Young John, and again handed the basket.

It was so like handing green meat into the cage of a dull, imprisoned bird, and John had so evidently bought the little basket as a handful of fresh relief from the stale, hot paving-stones and bricks of the jail that Clennam said, with a smile, "It was very kind of you to think of putting this between the wires; but I can not even get this down to-day."

As if the difficulty were contagious, Young John soon pushed away his own plate, and fell to folding the cabbage-leaf that had contained the ham. When he had folded it into a number of layers, one over another, so that it was small in the palm of his hand, he began to flatten it between both his hands, and to eye Clennam attentively.

"I wonder," he at length said, compressing his green packet with some force, "that if it's not worth your while to take care of yourself for your own sake, it's not worth doing for some one else's."

"Truly," returned Arthur, with a sigh and a smile, "I don't know for whose."

"Mr. Clennam," said John, warmly, "I'm surprised that a gentleman who is capable of the straightforwardness that you are capable of, should be capable of the mean action of making me such an answer. Mr. Clennam, I am surprised that a gentleman who is capable of having a heart of his own should be capable of the heartlessness of treating mine in that way. I am astonished at it, sir. Really and truly, I am astonished!"

Having got upon his feet to emphasize his concluding words, Young John sat down again, and fell to rolling his green packet on his right leg, never taking his eyes off Clennam, but surveying him with a fixed look of indignant reproach.

"I had got over it, sir," said John. "I had conquered it, knowing that it *must* be conquered, and had come to the resolution to think no more about it. I shouldn't have given my mind to it again, I hope, if to this prison you had not been brought, and in an hour unfortunate for me, this day!" (In his agitation Young John adopted his mother's powerful construction of sentences.) "When you first came upon me, sir, in the Lodge, this day, more as if a Upastree had been made a capture of than a private defendant, such mingled streams of feelings broke loose again within me that every thing was for the first few minutes swept away before them, and I was going round and round in a vortex. I got out of it. I struggled, and got out of it. If it was the last word I had to speak, against that vortex with my utmost powers I strove, and out of it I came. I argued that if I had been rude apologies was due, and those apologies, without a question of demeaning, I did make. And now, when I've been so wishful to show that one thought is next to being a holy one with me and goes before all others—now, after all, you dodge me when I ever so gently hint at it, and evadingly throw me back upon myself. For, do not, sir," said Young John, "do not be so base as to deny that dodge you do, and thrown me back upon myself you have!"

All amazement, Arthur gazed at him, like one lost, only saying, "What is it? What do you mean, John?" But John being in that state of mind in which nothing would seem to be more impossible to a certain class of people than the giving of an answer, went ahead blindly.

"I hadn't," said John, "no, I hadn't, and I never had, the audaciousness to think, I am sure, that all was any thing but lost. I hadn't, no, why should I say I hadn't if I ever had, any hope that it was possible to be so blessed, not after the words that passed, not even if barriers insurmountable had not been raised! But is that a reason why I am to have no memory, why I am to have no thoughts, why I am to have no sacred spots, nor any thing?"

"What can you mean?" cried Arthur.

"It's all very well to trample on it, sir," John went on, scouring a very prairie of wild words, "if a person can make up his mind to be guilty of the action. It's all very well to trample on it, but it's there. It may be that it couldn't be trampled upon if it wasn't there. But that doesn't make it gentlemanly, that doesn't make it honorable, that doesn't justify throwing a person back upon himself after he has struggled and strived out of himself, like a butterfly. The world may sneer at a turnkey, but he's a man—when he isn't a woman, which among female criminals he's expected to be."

Ridiculous as the incoherence of his talk was, there was yet a truthfulness in Young John's simple, sentimental character, and a sense of being wounded in some very tender respect, expressed in his burning face and in the agitation of his voice and manner, which Arthur must have been cruel to disregard. He turned his thoughts back to the starting-point of this unknown injury; and in the mean time Young John, having rolled his green packet pretty round, cut it carefully into three pieces, and laid it on a plate as if it were some particular delicacy.

"It seems to me just possible," said Arthur, when he had retraced the conversation to the water-cresses and back again, "that you have made some reference to Miss Dorrit?"

"It is just possible, sir," returned John Chivery.

"I don't understand it. I hope I may not be so unlucky as to make you think I mean to offend you again, for I never have meant to offend you yet, when I say I don't understand it."

"Sir," said Young John, "will you have the perfidy to deny that you know, and long have known, that I felt toward Miss Dorrit, call it not the presumption of love, but adoration and sacrifice?"

"Indeed, John, I will not have any perfidy if I know it; why should you suspect me of it. I am at a loss to think. Did you ever hear from Mrs. Chivery, your mother, that I went to see her once?"

"No, sir," returned John, shortly. "Never heard of such a thing."

"But I did. Can you imagine why?"

"No, sir," returned John shortly. "I can't imagine why."

"I will tell you. I was solicitous to promote Miss Dorrit's happiness; and if I could have supposed that Miss Dorrit returned your affection—"

Poor John Chivery turned crimson to the tips of his ears. "Miss Dorrit never did, sir. I wish to be honorable and true, so far as in my humble way I can, and I would scorn to pretend for a moment that she ever did, or that she ever led me to believe she did; no, nor even that it was ever to be expected in any cool reason that she would or could. She was far above me in all respects at all times. As likewise," added John, "similarly was her gen-teel family."

His chivalrous feeling toward all that belonged to her made

him so very respectable, in spite of his small stature and his rather weak legs, and his very weak hair and his poetical temperament, that a Goliath might have sat in his place demanding less consideration at Arthur's hands.

"You speak, John," he said, with cordial admiration, "like a man."

"Well, sir," returned John, brushing his hand across his eyes, "then I wish you'd do the same."

He was quick with this unexpected retort, and it again made Arthur regard him with a wondering expression of face.

"Leastways," said John, stretching his hand across the tea-tray, "if too strong a remark, withdrawn! But, why not, why not? When I say to you, Mr. Clennam, take care of yourself for some one else's sake, why not be open, though a turnkey? Why did I get you the room which I knew you'd like best? Why did I carry up your things? Not that I found 'em heavy; I don't mention 'em on that accounts; far from it. Why have I cultivated you in the manner I have done since the morning? On the ground of your own merits? No. They're very great, I've no doubt at all; but not on the ground of them. Another's merits have had their weight, and have had far more weight with Me. Then why not speak free!"

"Unaffectedly, John," said Clennam, "you are so good a fellow, and I have so true a respect for your character, that if I have appeared to be less sensible than I really am, of the fact that the kind services you have rendered me to-day are attributable to my having been trusted by Miss Dorrit as her friend—I confess it to be a fault, and I ask your forgiveness."

"Oh! why not," John repeated, with returning scorn, "why not speak free?"

"I declare to you," returned Arthur, "that I don't understand you. Look at me. Consider the trouble I have been in. Is it likely that I would willfully add to my other self-reproaches, that of being ungrateful or treacherous to you? I do not understand you."

John's incredulous face slowly softened into a face of doubt. He rose, backed into the garret-window of the room, beckoned Arthur to come there, and stood looking at him thoughtfully with quivering lips.

"Mr. Clennam, do you mean to say that you don't know ?"

"What, John?"

"Lord," said Young John, appealing with a gasp to the spikes on the wall. "He says, What!"

Clennam looked at the spikes, and looked at John.

"He says, What! And what is more," exclaimed Young John, surveying him in a doleful maze, "he appears to mean it! Do you see this window, sir?"

"Of course, I see this window."

"See this room?"

"Why of course I see this room.'

"That wall opposite, and that yard down below? They have all been witnesses of it, from day to day, from night to night, from week to week, from month to month. For, how often have I seen Miss Dorrit here when she has not seen me!"

"Witnesses of what?" said Clennam.

"Of Miss Dorrit's love."

"For whom?"

"You!" said John. And touched him with the back of his hand upon the breast, and backed to his chair, and sat down in it with a pale face, holding the arms, and shaking his head at him.

If he had dealt Clennam a heavy blow, instead of laying that light touch upon him, its effect could not have been to shake him more. He stood amazed; his eyes looking at John; his lips parted, and seeming now and then to form the word "Me!" without uttering it; his hands dropped at his sides: his whole appearance that of a man who has been awakened from sleep, and stupefied by intelligence beyond his full comprehension.

"Me!" he at length said, aloud.

"Ah!" groaned Young John. "You!"

He did what he could to muster a smile, and returned, "Your fancy. You are completely mistaken."

"I mistaken, sir!" said Young John. "*I* completely mistaken on that subject! No, Mr. Clennam, don't tell me so. On any other, if you like, for I don't set up to be a penetrating character, and am well aware of my own deficiencies. But, *I* mistaken on a point that has caused me more smart in my breast than a flight of savages' arrows could have done! *I* mistaken on a point that almost sent me into my grave, as I sometimes wished it would, if the grave could only have been made compatible with the tobacco-business and father and mother's feelings! I mistaken on a point that, even at the present moment, makes me take out my pocket-handkercher like a great girl, as people say; though I am sure I don't know why a great girl should be a term of reproach, for every rightly constituted male mind loves 'em great and small! Don't tell me so, don't tell me so!"

Still highly respectable at bottom, though absurd enough upon the surface, Young John took out his pocket-handkerchief, with a genuine absence both of display and concealment, which is only to be seen in a man with a great deal of good in him, when he takes out his pocket-handkerchief for the purpose of wiping his eyes. Having dried them, and indulged in the harmless luxury of a sob and a sniff, he put it up again.

The touch was still in its influence so like a blow that Arthur could not get many words together to close the subject with. He assured John Chivery when he had returned his handkerchief to his pocket, that he did all honor to his disinterestedness and to the fidelity of his remembrance of Miss Dorrit. As to the impression on his mind, of which he had just relieved it—Here John interposed, and said, "No impression! certainty!"—as to that, they might perhaps speak of it at another time, but would say no more now. Feeling low-spirited and weary he would go back to his room, with John's leave, and come out no more that night. John assented, and he crept back in the shadow of the wall to his own lodging.

The feeling of the blow was still so strong upon him, that when the dirty old woman was gone whom he found sitting on the stairs outside his door waiting to make his bed, and who gave him to understand while doing it that she had received her instructions from Mr. Chivery—"not the old 'un but the young 'un," he sat down in the faded arm-chair, pressing his head between his hands as if he had been stunned. Little Dorrit love him! More bewildering to him than his misery, far.

Consider the improbability. He had been accustomed to call her his child, and his dear child, and to invite her confidence, by dwelling upon the difference in their respective ages, and to speak of himself as one who was turning old. Yet she might not have thought him old. Something reminded him that he had not thought himself so, until the roses had floated away upon the river.

He had her two letters among other papers in his box, and he took them out and read them. There seemed to be a sound in them like the sound of her sweet voice. It fell upon his ear with many tones of tenderness that were not insusceptible of the new meaning. Now it was that the quiet desolation of her answer, "No, No, No," made to him that night in that very room—that night, when he had been shown the dawn of her altered fortune, and when other words had passed between them which he had been destined to remember, in humiliation and a prisoner—rushed into his mind.

Consider the improbability.

But it had a preponderating tendency, when considered, to become fainter. There was another and a curious inquiry of his own heart's that concurrently became stronger. In the reluctance he had felt to believe that she loved any one; in his desire to set that question at rest; in a half-formed consciousness he had had that there would be a kind of nobleness in his helping her love for any one; was there no suppressed something on his own side that he had hushed as it arose? Had he ever whispered to himself that he must not think of such a thing as her loving him, that he must not take advantage of her gratitude; that he must keep his experience in remembrance as a warning and reproof; that he must regard such youthful hopes as having passed away, as his friend's dead daughter had passed away; that he must be steady in saying to himself that the time had gone by him, and he was too saddened and old?

He had kissed her when he lifted her from the ground, on the day when she had been so consistently and expressively forgotten. Quite as he might have kissed her if she had been conscious? No difference?

The darkness found him occupied with these thoughts. The darkness also found Mr. and Mrs. Plornish knocking at his door. They brought with them a basket, filled with choice selections from that stock in trade which met with such a quick sale, and produced such a slow return. Mrs. Plornish was affected to tears. Mr. Plornish amiably growled, in his philosophical but not lucid manner, that there was ups, you see, and there was downs. It was in wain to ask why ups, why downs; there they was, you know. He had heered it given for a truth that accordin' as the world went round, which round it did rewolve, undoubted, even the best of gentlemen must take his turn of standing with his 'ed upside down, and all his air a flying the wrong way, into what you might call Space. Wery well then. What Mr. Plornish said was, wery well then. The gentleman's 'ed would come up'ards when his turn come, that gentleman's air would be a pleasure to look upon, being all smooth again, and wery well then!

It has been already stated that Mrs. Plornish, not being philosophical, wept It further happened that Mrs. Plornish, not being philosophical, was intelligible. It may have arisen out of her softened state of mind, out of her sex's wit, out of a woman's quick association of ideas, or out of a woman's no association of ideas, but it further happened somehow that Mrs. Plornish's intelligibility displayed itself upon the very subject of Arthur's meditations.

"The way father has been talking about you, Mr. Clennam," said Mrs. Plornish, "you hardly would believe. It's made him quite poorly. As to his voice, this misfortune has took it away. You know what a sweet singer father is; but he couldn't get a note out for the children at tea, if you will credit what I tell you."

While speaking, Mrs. Plornish shook her head and wiped her eyes, and looked retrospectively about the room.

"As to Mr. Baptist," pursued Mrs. Plornish, "whatever he'll do when he comes to know of it, I can't conceive nor yet imagine. He'd have been here before now, you may be sure, but that he's away on confidential business of your own. The persevering manner in which he follows up that business, and gives himself no rest from it—it really do," said Mrs. Plornish, winding up in the Italian manner, "as I say to him, Mooshattonisha padrona."

Though not conceited, Mrs. Plornish felt that she had turned this Tuscan sentence with peculiar elegance. Mr. Plornish could not conceal his exultation in her accomplishments as a linguist.

"But what I say is, Mr. Clennam," the good woman went on, "there's always something to be thankful for, as I am sure you will yourself admit. Speaking in this room, it's not hard to think what the present something is. It's a thing to be thankful for, indeed, that Miss Dorrit is not here to know it."

Arthur thought she looked at him with a particular expression.

"It's a thing," reiterated Mrs. Plornish, "to be thankful for, indeed, that Miss Dorrit is far away. It's to be hoped she is not likely to hear of it. If she had been here to see it, sir, it's not to be doubted that the sight of you," Mrs. Plornish repeated those words—"not to be doubted that the sight of *you*—in misfortune and trouble, would have been almost too much for her affectionate heart. There's nothing I can think of that would have touched Miss Dorrit so bad as that."

Of a certainty, Mrs. Plornish did look at him now, with a sort of quivering defiance in her friendly emotion.

"Yes!" said she. "And it shows what notice father takes, though at his time of life, that he says to me, this afternoon, which Happy Cottage knows I neither make it up nor anyways enlarge, 'Mary, it's much to be rejoiced in that Miss Dorrit is not on the spot to behold it.' Those were father's words. Father's own words was 'Much to be rejoiced in, Mary, that Miss Dorrit is not on the spot to behold it.' I says to father then, I says to him, 'Father, you are right!' That" Mrs. Plornish concluded with the air of a very precise legal witness, "is what passed betwixt father and me. And I tell you nothing but what did pass betwixt me and father."

Mr. Plornish, as being of a more laconic temperament, embraced this opportunity of interposing with the suggestion that she should now leave Mr. Clennam to himself. "For, you see," said Mr. Plornish, gravely, "I know what it is, old gal;" repeating that valuable remark several times, as if it appeared to him to include some great moral secret. Finally the worthy couple went away arm in arm.

Little Dorrit, Little Dorrit. Again for hours. Always Little Dorrit!

Happily, if it ever had been so, it was over, and better over. Granted, that she had loved him, and he had known it and had suffered himself to love her, what a road to have led her away upon—the road that would have brought her back to this miserable place! He ought to be much comforted by the reflection that she was quit of it forever; that she was, or would soon be, married (vague rumors of her father's projects in that direction had reached Bleeding Heart Yard, with the news of her sister's marriage); and that the Marshalsea gate had shut forever on all those perplexed possibilities of a time that was gone.

Dear Little Dorrit!

Looking back upon his own poor story, she was its vanishing point. Every thing in its perspective led to her innocent figure. He had traveled thousands of miles toward it; previous unquiet hopes and doubts had worked themselves out before it; it was the centre of the interest of his life; it was the termination of every thing that was good and pleasant in it; beyond there was nothing but mere waste, and darkened sky.

As ill at ease as on the first night of his lying down to sleep within those dreary walls, he wore the night out with such thoughts. What time, Young John lay wrapt in peaceful slumber, after composing and arranging the following monumental inscription on his pillow:

STRANGER!
RESPECT THE TOMB OF
JOHN CHIVERY, JUNIOR,
WHO DIED AT AN ADVANCED AGE
NOT NECESSARY TO MENTION.
HE ENCOUNTERED HIS RIVAL, IN A DISTRESSED STATE,
AND FELT INCLINED
TO HAVE A ROUND WITH HIM;
BUT, FOR THE SAKE OF THE LOVED ONE,
CONQUERED THOSE FEELINGS OF BITTERNESS,
AND BECAME
MAGNANIMOUS.

CHAPTER LXIV.

AN APPEARANCE IN THE MARSHALSEA.

THE opinion of the community outside the prison gates bore hard on Clennam as time went on, and he made no friends among the community within. Too depressed to associate with the herd in the yard, who got together to forget their cares, too retiring and too unhappy to join in the poor socialities of the tavern, he kept his own room, and was held in distrust. Some said he was proud; some objected that he was sullen and reserved; some were contemptuous of him, for that he was a poor-spirited dog who pined under his debts. The whole population were shy of him on these various counts of indictment, but especially the last, which involved a species of domestic treason; and he soon became so confirmed in his seclusion, that his only time for walking up and down was when the evening Club were assembled at their songs, and toasts, and sentiments, and when the yard was nearly left to the women and children.

Imprisonment began to tell upon him. He knew that he idled and moped. After what he had known of the influences of imprisonment within the four small walls of the very room he occupied, this consciousness made him afraid of himself. Shrinking from the observation of other men, and shrinking from his own, he began to change very sensibly. Any body might see that the shadow of the wall was dark upon him.

One day, when he might have been some ten or twelve weeks in jail, and when he had been trying to read, and had not been able to release even the imaginary people of the book from the Marshalsea, a footstep stopped at his door, and a hand tapped at it. He arose and opened it, and an agreeable voice accosted him with, "How do you do, Mr. Clennam? I hope I am not unwelcome in calling to see you."

It was the sprightly young Barnacle, Ferdinand. He looked

very good-natured and prepossessing, though overpoweringly gay and free, in contrast with the squalid prison.

"You are surprised to see me, Mr. Clennam," he said, taking the seat which Clennam offered him.

"I must confess to being much surprised."

"Not disagreeably, I hope?"

"By no means."

"Thank you. Frankly," said the engaging young Barnacle, "I have been excessively sorry to hear that you were under the necessity of a temporary retirement here, and I hope (of course as between two private gentlemen) that our place has had nothing to do with it?"

"Your office?"

"Our Circumlocution place."

"I can not charge any part of my reverses upon that remarkable establishment."

"Upon my life," said the vivacious young Barnacle, "I am heartily glad to know it. It is quite a relief to me to hear you say it. I should have so exceedingly regretted our place having had any thing to do with your difficulties."

Clennam again assured him that he absolved it of the responsibility.

"That's right," said Ferdinand. "I am very happy to hear it. I was rather afraid in my own mind that we might have helped to floor you, because there is no doubt that it is our misfortune to do that kind of thing now and then. We don't want to do do it; but if men will be graveled, why—we can't help it."

"Without giving an unqualified assent to what you say," returned Arthur, gloomily, "I am much obliged to you for your interest in me."

"No, but really! Our place is," said the easy young Barnacle, "the most inoffensive place possible. You'll say we are a Humbug. I won't say we are not; but all that sort of thing is intended to be, and must be. Don't you see?"

"I do not," said Clennam.

"You don't regard it from the right point of view. It is the point of view that is the essential thing. Regard our place from the point of view that we only ask you to leave us alone, and we are as capital a Department as you'll find any where."

"Is your place there to be left alone?" asked Clennam.

"You exactly hit it," returned Ferdinand. "It is there with the express intention that every thing shall be left alone. That is what it means. That is what it's for. No doubt there's a certain form to be kept up that it's for something else, but it's only a form. Why, good Heaven, we are nothing but forms! Think what a lot of our forms you have gone through. And you have never got any nearer to an end?"

"Never!" said Clennam.

"Look at it from the right point of view, and there you have us—official and effectual. It's like a limited game of cricket. A field of outsiders are always going in to bowl at the Public Service, and we block the balls."

Clennam asked what became of the bowlers? The airy Young Barnacle replied that they grew tired, got dead beat, got lamed, got their backs broken, died off, gave it up, went in for other games.

"And this occasions me to congratulate myself again," he pursued, "on the circumstance that our place has had nothing to do with your temporary retirement. It very easily might have had a hand in it; because it is undeniable that we are sometimes a most unlucky place, in our effects upon people who will not leave us alone. Mr. Clennam, I am quite unreserved with you. As between yourself and myself, I know I may be. I was so, when I first saw you making the mistake of not leaving us alone; because I perceived that you were inexperienced and sanguine, and had—I hope you'll not object to my saying—some simplicity?"

"Not at all."

"Some simplicity. Therefore I felt what a pity it was, and I went out of my way to hint to you (which really was not official, but I never am official when I can help it), something to the effect that if I were you, I wouldn't bother myself. However, you did bother yourself, and you have since bothered yourself. Now, don't do it any more."

"I am not likely to have the opportunity," said Clennam.

"Oh yes, you are! You'll leave here. Every body leaves

here. There are no ends of ways of leaving here. Now, don't come back to us. That entreaty is the second object of my call. Pray, don't come back to us. Upon my honor," said Ferdinand, in a very friendly and confiding way, "I shall be greatly vexed if you don't take warning by the past and keep away from us."

"And the invention?" said Clennam.

"My good fellow," returned Ferdinand, "if you'll excuse the freedom of that form of address, nobody wants to know of the invention, and nobody cares twopence-halfpenny about it."

"Nobody in the Office, that is to say?"

"Nor out of it. Every body is ready to dislike and ridicule any invention. You have no idea how many people want to be left alone. You have no idea how the Genius of the country (overlook the Parliamentary nature of the phrase, and don't be bored by it) tends to being left alone. Believe me, Mr. Clennam," said the sprightly young Barnacle, in his pleasantest manner, "our place is not a wicked Giant to be charged at full tilt; but, only a windmill showing you, as it grinds immense quantities of chaff, which way the country wind blows."

"If I could believe that," said Clennam, "it would be a dismal prospect for all of us."

"Oh! Don't say so!" returned Ferdinand. "It's all right. We must have humbug, we all like humbug, we couldn't get on without humbug. A little humbug and a groove, and every thing goes on admirably, if you leave it alone."

With this hopeful confession of his faith as the head of the rising Barnacles who were born of woman, to be followed under a variety of watchwords which they utterly repudiated and disbelieved, Ferdinand rose. Nothing could be more agreeable than his frank and courteous bearing, or adapted with a more gentlemanly instinct to the circumstances of his visit.

"Is it fair to ask," he said, as Clennam gave him his hand with a real feeling of thankfulness for his candor and good humor, "whether it is true that our late lamented Merdle is the cause of this passing inconvenience?"

"I am one of the many he has ruined. Yes."

"He must have been an exceedingly clever fellow," said Ferdinand Barnacle.

Arthur, not being in a mood to extol the memory of the deceased, was silent.

"A consummate rascal, of course," said Ferdinand, "but remarkably clever! One can not help admiring the fellow. Must have been such a master of humbug. Knew people so well—got over them so completely—did so much with them!"

In his easy way, he was really moved to genuine admiration.

"I hope," said Arthur, "that he and his dupes may be a warning to people not to have so much done with them again."

"My dear Mr. Clennam," returned Ferdinand, laughing, "have you really such a verdant hope? The next man who has as large a capacity and as genuine a taste for swindling, will succeed as well. Pardon me, but I think you really have no idea how the human bees will swarm to the beating of any old tin kettle; in that fact lies the complete manual of governing them. When they can be got to believe that the kettle is made of the precious metals, in that fact lies the whole power of men like our late lamented. No doubt there are, here and there," said Ferdinand, politely, "exceptional cases, where people have been taken in for what appeared to them to be much better reasons; and I need not go far to find such a case; but they don't invalidate the rule. Good-day! I hope that when I have the pleasure of seeing you next, this passing cloud will have given place to sunshine. Don't come a step beyond the door. I know the way out perfectly. Good-day!"

With those words, the best and brightest of the Barnacles went down stairs, hummed his way through the Lodge, mounted his horse in the front court-yard, and rode off to keep an appointment with his noble kinsman; who wanted a little coaching before he could triumphantly answer certain infidel Snobs, who were going to question the Nobs about their statesmanship.

He must have passed Mr. Rugg on his way out, for, a minute or two afterward, that ruddy-headed gentleman shone in at the door like an elderly Phœbus.

"How do you do to-day, sir?" said Mr. Rugg. "Is there any little thing I can do for you to-day, sir?"

"No, I thank you."

Mr. Rugg's enjoyment of embarrassed affairs was like a housekeeper's enjoyment in pickling and preserving, or a washerwoman's enjoyment of a heavy wash, or a dustman's enjoyment of an overflowing dust-binn, or any other professional enjoyment of a mess in the way of business.

"I still look round, from time to time, sir," said Mr. Rugg, cheerfully, "to see whether any lingering Detainers are accumulating at the gate. They have fallen in pretty thick, sir; as thick as we could have expected."

He remarked upon the circumstance as if it were a matter of congratulation; rubbing his hands briskly, and rolling his head a little.

"As thick," repeated Mr. Rugg, "as we could reasonably have expected. Quite a shower-bath of 'em. I don't often intrude upon you, now, when I look round, because I know you are not inclined for company, and that if you wished to see me, you would leave word in the Lodge. But I am here pretty well every day, sir. Would this be an unseasonable time, sir," asked Mr. Rugg, coaxingly, "for me to offer an observation?"

"As seasonable a time as any other."

"Hum! Public opinion, sir," said Mr. Rugg "has been busy with you."

"I don't doubt it."

"Might it not be advisable, sir," said Mr. Rugg, more coaxingly yet, "now to make, at last and after all, a trifling concession to public opinion? We all do it in one way or another. The fact is, we must do it."

"I can not set myself right with it, Mr. Rugg, and have no business to expect that I ever shall."

"Don't say that, sir; don't say that. The cost of being moved to the Bench is almost insignificant, and if the general feeling is strong that you ought to be there, why—really—"

"I thought you had settled, Mr. Rugg," said Arthur, "that my determination to remain here was a matter of taste."

"Well, sir, well! But is it good taste, is it good taste? That's the question." Mr. Rugg was so soothingly persuasive as to be quite pathetic. "I was almost going to say, is it good feeling? This is an extensive affair of yours; and your remaining here where a man can come for a pound or two, is remarked upon as not in keeping. It is *not* in keeping. I can't tell you, sir, in how many quarters I hear it mentioned. I heard comments made upon it last night in a Parlor frequented by what I should call, if I did not look in there now and then myself, the best legal company—I heard, there, comments on it that I was sorry to hear. They hurt me on your account.. Again, only this morning at breakfast. My daughter (but a woman, you'll say: yet still with a feeling for these things, and even with some little personal experience, as the plaintiff in Rugg and Bawkins) was expressing her great surprise—her great surprise. Now, under these circumstances, and considering that none of us can quite set ourselves above public opinion, wouldn't a trifling concession to that opinion be—Come, sir!" said Rugg, "I will put it on the lowest ground of argument, and say, Amiable?"

Arthur's thoughts had once more wandered away to Little Dorrit, and the question remained unanswered.

"As to myself, sir," said Mr. Rugg, hoping that his eloquence had reduced him to a state of indecision, "it's a principle of mine not to consider myself when a client's inclinations are in the scale. But, knowing your considerate character and general wish to oblige, I will repeat that I should prefer your being in the Bench. Your case makes a noise; it is a creditable case to be professionally concerned in; I should feel on a better standing with my connection, if you went to the Bench. Don't let that influence you, sir. I merely state the fact."

So errant had the prisoner's attention already grown in solitude and dejection, and so accustomed had it become to commune with only one silent figure within the ever-frowning walls, that Clennam had to shake off a kind of stupor before he could look at Mr. Rugg, recall the thread of his talk, and hurriedly say, "I am unchanged, and unchangeable in my decision. Pray, let it be; let it be!" Mr. Rugg, without concealing that he was nettled and mortified, replied,

"Oh! Beyond a doubt, sir! I have traveled out of the record, sir, I am aware, in putting the point to you. But really, when I hear it remarked in several companies, and in very good company, that, however worthy of a foreigner, it is not worthy of the spirit of an Englishman to remain in the

Marshalsea when the glorious liberties of his island home admit of his removal to the Bench, I thought I would depart from the narrow professional line marked out to me, and mention it. Personally," said Mr. Rugg, "I have no opinion on the topic."

"That's well," returned Arthur.

"Oh! None at all, sir!" said Mr. Rugg. "If I had, I should have been unwilling, some minutes ago, to see a client of mine visited in this place by a gentleman of high family riding a saddle-horse. But it was not my business. If I had, I might have wished to be now empowered to mention to another gentleman, a gentleman of military exterior at present waiting in the Lodge, that my client had never intended to remain here, and was on the eve of removal to a superior abode. But my course, as a professional machine, is clear; I have nothing to do with it. Is it your good pleasure to see the gentleman, sir?"

"Who is waiting to see me, did you say?"

"I did take that unprofessional liberty, sir. Hearing that I was your professional adviser, he declined to interpose before my very limited function was performed. Happily," said Mr. Rugg, with sarcasm, "I did not so far travel out of the record as to ask the gentleman for his name."

"I suppose I have no resource but to see him," sighed Clennam, wearily.

"Then it *is* your good pleasure, sir?" retorted Rugg. "Am I honored by your instructions to mention as much to the gentleman as I pass out? I am? Thank you, sir. I take my leave." His leave he took, accordingly, in dudgeon.

The gentleman of military exterior had so imperfectly awakened Clennam's curiosity, in the existing state of his mind, that a half forgetfulness of such a visitor's having been referred to, was already creeping over it as a part of the sombre vail which almost always dimmed it now, when a heavy footstep on the stairs aroused him. It appeared to ascend them, not very promptly or spontaneously, yet with a display of stride and clatter meant to be insulting. As it paused for a moment on the landing outside his door, he could not recall his association with the peculiarity of its sound, though he thought he had one. Only a moment was given him for consideration. His door was immediately swung open by a thump, and in the door-way stood the missing Blandois, the cause of many anxieties.

"Salve, fellow jail-bird!" said he. "You want me, it seems. See me here!"

Before Arthur could speak to him in his indignant wonder, Cavalletto followed him into the room. Mr. Pancks followed Cavalletto. Neither of the two had been there since its present occupant had had possession of it. Mr. Pancks, breathing hard, sidled near the window, put his hat on the ground, stirred his hair up with both hands, and folded his arms, like a man who had come to a pause in a hard day's work. Mr. Baptist, never taking his eyes from his dreaded chum of old, softly sat down on the floor, with his back against the door, and one of his ankles in each hand: resuming the attitude (except that it was now expressive of unwinking watchfulness) in which he had sat before the same man in the deeper shade of another prison, one hot morning at Marseilles.

"I have it on the witnessing of these two madmen," said Monsieur Blandois, otherwise Lagnier, otherwise Rigaud, "that you want me, brother-bird. Here I am!"

Glancing round contemptuously at the bedstead, which was turned up by day, he leaned his back against it as a resting-place, without removing his hat from his head, and stood defiantly lounging with his hands in his pockets.

"You villain of ill-omen!" said Arthur. "You have purposely cast a dreadful suspicion upon my mother's house. Why have you done it? What prompted you to the devilish invention?"

Monsieur Rigaud, after frowning at him for a moment, laughed. "Hear this noble gentleman! Listen, all the world, to this creature of Virtue! But, take care, take care. It is possible, my friend, that your ardor is a little compromising. Holy Blue! It is possible."

"Signore!" interposed Cavalletto, also addressing Arthur: "for to commence, hear me! I received your instructions to find him, Rigaud; is it not?"

"It is the truth."

"I go, consequentementally,"—it would have given Mrs. Plornish great concern if she could have been persuaded that his occasional lengthening of an adverb in this way was the chief fault of his English—"first, among my own countrymen. I ask them what news in Londra, of foreigners arrived. Then, I go among the French. Then, I go among the Germans. They all tell me. The great part of us know well the other, and they all tell me. But!—no person can tell me nothing of him, Rigaud. Fifteen times," said Cavalletto, thrice throwing out his left hand with all its fingers spread, and doing it so rapidly that the sense of sight could hardly follow the action, "I ask of him in every place where go the foreigners; and fifteen times," repeating the same swift performance, "they know nothing. But!—"

At his significant Italian rest on the word "But," his back-handed shake of his right fore-finger came into play; a very little, and very cautiously.

"But!—After long time when I have not been able to find that he is here in Londra, some one tells me of a soldier with white hair—hey?—not hair like this that he carries—white—who lives retired secretementally, in a certain place. But!—" with another rest upon the word, "who sometimes in the after-dinner, walks and smokes. It is necessary, as they say in Italy (and as they know, poor people), to have patience. I have patience. I ask where is this certain place. One believes it is here, one believes it is there. Eh, well! It is not here, it is not there. I wait patientissementally. At last I find it. Then I watch; then I hide, until he walks and smokes. He is a soldier with gray hair—But!—" a very decided rest, indeed, and a very vigorous play from side to side of the back-handed fore-finger—"he is also this man that you see."

It was noticeable that, in his old habit of submission to one who had been at the trouble of asserting superiority over him, he even then bestowed upon Rigaud a confused bend of his head, after thus pointing him out.

"Eh well, Signore!" he cried, in conclusion, addressing Arthur again. "I waited for a good opportunity. I writed some words to Signor Panco"—an air of novelty came over Mr. Pancks with this designation—"to come and help. I showed him, Rigaud, at his window to Signor Panco, who was often the spy in the day. I slept at night near the door of the house.

At last we entered, only this to-day, and now you see him! As he would not come up in presence of the illustrious Advocate,"—such was Mr. Baptist's honorable mention of Mr. Rugg—"we waited down below there together, and Signor Panco guarded the street."

At the close of this recital, Arthur turned his eyes upon the impudent and wicked face. As it met his the nose came down over the mustache, and the mustache went up under the nose. When nose and mustache had settled into their places again, Monsieur Rigaud loudly snapped his fingers half a dozen times, bending forward to jerk the snaps at Arthur, as if they were palpable missiles which he jerked into his face.

"Now, Philosopher!" said Rigaud. "What do you want with me?"

"I want to know," returned Arthur, without disguising his abhorrence, "how you dare direct a suspicion of murder against my mother's house?"

"Dare!" cried Rigaud. "Ho, ho! Hear him! Dare? Is it dare? By Heaven, my small boy, but you are a little compromising!"

"I want that suspicion to be cleared away," said Arthur. "You shall be taken there, and be publicly seen. I want to know, moreover, what business you had there, when I had a burning desire to fling you down stairs. Don't frown at me, man! I have seen enough of you to know that you are a bully and a coward. I need no revival of my spirits from the effects of this wretched place, to tell you so plain a fact, and one that you know so well."

White to the lips, Rigaud stroked his mustache, muttering, "By Heaven, my small boy, but you are a little compromising of my lady, your respectable mother," and seemed for a minute undecided how to act. His indecision was soon gone. He sat himself down with a threatening swagger, and said,

"Give me a bottle of wine. You can buy wine here. Send one of your madmen to get me a bottle of wine. I won't talk to you without wine. Come! Yes or no?"

"Fetch him what he wants, Cavalletto," said Arthur, scornfully, producing the money.

"Contraband beast," added Rigaud, "bring port wine! I'll drink nothing but Porto-Porto."

The contraband beast, however, assuring all present, with his significant finger, that he peremptorily declined to leave his post at the door, Signor Panco offered his services. He soon returned with the bottle of wine, which, according to the custom of the place, originating in a scarcity of corkscrews among the Collegians (in common with a scarcity of much else), was already opened for use.

"Madman! A large glass," said Rigaud.

Signor Panco put a tumbler before him; not without a visible conflict of feeling on the question of throwing it at his head.

"Haha!" boasted Rigaud. "Once a gentleman, and always a gentleman. A gentleman from the beginning, and a gentleman to the end. What the devil! A gentleman must be waited on, I hope? It's a part of my character to be waited on!"

He half filled the tumbler as he said it, and drank off the contents when he had done saying it.

"Hah!" smacking his lips. "Not a very old prisoner *that!* I judge by your looks, brave sir, that imprisonment will subdue your blood much sooner than it softens this hot wine. You are mellowing—losing body and color already. I salute you?"

He tossed off another half glass; holding it up both before and afterward, so as to display his small, white hand.

"To business," he then continued. "To conversation. You have shown yourself more free of speech than body, sir."

"I have used the freedom of telling you what you know yourself to be. You know yourself, as we all know you, to be far worse than that, however."

"Add, always a gentleman, and it's no matter. Except in that regard, we are all alike. You couldn't, for your life, be a gentleman, for example; I couldn't for my life be otherwise. How great the difference! Let us go on. Words, sir, never influenced the course of cards, or the course of the dice. Do you know that? You do? I also play a game, and words are without power over it."

Now that he was confronted with Cavalletto, and knew that his story was known, whatever thin disguise he had worn he dropped, and faced it out with a bare face, as the infamous wretch he was.

"No, my son," he resumed, with a snap of his fingers. "I play my game to the end, in spite of words; and Death of my Body and Death of my Soul! I'll win it. You want to know why I played this little trick that you have interrupted? Know, then, that I had, and that I have—do you understand me? have—a commodity to sell my lady, your respectable mother. I described my precious commodity, and fixed my price. Touching the bargain, your admirable mother was a little too calm, too stolid, too immovable and statue-like. In fine, your admirable mother vexed me. To make variety in my position, and to amuse myself—what! a gentleman must be amused at somebody's expense!—I conceived the happy idea of disappearing. An idea, you see, that your characteristic mother and my Flintwinch would have been well enough pleased to execute. Ah! Bah, bah, bah, don't look as from high to low at me! I repeat it. Well enough pleased, excessively enchanted, with all their hearts ravished. How strongly will you have it?"

He threw out the lees of his glass on the ground, so that they nearly spattered Cavalletto. This seemed to draw his attention to him anew. He set down his glass and said:

"I'll not fill it. What! I am born to be served. Come, then, you Cavalletto, and fill!"

The little man looked at Clennam, whose eyes were occupied with Rigaud, and seeing no prohibition, got up from the ground, and poured out from the bottle into the glass. The blending, as he did so, of his old submission with a sense of something humorous; the striving of that with a certain smouldering ferocity, which might have flashed fire in an instant (as the born gentleman seemed to think, for he had a wary eye upon him); and the easy yielding of all to a good-natured, careless, predominant propensity to sit down on the ground again; formed a very remarkable combination of character.

"This happy idea, brave sir," Rigaud resumed, after drinking, "was a happy idea for several reasons. It amused me, it worried your dear mamma and my Flintwinch, it caused you agonies (my terms for a lesson in politeness toward a gentleman), and it suggested to all the amiable persons interested that your entirely devoted is a man to fear! By heaven he is a man to fear! Beyond this; it might have restored her wit to my lady your mother—might, under the pressing little suspicion your wisdom has recognized, have persuaded her at last to announce, covertly, in the journals that the difficulties of a certain contract would be removed by the appearance of a certain important party to it. Perhaps yes, perhaps no. But, that you have interrupted. Now, what is it you say? What is it you want?"

Never had Clennam felt more acutely that he was a prisoner in bonds than when he saw this man before him, and could not accompany him to his mother's house. All the undiscernible difficulties and dangers he had ever feared were closing in, when he could not stir hand or foot.

"Perhaps, my friend, philosopher, man of virtue, Imbecile, what you will; perhaps," said Rigaud, pausing in his drink to look out of his glass with his horrible smile upon him, "you would have done better to leave me alone?"

"No! At least," said Clennam, "you are known to be alive and unharmed. At least you cannot escape from these two witnesses; and they can produce you before any public authorities, or before hundreds of people."

"But will not produce me before one," said Rigaud, snapping his fingers again, with an air of triumphant menace. "To the Devil with your witnesses! To the Devil with your produced! To the Devil with yourself! What? Do I know what I know, for that? Have I my commodity on sale, for that? Bah, poor debtor! You have interrupted my little project. Let it pass. How then? What remains? To you, nothing; to me, all. Produce *me*? Is that what you want? I will produce myself, only too quickly. Contrabandist! Give me pen, ink and paper."

Cavaletto got up again as before, and laid them before him in his former manner. Rigaud, after some villainous thinking and smiling, wrote and read aloud as follows:

"To MRS. CLENNAM.

"Wait answer.

"PRISON OF THE MARSHALSEA.

"At the apartment of your son.

"DEAR MADAM:—I am in despair to-day to be informed

IN THE OLD ROOM.

by our estimable prisoner here (who has had the goodness to employ spies to seek me, living for politic reasons *en retraite*), that you have had fears for my safety.

"Reassure yourself, dear madam. I am well, I am strong and resolute.

"With the strongest impatience I should fly to your house, but that I foresee it to be possible, under the circumstances, that you will not yet have quite definitively arranged the little proposition I have had the honor to submit to you. I name one week from this day, for a last final visit on my part; when you will unconditionally accept it or reject it, with its train of consequences.

"I suppress my ardor to embrace you and achieve this interesting business in order that you may have leisure to adjust its details to our perfect mutual satisfaction.

"In the meanwhile, it is not too much to propose (our estimable prisoner having deranged my housekeeping) that my expenses of lodging and nourishment at an hotel shall be paid by you.

"Receive, dear madam, the assurance of my highest and most distinguished consideration.

RIGAUD BLANDOIS.

"A thousand friendships to that dear Flintwinch.

"I kiss the hands of Madame F——"

When he had finished this epistle, Rigaud folded it, and tossed it with a flourish at Clennam's feet. "Hola you! Apropos of producing, let somebody produce that at its address, and produce the answer here."

"Cavalletto," said Arthur. "Will you take this fellow's letter?"

But Cavalletto's significant finger again expressing that his post was at the door to keep watch over Rigaud, now he had found him with so much trouble, and that the duty of his post was to sit on the floor backed up by the door, looking at Rigaud and holding his own ankles—Signor Panco once more volunteered. His services being accepted, Cavalletto suffered the door to open barely wide enough to admit of his squeezing himself out, and immediately shut it on him.

"Touch me with a finger, touch me with an epithet, question

my superiority as I sit here drinking my wine at my pleasure," said Rigaud, "and I follow the letter and cancel my week's grace. *You* wanted me! You have got me! How do you like me?"

"You know," returned Clennam, with a bitter sense of his helplessness, "that when I sought you, I was not a prisoner."

"To the devil with you and your prison," retorted Rigaud, leisurely, as he took from his pocket a case containing the materials for making cigarettes, and employed his facile hands in folding a few for present use; "I care for neither of you. Contrabandist! A light."

Again Cavalletto got up, and gave him what he wanted. There had been something dreadful in the noiseless skill of his cold, white hands, with the fingers lithely twisting about and twining over one another like serpents. Clennam could not prevent himself from shuddering inwardly, as if he had been looking on at a nest of those creatures.

"Hola, Pig!" cried Rigaud, with a noisy, stimulating cry, as if Cavalletto were an Italian horse or mule. "What! The infernal old jail was a respectable one to this. There was dignity in the bars and stones of that place. It was a prison for men. But this! Bah! A hospital for imbeciles!"

He smoked his cigarette out, with his ugly smile so fixed upon his face that he looked as though he were smoking with his drooping beak of a nose rather than his mouth—like a fancy in a weird picture. When he had lighted a second cigarette at the still burning end of the first, he said to Clennam:

"One must pass the time in the madman's absence. One must talk. One can't drink strong wine all day long, or I would have another bottle. She's handsome, sir. Though not exactly to my taste, still, by the Thunder and the Lightning! very handsome. I felicitate you on your admiration."

"I neither know nor ask," said Clennam, "of whom you speak."

"Della bella Gowana, sir, as they say in Italy. Of the Gowan, the fair Gowan."

"Of whose husband you were the—follower, I think?"

"Sir? Follower? You are insolent. The friend."

"Do you sell all your friends?"

Rigaud took his cigarette from his mouth, and eyed him with a momentary revelation of surprise. But he put it between his lips again, as he answered with coolness :

"I sell any thing that commands a price. How do your lawyers live, your politicians, your intriguers, your men of exchange? How do you live? How do you come here? Have you sold no friend? Lady of mine! I rather think, yes!"

Clennam turned away from him toward the window, and sat looking out at the wall.

"Effectively, sir," said Rigaud. "Society sells itself and sells me: and I sell Society. I perceive you have acquaintance with another lady. Also handsome. A strong spirit. Let us see. How do they call her? Wade."

He received no answer, but could easily discern that he had hit the mark.

"Yes!" he went on; "that handsome lady and strong spirit addresses me in the street, and I am not insensible. I respond. That handsome lady and strong spirit does me the favor to remark, in full confidence, 'I have my curiosity, and I have my chagrins. You are not more than ordinarily honorable, perhaps?' I announce myself, 'Madam, a gentleman from birth, and a gentleman to the death; but *not* more than ordinarily honorable. I despise such a weak fantasy.' Thereupon she is pleased to compliment. 'The difference between you and the rest is,' she answers, 'that you say so.' For she knows society. I accept her congratulations with gallantry and politeness. Politeness and little gallantries are inseparable from my character. She then makes a proposition, which is, in effect, that she has seen us much together; and it appears to her that I am for the passing time the cat of the house, the friend of the family; that her curiosity and her chagrins awaken the fancy to be acquainted with their movements, to know the manner of their life, how the fair Gowana is beloved, how the fair Gowana is cherished, and so on. She is not rich, but offers such and such little recompenses for the little cares and derangements of such services; and I graciously—to do every thing graciously is a part of my character—consent to accept them. Oh, yes! So goes the world. It is the mode."

Though Clennam's back was turned while he spoke, and

thenceforth to the end of the interview, he kept those glittering eyes of his, that were too near together, upon him, and evidently saw in the very carriage of the head, as he passed, with his braggart recklessness, from clause to clause of what he said, that he was saying nothing which Clennam did not already know."

"Whoof! The fair Gowana!" he said, lighting a third cigarette, with a sound as if his lightest breath could blow her away. "Charming, but imprudent! For it was not well of the fair Gowana to make mysteries of letters from old lovers, in her bed-chamber on the mountain, that her husband might not see them. No, no. That was not well. Whoof! The Gowana was mistaken there."

"I pray Heaven," cried Arthur aloud, "that Pancks may not be long gone, for this man's presence pollutes the room."

"Ay! But he'll flourish here, and every where," said Rigaud, with an exulting look and snap of his fingers. "He always has; he always will!" Stretching his body out on the only three chairs in the room besides that on which Clennam sat, he sang, smiting himself on the breast as the gallant personage of the song

"'Who passes by this road so late?
Compagnon de la Majolaine:
Who passes by this road so late?
Always gay!'

Sing the refrain, Pig! You could sing it once, in another jail. Sing it! Or, by every Saint who was stoned to death, I'll be affronted and compromising; and then some people who are not dead yet, had better have been stoned along with them!"

"'Of all the king's knights 'tis the flower,
Compagnon de la Majolaine:
Of all the king's knights 'tis the flower,
And he's always gay!'"

Partly in his old habit of submission, partly because his not doing it might injure his benefactor, and partly because he would as soon do it as any thing else, Cavalletto took up the refrain this time. Rigaud laughed, and fell to smoking with his eyes shut.

Possibly another quarter of an hour elapsed before Mr. Pancks's step was heard upon the stairs, but the interval seemed to Clennam insupportably long. His step was attended by another step; and when Cavalletto opened the door, he admitted Mr. Pancks and Mr. Flintwinch. The latter was no sooner visible than Rigaud rushed at him and embraced him boisterously.

"How do you find yourself, sir?" said Mr. Flintwinch, as soon as he could disengage himself, which he struggled to do with very little ceremony. "Thank you, no; I don't want any more." This was in reference to another menace of affection from his recovered friend. "Well, Arthur. You remember what I said to you about sleeping dogs and missing ones. It's come true, you see."

He was as imperturbable as ever, to all appearance, and nodded his head in a moralizing way as he looked round the room.

"And this is the Marshalsea prison for debt!" said Mr. Flintwinch. "Ha! You have brought your pigs to a very indifferent market, Arthur."

If Arthur had patience, Rigaud had not. He took his little Flintwinch, with fierce playfulness, by the two lappels of his coat, and cried:

"To the Devil with the Market, to the Devil with the Pigs, and to the devil with the Pig-Driver! Give me the answer to my letter."

"If you can make it convenient to let go a moment, sir," returned Mr. Flintwinch, "I'll first hand Mr. Arthur a little note that I have for him."

He did so. It was in his mother's maimed writing, on a slip of paper, and contained only these words:

"I hope it is enough that you have ruined yourself. Rest contented without more ruin. Jeremiah Flintwinch is my messenger and representative. Your affectionate M. C."

Clennam read this twice, in silence, and then tore it in pieces. Rigaud in the meanwhile stepped into a chair, and sat himself upon the back, with his feet upon the seat.

"Now, Beau Flintwinch," he said, when he had closely watched the note to its destruction, "the answer to my letter?"

"Mrs. Clennam did not write it, Mr. Blandois, her hands being cramped, and she thinking it as well to send it verbally by me." Mr. Flintwinch screwed this out of himself, unwillingly and rustily. "She sends her compliments and says she doesn't on the whole wish to term you unreasonable, and that she agrees. But without prejudicing the appointment that stands for this day week."

Monsieur Rigaud, after indulging in a fit of laughter, descended from his throne, saying, "Good! I go to seek an hotel!" But there his eyes encountered Cavalletto, who was still at his post.

"Come, Pig," he added, "I have had you for a follower against my will; now, I'll have you against yours. I tell you, my little reptiles, I am born to be served. I demand the service of this contrabandist as my domestic, until this day week."

In answer to Cavalletto's look of inquiry, Clennam made him a sign to go; but he added aloud, "unless you are afraid of him." Cavalletto replied with a very emphatic finger-negative. "No, master, I am not afraid of him, when I no more keep it secretementally that he was once my comrade." Rigaud took no notice of either remark, until he had lighted his last cigarette and was quite ready for walking.

"Afraid of him," he said then, looking round upon them all. "Whoof! My children, my babies, my little dolls, you are all afraid of him. You give him his bottle of wine here; you give him meat, drink, and lodging, there; you dare not touch him with a finger or an epithet. No. It is his character to triumph! Whoof!

"'Of all the king's knights he's the flower,
And he's always gay!'"

With the refrain, he stalked out of the room, closely followed by Cavalletto, whom perhaps he had pressed into his service because he tolerably well knew it would not be easy to get rid of him. Mr. Flintwinch, after scraping his chin and looking about with caustic disparagement of the Pig-Market, nodded to

Arthur, and followed. Mr. Pancks, still penitent and depressed, followed too; after whispering that, on the possibility of being useful, he would see this affair out, and stand by it to the end. So the prisoner—with the feeling that he was more despised, more scorned and repudiated, more helpless, altogether more miserable and fallen, than before—was left alone again.

CNAPTER LXV

A PLEA IN THE MARSHALSEA.

HAGGARD anxiety and remorse are bad companions to be barred up with.. Brooding all day, and resting very little indeed at night, will not arm a man against misery. Next morning, Clennam felt that his health was sinking, as his spirits had already sunk, and that the weight under which he bent was bearing him down.

Night after night he had arisen from his bed of wretchedness at twelve or one o'clock, and had sat at his window watching the sickly lamps in the yard, and looking upward for the first wan trace of day, hours before it was possible that the sky could show it. Now when the night came, he could not even persuade himself to undress.

For a burning restlessness set in, an agonized impatience of the prison, and a conviction that he was going to break his heart and die there, which caused him indescribable suffering. His dread and hatred of the place became so intense that he felt it a labor to draw his breath in it. The sensation of being stifled sometimes so overpowered him, that he would stand at the window holding his throat and gasping. At the same time a longing for other air, and a yearning to be beyond the blind, blank wall, made him feel as if he must go mad with the ardor of the desire.

Many other prisoners had had experience of this condition before him, and its violence and continuity had worn themselves out in their cases as they did in his. Two nights and a day exhausted it. It came back by fits, but those grew fainter, and returned at lengthened intervals. A desolate calm succeeded, and the middle of the week found him settled down in the despondency of low, slow fever.

With Cavalletto and Pancks away, he had no visitors to fear but Mr. and Mrs. Plornish. His anxiety, in reference to that worthy pair, was that they should not come near him; for, in the morbid state of his nerves, he sought to be left alone, and spared the being seen so subdued and weak. He wrote a note to Mrs. Plornish, representing himself as occupied by his affairs, and bound by the necessity of devoting himself to them to remain for a time even without the pleasant interruption of a sight of her kind face. As to Young John, who looked in daily at a certain hour when the turnkeys were to be relieved, to ask if he could do any thing for him, he always made a pretense of being engaged in writing, and to answer cheerfully in the negative. The subject of their only long conversation had never been revived between them. Through all these changes of unhappiness, however, it had never for a moment lost its hold on Clennam's mind.

The sixth day of the appointed week was a moist, hot, misty day. It seemed as though the prison's poverty, and shabbiness, and dirt, were growing in the sultry atmosphere. With an aching head and a weary heart Clennam had watched the miserable night out, listening to the fall of the rain on the yard pavement, thinking of its softer fall upon the country earth. A blurred circle of yellow haze had risen up in the sky in lieu of sun, and he had watched the patch it put upon his wall, like a bit of the prison's raggedness. He had heard the gates open, and the badly-shod feet that waited outside shuffle in; and the sweeping, and pumping, and moving about, begin, which commenced the prison morning. So ill and faint that he was obliged to rest himself many times in the process of getting himself washed, he had at length crept to his chair by the open window. In it he sat dozing, while the old woman who arranged his room went through her morning's work.

Light of head with want of sleep and want of food (his appetite and even his sense of taste having quite forsaken him), he had been two or three times conscious, in the night, of going astray. He had heard fragments of tunes and songs, in the warm wind, which he he knew had no existence. Now that he had begun to doze in exhaustion, he heard them again; and voices seemed to address him, and he answered and started.

Dozing and dreaming, without the power of reckoning time, so that a minute might have been an hour and an hour a minute, some abiding impression of a garden stole over him—a garden of flowers, with a damp, warm wind gently stirring their scents. It required such a painful effort to lift his head for the purpose of inquiring into this, or inquiring into any thing, that the impression appeared to have become quite an old and importunate one when he looked round. Beside the tea-cup on his table he saw, then, a blooming nosegay; a wonderful handful of the choicest and most lovely flowers.

Nothing had ever appeared so beautiful in his sight. He took them up and inhaled their fragrance, and he lifted them to his hot head, and he put them down and opened his parched hands to them, as cold hands are opened to receive the cheering of a fire. It was not until he had delighted in them for some time that he wondered who had sent them, and opened his door to ask the woman who must have put them there how they had come into her hands. But she was gone, and seemed to have been long gone; for the tea she had left for him on the table was cold. He tried to drink some, but could not bear the odor of it; so he crept back to his chair by the open window, and put the flowers on the little round table of old.

When the first faintness consequent on having moved about had left him, he subsided into his former state. One of the night-tunes was playing in the wind, when the door of his room seemed to open to a light touch, and after a moment's pause, a quiet figure seemed to stand there with a black mantle on it. It seemed to draw the mantle off and drop it on the ground, and then it seemed to be his Little Dorrit in her old, worn dress. It seemed to tremble and to clasp its hands, and to smile, and to burst into tears.

He roused himself, and cried out. And then he saw, in the loving, pitying, sorrowing dear face, as in a mirror, how changed he was; and she came toward him; and with her hands laid on his breast to keep him in his chair, and with her knees upon the floor at his feet, and with her lips raised up to kiss him, and with her tears dropping on him as the rain from heaven had dropped upon the flowers, Little Dorrit, a living presence, called him by his name.

"Oh, don't cry! Dear Mr. Clennam, don't let me see you

cry! Unless you cry with pleasure to see me. I hope you do. Your own poor child come back!"

So faithful, tender, and unspoiled by fortune. In the sound of her voice, in the light of her eyes, in the touch of her hands, so Angelically comforting and true!

As he embraced her, she said to him, "They never told me you were ill," and drawing an arm softly around his neck, laid his head upon her bosom, put a hand upon his head, and resting her cheek upon that hand, nursed him as lovingly, and God knows as innocently, as she had nursed her father in that room, when she had been but a baby, needing all the care from others that she took of them.

When he could speak, he said, "Is it possible that you have come to me? And in this dress?"

"I hoped you would like me better in this dress than any other. I have always kept it by me to remind me: though I wanted no reminding. I am not alone, you see. I have brought an old friend with me."

Looking round, he saw Maggy in her big cap which had been long abandoned, with a basket on her arm as in by-gone days, chuckling rapturously.

"It was only yesterday evening that I came to London with my brother. I sent round to Mrs. Plornish almost as soon as we arrived that I might hear of you and let you know I had come. Then I heard that you were here. Did you happen to think of me in the night? I almost believe you must have thought of me a little. I thought of you so anxiously, and it appeared so long to morning."

"I have thought of you—" He hesitated what to call her. She perceived it in an instant.

"You have not spoken to me by my right name yet. You know what my right name always is with you."

"I have thought of you, Little Dorrit, every day, every hour, every minute, since I have been here."

"Have you? Have you?"

He saw the bright delight of her face, and the flush that kindled in it, with a feeling of shame. He, a broken, bankrupt, sick, dishonored prisoner.

"I was here before the gates were opened, but I was afraid

to come straight to you. I should have done you more harm than good, at first; for the prison was so familiar and yet so strange, and it brought back so many remembrances of my poor father, and of you too, that, at first, it overpowered me. But we went to Mr. Chivery before we came to the gate, and he brought us in, and got John's room for us—my poor old room, you know—and we waited there a little. I brought the flowers to the door, but you didn't hear me."

She looked something more womanly than when she had gone away, and the ripening touch of the Italian sun was visible upon her face. But otherwise she was quite unchanged. The same deep, timid earnestness that he had always seen in her, and never without emotion, he saw still. If it had a new meaning that smote him to the heart, the change was in his perception, not in her.

She took off her old bonnet, hung it in the old place, and noiselessly began, with Maggy's help, to make his room as fresh and neat as it could be made, and to sprinkle it with a pleasant smelling water. When that was done, the basket which was filled with grapes and other fruit, was unpacked, and all its contents were quietly put away. When that was done, a moment's whisper dispatched Maggy to dispatch somebody else to fill the basket again, which soon came back replenished with new stores, from which a present provision of cooling drink and jelly, and a prospective supply of roast chicken and wine and water, were the first extracts. These various arrangements completed, she took out her old needle-case to make him a curtain for his window; and thus, with a quiet reigning in the room that seemed to diffuse itself through the else noisy prison, he found himself composed in his chair with Little Dorrit working at his side.

To see the modest head again bent down over its task, and the nimble fingers busy at their old work—though she was not so absorbed in it but that her compassionate eyes were often raised to his face, and, when they drooped again, had tears in them—to be so consoled and comforted, and to believe that all the devotion of this great nature was turned to him in his adversity, to pour out its inexhaustible wealth of goodness upon him, did not steady Clennam's trembling voice or hand, or strengthen him in his weakness. Yet it inspired him with an inward fortitude that rose with his love. And how dearly he loved her now what words can tell!

As they sat side by side, in the shadow of the wall, the shadow fell like light upon him. She would not let him speak much, and he lay back in his chair, looking at her. Now and again she would rise and give him the glass that he might drink, or would smooth the resting-place of his head; then she would gently resume her seat by him, and bend over her work again.

The shadow moved with the sun, but she never moved from his side, except to wait upon him. The sun went down, and she was still there. She had done her work now, and her hand, faltering on the arm of his chair since its last tending of him, was hesitating there yet. He laid his hand upon it, and it clasped him with a trembling supplication.

"Dear Mr. Clennam, I must say something to you before I go. I have put it off from hour to hour, but I must say it."

"I, too, dear Little Dorrit. I have put off what I must say."

She nervously moved her hand toward his lips, as if to stop him; then it dropped, trembling into its former place.

"I am not going abroad again. My brother is, but I am not. He was always attached to me, and he is so grateful to me now—so much too grateful, for it is only because I happened to be with him in his illness—that he says I shall be free to stay where I like best, and to do what I like best. He only wishes me to be happy, he says."

There was one bright star shining in the sky. She looked up at it while she spoke, as if it were the fervent purpose of her own heart shining before her.

"You will understand, I dare say, without my telling you, that my brother has come home to find my dear father's will, and to take possession of his property. He says, if there is a will, he is sure I shall be left rich; and if there is none, that he will make me so."

He would have spoken; but she put up her trembling hand again, and he stopped.

"I have no use for money, I have no wish for it. It would be of no value at all to me, but for your sake. I could not be rich, and you here. I must always be much worse than poor, with you distressed. Will you let me lend you all I have? Will you let me give it you? Will you let me show you that I never have forgotten, that I never can forget, your protection of me when this was my home? Dear Mr. Clennam, make me of all the world the happiest, by saying Yes! Make me as happy as I can be in leaving you here, by saying nothing to-night, and letting me go away with the hope that you will think of it kindly; and that for my sake—not for yours, for mine, for nobody's but mine!—you will give me the greatest joy I can experience on earth, the joy of knowing that I have been serviceable to you, and that I have paid some little of the great debt of my affection and gratitude. I can't say what I wish to say. I can't visit you here where I have lived so long, I can't think of you here where I have seen so much, and be as calm and comforting as I ought. My tears will make their way. I can not keep them back. But pray, pray, pray, do not turn from your Little Dorrit, now, in your affliction! Pray, pray, pray, I beg you and implore you, with all my grieving heart, my friend—my dear!—take all I have, and make it a Blessing to me!"

The star had shone on her face until now, when her face sank upon his hand and her own.

It had grown darker when he raised her in his encircling arm, and softly answered her:

"No, darling Little Dorrit. No, my child. I must not hear of such a sacrifice. Liberty and hope would be so dear bought at such a price that I could never support their weight—never bear the reproach of possessing them. But, with what ardent thankfulness and love I say this, I may call heaven to witness!"

"And yet you will not let me be faithful to you in your affliction?"

"Stay, dearest Little Dorrit, and yet I will try to be faithful to you. If, in the by-gone days when this was your home and when this was your dress, I had understood myself (I speak only of myself) better, and had read the secrets of my own breast more distinctly; if, through my reserve and self-distrust, I had discerned a light that I see brightly now when it has passed far away, and my weak footsteps can never overtake it; if I had then known, and told you, that I loved and honored you, not as the poor child I used to call you, but as a woman whose true hand would raise me high above myself, and make me a far happier and better man; if I had so used the opportunity there is no recalling—as I wish I had, oh, I wish I had!—and if something had kept us apart then, when I was moderately thriving, and when you were poor; I might have met your noble offer of your fortune, dearest girl, with other words than these, and still have blushed to touch it. But, as it is, I must never touch it—never!"

She besought him more pathetically and earnestly with her little supplicatory hand than she could have done in any words.

"I am disgraced enough, my Little Dorrit. I must not descend so low as that, and carry you—so dear, so generous, and so good, down with me. God bless you, God reward you! It is past."

He took her in his arms, as if she had been his daughter.

"Always so much older, so much rougher, and so much less worthy, even what I was must be dismissed by both of us, and you must see me only as I am. I put this parting kiss upon your cheek, my child—who might have been more near to me, who never could have been more dear—a ruined man, far removed from you, forever separated from you, whose course is run, while yours is but beginning. I have not the courage to ask to be forgotten by you in my humiliation, but I ask to be remembered only as I am."

The bell began to ring, warning visitors to depart. He took her mantle from the wall, and tenderly wrapped it round her.

"One other word, my Little Dorrit. A hard one to me, but it is a necessary one. The time when you and this prison had any thing in common has long gone by. Do you understand?"

"Oh, you will never say to me," she cried, weeping bitterly, and holding up her clasped hands in entreaty, "that I am not to come back any more! You will surely not desert me so!"

"I would say it if I could; but I have not the courage quite to shut out this dear face, and abandon all hope of its return. But do not come soon! do not come often! This is now a tainted place, and I well know the taint of it clings to me.

You belong to much brighter and better scenes. You are not to look back here, my Little Dorrit; you are to look away to very different and much happier paths. Again, God bless you in them! God reward you!"

Maggy, who had fallen into very low spirits, here cried, "Oh, get him into a hospital; do get him into a hospital, Mother! He'll never look like his self again if he an't got into a hospital. And then the little woman as was always spinning at her wheel, she can go to the cupboard with the Princess and say, What do you keep the Chicking there for? and then they can take it out and give it to him, and then all will be happy!"

The interruption was seasonable, for the bell had nearly rung itself out. Again tenderly wrapping her mantle about her, and taking her on his arm (though but for her visit he was almost too weak to walk), Arthur led Little Dorrit down stairs. She was the last visitor to pass out at the Lodge, and the gate jarred heavily and hopelessly upon her.

With the funeral clang that it sounded into Arthur's heart, his sense of weakness returned. It was a toilsome journey up stairs to his room, and he re-entered its dark, solitary precincts in unutterable misery.

When it was almost midnight, and the prison had long been quiet, a cautious creak came up the stairs, and a cautious tap of a key was given at his door. It was Young John. He glided in in his stockings, and held the door closed, while he spoke in a whisper,

"It's against all rules, but I don't mind. I was determined to come through, and come to you."

"What is the matter?"

"Nothing's the matter, sir. I was waiting in the court-yard for Miss Dorrit when she came out. I thought you'd like some one to see that she was safe."

"Thank you, thank you! You took her home, John?"

"I saw her to her hotel. The same that Mr. Dorrit was at. Miss Dorrit walked all the way, and was just the same. Talked to me so kind, it quite knocked me over. Why do you think she walked instead of riding?"

"I don't know, John."

"To talk about you. She said to me, 'John, you was always

honorable, and if you'll promise me that you will take care of him, and never let him want for help and comfort when I am not there, my mind will be at rest so far.' I promised her. And I'll stand by you," said John Chivery, "forever!"

Clennam, much affected, stretched out his hand to this honest spirit.

"Before I take it," said John, looking at it, without coming from the door, "guess what message Miss Dorrit gave me."

Clennam shook his head.

"'Tell him,'" repeated John, in a distinct, though quavering voice, "'that his Little Dorrit sent him her undying love.' Now it's delivered. Have I been honorable, sir?"

"Very, very!"

"Will you tell Miss Dorrit I've been honorable, sir?"

"I will, indeed."

"There's my hand, sir," said John, "and I'll stand by you forever!"

After a hearty squeeze, he disappeared with the same cautious creak upon the stair, crept shoeless over the pavement of the yard, and, locking the gates behind him, passed out into the front, where he had left his shoes. If the same way had been paved with burning plow-shares, it is not at all improbable that John would have traversed it with the same devotion, for the same purpose.

CHAPTER LXVI.

CLOSING IN.

THE last day of the appointed week touched the bars of the Marshalsea gate. Black, all night, since the gate had clashed upon Little Dorrit, its iron stripes were turned by the early-glowing sun into stripes of gold. Far aslant across the city, over its jumbled roofs, and through the open tracery of its church towers, struck the long bright rays, bars of the prison of this lower world.

Throughout the day, the old house within the gateway remained untroubled by any visitors. But, when the sun was low, three men turned in at the gateway and made for the dilapidated house.

Rigaud was the first, and walked by himself, smoking. Mr. Baptist was the second, and jogged close after him, looking at no other object. Mr. Pancks was the third, and carried his hat under his arm for the liberation of his restive hair; the weather being extremely hot. They all came together at the door-steps.

"You pair of madmen!" said Rigaud, facing about. "Don't go yet!"

"We don't mean to," said Mr. Pancks.

Giving him a dark glance in acknowledgment of his answer, Rigaud knocked loudly. He had charged himself with drink for the playing out of his game, and was impatient to begin. He had hardly finished one long-resounding knock, when he turned to the knocker again and began another. That was not yet finished, when Jeremiah Flintwinch opened the door, and they all clanked into the stone hall. Rigaud, thrusting Mr. Flintwinch aside, proceeded straight up-stairs. His two attendants followed him, Mr. Flintwinch followed them, and they all came trooping into Mrs. Clennam's quiet room. It was in its usual state; except that one of the windows was wide open, and Affery sat on its old-fashioned window-seat, mending a stocking. The usual articles were on the little table; the usual deadened fire was in the grate; the bed had its usual pall upon it; and the mistress of all sat on her black bier-like sofa, propped up by her black angular bolster that was like the headsman's block.

Yet there was a nameless air of preparation in the room, as if it were strung up for an occasion. From what the room derived it—every one of its small variety of objects being in the fixed spot it had occupied for years—no one could have said without looking attentively at its mistress, and that, too, with a previous knowledge of her face. Although her unchanging black dress was in every plait precisely as of old, and her unchanging attitude was rigidly preserved, a very slight additional setting of her features and contraction of her gloomy forehead was so powerfully marked, that it marked every thing about her.

"Who are these !" she said, wonderingly, as the two attendants entered. "What do these people want here?"

"Who are these, dear madam, is it?" returned Rigaud. "Faith, they are friends of your son, the prisoner. And what do they want here, is it? Death, madam, I don't know. You will do well to ask them."

"You know you told us, at the door, not to go yet," said Pancks.

"And you know you told me, at the door, you didn't mean to go," retorted Rigaud. "In a word, madame, permit me to present two spies of the prisoner's—madmen, but spies. If you wish them to remain here during our little conversation, say the word. It is nothing to me."

"Why should I wish them to remain here?" said Mrs. Clennam. "What have I to do with them?"

"Then, dearest madame," said Rigaud, throwing himself into an arm-chair so heavily that the old room trembled, "you will do well to dismiss them. It is your affair. They are not *my* spies, not *my* rascals."

"Hark! You, Pancks," said Mrs. Clennam, bending her brows upon him angrily, "you Casby's clerk! Attend to your employer's business and your own. Go. And take that other man with you."

"Thank you, ma'am," returned Mr. Pancks, "I am glad to say I see no objection to our both retiring. We have done all we undertook to do for Mr. Clennam. His constant anxiety has been (and it grew worse upon him when he became a prisoner), that this agreeable gentleman should be brought back here, to the place from which he slipped away. Here he is—brought back. And I will say," added Mr. Pancks, "to his ill-looking face, that in my opinion the world would be no worse for his slipping out of it altogether."

"Your opinion is not asked," answered Mrs. Clennam. "Go!"

"I am sorry not to leave you in better company, ma'am," said Pancks; "and sorry, too, that Mr. Clennam can't be present. It's my fault, that is."

"You mean his own," she returned.

"No, I mean mine, ma'am," said Pancks, "for it was my misfortune to lead him into a ruinous investment." (Mr. Pancks still clung to that word, and never said speculation.) "Though I can prove by figures," added Mr. Pancks, with an anxious countenance, "that it ought to have been a good investment. I have gone over it since it failed, every day of my life, and it comes out—regarded as a question of figures—triumphant. The present is not a time or place," Mr. Pancks pursued, with a longing glance into his hat, where he kept his calculations, "for entering upon the figures; but the figures are not to be disputed. Mr. Clennam ought to have been at this moment in his carriage-and-pair, and I ought to have been worth from three to five thousand pound."

Mr. Pancks put his hair erect with a general aspect of confidence, that could hardly have been surpassed if he had had the amount in his pocket. These incontrovertible figures had been the occupation of every moment of his leisure since he had lost his money, and were destined to afford him consolation to the end of his days.

"However," said Mr. Pancks, "enough of that. Altro, old boy, you have seen the figures, and you know how they come out." Mr. Baptist, who had not the slightest arithmetical power of compensating himself in this way, nodded, with a fine display of bright teeth.

At whom Mr. Flintwinch had been looking, and to whom he then said:

"Oh! It's you, is it? I thought I remembered your face, but I wasn't certain till I saw your teeth. Ah! yes, to be sure. It was this officious refugee," said Jeremiah to Mrs. Clennam, "who came here knocking at the door, on the night when Arthur and Chatterbox were here, and who asked me a whole catechism of questions about Mr. Blandois."

"It is true," Mr. Baptist cheerfully admitted. "And behold him, padrone! I have found him consequentementally."

"I shouldn't have objected," returned Mr. Flintwinch, "to your having broken your neck consequentementally."

"And now," said Mr. Pancks, whose eye had often stealthily wandered to the window-seat, and the stocking that was being mended there, "I've only one other word to say before I go. If Mr. Clennam was here—but unfortunately, though he has so far got the better of this fine gentleman as to return him to this place against his will, he is ill and in prison—ill and in prison, poor fellow—if he was here," said Mr. Pancks, taking one step aside toward the window-seat, and laying his right hand upon the stocking; "he would say, 'Affery, tell your dreams!'"

Mr. Pancks held up his right forefinger between his nose and the stocking, with a ghostly air of warning, turned, steamed out, and towed Mr. Baptist after him. The house-door was heard to close upon them, their steps were heard passing over the dull pavement of the echoing court-yard, and still nobody had added a word. Mrs. Clennam and Jeremiah had exchanged a look; and had then looked, and looked still at Affery, who sat mending the stocking with great assiduity.

"Come!" said Mr. Flintwinch at length, screwing himself a curve or two in the direction of the window-seat, and rubbing the palms of his hands on his coat-tails as if he were preparing them to do something: "Whatever has to be said among us, had better be begun to be said, without more loss of time.—So, Affery, my woman, take yourself off!"

In a moment, Affery had thrown the stocking down, started up, caught hold of the window-sill with her right hand, lodged herself upon the window-seat with her right knee, and was flourishing her left hand, beating expected assailants off.

"No, I won't, Jeremiah—no I won't—no I won't! I won't go, I'll stay here. I'll hear all I don't know, and say all I know. I will, at last, if I die for it. I will, I will, I will, I will!"

Mr. Flintwinch, stiffening with indignation and amazement, moistened the fingers of one hand at his lips, softly described a circle with them in the palm of the other hand, and continued with a menacing grin to screw himself in the direction of his wife: gasping some remark as he advanced, of which, in his choking anger, only the words, "Such a dose!" were audible.

"Not a bit nearer, Jeremiah!" cried Affery, never ceasing to beat the air. "Don't come a bit nearer to me, or I'll rouse the neighborhood! I'll throw myself out of window! I'll scream Fire and murder! I'll wake the dead! Stop where you are, or I'll make shrieks enough to wake the dead!"

The determined voice of Mrs. Clennam echoed "Stop!" Jeremiah had stopped already.

"It is closing in, Flintwinch. Let her alone. Affery, do you turn against me after these many years?"

"I do, if it's turning against you to hear what I don't know, and say what I know. I have broke out now, and I can't go back. I am determined to do it. I will do it, I will, I will, I will! If that's turning against you, yes, I turn against both of you two clever ones. I told Arthur, when he first come home, to stand up against you. I told him it was no reason, because I was afeard of my life of you, that he should be. All manner of things have been a going on since then, and I won't be run up by Jeremiah, nor yet I won't be dazed and scared, nor made a party to I don't know what, no more. I won't, I won't, I won't! I'll up for Arthur when he has nothing left, and is ill, and in prison, and can't up for himself. I will, I will, I will, I will!"

"How do you know, you heap of confusion," asked Mrs. Clennam, sternly, "that in doing what you are doing now, you are even serving Arthur?"

"I don't know nothing rightly about any thing," said Affery; "and if ever you said a true word in your life, it's when you call me a heap of confusion, for you two clever ones have done your most to make me such. You married me whether I liked it or not, and you've led me, pretty well ever since, such a life of dreaming and frightening as never was known, and what do you expect me to be but a heap of confusion? You wanted to make me such, and I am such; but I won't submit no longer; no, I won't, I won't, I won't, I won't!" She was still beating the air against all comers.

After gazing at her in silence, Mrs. Clennam turned to Rigaud. "You see and hear this foolish creature. Do you object to such a piece of distraction remaining where she is?"

"I, madame?" he replied; "do I? That's a question for you."

"I do not," she said, gloomily. "There is little left to choose now. Flintwinch, it is closing in."

Mr. Flintwinch replied by directing a look of red vengeance at his wife, and then, as if to pinion himself from falling upon her, screwed his crossed arms into the breast of his waistcoat, and with his chin very near one of his elbows stood in the corner watching Rigaud in the oddest attitude. Rigaud for his part arose from his chair, and seated himself on the table, with his legs dangling. In this easy attitude, he met Mrs. Clennam's set face, with his mustache going up, and his nose coming down.

"Madame, I am a gentleman——"

"Of whom," she interrupted in her steady tones, "I have heard disparagement, in connection with a French jail, and an accusation of murder!"

He kissed his hand to her, with his exaggerated gallantry. "Perfectly. Exactly; of a lady too! What absurdity! How incredible! I had the honor of making a great success then; I hope to have the honor of making a great success now. I kiss your hands. Madame, I am a gentleman (I was going to observe), who when he says, 'I will definitely finish this or that affair at this present sitting,' does definitely finish it. I announce to you, that we are arrived at our last sitting, on our little business. You do me the favor to follow, and to comprehend?"

She kept her eyes fixed upon him with a frown. "Yes."

"Further, I am a gentleman to whom mere mercenary trade-bargains are unknown, but to whom money is always acceptable as the means of pursuing his pleasures. You do me the favor to follow, and to comprehend?"

"Scarcely necessary to ask, one would say. Yes."

"Further, I am a gentleman of the softest and sweetest disposition, but who, if trifled with, becomes enraged. Noble natures under such circumstances become enraged. I possess a noble nature. When the lion is awakened—that is to say, when I enrage—the satisfaction of my animosity is as acceptable to me as money. You always do me the favor to follow, and to comprehend?"

"Yes," she answered somewhat louder than before.

"Do not let me derange you; pray be tranquil. I have said we are now arrived at our last sitting. Allow me to recall the two sittings we have held."

"It is not necessary."

"Death, madame," he burst out, "it's my fancy! Besides, it clears the way. The first sitting was limited. I had the honor of making your acquaintance—of presenting my letter; I am a Knight of Industry, at your service, madame, but my polished manners had won me so much of success, as a master of languages, among your compatriots, who are as stiff as their own starch is to one another, but ever ready to relax to a foreign gentleman of polished manners—and of observing one or two little things," he glanced around the room and smiled, "about this honorable house, to know which was necessary to assure me, and to convince me that I had the distinguished pleasure of making the acquaintance of the lady I sought. I achieved this. I gave my word of honor, to our dear Flintwinch, that I would return. I gracefully departed."

Her face neither acquiesced nor demurred. The same when he paused and when he spoke, it as yet showed him always the one attentive frown, and the dark revelation before mentioned of her being nerved for the occasion.

"I say, gracefully departed, because it was graceful to retire without alarming a lady. To be morally graceful, not less than physically, is a part of the character of Rigaud Blandois. It was also politic, as leaving you, with something overhanging you, to expect me again with a little anxiety, on a day not named. But your slave is politic. By Heaven, madame, politic! Let us return. On the day not named, I have again the honor to render myself at your house. I intimate that I have something to sell, which if not bought, will compromise madame whom I highly esteem. I explain myself generally. I demand —I think it was a thousand pounds. Will you correct me?"

Thus forced to speak, she replied, with constraint, "You demanded as much as a thousand pounds."

"I demand at present, Two. Such are the evils of delay. But to return once more. We are not accordant; we differ on that occasion. I am playful; playfulness is a part of my amiable character. Playfully, I become as one slain and hidden. For, see you, it may alone be worth half the sum, to madame, to be freed from the suspicions that my droll idea awakens. Accident and spies intermix themselves against my playfulness, and spoil the fruit, perhaps—who knows? only you and Flintwinch —when it is just ripe. Thus, madame, I am here for the last time. Listen! Definitely the last."

As he struck his straggling boot-heels against the flap of the table, meeting her frown with an insolent gaze, he began to change his tone for a fiercer one.

"Bah! Stop an instant! Let us advance by steps. Here is my Hotel-note to be paid, according to contract. Five minutes hence we may be at daggers' points. I'll not leave it till then, or you'll cheat me. Pay it! Count me the money!"

"Take it from his hand and pay it, Flintwinch," said Mrs. Clennam.

He spirted it into Mr. Flintwinch's face, when the old man advanced to take it; and held forth his hand, repeating noisily, "Pay it! Count it out! Good money!" Jeremiah picked the bill up, looked at the total with a bloodshot eye, took a small canvas bag from his pocket, and told the amount into his hand.

Rigaud chinked the money, weighed it in his hand, threw it up a little way and caught it, chinked it again.

"The sound of it, to the bold Rigaud Blandois, is like the taste of fresh meat to the tiger. Say, then, madame. How much?"

He turned upon her suddenly, with a menacing gesture of the weighted hand that clutched the money, as if he were going to strike her with it.

"I tell you again, as I told you before, that we are not rich here, as you suppose us to be, and that your demand is excessive. I have not the present means of complying with such a demand, if I had ever so great an inclination."

"If!" cried Blandois. "Hear this lady with her If! Will you say that you have not the inclination?"

"I will say what presents itself to me, and not what presents itself to you."

"Say it then. As to the inclination. Quick! Come to the inclination, and I know what to do."

She was no quicker, and no slower, in her reply. "It would seem that you have obtained possession of a paper—or of papers—which I assuredly have the inclination to recover."

Rigaud, with a loud laugh, drummed his heels against the table, and chinked his money. "I think so. I believe you there!"

"The paper might be worth, to me, a sum of money. I cannot say how much, or how little."

"What, the Devil!" he asked, savagely. "Not after a week's grace to consider?"

"No! I will not, out of my scanty means—for I tell you again, we are poor here, and not rich—I will not offer any price for a power that I do not know the worst and the fullest extent of. This is the third time of your hinting and threatening. You must speak explicitly, or you may go where you will, and do what you will. It is better to be torn to pieces at a spring, than to be a mouse at the caprice of such a cat."

He looked at her so hard with those eyes too near together, that the sinister sight of each crossing that of the other, seemed to make the bridge of his hooked nose crooked. After a long survey, he said, with the further setting-off of his infernal smile:

"You are a bold woman!"

"I am a resolved woman."

"You always were. What? She always was; is it not so, my little Flintwinch?"

"Flintwinch, say nothing to him. It is for him to say here, and now, all he can; or to go hence, and do all he can. You know this to be our determination. Leave him to his action on it."

She did not shrink under his evil leer, or avoid it. He turned it upon her again, but she remained steady at the point to which she had fixed herself. He got off the table, placed a chair near the sofa, sat down in it, and leaned an arm upon the sofa close to her own, which he touched with his hand. Her face was ever frowning, attentive, and settled.

"It is your pleasure, then, madame, that I shall relate a morsel of family history in this little family society," said Rigaud, with a warning play of his lithe fingers on her arm. "I am something of a doctor. Let me touch your pulse."

She suffered him to take her wrist in his hand. Holding it, he proceeded to say:

"A history of a strange marriage, and a strange mother, and a revenge, and a suppression.——Aye, aye, aye? This pulse is beating curiously! It appears to me that it doubles while I touch it. Are these the usual changes of your malady, madame?"

There was a struggle in her maimed arm as she twisted it away, but there was none in her face. On his face there was his own smile.

"I have lived an adventurous life. I am an adventurous character. I have known many adventurers; interesting spirits—amiable society! To one of them I owe my knowledge, and my proofs—I repeat it, estimable lady—proofs—of the ravishing little family history I go to commence. You will be charmed with it. But, bah! I forget. One should name a history. Shall I name it the history of a house? But, bah, again. There are so many houses. Shall I name it the history of this house?"

Leaning over the sofa, poised on two legs of his chair and his left elbow; that hand often tapping her arm, to beat his words home; his legs crossed; his right hand sometimes arranging his hair, sometimes smoothing his mustache, sometimes striking his nose, always threatening her whatever it did; coarse insolent, rapacious, cruel, and powerful; he pursued his narrative at his ease.

"In fine, then, I name it the history of this house. I commence it. There live here, let us suppose, an uncle and nephew. The uncle, a rigid old gentleman, of strong force of character; the nephew, habitually timid, repressed, and under constraint."

Mistress Affery, fixedly attentive in the window-seat, biting the rolled-up end of her apron, and trembling from head to foot, here cried out, "Jeremiah, keep off from me! I've heerd in my dreams, of Arthur's father and his uncle. He's a talking of them. It was before my time here; but I've heerd in my dreams that Arthur's father was a poor, irresolute, frightened chap, who had had every thing but his orphan life scared out of him when he was young, and that he had no voice in the choice of his wife, even, but his uncle chose her. There she sits! I heard it in my dreams, and you said it to her own self."

As Mr. Flintwinch shook his fist at her, and as Mrs. Clennam gazed upon her, Rigaud kissed his hand to her.

"Perfectly right, dear Madame Flintwinch. You have a genius for dreaming."

"I don't want none of your praises," returned Affery. "I don't want to have nothing at all to say to you. But Jeremiah said they was dreams, and I'll tell 'em as such!" Here she put her apron in her mouth again, as if she were stopping some body's else's mouth—perhaps Jeremiah's, which was chattering with threats as if he were grimly cold.

"Our beloved Madame Flintwinch," said Rigaud, "developing all of a sudden a fine susceptibility and spirituality, is right to a marvel. Yes. So runs the history. Monsieur, the uncle, commands the nephew to marry. Monsieur says to him in effect, 'My nephew, I introduce to you a lady of strong force of character, like myself: a resolved lady, a stern lady, a lady who has a will that can break the weak to powder; a lady without pity, without love, implacable, revengeful, cold as the stone, but raging as the fire.' Ah! what fortitude! Ah, what superiority of intellectual strength! Truly, a proud and noble character that I describe in the supposed words of Monsieur, the uncle. Ha, ha, ha! Death of my soul, I love the sweet young lady!"

Mrs. Clennam's face had changes. There was a remarkable darkness of color on it, and the brow was more contracted. "Madame, madame," said Rigaud, tapping her on the arm, as if his cruel hand were sounding a musical instrument, "I perceive I interest you. I perceive I awaken your sympathy. Let us go on!"

The drooping nose and the ascending mustache had, however, to be hidden for a moment with the white hand, before he could go on; he enjoyed the effect he made, so much.

"The nephew being, as the lucid Madame Flintwinch has remarked, a poor devil, who has had every thing but his orphan life frightened and famished out of him—the nephew abases his head, and makes response! 'My uncle, it is to you to command. Do as you will!' Monsieur, the uncle, does as he will. It is what he always does. The auspicious nuptials take place; the newly-married come home to this charming mansion; the lady is received, let us suppose, by Flintwinch. Hey, old intriguer?"

Jeremiah, with his eyes upon his mistress, made no reply. Rigaud looked from one to the other, struck his ugly nose, and made a cluckling with his tongue.

"Soon, the lady makes a singular and exciting discovery. Thereupon, full of anger, full of jealousy, full of vengeance, she forms—see you, madame!—a scheme of retribution, the weight of which she ingeniously forces her crushed husband to bear himself, as well as execute upon her enemy. What superior intelligence!"

"Keep off, Jeremiah!" cried the palpitating Affery, taking her apron from her mouth again. "But it was one of my dreams that you told her, when you quarreled with her one winter evening at dusk—there she sits and you looking at her—that she oughtn't to have let Arthur, when he come home, suspect his father only; that she had always the strength and the power; and that she ought to have stood up more, to Arthur, for his father. It was in the same dream where you said to her that she was not—not something, but I don't know what, for she burst out tremendous and stopped you. You know the dream as well as I do. When you come down stairs into the kitchen with the candle in your hand, and hitched my apron off my head. When you told me I had been dreaming. When you wouldn't believe the noises." After this explosion Affery put her apron into her mouth again; always keeping her hand on the window-sill, and her knee on the window-seat, ready to cry out or jump out, if her lord and master approached.

Rigaud had not lost a word of this.

"Haha!" he cried, lifting his eyebrows, folding his arms, and leaning back in his chair. "Assuredly, Madame Flintwinch is an oracle! How shall we interpret the oracle, you and I, and the old intriguer? He said that you were not ——? And you burst out and stopped him! What was it you were not? What is it you are not? Say, then, madame!"

Under this ferocious banter, she sat breathing harder, and her mouth was disturbed. Her lips quivered and opened, in spite of her utmost efforts to keep them still.

"Come, then, madame! Speak, then! Our old intriguer said that you were not ——, and you stopped him. He was going to say that you were not—what? I know already, but I want a little confidence from you. How, then? You are not what?"

She tried again to repress herself, but broke out vehemently, "Not Arthur's mother!"

"Good," said Rigaud. "You are amenable."

With the set expression of her face all torn away by the explosion of her passion, and with a bursting from every rent feature of the smoldering fire so long pent up, she cried out, "I will tell it myself! I will not hear it from your lips, and with the taint of your wickedness upon it. Since it must be seen, I will have it seen by the light I stood in. Not another word. Hear me!"

"Unless you are a more obstinate and more persisting woman than even I know you to be," Mr. Flintwinch interposed, "you had better leave Mr. Rigaud, Mr. Blandois, Mr. Beelzebub, to tell it in his own way. What does it signify when he knows all about it?"

"He does not know all about it."

"He knows all he cares about it," Mr. Flintwinch testily urged.

"He does not know *me*."

"What do you suppose he cares for you, you conceited woman?" said Mr. Flintwinch.

"I tell you, Flintwinch, I will speak. I tell you, when it has come to this, I will tell it with my own lips, and will express myself throughout it. What! Have I suffered nothing in this room, no deprivation, no imprisonment, that I should condescend at last to contemplate myself in such a glass as *that!* Can you see him? Can you hear him? If your wife were a hundred times the ingrate that she is, and if I were a thousand times more hopeless than I am of inducing her to be silent if this man is silenced, I would tell it myself, before I would bear the torment of hearing it from him."

Rigaud pushed his chair a little back; pushed his legs out straight before him; and sat with his arms folded, over against her.

"You do not know what it is," she went on, addressing him, "to be brought up strictly and straitly. I was so brought up. Mine was no light youth of sinful gayety and pleasure. Mine were days of wholesome repression, punishment, and fear. The corruption of our hearts, the evil of our ways, the curse that is upon us, the terrors that surround us—these were the themes of my childhood. They formed my character, and filled me with an abhorrence of evil-doers. When old Mr. Gilbert Clennam proposed his orphan nephew to my father for my husband, my father impressed upon me that his bringing-up had been, like mine, one of severe restraint. He told me, that besides the discipline his spirit had undergone, he had lived in a starved house, where rioting and gayety were unknown, and where every day was a day of toil and trial like the last. He told me that he had been a man in years, long before his uncle had acknowledged him as one; and that from his schooldays to that hour, his uncle's roof had been a sanctuary to him from the contagion of the irreligious and dissolute. When, within a twelvemonth of our marriage, I found my husband, at that time when my father spoke of him, to have sinned against the Lord and outraged me by holding a guilty creature in my place, was I to doubt that it had been appointed to me to make the discovery, and that it was appointed to me to lay the hand of punishment upon that creature of perdition?

Was I to dismiss in a moment—not my own wrongs—for what was I! but all the rejection of sin, and all the war against it, in which I had been bred?"

She laid her wrathful hand upon the watch on the table.

"No! 'Do not forget.' The initials of those words are within here now, and were within here then. I was appointed to find the old letter that referred to them, and that told me what they meant, and whose work they were, and why they were worked, lying with this watch in his secret drawer. But for that appointment, there would have been no discovery. 'Do not forget.' It spoke to me like a voice from an angry cloud. Do not forget the deadly sin, do not forget the appointed discovery, do not forget the appointed suffering. I did not forget. Was it my own wrong I remembered? Mine! I was but a servant and a minister. What power could I have had over them, but that they were bound in the bonds of their sin, and delivered to me!"

More than forty years had passed over the gray head of this determined woman, since the time she recalled. More than forty years of strife and struggle with the whisper that, by whatever name she called her vindictive pride and rage, nothing through all eternity could change their nature. Yet, gone those more than forty years, and come this Nemesis now looking her in the face, she still abided by her old impiety—still reversed the order of Creation, and breathed her own breath into a clay image of her Creator. Verily, verily, travelers have seen many monstrous idols in many countries, but no human eyes have ever seen more daring, gross, and shocking images of the Divine nature, than we creatures of the dust make in our own likenesses, of our own bad passions.

"When I forced him to give her up to me, by her name and place of abode," she went on in her torrent of indignation and defense; "when I accused her, and she fell hiding her face at my feet, was it my injury that I asserted, were they my reproaches that I poured upon her? Those who were appointed of old to go to wicked kings and accuse them—were they not ministers and servants? And had not I, unworthy, and far-removed from them, sin to denounce? When she pleaded to me her youth, and his wretched and hard life (that was her phrase for the virtuous training he had belied) and the desecrated ceremony of marriage there had secretly been between them, and the terrors of want and shame that had overwhelmed them both, when I was first appointed to be the instrument of their punishment, and the love (for she said the word to me, down at my feet) in which she had abandoned him and left him to me, was it *my* enemy that became my footstool, were they the words of *my* wrath that made her shrink and quiver! Not unto me the strength be ascribed; not unto me the wringing of the expiation!"

Many years had come and gone, since she had had the free use even of her fingers; but it was noticeable that she had already more than once struck her clenched hand vigorously upon the table, and that when she said these words she raised her whole arm in the air, as though it had been a common action with her.

"And what was the repentance that was extorted from the hardness of her heart and the blackness of her depravity? I, vindictive and implacable? It may seem so to such as you who know no righteousness, and no appointment except Satan's. Laugh; but I will be known as I know myself, and as Flintwinch knows me, though it is only to you and this half-witted woman."

"Add, to yourself, madame," said Rigaud. "I have my little suspicions, that madame is rather solicitous to be justified to herself."

"It is false. It is not so. I have no need to be" she said, with great energy and anger.

"Truly?" retorted Rigaud. "Hah!"

"I ask, what was the penitence, in works, that was demanded of her? 'You have a child; I have none. You love that child. Give him to me. He shall believe himself to be my son, and he shall be believed by every one to be my son. To save you from exposure, his father shall swear never to see or communicate with you more; equally to save him from being stripped by his uncle, and to save your child from being a beggar, you shall swear never to see or communicate with either of them more. That done, and your present means, derived from my husband, renounced, I charge myself with your support. You may, with your place of retreat unknown, then leave, if you please, uncontradicted by me the lie that when you passed out of all knowledge but mine, you merited a good name.' That was all. She had to sacrifice her sinful and shameful affections; no more. She was then free to bear her load of guilt in secret, and to break her heart in secret; and through such present misery (light enough for her, I think!) to purchase her redemption from endless misery, if she could. If, in this, I punished her here, did I not open to her a way hereafter? If she knew herself to be surrounded by insatiable vengeance and unquenchable fires, were they mine? If I threatened her, then and afterward, with the terrors that encompassed her, did I hold them in my right hand?"

She turned the watch upon the table, and opened it, and with an unsoftening face, looked at the worked letters within.

"They did *not* forget. It is appointed against such offenses that the offenders shall not be able to forget. If the presence of Arthur was a daily reproach to his father, and if the absence of Arthur was a daily agony to his mother, that was a just dispensation of Jehovah. As well might it be charged upon me, that the stings of an awakened conscience drove her mad, and that it was the will of the Disposer of all things that she should live so many years. I devoted myself to reclaim the otherwise predestined and lost boy; to give him the reputation of an honest origin; to bring him up in fear and trembling, and in a life of practical contrition for the sins that were heavy on his head before his entrance into this condemned world. Was that a cruelty? Was I not visited with consequences of the original offense, in which I had no complicity? Arthur's father and I lived no further apart, with half the globe between us, than when we were together in this house. He died, and sent this watch back to me, with its Do not forget. I do NOT forget, though I do not read it as he did. I read, in it, that I was appointed to do these things. I have so read these three letters since I have had them lying on this table, and I did so read them, with equal distinctness, when they were thousands of miles away."

As she took the watch-case in her hand, with that new freedom in the use of her hand of which she showed no consciousness whatever, bending her eyes upon it as if she were defying it to move her, Rigaud cried with a loud and contemptuous snapping of his fingers, "Come, madame! Time runs out. Come, lady of piety, it must be! You can tell nothing I don't know. Come to the money stolen, or I will! Death of my soul, I have had enough of your other jargon. Come straight to the stolen money!"

"Wretch that you are," she answered, and now her hands clasped her head; "through what fatal error of Flintwinch's, through what incompleteness on his part, who was the only other person helping in these things and trusted with them, through whose and what bringing together of the ashes of a burnt paper, you have become possessed of that codicil, I know no more than how you acquired the rest of your power here——"

"And yet," interrupted Rigaud, "it is my odd fortune to have by me, in a convenient place that I know of, that same short little addition to the will of Monsieur Gilbert Clennam, written by a lady and witnessed by the same lady, and our old intriguer! Ah, bah, old intriguer, crooked little puppet! Madame, let us go on. Time presses. You or I to finish?"

"I!" she answered, with increased determination, if it were possible. "I, because I will not endure to be shown myself, and have myself shown to any one, with your horrible distortion upon me. You, with your practices of infamous foreign prisons and galleys, would make it the money that impelled me. It was not the money."

"Bah, bah, bah! I repudiate, for the moment, my politeness, and say, Lies, lies, lies. You know you suppressed the deed, and kept the money."

"Not for the money's sake, wretch!" She made a struggle as if she were starting up; even as if, in her vehemence, she had almost risen on her disabled feet. "If Gilbert Clennam, reduced to imbecility, at the point of death, and laboring under the delusion of some imaginary relenting toward a girl, of whom he had heard that his nephew had once had a fancy for her, which he had crushed out of him, and that she afterward dropped away into melancholy and withdrawal from all who knew her—if, in that state of weakness, he dictated to me, whose life she had darkened with her sin, and who had been appointed to know her wickedness from her own hand and her own lips, a bequest meant as a recompense to her for supposed unmerited suffering; was there no difference between my spurning that injustice, and coveting mere money—a thing which you, and your comrades in the prisons, may steal from any one?"

"Time presses, madame. Take care!"

"If this house was blazing from the roof to the ground," she returned, "I would stay in it to justify myself, against my righteous motives being classed with those of stabbers and thieves."

Rigaud snapped his fingers tauntingly in her face. "One thousand guineas to the little beauty you slowly hunted to death. One thousand guineas to the youngest daughter her patron might have at fifty, or (if he had none) brother's youngest daughter, on her coming of age, 'as the remembrance his disinterestedness may like best of his protection of a friendless young orphan girl.' Two thousand guineas. What! You will never come to the money?"

"That patron," she was vehemently proceeding, when he checked her.

"Names! Call him Mr. Frederick Dorrit. No more evasions!"

"That Frederick Dorrit was the beginning of it all. If he had not been a player of music, and had not kept, in those days of his youth and prosperity, an idle house where singers, and players, and such like children of Evil, turned their backs on the Light and their faces to the Darkness, she might have remained in her lowly station, and might not have been raised out of it to be cast down. But, no. Satan entered into that Frederick Dorrit, and counseled him that he was a man of innocent and laudable tastes who did kind actions, and that here was a poor girl with a voice for singing music with. Then he is to have her taught. Then Arthur's father, who has all along been secretly pining, in the ways of virtuous ruggedness, for those accursed snares which are called the Arts, becomes acquainted with her. And so, a graceless orphan, training to be a singing girl, carries it, by that Frederick Dorrit's agency, against me, and I am humbled and deceived! Not I, that is to say," she added quickly, as color flushed into her face; "a greater than I. What am I?"

Jeremiah Flintwinch, who had been gradually screwing himself toward her, and who was now very near her elbow without her knowing it, made a specially wry face of objection when she said these words, and moreover twitched his gaiters, as if such pretensions were equivalent to little barbs in his legs.

"Lastly," she continued, "for I am at the end of these things, and I will say no more of them, and you shall say no more of them, and all that remains will be to determine whether the knowledge of them can be kept among us who are here present; lastly, when I suppressed that paper, with the knowledge of Arthur's father—"

"But not with his consent, you know," said Mr. Flintwinch.

"Who said with his consent?" She started to find Jeremiah so near her, and drew back her head, looking at him with some rising distrust. "You were often enough between us, when he would have had me produce it and I would not, to have contradicted me if I had said, with his consent. I say, when I suppressed that paper, I made no effort to destroy it, but kept it by me, here in this house, many years. The rest of the Gilbert property being left to Arthur's father, I could at any time, without unsettling more than the two sums, have made a pretense of finding it. But, besides that I must have supported such by a direct falsehood, (a great responsibility,) I have seen no new reason, in all the time I have been tried here, to bring it to light. It was a rewarding of sin; the wrong result of a delusion. I did what I was appointed to do, and I have undergone within these four wall what I was appointed to undergo. When the paper was at last destroyed—as I thought—in my presence, she had long been dead, and her patron, Frederick Dorrit, had long been deservedly ruined and imbecile. He had no daughter. I had found the niece before then; and what I did for her was better for her, far, than the money, of which she would have had no good." She added, after a moment, as though she addressed the watch: "She herself was innocent, and I might not have forgotten to relinquish it to her, at my death;" and sat looking at it.

"Shall I recall something to you, worthy madame?" said Rigaud. "The little paper was in this house on the night when our friend the prisoner—jail-comrade of my soul—came home from foreign countries. Shall I recall yet something more to you? The little singing-bird that never was fledged, was long kept in a cage, by a guardian of your appointing, well enough known to our old intriguer here. Shall we coax our old intriguer to tell us when he saw him last?"

"I'll tell you!" cried Affery, unstopping her mouth. "I dreamed it, first of all my dreams. Jeremiah, if you come a-nigh me now, I'll scream to be heard at St. Paul's! The person as this man has spoken of, was Jeremiah's own twin brother; and he was here in the dead of the night, on the night when Arthur come home, and Jeremiah with his own hands give him this paper along with I don't know what more, and he took it away in an iron box.—Help! Murder! Save me from Jere-*mi*-ah!"

Mr. Flintwinch had made a run at her, but Rigaud had caught him in his arms midway. After a moment's wrestle with him, Flintwinch gave up, and put his hands in his pockets.

"What!" cried Rigaud, rallying him as he poked and jerked him back with his elbows. "Assault a lady with such a genius for dreaming? Ha, ha, ha! Why, she'll be a fortune to you as an exhibition. All that she dreams comes true. Ha, ha, ha! You're so like him, Little Flintwinch. So like him, as I knew him (when I first spoke English for him to the host) in the Cabaret of the Three Billiard Tables, in the little street of the high roofs, by the wharf at Antwerp! Ah, but he was a brave boy to drink. Ah, but he was a brave boy to smoke! Ah, but he lived in a sweet bachelor-apartment—furnished, on the fifth floor, above the wood and charcoal merchants, and the dress-makers, and the chair-makers, and the maker of tubs—where I knew him too, and where, with his cognac and tobacco, he had twelve sleeps a day and one fit, until he had a fit too much, and ascended to the skies. Ha, ha, ha! What does it matter how I took possession of the papers in his iron box? Perhaps he confided it to my hands for you, perhaps it was locked and my curiosity was piqued, perhaps I suppressed it. Ha, ha, ha! What does it matter, so that I have it safe? We are not particular here; hey, Flintwinch? We are not particular here; is it not so, madame?"

Retiring before him with vicious counter-jerks of his own elbows, Mr. Flintwinch had got back into his corner, where he now stood with his hands in his pockets, taking breath, and returning Mrs. Clennman's stare. "Ha, ha, ha! But what's this ?" cried Rigaud. " It appears as if you don't know, one the other. Permit me, Madame Clennam, who suppresses, to present Monsieur Flintwinch, who intrigues."

Mr. Flintwinch, unpocketing one of his hands to scrape his jaw, advanced a step or so in that attitude, still returning Mrs. Clennam's look, and thus addressed her:

" Now, I know what you mean by opening your eyes so wide at me, but you needn't take the trouble, because I don't care for it. I've been telling you, for how many years, that you're one of the most opiniated and obstinate of women. That's what *you* are. You call yourself humble and sinful, but you are the most Bumptious of your sex. That's what *you* are. I have told you, over and over again when we have had a tiff, that you wanted to make every thing go down before you, but I wouldn't go down before you—that you wanted to swallow up every body alive, but I wouldn't be swallowed up alive. Why didn't you destroy the paper when you first laid hands upon it ? I advised you to ; but no ; it's not your way to take advice. You must keep it, forsooth. Perhaps you may carry it out at some other time, forsooth. As if I didn't know better than that ! I think I see your pride carrying it out, with a chance of being suspected of having kept it by you. But that's the way you cheat yourself. Just as you cheat yourself into making out, that you didn't do all this business because you were a rigorous woman, all slight, and spite, and power, and unforgivingness, but because you were a servant and a minister, and were appointed to do it. Who are you, that you should be appointed to do it ? That may be your religion, but it's my gammon. And, to tell you all the truth while I am about it," said Mr. Flintwinch, crossing his arms, and becoming the express image of irascible doggedness, " I have been rasped—rasped these forty years—by your taking such high ground even with me, who knows better ; the effect of it being coolly to put me on low ground. I admire you very much ; you are a woman of strong head and great talent ; but the strongest head, and the greatest talent, can't rasp a man for forty years without making him sore. So I don't care for your present eyes. Now, I am coming to the paper, and mark what I say. You put it away somewhere, and you keep your counsel where. You're an active woman at that time, and if you want to get that paper, you can get it. But, mark! There comes a time when you are struck into what you are now, and then, if you want to get that paper you can't get it. So it lies, long years in its hiding-place. At last, when we are expecting Arthur home every day, and when any day may bring him home, and it's impossible to say what rummaging he may make about the house, I recommend you five thousand times, if you can't get at it, to let me get at it, that it may be put in the fire. But no—no one but you knows where it is, and that's power; and, call yourself whatever humble names you will, I call you a female Lucifer in appetite for power! On a Sunday night, Arthur comes home. He has not been in this room ten minutes, when he speaks of his father's watch. You know very well that the Do Not Forget, at the time when his father sent that watch to you, could only mean, the rest of the story being then all dead and over, Do Not Forget the suppression. Make restitution! Arthur's ways have frightened you a bit, and the paper shall be burnt after all. So, before that jumping jade and Jezabel," Mr. Flintwinch grinned at his wife, "has got you into bed, you at last tell me where you have put the paper, among the old ledgers in the cellars, where Arthur himself went prowling the very next morning. But, it's not to be burnt on a Sunday night. No; you are strict, you are; we must wait over twelve o'clock, and get into Monday. Now, all this is a swallowing of me up alive, that rasps me; so, feeling a little out of temper, and not being as strict as yourself, I take a look at the document before twelve o'clock, to refresh my memory as to its appearance—fold up one of the many yellow old papers in the cellar like it—and afterward, when we have got into Monday morning, and I have, by the light of your lamp, to walk from you, lying on that bed, to this grate, make a little exchange like the conjurer, and burn accordingly. My brother Ephraim, the lunatic-keeper (I wish he had himself to keep in a straight-waistcoat), had had many jobs since the close of the long job he got from you, but had not done well. His wife died (not that that was much; mine might have died instead, and welcome), he speculated unsuccessfully in lunatics, he got into difficulty about over-roasting a patient to bring him to reason, and he got into debt. He was going out of the way, on what he had been able to scrape up, and a trifle from me. He was here that early Monday morning, waiting for the tide; in short, he was going to Antwerp, where (I am afraid you'll be shocked at my saying, And be damned to him!) he made the acquaintance of this gentleman. He had come a long way, and, I thought then, was only sleepy; but, I suppose now, was drunk. When Arthur's mother had been under the care of him and his wife, she had been always writing, incessantly writing,—mostly letters of confession to you, and prayers for forgiveness. My brother had handed, from time to time, lots of these sheets to me. I thought I might as well keep them to myself, as have them swallowed up alive too; so I kept them in a box, looking them over when I felt in the humor. Convinced that it was advisable to get the paper out of the place, with Arthur coming about it, I put it into this same box, and I locked the whole up with two locks, and I trusted it to my brother to take away and keep, till I should write about it. I did write about it, and never got an answer. I didn't know what to make of it, till this gentleman favored us with his first visit. Of course, I began to suspect how it was, then; and I don't want his word for it now, to understand how he gets his knowledge from my papers, and from your paper, and my brother's cognac and tobacco talk (I wish he'd had to gag himself). Now, I have only one thing more to say, you hammer-headed woman, and that is, that I haven't altogether made up my mind whether I might, or might not, have ever given you any trouble about the codicil. I think not; and that I should have been quite satisfied with knowing I had got the better of you, and that I held the power over you. In the present state of circumstances, I have no more explanation to give you till this time to-morrow night. So you may as well," said Mr. Flintwinch, terminating his oration with a screw, "keep your eyes open at somebody else, for it's no use keeping 'em open at me."

She slowly withdrew them when he had ceased, and dropped her forehead on her hand. Her other hand pressed hard upon the table, and again the curious stir was observable in her, as if she were going to rise.

"This box can never bring, elsewhere, the price it will bring here. This knowledge can never be of the same profit to you, sold to any other person, as sold to me. But I have not the present means of raising the sum you have demanded. I have not prospered. What will you take now, and what at another time, and how am I to be assured of your silence?"

"My angel," replied Rigaud, "I have said what I will take, and time presses. Before coming here, I placed copies of the most important of these papers in another hand. Put off the time till the Marshalsea gate shall be shut for the night, and it will be too late to treat. The prisoner will have read them."

She put her two hands to her head again, uttered a loud exclamation, and started to her feet. She staggered for a moment, as if she would have fallen; then stood firm.

"Say what you mean. Say what you mean, man!"

Before her ghostly figure, so long unused to its erect attitude, and so stiffened in it, Rigaud fell back and dropped his voice. It was, to all the three, as if a dead woman had risen.

"Miss Dorrit," answered Rigaud, "the little niece of Monsieur Frederick, whom I have known across the water, is attached to the prisoner. Miss Dorrit, little niece of Monsieur Frederick, watches at this moment over the prisoner, who is ill. For her, I with my own hands left a packet at the prison, on my way here, with a letter of instructions, '*for his sake*'—she will do any thing for his sake—to keep it without breaking the seal, in case of its being reclaimed before the hour of shutting up to-night—if it should not be reclaimed before the ringing of the prison bell, to give it to him; and it encloses a second copy for herself, which he must give to her. What! I don't trust myself among you, now we have got so far without giving my secret a second life. And as to its not bringing me, elsewhere the price it will bring here, say then, madame, have you limited and settled the price the little niece will give—for his sake—to hush it up? Once more I say, time presses. The packet not reclaimed before the ringing of the bell to-night, you cannot buy. I sell, then, to the little girl!"

Once more the stir and struggle in her, and she ran to a closet, tore the door open, took down a hood or shawl, and wrapped it over her head. Affery, who had watched her in terror, darted to her in the middle of the room, caught hold of her dress, and went on her knees to her.

"Don't, don't, don't! What are you doing? Where are you going? You're a fearful woman, but I don't bear you no ill-

DAMOCLES.

will. I can do poor Arthur no good now, that I see; and you needn't be afraid of me. I'll keep your secret. Don't go out, you'll fall dead in the street. Only promise me, that, if it's the poor thing that's kept here, secretly, you'll let me take charge of her and be her nurse. Only promise me that, and never be afraid of me."

Mrs. Clennam stood still for an instant, at the height of her rapid haste, saying in stern amazement:

"Kept here? She has been dead a score of years and more. Ask Flintwinch—ask *him*. They can both tell you that she died, when Arthur went abroad."

"So much the worse," said Affery, with a shiver, "for she haunts the house then. Who else rustles about it, making signals by dropping dust so softly? Who else comes and goes, and marks the walls with long crooked touches, when we are all a-bed? Who else holds the door sometimes? But don't go out—don't go out! Mistress, you'll die in the street!"

Her mistress only disengaged her dress from the beseeching hands, said to Rigaud, "Wait here till I come back!" and ran out of the room. They saw her, from the window, run wildly through the courtyard and out at the gateway.

For a few moments they stood motionless. Affery was the first to move, and she, wringing her hands, pursued her mistress. Next Jeremiah Flintwinch slowly backing to the door, with one hand in a pocket and the other rubbing his chin, twisted himself out in his reticent way, speechlessly. Rigaud, left alone, composed himself upon the window-seat of the open window, in the old Marseilles-Jail attitude. He laid his cigarettes and fire-box ready to his hand, and fell to smoking.

"Whoof! Almost as dull as the infernal old jail. Warmer, but almost as dismal. Wait till she comes back? Yes, certainly; but where is she gone, and how long will she be gone? No matter! Rigaud Lagnier Blandois, my amiable subject, you will get your money. You will enrich yourself. You have lived a gentleman; you will die a gentleman. You triumph, my little boy; but it is your character to triumph. Whoof!"

In the hour of his triumph, his mustache went up and his nose came down, as he ogled a great beam over his head with particular satisfaction.

CHAPTER LXVII.

CLOSED.

The sun had set, and the streets were dim in the dusty twilight, when the figure so long unused to them hurried on its way. In the immediate neighborhood of the old house, it attracted little attention, for there were only a few straggling people to notice it; but, ascending from the river, by the crooked ways that led to London Bridge, and passing into the great main road, it became surrounded by astonishment.

Resolute and wild of look, rapid of foot, and yet weak and uncertain, conspicuously dressed in its black garments and with its hurried head-covering, gaunt and of an unearthly paleness, it pressed forward, taking no more heed of the throng than a sleep-walker. More remarkable by being so removed from the crowd it was among, than if it had been lifted on a pedestal to be seen, the figure attracted all eyes. Saunterers pricked up their attention to observe it; busy people crossing it, slackened their pace and turned their heads; companions pausing and standing aside, whispered one another to look at this spectral woman who was coming by; and the sweep of the figure as it passed seemed to create a vortex, drawing the most idle and most curious after it.

Made giddy by the turbulent irruption of this multitude of staring faces into her cell of years, by the confusing sensation of being in the air and the yet more confusing sensation of being afoot, by the unexpected changes in half-remembered objects, and the want of likeness between the controllable pictures her imagination had often drawn of the life from which she was secluded, and the overwhelming rush of the reality, she held ner way as if she were environed by distracting thoughts, rather than by external humanity and observation. But, having crossed the bridge, and gone some distance straight onward, she remembered that she must ask for a direction; and it was only then, when she stopped and turned to look about her for a hopeful place of inquiry, that she found herself surrounded by an eager glare of faces.

"Why are you encircling me?" she asked, trembling.

None of those who were nearest answered; but, from the outer ring, there arose a shrill cry of "'Cause you're mad!"

"I am as sane as any one here. I want to find the Marshalsea prison."

The shrill outer circle again retorted, "Then that 'ud show you was mad if nothing else did, 'cause it's right opposite!"

A short, mild, quiet-looking young man, made his way through to her, as a whooping ensued on this reply, and said: "Was it the Marshalsea you wanted? I'm going on duty there. Come across with me."

She laid her hand upon his arm, and he took her over the way; the crowd, rather injured by the near prospect of losing her, pressing before and behind and on either side, and recommending an adjournment to Bedlam. After a momentary whirl in the outer courtyard, the prison-door opened, and shut upon them. In the lodge, which seemed by contrast with the outer noise a place of refuge and peace, a yellow lamp was already striving with the prison shadows.

"Why, John!" said the turnkey who had admitted them. "What is it?"

"Nothing, father; only this lady not knowing her way, and being badgered by the boys. Who did you want, ma'am?"

"Miss Dorrit. Is she here?"

The young man became more interested. "Yes, she is here. What might your name be?"

"Mrs. Clennam."

"Mr. Clennam's mother?" asked the young man.

"She pressed her lips together, and hesitated. "Yes. She had better be told it is his mother."

"You see," said the young man, the Marshal's family living in the country at present, the Marshal has given Miss Dorrit one of the rooms in his house, to use when she likes. Don't you think you had better come up there, and let me bring Miss Dorrit?"

She signified her assent, and he unlocked a door, and conducted her up a side staircase into a dwelling-house above. He showed her into a darkening room, and left her. The room looked down into the darkening prison-yard, with its inmates strolling here and there, leaning out of windows, communing as much apart as they could with friends who were going away, and generally wearing out their imprisonment as they best might, that summer evening. The air was heavy and hot; the closeness of the place, oppressive; and from without there arose a rush of free sounds, like the jarring memory of such things in a headache and heartache. She stood at the window, bewildered, looking down into this prison as it were out of her own different prison, when a soft word or two of surprise made her start, and Little Dorrit stood before her.

"Is it possible, Mrs. Clennam, that you are so happily recovered as——"

Little Dorrit stopped, for there was neither happiness nor health in the face that turned to her.

"This is not recovery; it is not strength; I don't know what it is." With an agitated wave of her hand, she put all that aside. "You have had a packet left with you, which you were to give to Arthur if it was not reclaimed before this place closed to-night."

"Yes."

"I reclaim it."

Little Dorrit took it from her bosom, and gave it into her hand, which remained stretched out, after receiving it.

"Have you any idea of its contents?"

Frightened by her being there, with that new power of movement in her, which, as she had said herself, was not strength, and which was unreal to look upon, as though a picture or a statue had been animated, Little Dorrit answered, "No."

"Read them."

Little Dorrit took the packet from the still outstretched hand, and broke the seal. Mrs. Clennam then gave her the inner packet that was addressed to herself, and held the other. The shadow of the wall and of the prison-buildings, which made the room sombre at noon, made it too dark to read there, with the dusk deepening apace, save in the window. In the window, where a little of the bright summer evening sky could shine upon her, Little Dorrit stood and read. After a broken exclamation or so of wonder and of terror, she read in silence. When she had finished, she looked around and her old mistress bowed herself before her.

"You know, now, what I have done."

"I think so. I am afraid so; though my mind is so hurried, and so sorry, and has so much to pity, that it has not been able to follow all I have read," said Little Dorrit, tremulously.

"I will restore to you what I have withheld from you. Forgive me. Can you forgive me?"

"I can, and Heaven knows I do! Do not kiss my dress and kneel to me; you are too old to kneel to me; I forgive you freely, without that."

"I have more to ask yet."

"Not in that posture," said Little Dorrit. "It is unnatural to see your gray hair lower than mine. Pray rise; let me help you." With that she raised her up, and stood rather shrinking from her, but looking at her earnestly.

"The great petition that I make to you (there is another which grows out of it,) the great supplication that I address to your meriful and gentle heart, is, that you will not disclose this to Arthur until I am dead. If you think, when you have had time for consideration, that it can do him any good to know it while I am yet alive, then tell him. But, you will not think that; and in such case, will you promise me to spare me until I am dead?"

"I am so sorry, and what I have read has so confused my thoughts," returned Little Dorrit, "that I can scarcely give you a steady answer. If I should be quite sure that to be acquainted with it will do Mr. Clennam no good——"

"I know you are attached to him, and will make him the first consideration. It is right that he should be the first consideration; I ask that. But, having regarded him, and still finding that you may spare me for the little time I shall remain on earth, will you do it?"

"I will."

"God bless you!"

She stood in the shadow so that she was only a vailed form to Little Dorrit in the light; but the sound of her voice, in saying those three grateful words, was at once fervent and broken. Broken by emotion as unfamiliar to her frozen eyes as action to her frozen limbs.

"You will wonder, perhaps," she said in a stronger tone, "that I can better bear to be known to you whom I have wronged, than to the son of my enemy who wronged me. For, she did wrong me! She not only sinned grievously against the Lord, but she wronged me. What Arthur's father was to me, she made him. From our marriage-day I was his dread, and that she made me. I was the scourge of both, and that is referable to her. You love Arthur (I can see the blush upon your face; may it be the dawn of happier days to both of you!), and you will have thought already that he is as merciful and kind as you, and why do I not trust myself to him as soon as to you. Have you not thought so?"

"No thought," said Little Dorrit, "can be quite a stranger to my heart, that springs out of the knowledge that Mr. Clennam is always to be relied upon for being kind, and generous, and good."

"I do not doubt it. Yet Arthur is, of the whole world, the one person from whom I would conceal this while I am in it. I kept over him as a child, in the days of his first remembrance, my restraining and correcting hand. I was stern with him, knowing that the transgressions of the parents are visited on their offspring, and that there was an angry mark upon him at his birth. I have sat with him and his father, seeing the weakness of his father yearning to unbend to him; and forcing it back, that the child might work out his release in bondage and hardship. I have seen him, with his mother's face, looking up at me in awe from his little books, and trying to soften me with his mother's ways that hardened me."

The shrinking of her auditress stopped her for a moment in her flow of words, delivered in a retrospective, gloomy voice.

"For his good. Not for the satisfaction of my injury. What was I, and what was the worth of that, before the curse of Heaven? I have seen that child grow up; not to be pious in a chosen way (his mother's offense lay too heavy on him for that), but still to be just and upright, and to be submissive to me. He never loved me, as I once half-hoped he might—so frail we are, and so do the corrupt affections of the flesh war with our trusts and tasks; but he always respected me, and ordered himself dutifully to me. He does to this hour. With an empty place in his heart that he has never known the meaning of, he has turned away from me, and gone his separate road; but even that he has done considerately and with deference. These have been his relations toward me. Yours have been of a much slighter kind, spread over a much shorter time. When you have sat at your needle in my room, you have been in fear of me, but you have supposed me to have been doing you a kindness; you are better informed now, and know me to have done you an injury. Your misconstruction and misunderstanding of the cause in which, and the motives with which, I have worked out this work, is lighter to endure than his would be. I would not, for any worldly recompense I can imagine, have him in a moment, however blindly, throw me down from the station I have held before him all his life, and change me altogether, into something he would cast out of his respect, and think detected and exposed. Let him do it, if it must be done, when I am not here to see it. Let me never feel, while I am still alive, that I die before him, and utterly perish away from him, like one consumed by lightning and swallowed by an earthquake."

Her pride was very strong in her, the pain of it and of her old passions was very sharp with her, when she thus expressed herself. Not less so, when she added:

"Even now, I see *you* shrink from me as if I had been cruel."

Little Dorrit could not gainsay it. She tried not to show it, but she recoiled with dread from the state of mind that had burnt so fiercely and lasted so long. It presented itself to her with no sophistry upon it, in its own plain nature.

"I have done," said Mrs. Clennam, "what it was given to me to do. I have set myself against evil; not against good. I have been an instrument of severity against sin. Have not mere sinners like myself been commissioned to lay it low in all time?"

"In all time?" repeated Little Dorrit.

"Even if my own wrong had prevailed with me, and my own

vengeance had moved me, could I have found no justification? None in the old days when the innocent perished with the guilty, a thousand to one? When the wrath of the hater of the unrighteous was not slaked even in blood, and yet found favor?"

"O, Mrs. Clennam, Mrs. Clennam," said Little Dorrit, "angry feelings and unforgiving deeds are no comfort and no guide to you and me. My life has been passed in this poor prison, and my teaching has been very defective; but let me implore you to remember later and better days. Be guided only by the healer of the sick, the raiser of the dead, the friend of all who were afflicted and forlorn, the patient Master who shed tears of compassion for our infirmities. We cannot but be right if we put all the rest away, and do every thing in remembrance of Him. There is no vengeance and no infliction of suffering in His life I am sure. There can be no confusion in following Him, and seeking for no other footsteps, I am certain!"

In the softened light of the window, looking from the scene of her early trials to the shining sky, she was not in stronger opposition to the black figure in the shade, than the life and doctrine on which she rested were to that figure's history. It bent it's head low again, and said not a word. It remained thus, until the first warning bell began to ring.

"Hark!" cried Mrs. Clennam, starting. "I said I had another petition. It is one that does not admit of delay. The man who brought you this packet and possesses these proofs, is now waiting at my house, to be bought off. I can keep this from Arthur, only by buying him off. He asks a large sum; more than I can get together to pay him, without having time. He refuses to make any abatement, because his threat is that if he fails with me he will come to you. Will you return with me and show him that you already know it? Will you return with me and try to prevail with him? Will you come and help me with him? Do not refuse what I ask in Arthur's name, though I dare not ask it for Arthur's sake!"

Little Dorrit yielded willingly. She glided away into the prison for a few moments, returned, and said she was ready to go. They went out by another staircase, avoiding the lodge; and, coming into the front courtyard, now all quiet and deserted, gained the street.

It was one of those summer evenings when there is no greater darkness than a long twilight. The vista of street and bridge was plain to see, and the sky was serene and beautiful. People stood and sat at their doors, playing with children and enjoying the evening; numbers were walking for air; the worry of the day had almost worried itself out, and few but themselves were hurried. As they crossed the bridge, the clear steeples of the many churches looked as if they had advanced out of the murk that usually enshrouded them and come much nearer. The smoke that rose into the sky had lost its dingy hue, and taken a brightness upon it. The beauties of the sunset had not faded from the long light films of cloud that lay at peace in the horizon. From a radiant centre, over the whole length and breadth of the tranquil firmament, great shoots of light streamed among the early stars, like signs of the blessed later covenant of peace and hope that changed the crown of thorns into a glory.

Less remarkable now that she was not alone and it was darker, Mrs. Clennam hurried on at Little Dorrit's side, unmolested. They left the great thoroughfare at the turning by which she had entered it, and wound their way down among the silent, empty, cross-streets. Their feet were at the gateway, when there was a sudden noise like thunder.

"What was that! Let us make haste in," said Mrs. Clennam.

They were in the gateway. Little Dorrit, with a piercing cry, held her back.

In one swift instant, the old house was before them, with the man lying smoking in the window; another thundering sound, and it heaved, surged outward, opened asunder in fifty places, collapsed and fell. Deafened by the noise, stifled, choked, and blinded by the dust, they hid their faces and stood rooted to the spot. The dust storm, driving between them and the placid sky, parted for a moment and showed them the stars. As they looked up wildly crying for help, the great pile of chimneys, which was then alone left standing, like a tower in a whirlwind, rocked, broke, and hailed itself down upon the heap of ruin, as if every tumbling fragment were intent on burying the crushed wretch deeper.

So blackened by the flying particles of rubbish as to be unrecognizable, they ran back from the gateway into the street, crying and shrieking. There, Mrs. Clennam dropped upon the stones; and she never from that hour moved so much as a finger again, or had the power to speak one word. For upward of three years she reclined in her wheeled chair, looking attentively at those about her, and appearing to understand what they said; but the rigid silence she had so long held was evermore enforced upon her, and, except that she could move her eyes and faintly express a negative and affirmative with her head, she lived and died a statue.

Affery had been looking for them at the prison, and had caught sight of them at a distance on the bridge. She came up to receive her old mistress in her arms, to help to carry her into a neighboring house, and to be faithful to her. The mystery of the noises was out now; Affery, like greater people, had always been right in her facts, and always wrong in the theories she deduced from them.

When the storm of dust had cleared away and the summer night was calm again, numbers of people choked up every avenue of access, and parties of diggers were formed to relieve one another in digging among the ruins. There had been a hundred people in the house at the time of its fall, there had been fifty, there had been fifteen, there had been two. Rumor finally setted the number at two: the foreigner and Mr. Flintwinch.

The diggers dug all through the short night by flaring pipes of gas, and on a level with the early sun, and deeper and deeper below it as it rose into its zenith, and aslant of it as it declined, and on a level with it again as it departed. Sturdy digging, and shoveling, and carrying away, in carts, barrows, and baskets, went on without intermission, by night and by day; but it was night for the second time when they found the dirty heap of rubbish that had been the foreigner, before his head had been shivered to atoms, like so much glass, by the great beam that lay upon him, crushing him.

Still, they had not come upon Flintwinch yet; so, the sturdy digging and shoveling and carrying away went on without intermission by night and by day. It got about that the old house had had famous cellarage (which indeed was true), and that Flintwinch had been in a cellar at the moment, or had had time to escape into one, and that he was safe under its strong arch, and even that he had been heard to cry, in hollow, subterranean, suffocated notes, "Here I am!" At the opposite extremity of the town it was even known that the excavators had been able to open a communication with him through a pipe, and that he had received both soup and brandy by that channel, and that he had said with admirable fortitude that he was All right, my lads! with the exception of his collar-bone. But, the digging and shoveling and carrying away went on without intermission, until the ruins were all dug out, and the cellars opened to the light, and still no Flintwinch, living or dead, all right or all wrong, had been turned up by pick or spade.

It began, then, to be perceived that Flintwinch had not been there at the time of the fall; and it began then to be perceived that he had been rather busy elsewhere, converting securities into as much money as could be got for them on the shortest notice, and turning to his own exclusive account his authority to act for the Firm. Affery remembering that the clever one had said he would explain himself further in four-and-twenty hours' time, determined for her part that his taking himself off within that period with all he could get, was the final satisfactory sum and substance of his promised explanation; but she held her peace, devoutly thankful to be quit of him. As it seemed reasonable to conclude that a man who had never been buried could not be unburied, the diggers gave him up when their task was done, and did not dig down for him into the depths of the earth.

This was taken in ill part by a great many people, who persisted in believing that Flintwinch was lying somewhere among the London geological formations. Nor was their belief much shaken by repeated intelligence which came over in course of time, that an old man, who wore the tie of his neckcloth under one ear, and who was very well known to be an Englishman, consorted with the Dutchmen, on the quaint banks of the canals at the Hague, and in the drinking-shops of Amsterdam, under the style and designation of Mynheer von Flyntevynge.

CHAPTER LXVIII.

GOING.

ARTHUR continuing to lie very ill in the Marshalsea, and Mr. Rugg descrying no break in the legal sky affording a hope of his enlargement, Mr. Pancks suffered desperately from self-reproaches. If it had not been for those infallible figures which proved that Arthur, instead of pining in imprisonment, ought to be promenading in a carriage and pair, and that Mr. Pancks, instead of being restricted to his clerkly wages, ought to have from three to five thousand pounds of his own, at his immediate disposal, that unhappy arithmetician would probably have taken to his bed, and there have made one of the many obscure persons who turned their faces to the wall and died, as a last sacrifice to the late Mr. Merdle's greatness. Solely supported by his unimpugnable calculations, Mr. Pancks led an unhappy and restless life; constantly carrying his figures about with him in his hat, and not only going over them himself on every possible occasion, but entreating every human being he could lay hold of to go over them with him, and observe what a clear case it was. Down in Bleeding Heart Yard, there was scarcely an inhabitant of any note to whom Mr. Pancks had not imparted his demonstration, and, as figures are catching, a kind of ciphering measles broke out in that locality, under the influence of which the whole yard was light-headed.

The more restless Mr. Pancks grew in his mind, the more impatient he became of the Patrarch. In their later conferences, his snorting had assumed an irritable sound which boded the Patriarch no good; likewise, Mr. Pancks had on several occasions looked harder at the Patriarchal bumps than was quite reconcilable with the fact of his not being a painter or a peruke-maker in search of the living model.

However, he had steamed in and out of his little back dock, according as he was wanted or not wanted in the Patriarchal presence, and business had gone on in its customary course. Bleeding Heart Yard had been harrowed by Mr. Pancks, and cropped by Mr. Casby, at the regular seasons; Mr. Pancks had taken all the drudgery and all the dirt of the business as his share; Mr. Casby had taken all the profits, all the ethereal vapor, and all the moonshine, as *his* share; and, in the form of words which that benevolent beamer generally employed on Saturday evenings, when he twirled his fat thumbs after striking the week's balance, "every thing had been satisfactory to all parties—all parties—satisfactory, sir, to all parties."

The Dock of the Steam-Tug, Pancks, had a leaden roof, which, boiling in the very hot sunshine, may have heated the vessel. Be that as it may, one glowing Saturday evening, on being hailed by the lumbering bottle-green ship, the Tug instantly came working out of the Dock in a highly heated condition.

"Mr. Pancks," was the Patriarchal remark, "you have been remiss, you have been remiss, sir."

"What do you mean by that?" was the short rejoinder.

The Patriarchal state, always a state of calmness and composure, was so particularly serene that evening as to be provoking. Every body else within the bills of mortality was hot; but the Patriarch was perfectly cool. Every body was thirsty, and the Patriarch was drinking. There was a fragrance of limes or lemons about him; and he had made a drink of golden sherry, which shone in a large tumbler, as if he were drinking the evening sunshine. This was bad, but not the worst. The worst was, that with his big blue eyes, and his polished head, and his long white hair, and his bottle-green legs stretched out before him, terminating in his easy shoes easily crossed at the instep, he had a radiant appearance of having in his extensive benevolence made the drink for the human species, while he himself wanted nothing but his own milk of human kindness.

Wherefore, Mr. Pancks said, "What do you mean by that?" and put his hair up with both hands, in a highly portentous manner.

"I mean, Mr. Pancks, that you must be sharper with the people, sharper with the people, much sharper with the people, sir. You don't squeeze them. You don't squeeze them. Your receipts are not up to the mark. You must squeeze them, sir, or our connection will not continue to be as satisfactory as I could wish it to be, to all parties. All parties."

"*Don't* I squeeze 'em?" retorted Mr. Pancks. "What else am I made for?"

"You are made for nothing else, Mr. Pancks. You are made to do your duty, but you don't do your duty. You are paid to squeeze, and you must squeeze to pay." The Patriarch so much surprised himself by this brilliant turn, after Dr. Johnson, which he had not in the least expected or intended, that he laughed aloud; and repeated with great satisfaction, as he twirled his thumbs and nodded at his youthful portrait, "Paid to squeeze, sir, and must squeeze to pay."

"Oh!" said Pancks. "Any thing more?"

"Yes, sir; yes, sir. Something more. You will please, Mr. Pancks, to squeeze the yard again, the first thing on Monday morning."

"Oh!" said Pancks. "An't that too soon? I squeezed it dry to-day."

"Nonsense, sir. Not near the mark, not near the mark."

"Oh!" said Pancks, watching him as he benevolently gulped down a good draught of his mixture. "Any thing more?"

"Yes, sir; yes sir; something more. I am not at all pleased, Mr. Pancks, with my daughter; not at all pleased. Besides calling much too often to inquire for Mrs. Clennam, Mrs. Clennam, who is not just now in circumstances that are by no means calculated to—to be satisfactory to all parties, she goes, Mr. Pancks, unless I am much deceived, to inquire for Mr. Clennam in jail. In jail."

"He's laid up, you know," said Pancks. "Perhaps it's kind."

"Pooh, pooh, Mr. Pancks. She has nothing to do with that, nothing to do with that. I can't allow it. Let him pay his debts and come out, come out; pay his debts, and come out."

Although Mr. Pancks's hair was standing up like strong wire, he gave it another double-handed impulse in the perpendicular direction, and smiled at his proprietor in a most hideous manner.

"You will please to mention to my daughter, Mr. Pancks, that I can't allow it, can't allow it," said the Patriarch, blandly.

"Oh!" said Pancks. "You couldn't mention it yourself?"

"No, sir, no; you are paid to mention it," the blundering old booby could not resist the temptation of trying it again, "and you must mention it to pay, mention it to pay."

"Oh!" said Pancks. "Any thing more?"

"Yes, sir. It appears to me, Mr. Pancks, that you yourself are too often and too much in that direction, that direction. I recommend you, Mr. Pancks, to dismiss from your attention both your own losses and other people's losses, and to mind your business, mind your business."

Mr. Pancks acknowledged this recommendation with such an extraordinarily abrupt, short, and loud utterance of the monosyllable "Oh!" that even the unwieldy Patriarch moved his blue eyes in something of a hurry to look at him. Mr. Pancks, with a sniff of corresponding intensity, then added, "Any thing more?"

"Not at present, sir; not at present. I am going," said the Patriarch, finishing his mixture, and rising with an amiable air, "to take a little stroll, little stroll. Perhaps I shall find you here when I come back. If not, sir, duty, duty; squeeze, squeeze, squeeze, on Monday; squeeze on Monday!"

Mr. Pancks, after another stiffening of his hair, looked on at the Patriarchal assumption of the broad-brimmed hat, with a momentary appearance of indecision contending with a sense of injury. He was also hotter than at first, and breathed harder. But he suffered Mr. Casby to go out, without offering any further remark, and then took a peep at him over the little green window-blinds. "I thought so," he observed. "I knew where you were bound to. Good." He then steamed back to his Dock, put it carefully in order, took down his hat, looked round the Dock, said "Good-by!" and puffed away on his own account. He steered straight for Mrs. Plornish's end of Bleeding Heart Yard, and arrived there, at the top of the steps, hotter than ever.

At the top of the steps, resisting Mrs. Plornish's invitations to come and sit along with father in Happy Cottage—

which to his relief was not so numerously filled as it would have been on any other night than Saturday, when the connection who so gallantly supported the business with every thing but money, gave their orders freely—at the top of the steps, Mr. Pancks remained until he beheld the Patriarch, who always entered the Yard at the other end, slowly advancing, beaming, and surrounded by suitors. Then Mr. Pancks descended and bore down upon him, with his utmost pressure of steam on.

The Patriarch, approaching with his usual benignity, was surprised to see Mr. Pancks, but supposed him to have been stimulated to an immediate squeeze instead of postponing that operation until Monday. The population of the Yard were astonished at the meeting, for the two powers had never been seen there together, within the memory of the oldest Bleeding Heart. But they were overcome by unutterable amazement when Mr. Pancks, going close up to the most venerable of men, and halting in front of the bottle-green waistcoat, made a trigger of his right thumb and forefinger, applied the same to the brim of the broad-brimmed hat, and, with singular smartness and precision, shot it off the polished head as if it had been a large marble.

Having taken this little liberty with the Patriarchal person, Mr. Pancks further astounded and attracted the Bleeding Hearts by saying, in an audible voice, "Now, you sugary swindler, I mean to have it out with you!"

Mr. Pancks and the Patriarch were instantly the centre of a press, all eyes and ears; windows were thrown open, and door-steps were thronged.

"What do you pretend to be?" said Mr. Pancks. "What's your moral game? What do you go in for? Benevolence, an't it? You benevolent!" Here Mr. Pancks, apparently without the intention of hitting him, but merely to relieve his mind and expend his superfluous power in wholesome exercise, aimed a blow at the bumpy head, which the bumpy head ducked to avoid. This singular performance was repeated, to the ever increasing admiration of the spectators, at the end of every succeeding article of Mr. Pancks's oration.

"I have discharged myself from your service," said Pancks, "that I may tell you what you are. You're one of a lot of impostors that are the worst lot of all the lots to be met with. Speaking as a sufferer by both, I don't know that I wouldn't as soon have the Merdle lot as your lot. You're a driver in disguise, a screwer by deputy, a wringer, and squeezer, and shaver by substitute. You're a philanthropic sneak. You're a shabby deceiver!"

(The repetition of the performance at this point was received with a burst of laughter.)

"Ask these good people who's the hard man here. They'll tell you Pancks, I believe."

This was confirmed with cries of "Certainly," and "Hear!"

"But I tell you, good people—Casby! This mound of meekness, this lump of love, this bottle-green smiler, this is your driver!" said Pancks. "If you want to see the man who would flay you alive—here he is! Don't look for him in me, at thirty shillings a-week, but look for him in Casby, at I don't know how much a-year!"

"Good!" cried several voices. "Hear Mr. Pancks!"

"Hear Mr. Pancks?" cried that gentleman (after repeating the popular performance), "yes, I should think so! It's almost time to hear Mr. Pancks. Mr. Pancks has come down into the Yard to-night, on purpose that you should hear him. Pancks is only the Works; but here's the Winder!"

The audience would have gone over to Mr. Pancks, as one man, woman, and child, but for the long, gray, silken locks, and the broad-brimmed hat.

"Here's the Stop," said Pancks, "that sets the tune to be ground. And there is but one tune, and its name is Grind, Grind, Grind! Here's the Proprietor, and here's his Grubber. Why, good people, when he comes smoothly spinning through the Yard to-night, like a slow-going benevolent Humming-Top, and when you come about him with your complaints of the Grubber, you don't know what a cheat the Proprietor is! What do you think of his showing himself to-night, that I may have all the blame on Monday? What do you think of his having had me over the coals this very evening, because I don't squeeze you enough? What do you think of my being at the present moment, under special orders to squeeze you dry on Monday?"

The repiy was given in a murmur of "Shame!" and "Shabby!"

"Shabby?" snorted Pancks. "Yes, I should think so. The lot that your Casby belongs to, is the shabbiest of all the lots. Setting their Grubbers on, at a wretched pittance, to do what they're ashamed and afraid to do and pretend not to do, but what they will have done, or give a man no rest! Imposing on you to give their Grubbers nothing but blame, and to give them nothing but credit! Why, the worst-looking cheat in all this town, who gets the value of eighteenpence under false pretenses, an't half such a cheat as this sign-post of The Casby's Head here!"

Cries of "That's true!" and "No more he an't!"

"And see what you get of these fellows, besides," said Pancks. "See what more you get of these precious Humming-Tops, revolving among you with such smoothness that you've no idea of the pattern painted on 'em, or the little window in 'em! I wish to call your attention to myself for a moment. I an't an agreeable style of chap, I know that very well."

The auditory were divided on this point; its more uncompromising members crying, "No, you are not," and its politer materials, "Yes, you are."

"I am, in general," said Mr. Pancks, "a dry, uncomfortable, dreary Plodder and Grubber. That's your humble servant.—There's his full-length portrait, painted by himself and presented to you, warranted a likeness! But what's a man to be, with such a man as this for his Proprietor? What can be expected of him? Did any body ever find boiled mutton and caper-sauce growing in a cocoa-nut?"

None of the Bleeding Hearts ever had, it was clear from the alacrity of their response.

"Well," said Mr. Pancks, "and neither will you find in Grubbers like myself, under Proprietors like this, pleasant qualities. I've been a Grubber from a boy. What has my life been? Fag and grind, fag and grind, turn the wheel, turn the wheel! I haven't been agreeable to myself, and I haven't been likely to be agreeable to any body else. If I was a shilling a week less useful in ten years' time, this impostor would give me a shilling a week less; if as useful a man could be got at sixpence cheaper, he would be taken in my place at sixpence cheaper. Bargain and sale, bless you! Fixed principles! It is a mighty fine sign-post, is The Casby's Head," said Mr. Pancks, surveying it with any thing rather than admiration; "but the real name of the House is The Sham's Arms. Its motto is, Keep the Grubber always at it. Is any gentleman present," said Mr. Pancks, breaking off and looking round, "acquainted with the English Grammar?"

Bleeding Heart Yard was shy of claiming that acquaintance.

"It's no matter," said Mr. Pancks. "I merely wish to remark that the task this Proprietor has set me, has been, never to leave off conjugating the Imperative Mood Present Tense of the verb To keep always at it. Keep thou always at it. Let him keep always at it. Keep we or do we keep always at it. Keep ye or do ye or you keep always at it. Let them keep always at it. Here is your benevolent Patriarch of a Casby, and there is his golden rule. He is uncommonly improving to look at, and I am not at all so. He is as sweet as honey, and I am as dull as ditch-water. He provides the pitch, and I handle it, and it sticks to me. Now," said Mr. Pancks, closing upon his late Proprietor again, from whom he had withdrawn a little for the better display of him to the Yard; "as I am not accustomed to speak in public, and as I have made a rather lengthy speech, all circumstances considered, I shall bring my observations to a close by requesting you to get out of this."

The Last of the Patriarchs had been so seized by assault, and required so much room to catch an idea in, and so much more room to turn it in, that he had not a word to offer in reply. He appeared to be meditating some Patriarchal way out of his delicate position, when Mr. Pancks, once more suddenly applying the trigger to his hat, shot it off again with his former dexterity. On the preceding occasion, one or two of the Bleeding Heart Yarders had obsequiously picked it up and handed it to its owner; but Mr. Pancks had now so far impressed his audience, that the Patriarch had to turn and stoop for it himself.

Quick as lightning, Mr. Pancks, who, for some moments, had

had his right hand in his coat pocket, whipped out a pair of shears, swooped upon the Patriarch behind, and snipped off short the sacred locks that flowed upon his shoulders. In a paroxysm of animosity and rapidity, Mr. Pancks then caught the broad-brimmed hat out of the astounded Patriarch's hand, cut it down into a mere stewpan, and fixed it on the Patriarch's head.

Before the frightful results of this desperate action, Mr. Pancks himself recoiled in consternation. A bare-polled, goggle-eyed, big-headed, lumbering personage stood staring at him, not in the least impressive, not in the least venerable, who seemed to have started out of the earth to ask what was become of Casby. After staring at this phantom in return, in silent awe, Mr. Pancks threw down his shears, and fled for a place of hiding, where he might lie sheltered from the consequences of his crime. Mr. Pancks deemed it prudent to use all possible dispatch in making off, though he was pursued by nothing but the sound of laughter in Bleeding Heart Yard, rippling through the air, and making it ring again.

CHAPTER LXIX.

GOING!

THE changes of a fevered room are slow and fluctuating; but the changes of the fevered world are rapid and irrevocable.

It was Little Dorrit's lot to wait upon both kinds of change. The Marshalsea walls, during a portion of every day, again embraced her in their shadows as their child while she thought for Clennam, worked for him, watched him, and only left him still to devote her utmost love and care to him. Her part in the life outside the gate urged its pressing claims upon her too, and her patience untiringly responded to them. Here was Fanny, proud, fitful, whimsical, further advanced in that disqualified state for going into society which had so much fretted her on the evening of the tortoise-shell knife, resolved always to want comfort, resolved not to be comforted, resolved to be deeply wronged, and resolved that nobody should have the audacity to think her so. Here was her brother, a weak, proud, tipsy, young old man, shaking from head to foot, talking as indistinctly as if some of the money he plumed himself upon had got into his mouth and couldn't be got out, unable to walk alone in any act of his life, and patronizing the sister whom he selfishly loved (he always had that negative merit, ill-starred, and ill-launched Tip!), because he suffered her to lead him. Here was Mrs. Merdle in gauzy mourning—the original cap whereof had possibly been rent to pieces in a fit of grief, but had certainly yielded to a highly becoming article from the Parisian market,—warring with Fanny foot to foot, and breasting her with her desolate bosom every hour in the day. Here was poor Mr. Sparkler, not knowing how to keep the peace between them, but humbly inclining to the opinion that they could do no better than agree that they were both remarkably fine women, and that there was no nonsense about either of them—for which gentle recommendation they united in falling upon him frightfully.

Then, too, here was Mrs. General, got home from foreign parts, sending a Prune and a Prism by post every other day, demanding a new Testimonial by way of recommendation to some vacant appointment or other. Of which remarkable gentlewoman it may be finally observed, that there surely never was a gentlewoman of whose transcendent fitness for any vacant appointment on the face of this earth, so many people were (as the warmth of her Testimonials evinced) so perfectly satisfied—or who was so very unfortunate in having a large circle of ardent and distinguished admirers, who never themselves happened to want her, in any capacity.

On the first crash of the eminent Mr. Merdle's decease, many important persons had been unable to determine whether they should cut Mrs. Merdle or comfort her. As it seemed, however, essential to the strength of their own case that they should admit her to have been cruelly deceived, they graciously made the admission and continued to know her. It followed that Mrs. Merdle, as a woman of fashion and good breeding, who had been sacrificed to the wiles of a vulgar barbarian (for Mr. Merdle was found out from the crown of his head to the sole of his foot, the moment he was found out in his pocket), must be actively championed by her order, for her order's sake. She returned this fealty, by causing it to be understood that she was even more incensed against the felonious shade of the deceased than any body else was ; thus on the whole she came out of her furnace like a wise woman, and did exceedingly well.

Mr. Sparkler's lordship was fortunately one of those shelves on which a gentleman is considered to be put away for life, unless there should be reasons for hoisting him up with the Barnacle crane to a more lucrative height. That patriotic servant accordingly stuck to his colors (the Standard of Four Quarterings), and was a perfect Nelson in respect of nailing them to the mast. On the profits of his intrepidity, Mrs. Sparkler and Mrs. Merdle, inhabiting different floors of the genteel little temple of inconvenience to which the smell of the day before yesterday's soup and coach-horses was as constant as Death to man, arrayed themselves to fight it out in the lists of Society, sworn rivals. And Little Dorrit, seeing all these things as they developed themselves, could not but wonder, anxiously, into what back corner of the genteel establishment Fanny's children would be poked by-and-by, and who would take care of those unborn little victims.

Arthur being far too ill to be spoken with on subjects of emotion or anxiety, and his recovery greatly depending on the repose into which his weakness could be hushed, Little Dorrit's sole reliance during this heavy period was on Mr. Meagles. He was still abroad; but she had written to him, through his daughter, immediately after first seeing Arthur in the Marshalsea, and since, confiding her uneasiness to him on the points on which she was most anxious, but especially on one. To that one, the continued absence of Mr. Meagles abroad, instead of his comforting presence in the Marshalsea, was referable.

Without disclosing the precise nature of the documents that had fallen into Rigaud's hands, Little Dorrit had confided the general outline of that story to Mr. Meagles, to whom she had also recounted his fate. The old cautious habits of the scales and scoop at once showed Mr. Meagles the importance of recovering the original papers; wherefore, he wrote back to Little Dorrit, strongly confirming her in the solicitude she expressed on that head, and adding that he would not come over to England "without making some attempt to trace them out."

By this time, Mr. Henry Gowan had made up his mind that it would be agreeable to him not to know the Meagleses. He was so considerate as to lay no injunctions on his wife in that particular; but he mentioned to Mr. Meagles that personally they did not appear to get on together, and that he thought it would be a good thing if—politely, and without any scene, or any thing of that sort—they agreed that they were the best fellows in the world, but were best apart. Poor Mr. Meagles, who was already sensible that he did not advance his daughter's happiness by being constantly slighted in her presence, said, "Good Henry! You are my pet's husband: you have displaced me, in the course of nature; if you wish it, good!" This arrangement involved the contingent advantage, which perhaps Henry Gowan had not foreseen, that both Mr. and Mrs. Meagles were more liberal than before to their daughter, when their communication was only with her and her young child; and that his high spirit found itself better provided with money, without being under ths degrading necessity of knowing whence it came.

Mr. Meagles, at such a period, naturally seized an occupation with great ardor. He knew from his daughter the various towns which Rigaud had been haunting, and the various hotels at which he had been living for some time back. The occupation he set himself was, to visit these with all discretion and speed and in the event of finding anywhere that he had left a bill unpaid, and a box or parcel behind, to pay such bill and bring away such box or parcel.

With no other attendant than Mother, Mr. Meagles went upon this pilgrimage, and encountered a number of adventures. Not the least of his difficulties was, that he never knew what was said to him, and that he pursued his inquiries among people who never knew what he said to them. Still, with an unshaken confidence that the English tongue was somehow the mother tongue of the whole world, only the people were too stupid to know it, Mr. Meagles harangued innkeepers in the most voluble manner, entered into loud explanations of the most complicated sort, and utterly renounced replies in the native language of the respondents, on the ground that they were "all bosh." Sometimes interpreters were called in; whom Mr. Meagles addressed in such idiomatic terms of speech, as instantly to extinguish and shut up —which made the matter worse. On a balance of the account, however, it may be doubted whether he lost much; for, although he found no property, he found so many debts and various associations of discredit with the proper name which was the only word he made intelligible, that he was almost everywhere overwhelmed with injurious accusations. On no fewer than four occasions, the police were called in to receive denunciations of Mr. Meagles as a Knight of Industry, a good-for-nothing, and a thief; all of which opprobrious language he bore with the best temper (having no idea what it meant), and was in the most ignominious manner escorted to steamboats and public carriages to be got rid of, talking all the while, like a cheerful and fluent Briton as he was, with Mother under his arm.

But, in his own tongue, and in his own head, Mr. Meagles was a clear, shrewd, persevering man. When he had "worked round," as he called it, to Paris in his pilgrimage, and had wholly failed in it so far, he was not disheartened. "The nearer to England I follow him, you see, Mother," argued Mr. Meagles, "the nearer I am likely to come to the papers, whether they turn up or no. Because it is only reasonable to conclude, that he would deposit them somewhere where they would be safe from people over in England, and where they would yet be accessible to himself, don't you see."

At Paris, Mr. Meagles found a letter from Little Dorrit, lying waiting for him; in which she mentioned that she had been able to talk for a minute or two with Mr. Clennam, about this man who was no more; and that when she told Mr. Clennam that his friend Mr. Meagles, who was on his way to see him, had an interest in ascertaining something about the man if he could, he had asked her to tell Mr. Meagles that he had been known to Miss Wade, then living in such a street at Calais. "Oho!" said Mr. Meagles.

As soon afterward as might be, in those Diligence days, Mr. Meagles rang the cracked bell at the cracked gate, and it jarred opened, and the peasant woman stood in the dark doorway, saying, "Ice-say! Seer! Who?" In acknowledgment of whose address, Mr. Meagles murmured to himself that there was some sense about these Calais people, who really did know something of what you and themselves were up to; and returned, "Miss Wade, my dear." He was then shown into the presence of Miss Wade.

"It's some time since we met," said Mr. Meagles, clearing his throat; "I hope you have been pretty well, Miss Wade?"

Without hoping that he or anybody else had been pretty well, Miss Wade asked him to what she was indebted for the honor of seeing him again? Mr. Meagles, in the meanwhile, glanced all round the room, without observing any thing in the shape of a box.

"Why, the truth is, Miss Wade," said Mr. Meagles, in a comfortable, managing, not to say coaxing, voice, "it is possible that you may be able to throw a light upon a little something that is at present dark. Any unpleasant bygones between us, are bygones, I hope. Can't be helped now. You recollect my daughter? Times change so! A mother!"

In his innocence, Mr. Meagles could not have struck a worse

key-note. He paused for any expression of interest, but paused in vain.

"That is not the subject you wished to enter on?" she said, after a cool silence.

"No, no," returned Mr. Meagles. "No. I thought your good-nature might——"

"I thought you knew," she interrupted, with a smile, "that my good-nature is not to be calculated upon."

"Don't say so," said Mr. Meagles; "you do yourself an injustice. However, to come to the point." For he was sensible of having gained nothing by approaching it in a roundabout way. "I have heard from my friend Clennam, who, you will be sorry to hear, has been and still is very ill——"

He paused again, and again she was silent.

"—that you had some knowledge of one Blandois, lately killed in London, by a violent accident. Now, don't mistake me! I know it was a slight knowledge," said Mr. Meagles, dexterously forestalling an angry interruption which he saw about to break. "I am fully aware of that. It was a slight knowledge, I know. But, the question is," Mr. Meagles's voice here became comfortable again, "did he, on his way to England last time, leave a box of papers, or a bundle of papers, or some papers or other in some receptacle or other—any papers —with you: begging you to allow him to leave them here for a short time, until he wanted them?"

"The question is?" she repeated. "Whose question is?"

"Mine," said Mr. Meagles. "And not only mine, but Clennam's question, and other people's question. Now, I am sure," continued Mr. Meagles, whose heart was overflowing with Pet, "that you can't have any unkind feeling toward my daughter; it's impossible. Well! It's her question, too; being one in which a particular friend of hers is nearly interested. So here I am, frankly to say that *is* the question, and to ask, Now, did he?"

"Upon my word," she returned, "I seem to be a mark for every body who knew any thing of a man I once in my life hired, and paid, and dismissed, to aim their questions at!"

"Now, don't," remonstrated Mr. Meagles, "don't! Don't take offense, because it's the plainest question in the world, and might be asked of any one. The documents I refer to were not his own, were wrongfully obtained, might at some time or other be troublesome to an innocent person to have in keeping, and are sought by the people to whom they really belong. He passed through Calais going to London, and there were reasons why he should not take them with him then, why he should wish to be able to put his hands upon them readily, and why he should distrust leaving them with people of his own sort. Did he leave them here? I declare, if I knew how to avoid giving you offense, I would take any pains to do it. I put the question personally, but there's nothing personal in it. I might put it to any one; I have put it already to many people. Did he leave them here? Did he leave any thing here?"

"No."

"Then, unfortunately, Miss Wade, you know nothing about them."

"I know nothing about them. I have now answered your unaccountable question. He did not leave them here, and I know nothing about them."

"There!" said Mr. Meagles, rising. "I am sorry for it; that's over; and I hope there is not much harm done. Tattycoram well, Miss Wade?"

"Harriet well? Oh yes!"

"I have put my foot in it again," said Mr. Meagles, thus corrected. "I can't keep my foot out of it, here, it seems. Perhaps, if I had thought twice about it, I might never have given her the jingling name. But, when one means to be good-natured and sportive with young people, one doesn't think twice. Her old friend leaves a kind word for her, Miss Wade, if you should think proper to deliver it."

She said nothing as to that; and Mr. Meagles, taking his honest face out of the dull room, where it shone like a sun, took it to the Hotel where he had left Mrs. Meagles, and where he made the Report: "Beaten, Mother; no effects!" He took it next to the London Steam Packet, which sailed in the night; and next to the Marshalsea.

The faithful John was on duty, when Father and Mother Meagles presented themselves at the wicket toward nightfall. Miss Dorrit was not there then, he said; but she had been there in the morning, and invariably came in the evening. Mr.

Clennam was slowly mending; and Maggy and Mrs. Plornish and Mr. Baptist took care of him by turns. Miss Dorrit was sure to come back that evening before the bell rang. There was the room the Marshal had lent her, up-stairs, in which they could wait for her, if they pleased. Mistrustful that it might be hazardous to Arthur to see him without preparation, Mr. Meagles accepted the offer: and they were left shut up in the room, looking down through its barred window into the jail.

The cramped area of the prison had such an effect on Mrs. Meagles that she began to weep, and such an effect on Mr. Meagles that he began to gasp for air. He was walking up and down the room, panting, and making himself worse by laboriously fanning himself with his handkerchief, which he turned toward the opening door.

"Eh? Good Gracious!" said Mr. Meagles, "this is not Miss Dorrit! Why, Mother, look! Tattycoram!"

No other. And in Tattycoram's arms was an iron box some two feet square. Such a box had Affery Flintwinch seen in the first of her dreams, going out of the old house in the dead of the night, under Double's arm. This, Tattycoram put on the ground at her old master's feet; this, Tattycoram fell on her knees by, and beat her hands upon, crying half in exultation and half in despair, half in laughter and half in tears, "Pardon, dear Master, take me back dear Mistress, here it is!"

"Tatty!" exclaimed Mr. Meagles.

"What you wanted!" said Tattycoram. "Here it is! I was put in the next room not to see you. I heard you ask her about it, I heard her say she hadn't got it, I was there when he left it, and I took it at bedtime and brought it away. Here it is!"

"Why, my girl," cried Mr. Meagles, more breathless than before, "how did you come over?"

"I came in the boat with you. I was sitting wrapped up at the other end. When you took a coach at the wharf, I took another coach, and followed you here. She never would have given it up, after what you had said to her about its being wanted; she would sooner have sunk it in the sea, or burnt it. But, here it is!"

The glow and rapture that the girl was in, with her "Here it is!"

"She never wanted it to be left, I must say that for her; but he left it, and I know well that after what you said, and after her denying it, she never would have given it up. But here it is! Dear Master, dear Mistress, take me back again, and give me back the dear old name! Let this intercede for me. Here it is!"

Father and Mother Meagles never deserved their names better, than when they took the headstrong foundling-girl into their protection again.

"Oh! I have been so wretched," cried Tattycoram, weeping much more after that, than before; "always so unhappy, and so repentant! I was afraid of her, from the first time I ever saw her. I knew she had got a power over me, through understanding what was bad in me, so well. It was a madness in me, and she could raise it whenever she liked. I used to think, when I got into that state, that people were all against me because of my first beginning; and the kinder they were to me, the worse fault I found in them. I made it out that they triumphed above me, and that they wanted to make me envy them, when I know—when I even knew then, if I would—that they never thought of such a thing. And my beautiful young mistress not so happy as she ought to have been, and I gone away from her! Such a brute and wretch as she must think me! But you'll say a word to her for me, and ask her to be as forgiving as you two are? For, I am not so bad as I was," pleaded Tattycoram; "I am bad enough, but not so bad as I was, indeed. I have had Miss Wade before me all this time, as if it was my own self grown ripe—turning every thing the wrong way, and twisting all good into evil. I have had her before me all this time, finding no pleasure in any thing but in keeping me as miserable, suspicious, and tormenting as herself. Not that she had much to do, to do that," cried Tattycoram, in a closing great burst of distress, "for I was bad as bad could be. I only mean to say, that, after what I have gone through, I hope I shall never be quite so bad again, and that I shall get better by very slow degrees. I'll try very hard. I won't stop at five and twenty, sir. I'll count five and twenty hundred, five and twenty thousand!"

Another opening of the door, and Tattycoram subsided, and Little Dorrit came in, and Mr. Meagles with pride and joy produced the box, and her gentle face was lighted up with grateful happiness and joy. The secret was safe now! She could keep her own part of it from him; he should never know of her loss; in time to come, he should know all that was of import to himself; but he should never know what concerned her, only. That was all past, all forgiven, all forgotten.

"Now, my dear Miss Dorrit," said Mr. Meagles; "I am a man of business—or at least was—and I am going to take my measures, promptly, in that character. Had I better see Arthur to-night?"

"I think not to-night. I will go to his room and ascertain how he is. But I think it will be better not to see him to-night."

"I am much of your opinion, my dear," said Mr. Meagles, "and therefore I have not been any nearer to him than this dismal room. Then I shall probably not see him for some little time to come. But I'll explain what I mean when you come back."

She left the room. Mr. Meagles looking through the bars of the window, saw her pass out of the Lodge below him into the prison-yard. He said gently, "Tattvcoram, come to me a moment, my good girl."

She went up to the window.

"You see that young lady who was here just now—that little, quiet, fragile figure passing along there, Tatty? Look. The people stand out of the way to let her go by. The men —see the poor, shabby fellows—pull off their hats to her quite politely, and now she glides in at that doorway. See her, Tattycoram?"

"Yes, sir."

"I have heard tell, Tatty, that she was once regularly called the child of this place. She was born here, and lived here many years. I can't breathe here. A doleful place to be born and bred in, Tattycoram?"

"Yes indeed, sir!"

"If she had constantly thought of herself, and settled with herself that every body visited this place upon her, turned it against her, and cast it at her, she would have led an irritable and probably a useless existence. Yet I have heard tell, Tattycoram, that her young life has been one of active resignation, goodness, and noble service. Shall I tell you what I consider those eyes of hers that were here just now, to have always looked at, to get that expression?"

"Yes, if you please, sir."

"Duty, Tattycoram. Begin it early, and do it well; and there is no antecedent to it, in any origin or station, that will tell against us with the Almighty, or with ourselves."

They remained at the window, Mother joining them and pitying the prisoners, until she was seen coming back. She was soon in the room, and recommended that Arthur, whom she had left calm and composed, should not be visited that night.

"Good!" said Mr. Meagles, cheerily. "I have not a doubt that's best. I shall trust my remembrances then, my sweet nurse, in your hands, and I well know they couldn't be in better. I am off again to-morrow morning."

Little Dorrit, surprised, asked him where?

"My dear," said Mr. Meagles, "I can't live without breathing. This place has taken my breath away, and I shall never get it back again until Arthur's out of this place."

"How is that a reason for going off again to-morrow morning?"

"You shall understand," said Mr. Meagles. "To-night we three will put up at a City Hotel. To-morrow morning, Mother and Tattycoram will go down to Twickenham, where Mrs. Tickit, sitting attended by Dr. Buchan in the parlor-window, will think them a couple of ghosts; and I shall go abroad again for Doyce. We must have Dan here. Now, I tell you, my love, it's of no use writing and planning and conditionally speculating, upon this and that and the other, at uncertain intervals and distance; we must have Doyce here. I devote myself, at daybreak to-morrow morning, to bringing Doyce here. It's nothing to me to go and find him. I'm an old traveler, and all foreign languages and customs are alike to me—I never understand any thing about any of 'em. Therefore I can't be put to any inconvenience. Go at once I must, it stands to reason; because I can't live, without breathing freely;

and I can't breathe freely, until Arthur is out of this Marshalsea. I am stifled at the present moment, and have scarcely breath enough to say this much, and to carry this precious box down stairs for you."

They got into the street as the bell began to ring, Mr. Meagles carrying the box. Little Dorrit had no conveyance there; which rather surprised him. He called a coach for her, and she got into it, and he placed the box beside her when she was seated. In her joy and gratitude she kissed his hand.

"I don't like that, my dear," said Mr. Meagles. "It goes against my feeling of what's right, that *you* should do homage to *me*—at the Marshalsea Gate."

She bent forward, and kissed his cheek.

"You remind me of the days," said Mr. Meagles, suddenly drooping—"but she's very fond of him, and hides his faults, and thinks that no one sees them—and he certainly is well connected, and of a very good family!"

It was the only comfort he had in the loss of his daughter, and if he made the most of it, who could blame him?

CHAPTER LXX.

GONE.

On a healthy autumn day, the Marshalsea prisoner, weak but otherwise restored, sat listening to a voice that read to him. On a healthy autumn day; when the golden fields had been reaped and plowed again, when the summer fruits had ripened and waned, when the green perspective of hops had been laid low by the busy pickers, when the apples clustering in the orchards were russet, and the berries of the mountain ash were crimson among the yellowing foliage. Already in the woods, glimpses of the hardy winter that was coming, were to be caught through unaccustomed openings among the boughs where the prospect shone defined and clear, free from the bloom of the drowsy summer weather, which had rested on it as the bloom lies on the plum. So, from the sea-shore the ocean was no longer to be seen lying asleep in the heat, but its thousand sparkling eyes were open, and its whole breadth was in joyful animation, from the cool sand on the beach to the little sails on the horizon, drifting away like autumn-tinted leaves that had drifted from the trees.

Changeless and barren, looking ignorantly at all the seasons with its fixed, pinched face of poverty and care, the prison had not a touch of any of these beauties on it. Blossom what would, its bricks and bars bore uniformly the same dead crop. Yet Clennam, listening to the voice as it read to him, heard in it all that great Nature was doing, heard in it all the soothing songs she sings to man. At no Mother's knee but hers, had he ever dwelt in his youth on hopeful promises, on playful fancies, on the harvests of tenderness and humility that lie hidden in the early-fostered seeds of the imagination; on the oaks of retreat from blighting winds, that have the germs of their strong roots in nursery acorns. But, in the tones of the voice that read to him, there were memories of an old feeling of such things, and echoes of every merciful and loving whisper that had ever stolen to him in his life.

When the voice stopped, he put his hand over his eyes, murmuring that the light was strong upon them.

Little Dorrit put the book by, and presently arose quietly to shade the window. Maggy sat at her needlework in her old place. The light softened, Little Dorrit brought her chair closer to his side.

"This will soon be over, now, dear Mr. Clennam. Not only are Mr. Doyce's letters to you so full of friendship and encouragement, but Mr. Rugg says his letters to him are so full of help, and that every body (now a little anger is past) is so considerate, and speaks so well of you, that it will soon be over now."

"Dear girl. Dear heart. Good angel!"

"You praise me far too much. And yet it is such an exquisite pleasure to me to hear you speak so feelingly, and to—and to see," said Little Dorrit, raising her eyes to his, "how deeply you mean it, that I cannot say don't."

He lifted her hand to his lips.

"You have been here many, many times, when I have not seen you, Little Dorrit?"

"Yes, I have been here sometimes when I have not come into the room."

"Very often?"

"Rather often," said Little Dorrit, timidly.

"Every day?"

"I think," said Little Dorrit, after hesitating, "that I have been here at least twice, every day."

He might have released the little light hand, after fervently kissing it again; but that, with a very gentle lingering where it was, it seemed to court being retained. He took it in both of his, and it lay softly on his breast.

"Dear Little Dorrit, it is not my imprisonment only that will soon be over. This sacrifice of yours must be ended. We must learn to part again, and to take our different ways so wide asunder. You have not forgotten what we said together, when you came back?"

"Oh no, I have not forgotten it. But something has—You feel quite strong to day, don't you?"

"Quite strong."

The hand he held crept up a little nearer to his face.

"Do you feel quite strong enough to know what a great fortune I have got?"

"I shall be very glad to be told. No fortune is too great or good for Little Dorrit."

"I have been anxiously waiting to tell you. I have been longing and longing to tell you. You are sure you will not take it?"

"Never!"

"You are quite sure you will not take half of it?"

"Never, dear Little Dorrit?"

As she looked at him silently, there was something in her affectionate face that he did not quite comprehend; something that was full of repressed feeling; that could have broken into tears in a moment, and yet that was happy and proud.

"You will be sorry to hear what I have to tell you about Fanny. Poor Fanny has lost every thing. She has nothing left but her husband's income. All that papa gave her when she married was lost as your money was lost. It was in the same hands, and it is all gone."

Arthur was more shocked than surprised to hear it. "I had hoped it might not be so bad," he said: "but I had feared a heavy loss there, knowing the connection between her husband and the defaulter."

"Yes. It is all gone. I am very sorry for Fanny; very, very, very sorry for poor Fanny. My poor brother, too!"

"Had *he* property in the same hands?"

"Yes! And it is all gone.—How much do you think my great fortune is?"

As Arthur looked at her inquiringly with a new apprehension on him, she withdrew her hand, and laid her face down on the spot where it had rested.

"I have nothing in the world. I am as poor as when I lived here. When papa came over to England, he confided every thing he had to the same hands, and it is all swept away. O, my dearest and best, are you quite sure you will not share my fortune with me now?"

Locked in his arms, held to his heart, with his manly tears upon her own cheek, she drew the slight hand round his neck, and clasped it in its fellow-hand.

"Never to part, my dearest Arthur; never any more until the last! I never was rich before, I never was proud before, I never was happy before. I am rich in being taken by you, I am proud in having been resigned by you, I am happy in being with you in this prison, as I should be happy in coming back to it with you, if it should be the will of God, and comforting and serving you with all my love and truth. I am yours anywhere, everywhere! I love you dearly! I would rather pass my life here with you, and go out daily, working for our bread, than I would have the greatest fortune that ever was told, and be the greatest lady that ever was honored. O, if poor papa may only know how blest at last my heart is, in this room where he suffered for so many years!"

Maggy had of course been staring from the first, and had of course been crying her eyes out, long before this. Maggy was now so overjoyed that, after hugging her little mother with all her might, she went down stairs like a clog-hornpipe to find some body or other to whom to impart her gladness. Whom should Maggy meet but Flora and Mr. F.'s Aunt opportunely coming in? And whom else, as a consequence of that meeting, should Little Dorrit find waiting for herself, when, a good two or three hours afterward, she went out?

Flora's eyes were a little red, and she seemed rather out of spirits. Mr. F.'s Aunt was so stiffened that she had the appearance of being past bending, by any means short of powerful mechanical pressure. Her bonnet was cocked up behind in a terrific manner; and her stony reticule was as rigid as if it had been petrified by the Gorgon's head, and had got it at that moment inside. With these imposing attributes, Mr. F.'s Aunt, publicly seated on the steps of the Marshal's official residence, had been for the two or three hours in question a great boon to the younger inhabitants of the Borough, whose sallies of humor she had considerably flushed herself by resenting, at the point of her umbrella, from time to time.

"Painfully aware, Miss Dorrit, I am sure," said Flora, "that to propose an adjournment to any place to one so far removed by fortune and so courted and caressed by the best society, must ever appear intruding even if not a pie-shop far below your present sphere and a back-parlor though a civil man but if for the sake of Arthur—can not overcome it more improper now than ever late Doyce and Clennam—one last remark I might wish to make, one last explanation I might wish to offer perhaps your good nature might excuse under pretense of three kidney ones the humble place of conversation."

Rightly interpreting this rather obscure speech, Little Dorrit returned that she was quite at Flora's disposition. Flora accordingly led the way across the road to the pie-shop in question; Mr. F.'s Aunt stalking across in the rear, and putting herself in the way of being run over, with a perseverance worthy of a better cause.

When the "three kidney ones," which were to be a blind to the conversation, were set before them on three little tin platters, each kidney one ornamented with a hole at the top, into which the civil man poured hot gravy out of a spouted can, as if he were feeding three lamps, Flora took out her pocket-handkerchief.

"If Fancy's fair dreams," she began, "have ever pictured that when Arthur—can not overcome it pray excuse me—was restored to freedom even a pie as far from flaky as the present and so deficient in kidney as to be in that respect like a minced nutmeg might not prove unacceptable if offered by the hand of true regard such visions have forever fled and all is canceled but being aware that tenderer relations are in contemplation beg to state that I heartily wish well to both and find no fault with either not the least, it may be withering to know that ere the hand of Time had made me much less slim than formerly and dreadfully red on the slightest exertion, particularly after eating, I well know when it takes the form of a rash, it might have been and was not through the interruption of parents and mental torpor succeeded until the mysterious clue was held by

Mr. F. still I would not be ungenerous to either and I heartily wish well to both."

Little Dorrit took her hand, and thanked her for all her old kindness.

"Call it not kindness," returned Flora, giving her an honest kiss, "for you always were the best and dearest little thing that ever was if I may take the liberty and even in a money point of view a saving being Conscience itself though I must add much more agreeable than mine ever was to me for though not I hope more burdened than other people's yet I have always found it far readier to make one one uncomfortable than comfortable and evidently taking a greater pleasure in doing it but I am wandering, one hope I wish to express ere yet the closing scene draws in and it is that I do trust for the sake of old times and old sincerity that Arthur will know that I didn't desert him in his misfortunes but that I came backward and forward constantly to ask if I could do any thing for him and that I sat in the pie-shop where they very civilly fetched something warm in a tumbler from the hotel and really very nice hours after hours to keep him company over the way without his knowing it."

Flora really had tears in her eyes now, and they showed her to great advantage.

"Over and above which," said Flora, "I earnestly beg you as the dearest thing that ever was if you'll still excuse the familiarity from one who moves in very different circles to let Arthur understand that I don't know after all whether it wasn't all nonsense between us though pleasant at the time and trying too and certainly Mr. F. did work a change and the spell being broken nothing could be expected to take place without weaving it afresh which various circumstances have combined to prevent of which perhaps not the least powerful was that it was not to be, I am not prepared to say that if it had been agreeable to Arthur and had brought itself about naturally in the first instance I should not have been very glad being of a lively disposition and moped at home where papa undoubtedly is the most aggravating of his sex and not improved since having been cut down by the hand of the incendiary into something of which I never saw the counterpart in all my life but jealousy is not my character nor ill-will though many faults."

Without having been able closely to follow Mrs. Finching through this labyrinth, Little Dorrit understood its purpose, and cordially accepted the trust.

"The withered chaplet my dear," said Flora, with great enjoyment, "is then perished the column is crumbled and the pyramid is standing upside down upon its what's-his-name call it not giddiness call it not weakness call it not folly I must now retire into privacy and look upon the ashes of departed joys no more but taking the further liberty of paying for the pastry which has formed the humble pretext of our interview will for ever say Adieu!"

Mr. F.'s aunt, who had eaten her pie with great solemnity, and who had been elaborating some grievous scheme of injury in her mind, since her first assumption of that public position on the Marshal's steps, took the present opportunity of addressing the following Sibyllic apostrophe to the relict of her late nephew.

"Bring him for'ard, and I'll chuck him out o' winder!"

Flora tried in vain to soothe the excellent woman, by explaining that they were going home to dinner. Mr. F.'s Aunt persisted in replying, "Bring him for'ard, and I'll chuck him out o' winder!" Having reiterated this demand an immense number of times, with a sustained glare of defiance at Little Dorrit, Mr. F.'s Aunt folded her arms, and sat down in the corner of the pie-shop parlor; steadfastly refusing to budge until such time as "he" should have been "brought for'ard," and the chucking portion of his destiny accomplished.

In this condition of things, Flora confided to Little Dorrit that she had not seen Mr. F.'s Aunt so full of life and character for weeks; that she would find it necessary to remain there "hours perhaps," until the inexorable old lady could be softened; and that she could manage her best alone. They parted therefore, in the friendliest manner, and with the kindest feeling on both sides.

Mr. F.'s Aunt holding out like a grim fortress, and Flora becoming in need of refreshment, a messenger was dispatched to the hotel for the tumbler already glanced at, which was afterward replenished. With the aid of its contents, a newspaper, and some skimming of the cream of the pie-stock, Flora got through the remainder of the day in perfect good humor; though occasionally embarrassed by the consequences of an idle rumor which circulated among the credulous infants of the neighborhood, to the effect that an old lady had sold herself to the pie-shop, to be made up, and was then sitting in the pie-shop parlor, declining to complete her contract. This attracted so many young persons of both sexes, and, when the shades of evening began to fall, occasioned so much interruption to the business, that the merchant became very pressing in his proposals that Mr. F.'s Aunt should be removed. A conveyance was accordingly brought to the door, which, by the joint efforts of the merchant and Flora, this remarkable woman was at last induced to enter; though not without even then putting her head out of the window, and demanding to have him "brought for'ard" for the purpose originally mentioned. As she was observed at this time to direct baleful glances toward the Marshalsea, it has been supposed that this admirably consistent female intended by "him," Arthur Clennam. This, however, is mere speculation; who the person was, who, for the satisfaction of Mr. F.'s Aunt's mind, ought to have been brought forward, and never was brought forward, will never be positively known.

The autumn days went on, and Little Dorrit never came to the Marshalsea now, and went away without seeing him. No, no, no.

One morning, as Arthur listened for the light feet, that every morning ascended winged to his heart, bringing the heavenly brightness of a new love into the room where the old love had wrought so hard and been so true; one morning, as he listened, he heard her coming, not alone."

"Dear Arthur," said her delighted voice outside the door, "I have some one here. May I bring some one in?"

He had thought from the tread there were two with her. He answered "Yes," and she came in with Mr. Meagles. Sunbrowned and jolly Mr. Meagles looked, and he opened his arms and folded Arthur in them, like a sunbrowned and jolly father.

"Now I am all right," said Mr. Meagles, after a minute or

so. "Now, it's over. Arthur, my dear fellow, confess at once that you expected me before."

"I did," said Arthur, "but Amy told me——"

"Little Dorrit. Never any other name." It was she who whispered it.

"—But my Little Dorrit told me that, without asking for any further explanation, I was not to expect you until I saw you."

"And now you see me, my boy," said Mr. Meagles, shaking him by the hand stoutly; "and now you shall have any explanation and every explanation. The fact is, I *was* here,—came straight to you from the Allongers and Marshongers, or I should be ashamed to look you in the face to-day,—but you were not in company trim at the moment, and I had to start off again to catch Doyce."

"Poor Doyce!" sighed Arthur.

"Don't call him names that he don't deserve," said Mr. Meagles. "*He*'s not poor; *he*'s doing well enough. Doyce is a wonderful fellow over there. I assure you he's a making out his case like a house a-fire. He has fallen on his legs, has Dan. Where they don't want things done and find a man to do 'em, that man's off his legs; but where they do want things done and find a man to do 'em, that man's on his legs. You won't have occasion to trouble the Circumlocution Office any more. Let me tell you, Dan has done without 'em!"

"What a load you take from my mind!" cried Arthur. "What happiness you give me!"

"Happiness?" retorted Mr. Meagles. "Don't talk about happiness till you see Dan. I assure you Dan is directing works and executing labors over yonder, that it would make your hair stand on end to look at. He's no public offender, bless you, now! He's medalled, and ribboned, and starred, and crossed, and I don't know what all'd, like a born nobleman. But we mustn't talk about that over here."

"Why not?"

"Oh, egad!" said Mr. Meagles, shaking his head very seriously, "he must hide all those things under lock and key when he comes over here. They won't do, over here. In that particular, Britannia is a Britannia in the Manger—won't give her children such distinctions herself, and won't allow them to be seen, when they're given by other countries. No, no, Dan!" said Mr. Meagles, shaking his head again. "That won't do here!"

"If you had brought me (except for Doyce's sake) twice what I have lost," cried Arthur, "you would not have given me the pleasure that you give me in this news."

"Why, of course, of course," assented Mr. Meagles. "Of course I know that, my good fellow, and therefore I came out with it in the first burst. Now, to go back, about catching Doyce. I caught Doyce. Ran against him, among a lot of those dirty brown dogs in women's nightcaps a great deal too big for 'em, calling themselves Arabs and all sorts of incoherent races. *You* know 'em! Well! He was coming straight to me, and I was going straight to him, and so we came back together."

"Doyce in England?" exclaimed Arthur.

"There!" said Mr. Meagles, throwing open his arms. "I am the worst man in the world to manage a thing of this sort. I don't know what I should have done if I had been in the diplomatic line—right, perhaps! The long and short of it is, Arthur, we have both been in England this fortnight. And if you go on to ask where Doyce is at the present moment, why, my plain answer is—here he is! And now I can breathe again, at last!"

Doyce darted in from behind the door, caught Arthur by both hands, and said the rest for himself.

"There are only three branches of my subject, my dear Clennam," said Doyce, proceeding to mould them severally, with his plastic thumb on the palm of his hand, "and they're soon disposed of. First, not a word more from you about the past. There was an error in your calculations. I know what that is. It affects the whole machine, and failure is the consequence. You will profit by the failure, and will avoid it another time. I have done a similar thing myself, in construction, often. Every failure teaches a man something, if he will learn; and you are too sensible a man not to learn from this failure. So much for firstly. Secondly. I was sorry you should have taken it so heavily to heart, and reproached yourself so severely; I was traveling home night and day to put matters right, with the assistance of our friend, when I fell in with our friend as he has informed you. Thirdly. We two agreed, that, after what you had undergone, after your distress of mind, and after your illness, it would be a pleasant surprise if we could so far keep quiet as to get things perfectly arranged without your knowledge, and then come and say that all the affairs were smooth, that every thing was right, that the business stood in greater want of you than it ever did, and that a new and prosperous career was opened before you and me as partners. That's thirdly. But you know we always make an allowance for friction, and so I have reserved space to close in. My dear Clennam, I thoroughly confide in you; you have it in your power to be quite as useful to me, as I have, or have had, it in my power to be useful to you; your old place awaits you, and wants you very much; there is nothing to detain you here, one half-hour longer."

There was a silence, which was not broken until Arthur had stood for some time at the window with his back toward them, and until his little wife that was to be, had gone to him and stayed by him.

"I made a remark a little while ago," said Daniel Doyce then, "which I am inclined to think was an incorrect one. I said there was nothing to detain you here, Clennam, half an hour longer. Am I mistaken in supposing that you would rather not leave here till to-morrow morning? Do I know, without being very wise, where you would like to go direct from these walls and from this room?"

"You do," returned Arthur. "It has been our cherished purpose."

"Very well," said Doyce. "Then, if this young lady will do me the honor of regarding me for four and twenty hours in the light of a father, and will take a ride with me now toward Saint Paul's Churchyard, I dare say I know what we want to get there."

Little Dorrit and he went out together soon afterward, and Mr. Meagles lingered behind to say a word to his friend.

"I think, Arthur, you will not want Mother and me in the morning, and we will keep away. It might set Mother thinking about Pet; she's a soft-hearted woman. She's best at the cottage, and I'll stay there and keep her company."

With that they parted for the time. And the day ended, and the night ended, and the morning came, and Little Dorrit, simply dressed as usual, and having no one with her but Maggy, came into the prison with the sunshine. The poor room was a happy room that morning. Where in the whole world was there a room so full of quiet joy!

"My dear love," said Arthur. "Why does Maggy light the fire? We shall be gone directly."

"I asked her to do it. I have taken such an odd fancy. I want you to burn something for me."

"What?"

"Only this folded paper. If you will put it in the fire with your own hand, just as it is, my fancy will be gratified."

"Superstitious, darling Little Dorrit? Is it a charm?"

"It is any thing you like best, my own," she answered laughing with glistening eyes and standing on tiptoe to kiss him, "if you will only humor me when the fire burns up."

So they stood before the fire, waiting; Clennam with his arm about her waist, and the fire shining, as fire in that same place had often shone, in Little Dorrit's eyes. "Isnit bright enough now?" said Arthur. "Quite bright enough, now," said Little Dorrit. "Does the charm want any words to be said?" asked Arthur, as he held the paper over the flame. "You can say (if you don't mind) 'I love you!'" answered Little Dorrit. So he said it, and the paper burned away.

They passed very quietly along the yard; for no one was there, though many heads were stealthily peeping from the windows. Only one face, familiar of old, was in the Lodge. When they had both accosted it, and spoken many kind words, Little Dorrit turned back one last time with her hand stretched out, saying, "Good-by, good John! I hope you will live very happy, dear!"

Then they went up the steps of the neighboring Saint George's Church, and went up to the altar, where Daniel Doyce was waiting in his paternal character. And there was Little Dorrit's old friend who had given her the Burial Register for a

THE THIRD VOLUME OF THE REGISTERS.

pillow, full of admiration that she should come back to them to be married, after all.

And they were married, with the sun shining on them through the painted figure of Our Saviour on the window. And they went into the very room where Little Dorrit had slumbered after her party, to sign the Marriage Register. And there Mr. Pancks (destined to be chief clerk to Doyce and Clennam, and afterward partner in the house), sinking the Incendiary in the peaceful friend, looked in at the door to see it done, with Flora gallantly supported on one arm and Maggy on the other, and a background of John Chivery and father, and other turnkeys who had run round for the moment, deserting the parent Marshalsea for its happy child. Nor had Flora the least signs of seclusion upon her, notwithstanding her recent declaration; but on the contrary was wonderfully smart, and enjoyed the ceremonies mightily, though in a fluttered way.

Little Dorrit's old friend held the inkstand as she signed her name, and the clerk paused in taking off the good clergyman's surplice, and all the witnesses looked on with special interest. "For you see," said Little Dorrit's old friend, "this young lady is one of our curiosities, and has come now to the third volume of our Registers. Her birth is in what I call the first volume; she lay asleep on this very floor, with her pretty head on what I call the second volume; and she's now a-writing her little name as a bride, in what I call the third volume."

They all gave place when the signing was done, and Little Dorrit and her husband walked out of the church alone. They paused for a moment on the steps of the portico, looking at the fresh perspective of the street in the autumn morning sun's bright rays, and then went down.

Went down into a modest life of usefulness and happiness. Went down to give a mother's care, in the fullness of time, to Fanny's neglected children no less than to their own, and to leave that lady going into Society forever and a day. Went down to give a tender nurse and friend to Tip for some few years, who was never vexed by the great exactions he made of her, in return for the riches he might have given her if he had ever had them, and who lovingly closed his eyes upon the Marshalsea and all its blighted fruits. They went quietly down into the roaring streets, inseparable and blessed; and as they passed along in sunshine and in shade, the noisy and the eager, and the arrogant and the froward and the vain, fretted, and chafed, and made their usual uproar.

THE END.

www.ingramcontent.com/pod-product-compliance
Lightning Source LLC
LaVergne TN
LVHW020921110826
845150LV00004B/727

* 9 7 8 1 4 2 5 5 5 4 8 2 8 *